MW00973149

A MONOGRAPH

OF

CHRISTMAS ISLAND

(INDIAN OCEAN):

PHYSICAL FEATURES

AND

GEOLOGY

BY

CHARLES W. ANDREWS, B.A., B.Sc., F.G.S.

WITH DESCRIPTIONS OF

THE FAUNA AND FLORA

BY

NUMEROUS CONTRIBUTORS.

ILLUSTRATED BY TWENTY-TWO PLATES, A MAP, AND NUMEROUS
ILLUSTRATIONS IN THE TEXT.

LONDON:

PRINTED BY ORDER OF THE TRUSTEES.

SOLD BY

LONGMANS AND CO., 39, PATERNOSTER ROW.
B. QUARITCH, 15, PICCADILLY. DULAU AND CO., 37, SOHO SQUARE, W.
KEGAN PAUL AND CO., CHARING CROSS ROAD, W.C.

AND AT THE

BRITISH MUSEUM (NATURAL HISTORY), CROMWELL ROAD, S.W.

(All rights reserved.)

1900.

HERTFORD

PRINTED BY STEPHEN AUSTIN AND SONS.

This scarce antiquarian book is included in our special *Legacy Reprint Series*. In the interest of creating a more extensive selection of rare historical book reprints, we have chosen to reproduce this title even though it may possibly have occasional imperfections such as missing and blurred pages, missing text, poor pictures, markings, dark backgrounds and other reproduction issues beyond our control. Because this work is culturally important, we have made it available as a part of our commitment to protecting, preserving and promoting the world's literature. Thank you for your understanding.

PREFACE.

THE Trustees having been pleased to authorize the preparation of a monograph embracing the scientific results of the exploration of Christmas Island by Mr. C. W. Andrews during a visit extending over ten months in 1897-98, I was requested by the Director to make the necessary arrangements, and obtain the assistance of the several members of the staff of the Natural History Departments in the British Museum and other gentlemen (whose names will be found in this work), without whose kind co-operation Mr. Andrews' task would have been an impossible one.

The valuable help of various special artists had also to be secured to illustrate the work, and within rather over a year from the time of inception the volume has been completed.

By Professor Lankester's desire, this monograph has been restricted to a description of the Physical Features and the Geology, together with the Land Fauna and Flora of the island.

It is hoped that the satisfactory manner in which this work has been accomplished may result in the issue of other equally valuable monographs under the auspices of the Trustees, by the staff of the Museum, dealing with similar geographical units hitherto neglected.

HENRY WOODWARD.

GEOLOGICAL DEPARTMENT,
    BRITISH MUSEUM (NATURAL HISTORY).
        February, 1900.

AUTHOR'S PREFACE.

THE present volume contains an account of the collections and observations made by me during a stay of about ten months in Christmas Island.

This period included all the seasonal changes, and it is hoped that the collections of plants and insects are fairly complete.

In a few instances specimens obtained by previous collectors are described.

The collections of marine animals are discussed elsewhere.

I wish especially to express my sincere thanks to the Trustees of the British Museum, who granted me the necessary leave of absence, which, owing to the difficulty of reaching the island and the still greater difficulty of getting away, was prolonged considerably beyond the time that was at first thought necessary; to Sir John Murray, whose generosity in defraying the necessary expenses rendered the expedition possible; to Mr. George Clunies Ross, of Cocos-Keeling Islands, and his brother, Mr. Andrew Ross, for their hospitality, and assistance in numberless ways during my stay; to their nephew, Mr. H. Ross, a resident for some years on the island, whose knowledge of bush-life in general was of the greatest assistance to me;

and lastly, to Mr. W. A. Wilkinson, the Engineer to the Christmas Island Phosphate Company.

I am also greatly indebted to the contributors of the various sections of this book for the trouble and care they have taken in working out the collections I was able to send home.

CHAS. W. ANDREWS.

GEOLOGICAL DEPARTMENT,
  BRITISH MUSEUM (NATURAL HISTORY).
    February, 1900.

INTRODUCTORY NOTE.

CHRISTMAS ISLAND, in the Indian Ocean, appears to have been known to navigators from about the middle of the seventeenth century. Dampier and other voyagers sent boats ashore, but, until the year 1887, no person appears to have been able to penetrate beyond a few hundred yards from the landing-places, because of the steep and rugged cliffs, covered with dense tropical vegetation, by which the island is everywhere surrounded.

In 1887 Captain (now Rear-Admiral) Pelham Aldrich, R.N., visited the island in H.M.S. " Egeria," and with the assistance of a party of blue-jackets cut a way up the cliffs, encamped on the highest point of the island, and made some explorations towards the interior. In consequence of Captain Aldrich's discoveries during this expedition, the island was formally annexed to the British Crown in the following year. In the year 1897 a Company acquired the lease of the island, and arrangements were immediately made for its thorough exploitation ;—an agricultural rent is paid to the Government, in addition to royalties on all minerals and timber that may be exported.

The total area of the island is about 43 square miles, and in some parts it rises to over 1,000 feet above the level of the sea. Besides being the home of numerous endemic and other species of animals, it is completely covered by a luxuriant tropical vegetation. Down to a few years ago it was probably the only existing tropical island of any large extent that had never been inhabited by man, savage or civilized. Its interest, from a scientific point of view, is further increased by the fact that it is at least 190 miles distant from any other land, and is surrounded by an ocean in which the depths exceed three English miles.

It seemed highly desirable that this interesting island—which was evidently an upraised coral atoll—should be carefully examined and described by a competent naturalist and geologist, before being opened up by Europeans for agricultural and commercial purposes. Accordingly it was arranged with the Trustees of the British Museum that Mr. C. W. Andrews, B.Sc., F.G.S., of the Geological Department, should be granted leave to carry out this exploration. I undertook to pay all the expenses, and to present a complete set of all specimens procured to the National Collection.

During the years 1897 and 1898 Mr. Andrews carried out the exploration with great success, notwithstanding many disappointments, drawbacks, and hardships. He has enriched the British Museum with unique and extensive collections, and it will, I think, be admitted that in the present elaborate report we have the best account of a true oceanic island that has ever been published.

It has not hitherto been possible to watch carefully the immediate effects produced by the immigration of civilized man —and the animals and plants which follow in his wake—upon the physical conditions and upon the indigenous fauna and flora of an isolated oceanic island. I hope to arrange that this shall be done in the case of Christmas Island, at the same time that further explorations are undertaken, for Mr. Andrews' detailed report will enable this to be carried out with every prospect of success, and in a scientific manner.

Mr. Andrews, and the other officials of the British Museum who have assisted him in his investigations, are to be congratulated on the production of this excellent monograph of an oceanic island, which forms a most valuable addition to natural knowledge.

JOHN MURRAY.

CHALLENGER LODGE, WARDIE,
    EDINBURGH.
    February 15, 1900.

TABLE OF CONTENTS.

BOTANY.

PALÆONTOLOGY AND GEOLOGY.

ERRATA.

p. 61, line 6, for *P. sepulchralis* read *V. sepulchralis.*

p. 88, line 5 from bottom, for *Syrpindæ* read *Syrphidæ.*

p. 142, third genus under ' BLATTIDÆ,' for *Periplanata* read
Periplaneta.

LIST OF FIGURES IN THE TEXT.

CHRISTMAS ISLAND (INDIAN OCEAN).

HISTORY AND PHYSICAL FEATURES.

By C. W. ANDREWS, B.Sc., F.G.S.

CHRISTMAS ISLAND, the subject of the present monograph, lies in the eastern part of the Indian Ocean, in S. lat. 10° 25′, E. long. 105° 42′. Java, the nearest land, is about 190 miles to the north, while some 900 miles to the south-east is the coast of North-West Australia. A little to the south of west, at a distance of 550 miles, are the two atolls of Cocos and North Keeling, and to the north of these Glendinning Shoal. The submarine slopes of the island are very steep, and soundings of upwards of 1,000 fathoms occur within two or three miles of the coast: at this depth the bottom was found to consist of globigerina ooze. To the north is Maclear Deep, in which 3,200 fathoms were found, and to the south and south-west is the more extensive Wharton Deep, with upwards of 3,000 fathoms. The island, in fact, forms the summit of a submarine peak, the base of which rises from the low saddle which separates these two abysses, and on the western end of which the Cocos-Keeling Islands are situated.

The first mention of Christmas Island occurs in a map by Pieter Goos, published in Holland in 1666, in which it is called Moni. In subsequent maps this name and that of Christmas Island are applied to it indifferently, but it is not known by whom the island was discovered and named. The earliest approach to a descriptive account is found in Dampier's " Voyages " [1],[1] in the following passage :—

" After leaving New Holland, the ship tried to make Cocos, but was driven to a more easterly course, and met nothing of remark till the twenty-eighth day. Then we fell in with a small woody island in lat. 10° 20′ S. It was deep-water about the island, and there was no anchoring; but we sent two canoes ashore, one of them with the carpenters to cut a tree to make another pump; the other canoe went to search for fresh water, and found a small brook near the south-west point of the island, but there the sea fell on the shore so high that they could not get it off. At noon both the canoes returned on board, and the

---

[1] The numbers in square brackets refer to the list of papers, etc., relating to Christmas Island given at the end of the volume.

carpenters brought on board a good tree; the other canoe brought aboard as many boobies and man-of-war birds as sufficed all the ship's company when they were boiled.

"They also got a sort of land animal, somewhat resembling a large crawfish without its great claws. The island is a good height, with steep cliffs against the south and south-west, and a sandy bay on the north side, but with very deep water steep to the shore."

The date of Dampier's visit was March, 1688. The next account of the island is given by Captain Daniel Beckman, in 1718 [2]. He remarks that "the island looks exceeding pleasant, being covered with lofty trees, and may be known by the following directions:—Coming from the north-westward, it appears pretty high, with a saddle in the middle; the westernmost land is the highest, trenching away to the northward to a low, flat point; the easternmost point is low, but bluff. I sounded within eight miles of the low point, but had no bottom with the 100-fathom line out. The island is about seven leagues from east to west."

This writer gives a remarkable sketch, in which the heights are ridiculously exaggerated, the hill over the north-western point being made to look like a mountain with three peaks; his estimate of the length of the island also is much in excess of the truth. In 1771 the "Pigot," East Indiaman, attempted to find an anchorage, but failed. The crews of this and other passing vessels reported the occurrence of wild pigs, coconut-palms, and lime-trees, none of which really existed. The first attempt at an exploration of the island was made by the frigate "Amethyst" in 1857, from which a boat's crew was landed with the object of attempting to reach the summit, but the inland cliffs proved an insuperable obstacle, and the ascent was abandoned.

In 1886 the surveying vessel, "Flying Fish" (Captain Maclear) was ordered to make an examination of the island. The coast was found to consist of limestone cliffs, and it was only after sailing nearly all round the island that an anchorage was found in a bay with a white shingle beach on the north coast. To this the name Flying Fish Cove was given, and it is now the site of a small settlement. Another white beach was seen towards the north-west point, but no anchorage was found near it. A number of men were landed, and collections of the plants and animals were obtained, but, since the island seemed of little value, no serious attempt at exploration was made [3].

In the following year H.M.S. "Egeria" (Captain Pelham Aldrich) called at the island, and remained about ten days. Captain Aldrich and his men cut a way to the top of the island, and sent home a number of rock specimens obtained on the way, and Mr. J. J. Lister, who accompanied the expedition as naturalist, made extensive collections both of the fauna and flora, but had not time to penetrate to the middle of the island [4-6].

The island was formally annexed by H.M.S. "Impérieuse" in June, 1888, and placed under the Straits Settlements Government.

In 1890 H.M.S. "Redpole" called at the island for a few hours, and Mr. H. N. Ridley, of the Singapore Botanical Gardens, who was on board, collected a number of plants not previously recorded, and has written an interesting account of his visit [8].

Although Messrs. Lister and Ridley had made valuable collections of the fauna and flora of the island, the shortness of the time at their disposal rendered it impossible for them to penetrate far into the interior, or to make any examination of the geological structure. Nevertheless, the rock specimens brought back by the "Egeria" showed that the island probably consisted mainly of coral and foraminiferal limestones, resting on a basis of volcanic rocks; and a very interesting paper, in which the results of the expedition were summarized, and the probable structure of the island discussed, was published by Rear-Admiral Sir W. J. L. Wharton in the proceedings of the Royal Geographical Society for 1888 [7].

It seemed desirable, however, that a more complete examination of the island should be undertaken, and, if possible, collections should be made at different seasons of the year, and in 1896 Sir John Murray generously offered to pay the expenses of such an expedition. I was fortunate enough to be able to avail myself of this opportunity, and, the Trustees of the British Museum having granted the necessary leave of absence, I left England at the beginning of May, 1897. At that time the only means of access to the island was by the sailing-vessels belonging to Mr. G. Clunies Ross, of the Cocos-Keeling Islands, which are employed in carrying various supplies from Batavia to those islands, and on their way down usually touch at Christmas Island to land stores for the little colony established in Flying Fish Cove. Unfortunately, one of these vessels had left shortly before I arrived in Java, and I therefore had to wait some weeks before an opportunity of getting to my destination occurred; but at length, on July 23rd, I sailed from Batavia in the "J. G. Clunies Ross," a yawl of about 46 tons burden. After a rough passage of five days we sighted the island from the south-west, having run past it in the night. We arrived off Flying Fish Cove soon after sunset, but did not anchor till the following morning (July 29th).

Seen from the south-west, the island appears as a long green ridge, nearly level at the top, there being only slight elevations at the north-west and south-east ends. The ridge descends seaward in a succession of terraces, the upper ones bounded by comparatively gentle slopes, the lower by a high and nearly vertical cliff, below which there is a narrow platform sloping gently down to the sea cliff. This is usually about 15 to 30 feet high, and is much undercut by the heavy swell that is continually breaking against its base. On approaching nearer, it can be seen that the whole island is covered by a dense forest, broken only by the grey face of the high inland cliff which runs round the greater part of the island, rising like a wall above the tall trees growing on the shore terrace.

FIGURE 1.

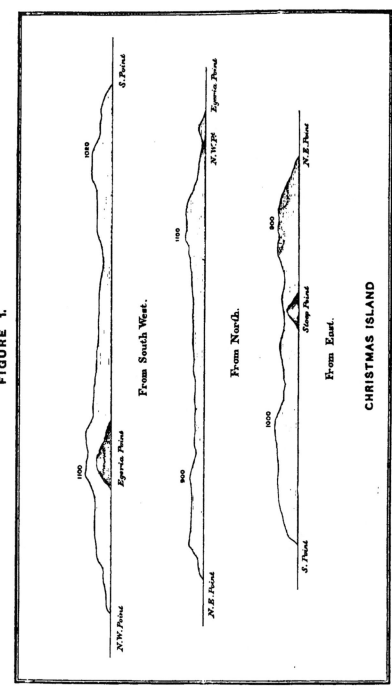

From South West.

From North.

From East.

CHRISTMAS ISLAND

The outlines of the land, as seen from the south-west, east, and north, and sections across it at various points, are shown in Figure 1 and in the map.

From these it can be gathered that the island consists of a central plateau, highest towards the north and east, and descending to the sea on all sides by a succession of terraces, separated by slopes or cliffs. In most places the arrangement of these, from the edge of the plateau downwards, is—(1) a steep slope strewn with blocks ; (2) a broad terrace, followed by a similar slope (this seems to be wanting on the south); (3) a second terrace, terminating in a cliff 200 or 300 feet high; (4) the shore terrace, sloping gently down to the sea cliff ; (5) the present fringing reef. There are, however, many local differences, the more important of which will be noticed below.

The greatest length of the island is from North-East Point to Egeria Point, a distance of about 12 miles. The greatest width is from North-East Point to South Point (see Map), about nine miles; the least on a line drawn north and south through Murray Hill, about three and a half miles. The total area of the island may be roughly stated as 43 square miles.

In giving a general account of the physical features of the island, it will be convenient to begin with the fringing reef, and then deal successively with the higher terraces, concluding with the plateau. There are, besides, one or two localities which will need a somewhat more detailed description.

The Fringing Reef. (Fig. 2.)

If the coast be examined in a boat, or from the edge of the sea cliff, it is found that round the greater part of the island there is a submarine terrace or shelf, which varies greatly in width and in its depth beneath the surface. At Flying Fish Cove this terrace consists of two portions—an inner, which is partly dry at low-water, and outside this and about two fathoms below it, a second, which slopes away seaward to about 20–30 fathoms, beyond which the water deepens suddenly. The upper reef is best developed at the northern and southern ends of the cove, and is almost absent in the middle. It exactly resembles the reef flat of an atoll. At low-water it can be seen to be composed of blocks of coral cemented together and forming a smooth, hard surface, like concrete, bored in all directions by marine worms. Some of the individual coral masses are of considerable size, and the section of one spherical mass was about four feet in diameter. On the surface of the reef are numerous loose blocks and large plate-like masses of coral, and towards the beach are a number of enormous masses of white foraminiferal limestone which have fallen from the high cliff above; some of these are 20 feet high and 30 or more long, and several have trees growing on them. In one case a block has rolled a distance of 50 or 60 yards out on to the reef flat. At the lowest tides the greater part of the surface of the reef is covered with water less than a foot deep, though there are a few holes of greater depth. In some places there are clumps of a small branching madrepore of considerable extent, the tops of which are exposed for nearly a foot for some time at low-water. Except for these there are only a few small corals in the deeper pools, and the chief inhabitants of this part of the reef are holothuria and small echinoids, which live in holes in the rock. The outer rim is raised from a foot to eighteen inches above the surface of the water of the lagoon. It consists mainly of flat blocks of coral overgrown and cemented together by a thick coating of bright red nullipores, and is cleft by numerous deep fissures and channels, through which the water thrown over it escapes; it is on the sides of these fissures that the corals seem to flourish best. The reef flat at the northern end of the cove is of much the same character.

Standing on the nullipore-covered edge of this upper reef, the outer lower reef can be seen through the one or two fathoms of clear water that cover it. Its surface is studded with masses of various species of corals, separated by areas of coral sand. As above mentioned, this reef slopes away gently to about 20 fathoms, beyond which the water deepens suddenly. At the southern end of the bay it is interrupted, and at Smith Point no bottom was found with 30 fathoms close to the cliffs.

A little south of the middle of the cove the reefs are interrupted by a boat-channel forty to fifty yards wide, which runs up to the beach. Its bottom slopes gently down to four or five fathoms, and is composed of coral shingle; beyond this patches of coral appear, and it passes into the general surface of the lower reef.

Except at West White Beach and a few small bays with beaches on the east coast, Flying Fish Cove is the only place where any part of the fringing reef is dry at low-water. Round the greater part of the island the foot of the cliff is washed by the sea at all times of the tide, and the fringing reef, if present at all, is from a yard to three or four fathoms below the surface, even at ebb-tide. Here it seems to consist, on its landward side, of a platform formed by the cutting back of the cliff by the sea, while on the seaward portion coral is luxuriant, and is, no doubt, growing outward on the talus resulting from the denudation of the coast.

The Sea Cliff and Beaches. (Fig. 3.)

Nearly the whole of the coastline is formed by limestone cliffs, varying in height from about 15 to 150 feet or more. The latter height only occurs at Steep Point, in consequence of certain movements which will be described elsewhere; in other places the height seldom exceeds 50 feet. The cliffs are nearly everywhere much undercut, and sometimes overhang to the extent of 30 feet or more. There are numerous caves, and occasionally these have openings on the shore terrace at some distance from the sea.

FIG. 2.
REEF-EDGE AT LOW-WATER, SOUTH SIDE OF FLYING FISH COVE.

FIG. 3.—NORTH COAST LOOKING TOWARDS SMITH POINT.

When a heavy sea strikes the cliffs, the air is driven through these passages with great violence, and sometimes accompanied by a column of spray 60 or 70 feet high. These blowholes are most numerous on the south coast, where the cliffs are exposed to the heavy ocean swell caused by the south-east trade-wind, which prevails during the greater part of the year. Along this coast the cliffs are cut up into narrow, finger-like masses, and their summit for some distance inland is bare of vegetation, being continually swept by the spray. Rock-pools containing small living fish sometimes occur on the cliff top. On the north coast, which is more rarely exposed to a heavy sea, the cliffs often form a continuous wall for long distances. The structure of the sea cliff will be described in more detail in the geological part of this memoir. Here it may be mentioned that by far the greater part of it is a section of a recently raised fringing reef; but in some places—e g., on the east coast—the sea has cut back to the older and more central parts of the island, and in such places the cliff may consist largely of volcanic, mostly basaltic, rocks; even when this is the case, however, the upper portion is usually formed of recent coral limestone.

In one or two places the sea cliff is interrupted by beaches of coral shingle. The most important of these is at Flying Fish Cove, where it forms a crescent some 500 yards long. Towards the southern end it is composed of sand, but to the northward it becomes coarser and coarser, till about the middle it consists of rolled blocks of coral, and on the foreshore masses of yellowish limestone, apparently part of the talus derived from the cliff behind. At the northern end it becomes finer again. In places the shingle has been cemented into hard, compact rock, in sheets several inches thick. The top of the beach is about 15 feet above low-tide level, and its slope varies much, being very steep after a northerly or north-easterly gale, and gentler during the prevalence of the trade-wind, when the sea in the cove is quiet.

Behind the beach there is a broad, nearly level platform, composed mainly of fragments and blocks of coral, but to some extent also of volcanic and other rock derived from the cliff above. Formerly the whole of this platform was forest-clad, and even now much of the beach down to high-water mark is fringed with a belt of Ironwoods (*Cordia*), Waroo (*Hibiscus*), and *Tournefortia*; but within this much of the forest has been cleared, fruit-trees (custard apples, limes, etc.) and coconut-palms planted, and a number of substantial houses built. At its northern end this platform is shut in by an inland continuation of the sea cliff (10–20 feet), which still shows traces of wave action; and at the back there rises in a semicircle a cliff covered almost entirely with forest, and towards the middle of the cove towering nearly 500 feet above the platform.

West White Beach is in some respects similar to Flying Fish Cove, but here the platform is much narrower, and the sea cliff is continued behind it; above this cliff there is a wide terrace, as on other parts of the coast. In many places the beach is covered with slabs of shore cement, but on the whole it consists of finer material than that at the cove. Between it and Smith Point there are three other small beaches, but these are shut in by cliffs and covered at high-water. On the east coast there are several similar beaches of various sizes. At one of these a bed of basalt comes out on the shore, and over it gushes a small stream of excellent fresh water, the volume of which seems to remain constant at all times of the year; this waterfall is called by the Malays " Panchorán," and the bay in which it occurs may be named Panchorán Bay. On the west coast, towards North-West Point, I saw a series of small white beaches, which are probably covered at high·tide.

The Shore Terrace.

By this is meant the terrace extending from the top of the sea cliff to the foot of the first inland cliff. It is the most persistent and best defined of the terraces, being interrupted, so far as I am aware, at Flying Fish Cove and Steep Point only. Its width varies from nearly half a mile to less than a hundred yards. As a rule, it slopes gently upwards to the foot of the first inland cliff, but probably its greatest elevation is less than a hundred feet, and its average height is not more than about fifty. At the outer border there is usually a belt of low, jagged pinnacles, often separated by channels running seaward, precisely like those seen in the present fringing reef; within this is a level area thickly covered with rich soil, and then, towards the foot of the inland cliff, another belt covered with pinnacles and blocks fallen from the heights above. Sometimes, however, the whole width is a chaos of jagged pinnacles and masses of limestone, which, when covered with jungle, is quite impassable. As already mentioned, along the sheltered part of the north coast the forest extends to the very edge of the cliff. Elsewhere there is usually an outer band, where only coarse grass and a few straggling bushes of *Pemphis* and *Scævola* will grow. Within this is a zone composed mainly of *Pandanus, Cordia, Calophyllum, Hibiscus, Pisonia*, and other sea-loving plants; these form a protection to the forest, covering the inner part of the platform. The trees found here are mostly large forest trees, such as occur in the higher parts of the island. The commonest forms are *Gyrocarpus, Berria, Erythrina, Ochrosia, Kleinhovia, Celtis, Terminalia*, and *Arenga*, but there are many others. The *Gyrocarpus*, which is completely bare of leaves during the last six months of the year, gives a very peculiar appearance to the forest during that time. Occasionally the fairly open forest is replaced by dense jungle of pandanus and thorny creepers.

In several places on the east coast the shore terrace is composed largely of volcanic rocks, and since these hold up the water which elsewhere sinks through the porous limestone, there are several small brooks. These are never more than two or three hundred yards long, and rise from springs, welling out at or near the base of the inland cliff. Their banks are very muddy, and are burrowed in all directions by a peculiar grey crab (*Cardiosoma*), which is provided with a sort of brush on each side of the mouth, apparently for filtering the water which enters the gill chamber.

The First Inland Cliff and Terrace. (Fig. 5.)

The first inland cliff is the most conspicuous feature in the scenery, and in one form or another it extends round nearly the whole island. In one place it forms a cliff with a nearly vertical face bare of vegetation; in another it is reduced to a talus slope of blocks of limestone piled up in wild confusion and covered with trailing plants and bushes; and in others, again, it is replaced by a succession of smaller cliffs and terraces of varying height and breadth, rising step-like one behind the other. Whatever form it may take, its summit is between 250 and 300 feet above the sea-level. On the east coast, about half a mile south of North-East Point, this cliff is absent for a short distance, and on the western coast it is much less distinctly developed than elsewhere. In many places where the cliff face is vertical, or nearly vertical, it shows distinct traces of wave action at two or three levels, the chief evidence of this being lines of small caves, and in places near the foot a very distinct and clearly comparatively recent undercutting of the face. For instance, on the north coast, at about 20 feet above the shore plat-form, the cliff is cut back into a shelf, above which it overhangs considerably, and from 150 to 200 feet higher up there are less distinct traces of a similar structure, the line of wave action being there marked by small caves. Where the single cliff face is replaced by a number of secondary cliffs and terraces, these also indicate that the surface of the sea has stood at successively lower levels with regard to the land, each cliff and terrace apparently marking such a change of level. In places these smaller cliffs and terraces are interrupted by gentler slopes, and one or more may disappear. Although the terraces may be continuous for considerable dis-tances, it is difficult to correlate those occurring in different parts of the island. Both the mode of origin and the composition of the first inland cliff seem to differ considerably in different places, but these points will be more fully considered in the geological section.

The terrace on the top of the first inland cliff varies much in width and general structure. It is widest opposite the principal headlands, where it is between a quarter and half a mile wide; elsewhere it may be any width from less than 100 to 400 or 500 yards. It usually slopes gently seawards, sometimes becoming steeper towards the cliff edge, which is nearly everywhere bordered with a belt of pinnacles of coral limestone, separated by clefts and channels often parallel to the cliff edge. In one or two places, notably near the middle of the north coast, the structure is more complex. Here, on descending the slope of the terrace towards the cliff edge, we come first to a narrow belt of pinnacles, beyond which is a sudden drop of about 50 feet; at the foot of the low cliff thus formed is a perfectly level, soil-clad terrace, some 50 yards broad, which is bounded on the outer side by lines of pinnacles 20–30 feet high, separated by winding channels with level floors; beyond these is a slope covered with piles of limestone blocks extending to the cliff edge. The channel included between the low cliff and the outer belt of pinnacles extends for half a mile or more roughly parallel to the coast, and may be either the result of a slip downward of the outer part of the cliff, or possibly a channel in a reef formed round the island when the sea was at that level. Whatever its structure, this terrace is always thickly covered with forest.

The Upper Cliffs and Terraces.

Above the first inland terrace, which, as just mentioned, varies greatly in width, we meet with a second inland cliff, or rather steep rock-covered slope, for an actual cliff is only found in a few places, as, for instance, west of the southern end of Flying Fish Cove. Usually the limestones composing this cliff show many traces of coral structure. At the summit there is a second terrace sloping gently upwards towards the foot of the third inland cliff, which forms its inland boundary. The width of this terrace, like that of the one below, varies very much, and is greatest opposite the headlands. It is occasionally partly covered with pinnacles and blocks of limestone, but usually is clothed with soil, which supports a luxuriant forest of great trees 150–200 feet high; in some places there is thick undergrowth of *Pandanus, Randia,* ferns, etc., but as a rule the forest is fairly open. The upper cliff, like that last described, is usually a steep talus-covered slope, with cliff faces showing in a few places only. Along the east coast, however, the upper 40 or 50 feet may be nearly vertical for long distances, forming a true cliff along the upper rim of the island. For the most part the rocks composing it show few traces of coral, and have been to a great extent dolomitized, as will be described in the geological section.

On the south coast one or other of the upper inland cliffs is wanting, or rather the two form a single declivity.

The Central Plateau and Hills.

Speaking generally, the whole of the upper part of the island consists of a plain, sloping gently to the south and west, and possessing a surface varied with shallow valleys, rounded flat-topped hills, and low ridges and reefs of coral limestone. On the northern and eastern sides the edge forms, in most places, a raised rim, bounded externally by a low cliff, below which comes the

uppermost of the inland cliffs above described. In other places
it passes into the inland cliff by a more gentle slope. The actual
margin is usually marked by a belt of limestone pinnacles of
greater or less width. Another notable feature is the occurrence
on the northern and eastern borders of several peculiar hills, the
long axis of which lies parallel to the edge of the plateau.

Of these hills Gannet Hill and Phosphate Hill (see Map and
Figs. 4 A, B) may be taken as typical. If the former be approached
from the westward, it will be found that the plateau slopes very
gently up to its foot; then there is a steep slope, from 50 to 60 feet
high, and above this a level surface from 100 to 200 yards wide.
On the outer edge of this, and rising abruptly from it, is a belt of
limestone pinnacles, some of which are more than 10 feet high;

FIGURE 4.

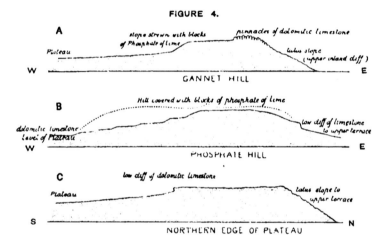

beyond these is a steep slope covered with a wild confusion of
blocks and pinnacles of limestone. The top of the hill is about
850 feet above the sea, while that of the plateau within is some
50 feet lower, at least at the northern end. Towards the south
the difference becomes less and less, till the ridge completely
disappears. The inland slope is strewn with blocks of phosphate
of lime, and the whole, as far as the belt of pinnacles, is covered
with a forest of lofty trees; the outer slopes are clothed with
thorny creepers and low trees.

Phosphate Hill, which forms the north-eastern angle of the
plateau, is much more extensive, and in the northern part at least
there is no distinct belt of pinnacles forming its outer border, but,
instead, a fairly gentle slope, terminating in a low limestone cliff,
below which is the level upper terrace. The whole of the summit,
as well as the northern and western flanks of this hill, is thickly

covered with a bed of blocks of phosphatic rock, which in a few
places can be seen to rest on a highly dolomitized limestone,
showing few or no traces of organic structure. The whole of the
slopes and terraces below this hill are thickly strewn with nodules
of the phosphate, and fragments of this substance are found enclosed
in the more recent limestones forming the lowest cliffs.

Another form assumed by the raised rim of the plateau occurs on
the northern side (Fig. 4 C). Here it forms a flat surface 200 or
300 yards broad, on the inner side of which there is a sudden
drop of 10–15 feet to the plateau, forming a low cliff of cavernous
dolomitic limestone, which can be traced some distance. On the
outer side is a steep slope, covered with talus, leading down to the
level upper terrace. The flat surface is similar to the reef flat of
an atoll, the inner cliff to the sudden drop of two or three fathoms
which often occurs on the lagoon side of the reef flat, and the
talus slope represents the reef slope on the seaward side. Much,
however, remains to be done in the examination of the limestones
before it can be definitely decided whether this interpretation of
the physical features described is the correct one.

Here and there on the surface of the plateau, particularly on the
northern portion, there are groups of limestone pinnacles of fan-
tastic shape, often 15 feet or more in height; these do not usually
show many traces of coral structure, but are largely composed of
fragments of branching *Lithothamnion*, *Halimeda*, and many pieces
of *Carpenteria*, all evidences of shallow-water conditions. In other
places in the northern angle of the plateau, just beneath the soil,
and forming slight ridges, is a chalk-like rock, showing, as a rule,
no trace of organic structure, but in the centre of the larger blocks
there is sometimes a hard unaltered core, which contains delicate
shelled foraminifera and some *Lithothamnion*. This rock was most
probably a chalky mud deposited in a quiet corner of the lagoon.
Another characteristic feature of this northern region is the
occurrence of rounded hills, often less than 50 feet high: their
lower portion is a soil-clad slope, and the flat-topped summit is
composed of much fissured limestone, forming lines by pinnacles
separated by deep fissures and channels. The whole is covered
with thick forest.

Farther south there are two or three ridges running in an
approximately east-and-west direction and having their longest
slope to the south, so that the plateau descends in that direction
to about 500 feet. It seems not impossible that these ridges may,
in part at least, represent the uppermost cliff of the northern
and eastern sides, and that when the sea stood at about this level
the coast, or more probably the submerged reef of the southern side
of the island, formed a wide bay opening towards the south-west.
The southern slopes of these ridges are largely formed by bare
limestone, often full of coral, and here and there, on the level
also, there are considerable areas covered with reefs split up into
pinnacles of rock by winding channels and deep fissures.

The western flank of the island differs considerably from the north and east, the upper cliffs being represented apparently by gentle slopes, and even the first inland cliff, except towards North-West Point (Fig. 5) and Egeria Point, is less clearly defined than elsewhere.   Another peculiar feature is the occurrence of several narrow dales or gorges running towards the coast in a direction a little south of west.   Some of these cut down to the sea-level, others open out on the shore terrace (as above defined).   In several cases their floor is formed by volcanic rock, and in the wet season they are traversed by a small stream which descends to the sea in a succession of falls and rapids.   At the time of my visit (October) there was no water in any of these valleys except one towards the north (see Map, Hugh's Dale); but the rounded steps and boulders, both of limestone and basalt, show that a considerable volume of water must pass during the rains.   The surface of the basalt is often covered with a thick coat of lime deposited from the water.   Some of the falls are of considerable size; one in Sidney's Dale, formed by the edge of a bed of basalt, is 40 feet high by about 30 broad.

The cliffs shutting in the valley are sometimes 50 to 60 feet high.   They are generally much more developed on one side than the other; and on the northern side there may be merely a steep slope, while on the southern there is a vertical cliff.   The mode of formation of these valleys will be considered in the geological section, but it may be here mentioned that although water has no doubt helped to deepen them—and in the case of those which reach the sea, has cut through the shore terrace and sea cliff— they do not appear to owe their origin to this agency.

From time to time a good deal of slipping and faulting has taken place round the flanks of the island, and in some localities has been so extensive as to materially modify the arrangement of the inland cliffs and terraces.

Perhaps the most extensive of the slips that have taken place is on the east coast a little south of North-East Point and beneath the eastern slopes of Phosphate Hill.   Here for some distance the first and second inland cliffs, or the slopes representing them, are interrupted by a precipice, the upper edge of which is from five to six hundred feet above the sea-level; the lower third or so is covered with a talus of immense blocks of limestone.   This cliff seems to be the result of the slipping down of an outer portion of the island, extending inland nearly as far as the cliff spoken of above as the third inland cliff.   This movement must have taken place before the elevation which gave rise to the present shore terrace and sea cliff, since these are continuous with those to the north and south, and can be seen to consist, here as elsewhere, of a raised fringing reef, which has here grown out upon the foot of the talus slope above mentioned, and sometimes has included fallen blocks within itself.

North of the high cliff just noticed the first inland cliff is

FIG. 5.—NORTH-WEST POINT FROM THE NORTH.

FIG. 6.—STEEP POINT FROM THE NORTH.

resumed; but it is of a different character from that found elsewhere on the north and east coast, and consists of Miocene limestones. It seems probable that this cliff likewise is the result of a slipping down of the seaward portions of the island, and on the terrace above it there are several ridges marking similar slips of less extent. The cliff on the southern side of the headland of Egeria Point shows signs of a similar origin, and there it can be clearly seen that a number of minor slips have occurred, giving rise to several small vertical cliffs which do not extend any great distance and occur at different levels; they are all situated above the main cliff face.

Although, as already stated, the main slipping occurred before the elevation of the present shore terrace, similar movements of small extent have taken place since, and at North-East Point itself a distinct fault, with a throw of about five feet, cuts across the shore terrace and runs out to sea in a north-easterly direction.

At Steep Point (Fig. 6) a dislocation of a somewhat different character has occurred. There little downward displacement has taken place, but the projecting angle of the island which forms the headland has split away from the main mass and tilted slightly outward in such a way that it is separated from the main mass of the island by a narrow valley. The result of this is that at the Point the shore terrace is interrupted for some distance, and the sea washes the base of what is elsewhere the first inland cliff, but which here forms a fine headland, with a vertical cliff some 150 to 200 feet high. This dislocation also took place before the elevation of the present shore terrace, and there is some evidence that the bottom of the narrow valley, marking the line of fracture, was for a time, at least in part, filled with water, and Steep Point Hill must then have formed a small island, or was perhaps joined to the mainland by a small isthmus formed by talus.

Besides Steep Point, Flying Fish Cove is the only place round the island where the shore terrace is interrupted, and here also this seems to have been the result of the slipping of the outer portion of the lofty cliff, but in this case the talus has accumulated in such a way as to form the foundation of the crescent-shaped platform on which the settlement stands, and to make the submarine slopes sufficiently gentle to allow the fairly broad fringing reef to grow outward, giving rise to the present anchorage. The structure of Flying Fish Cove will be described in greater detail in the geological section.

Cracking and slipping of the outer flanks of the island may be said to be universal, and in the neighbourhood of Flying Fish Cove both the sea cliff and even the present reef can be seen to be fissured by cracks, traceable for several hundred yards and running roughly parallel to the coastline. This circumstance gives a key to many peculiar, and at first incomprehensible, features on some of the higher terraces.

Climate.

The climate of Christmas Island is both pleasant and healthy. During the greater part of the year the weather is much like that of a hot, dry, English summer, tempered nearly always by a steady sea-breeze from the E.S.E., which is generally fairly cool, and keeps the temperature very even day and night. The maximum temperature (in the shade) recorded during my stay was 89° Fahr. on November 20th ; the minimum (night) was 70° Fahr. on February 13th, when it was raining heavily. The greatest range in twenty-four hours was 14°. The average daily maximum and minimum may be taken as about 84° Fahr. and 75° Fahr. respectively, the former occurring an hour or two after midday, the latter shortly before sunrise. The average temperature of the surface of the sea, deduced from several observations, is about 83°.

The prevalent wind is the S.E., or rather E.S.E., trade-wind, which blows the greater part of the year (about 300 days on an average). From May to December it is almost uninterrupted, but during the earlier months of the year, which are the rainy season in the island, the wind occasionally shifts round to the N. and N.E., and sometimes blows hard from these directions, accompanied by heavy rains. At such times Flying Fish Cove, which during the prevalence of the trade-wind forms a sheltered anchorage, is exposed to a heavy sea, which breaks on the reef with great violence, the spray filling the whole valley and drifting up the high cliff like smoke. The beach is piled up till it is nearly vertical, and at high tide a little water is sometimes spilled over its edge on to the platform behind. During these periods many birds of passage, such as wagtails, whimbrel, swallows, etc., reach the island, often in a very exhausted condition, and several new kinds of moths and butterflies, not seen at other times, were obtained. Even if the northerly wind only lasts a few hours swarms of dragon-flies nearly always arrive ; after two or three weeks they disappear again.

Except for showers at night on the higher parts of the island, almost the whole rainfall occurs from December to May inclusive : during these months there are sometimes heavy downpours lasting several days, but as a rule the mornings are fine. At these times the rain nearly always comes when the wind shifts round towards the north. In the dry season (May–December) the vegetation is kept fresh by very heavy dews and occasional showers at night. These latter often occur on the uplands of the island, and seem to be caused by the chilling of the E.S.E. wind, which results in the formation of clouds over the high land.

The meteorological peculiarities of the island no doubt depend on its situation close to the southern limit of the monsoon. From towards the end of the year till May the northern horizon is nearly always marked by a cloud-bank, even when the trade-wind is blowing on the island, and, as shown above, it is only occasionally

that the N. and N.E. wind extends as far south as the island,
bringing with it unsettled weather.

Unfortunately no rain-gauge[1] was taken, so that accurate
measurements of the rainfall were not made; but the luxuriance
of the vegetation over the whole island, the fact that under fallen
logs the soil is generally moist, and the presence of perennial
springs on the east coast, are sufficient evidences that the amount is
large. Owing to the porous nature of the limestones and the
depth of the soil, there is a complete absence of standing water
and of marshy ground, except close to the small stream on the east
coast; and though, no doubt, it is to this circumstance that the
island owes its extreme healthiness, still the lack of easily
accessible water on the higher ground is a drawback which has
to be reckoned with. Wherever water is found it is held up by
the volcanic rock, and since in many places this occurs at no great
depth, borings will probably give an abundant supply without
much difficulty.

The Soil.

The soil which covers the greater part of the terraces and
plateau, with the exception of the areas occupied by the reefs and
groups of pinnacles described above, is a rich brown loam, often
strewn with nodules of phosphate and here and there with fragments of volcanic rock. One of the most notable features about
the island is the great depth to which, in many places, the soil
extends. For instance, near the northern angle of the plateau
Mr. Ross sank a well nearly forty feet without reaching the bed
rock, and even on the shore terrace near Flying Fish Cove a shaft
some fifteen feet deep was entirely in soil in which some blocks of
limestone were embedded. Reefs of bare limestone may occur quite
close to such places, and it appears therefore that the soil fills great
inequalities in the surface of the island. It seems impossible that
a soil so abundant can have resulted merely from the disintegration
of limestone and the decay of vegetation, and no doubt it is to a
considerable extent the product of the decomposition of volcanic
rock which must have been exposed in many places on the higher
land, either in consequence of the incompleteness of the limestone
covering of the volcanic basis of the island, or through the removal
of portions of that covering through denudation, or possibly in a
few cases through the extrusion of volcanic material in the form
of lava-flows or tuff beds.

---

[1] In Colonial Report No. 257 on the Cocos-Keeling and Christmas Islands,
paragraph 35, it is stated that owing to injuries received by the meteorological
instruments while in my hands, Mr. A. Ross had been unable to keep the records
for the previous year. This is inaccurate. The thermometer by means of which
Mr. Ross recorded the temperatures in former years was never in my hands, and,
except perhaps a small pocket aneroid, there were not, to my knowledge, any
other meteorological instruments on the island.

It will be necessary in the future to exercise considerable care both in the clearing of the forest and in the introduction of animals, such as pigs and goats, likely to lead to its destruction, for if the disafforesting of the island were carried out to any very great extent the rainfall would be at once reduced, and there would be danger lest the torrential downpours of the wet season should lead to the gradual removal of much of the soil left unprotected by vegetation.

Inhabitants and Present Condition of the Island.

At the time of the visit of H.M.S. "Egeria" (Captain Aldrich), in 1887, the island was found to be entirely uninhabited, and there was no indication that it had ever been occupied. A few ships, probably whalers, seemed to have touched at Flying Fish Cove, for some of the large trees had letters cut on them [3], and Mr. Andrew Clunies Ross told me that there was a report current in Batavia that some thirty years ago five men of a Dutch vessel were cast away on the south-east coast, where they remained for several months. One of the party is said to have died, and the others were at last rescued by a Dutch ship. Captain Maclear also mentions [3] that one of his officers heard a similar report.

Towards the end of 1887 the rocks collected during the visit of H.M.S. "Egeria" were submitted to Dr. (now Sir John) Murray for examination, and he detected among the specimens from the higher parts of the island some which consisted of nearly pure phosphate of lime; it is to this discovery that the island owes its further development.

Early in 1888 Dr. Murray sent Dr. H. B. Guppy to explore the island and work out its structure. He went to Batavia, and thence paid a visit to the Cocos-Keeling Islands, of which he has given a valuable account; [1] but as far as Christmas Island was concerned the expedition miscarried, and he returned to England in February, 1889, without having reached it.

In the meanwhile Sir John Murray had given such information to the Government as led to the annexation of the island in June, 1888, as already mentioned above (p. 2), and in November of the same year a settlement was established at Flying Fish Cove by Mr. G. Clunies Ross, of Cocos-Keeling Island, and since that date this gentleman's brother, Mr. Andrew Clunies Ross, with his family and a few Cocos-Island Malays, have resided there almost continuously. By them houses were built, wells were dug, and small clearings for planting coffee, coconut-palms, bananas, and other plants were made in the neighbourhood of Flying Fish Cove.

---

[1] Scottish Geographical Magazine, vol. v (1889), pp. 281, 457, 569.

In February, 1891, Sir John Murray and Mr. G. Clunies Ross were granted a lease of the island by the British Government, and in 1895–6 Mr. Sidney Clunies Ross made explorations in the higher part of the island, resulting in the discovery of large deposits of phosphate of lime. Finally, in 1897 the leaseholders sold their lease to a small company, in the possession of which the island still remains.

During my visit a number of Malay coolies were imported to clear the forest for making roads. One of these roads was made from Flying Fish Cove to the east coast, another to Phosphate Hill, and a third from West White Beach to the west and south coast, and by these the further exploration of the island was much facilitated. Another result of these clearings is that the spread of various plants introduced for food is rendered much more rapid, and in the neighbourhood of the settlement several species have already run wild and are entering into competition with the native flora. The most successful of these newly introduced species are the 'chillie,' which already forms dense masses on the shore terrace near Flying Fish Cove, and the papaia, seedlings of which are very numerous in the same locality, and were also noticed here and there along the Phosphate Hill and south-east roads. In both these instances man, no doubt, has been mainly responsible for the dispersal of the seeds, but in the case of the chillies birds have probably assisted. Other plants will certainly follow, and in a few years a number will have established themselves at the expense of the native flora.

Since my stay in the island nearly two hundred Chinese have been imported, and the presence of these men will doubtless lead to the introduction and dispersal of other species of plants and animals, and at the same time, judging from recent reports, it will bring about a very considerable reduction in the numbers of the rats.

In addition to the Malays and Chinese, there are now on the island eight Europeans (including the wife and two children of Mr. W. A. Wilkinson, the Company's engineer) and five Sikh police.

At present the chief plants introduced include coconut-palm, date-palm, bamboo, sugar-cane, banana, pineapple, pomegranate, papaia, nutmeg, cacao, coffee, chillies, custard-apple, pumpkins, gourds, maize, tobacco, *Cassia siamea*, and probably several others. Of some of these only a few plants exist, and some no doubt will prove unsuitable to the new conditions of life.

Scarcely any domestic animals have been yet introduced. There are a few ducks and fowls, a number of dogs, necessary to keep down the rats in the settlement, a goat, and one or two pigs. The cat fortunately has not been taken to the island, and its introduction should certainly be avoided, for if it were to increase to any great extent the sea-birds, which are an important source of food, would probably be destroyed or their numbers greatly diminished. At present neither the Norway rat nor the house-mouse has reached the island ; but when large ships call at the island and stay there for some time, the arrival of these animals is inevitable. Probably a few insects, arachnids, and myriopods may have come from the Cocos-Keeling Islands and Java in Mr. Ross's vessels, and, in fact, I have seen two or three large centipedes which arrived in coconut-leaves which were imported for thatching. The number of forms thus introduced must, however, be very small, since the visits of these vessels only occur at intervals of several months.

It seems advisable to give these details as to the present condition of the island, because, although they are unimportant in themselves, they may be of considerable interest if the locality be again examined a few years hence.

CHRISTMAS ISLAND.

ZOOLOGY.

MAMMALIA.

By C. W. ANDREWS, B.Sc., F.Z.S.

As might be expected in an oceanic island, the mammals are both few in number and of small size. The collections brought back by the officers of H.M.S. "Flying Fish" and by Mr. Lister included two species of rat (*Mus macleari* and *M. nativitatis*), a large fruit-bat (*Pteropus natalis*), and a shrew (*Crocidura fuliginosa*, var. *trichura*); a small insectivorous bat was seen, but no specimens were obtained. Unfortunately no additions have been made to this list, but further information as to the habits and other points of interest have been obtained, and the small bat is now described for the first time.

The conditions of life are apparently extremely favourable, food being always abundant, and the hawk and owl, which are the only possible enemies, feeding mainly on birds and insects. The consequence of this is that all the species of mammals are extremely common, and the individuals are always exceedingly fat. Perhaps *Mus nativitatis*, the bull-dog rat as the Cocos Islanders have named it, is the least numerous, probably because of some competition with the much more active and versatile *M. macleari*, but most specimens of *M. nativitatis* have a layer of fat from half to three-quarters of an inch thick over most of the dorsal surface of the body. The fruit-bats are likewise invariably in remarkably good condition, and considerable quantities of oil can be obtained from them.

With the exception of the small bat, all the species have been described by Mr. O. Thomas in two papers[1] dealing with the collections made by the officers of H.M.S. "Flying Fish" and by Mr. J. J. Lister. His descriptions will be here reprinted, with such additions as the increased material renders possible and with some notes on the habits of the several species.

---

[1] P.Z.S., 1887, pp. 511–514, pls. xli, xlii; and 1888, pp. 532–534.

1. Pteropus natalis, Thomas. (Plate I.)

P.Z.S., 1887, p. 511.

Mr. Thomas's description of this species, founded upon two adult females and a new-born male, is given below:—

"Colour (♀) uniformly deep shining-black all over, the only variation in tone being that while the head is absolutely black there is a faint brownish tinge in the fur of the body. Fur thick, soft, woolly, more so, of course, upon the head and neck than on the back, but nowhere really straight; on the fore limbs above it extends along the humerus, and thinly along the proximal half of the forearm; on the back its least breadth is about 2½ inches; on the hind limbs it extends thinly to about half-way down the tibia. Below, the humerus, proximal half of forearms, hind limbs to just below the knee, and wing membranes between the body and

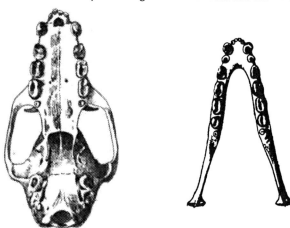

FIG. 7.—Skull and Mandible of *Pteropus natalis*, showing dentition.
Natural size.

a line drawn from the centre of the forearm to the knee, are all thinly clothed with scattered woolly black hairs. Muzzle broad and obtuse. Ears rather short; laid forward, they barely reach to the posterior canthus of the eye; their anterior edges evenly but slightly convex, their tips pointed or narrowly rounded off, their outer margins straight or faintly concave for their upper half, markedly convex for their lower; their basal half thinly hairy internally; their distal half quite naked, black. Wings arising on the back about an inch apart. Interfemoral membrane narrow, quite hidden in the fur.

"Teeth, especially the canines, small and short. Upper incisors, forming an evenly curved series, touching one another, their total breadth 5 mm. Canines short, 5 mm. from cingulum to tip behind, thin, and acutely pointed ; their postero - internal basal ledge proportionally rather broad. Anterior premolars minute or absent. Posterior premolars and first molar short, evenly oval in section ; the surface of the molars and last premolar singularly smooth and rounded ; the cusps but little developed, and merely consisting of low rounded ridges ; last molar circular in section, rather larger than one of the outer incisors, about 1·5 mm. in diameter.

" Lower incisors small, separated in the centre, the inner about half the size of the outer, the combined diameters of those of each side 2 mm. Canines proportionally still shorter than in the upper jaw, 3·5 mm. from cingulum to tip behind ; their basal ledge broad. Anterior premolar very large, nearly filling up the space between the canine and second premolar, its size in cross section nearly equal to that of the canine. Molars smooth and rounded, as in the upper jaw. Last molar in section about one-third the size of the anterior premolar, and three - quarters that of the last upper molar.

" Dimensions of the type, specimen *a*, an adult female in spirit : Head and body, 210 mm. ; head, 61 ; muzzle, 22 ; ear, above crown, 26 ; from notch at base, 28 ; forearm, 127 (▬ 5·0 inches) ; thumb, without claw, 43 ; index finger, 90 ; tibia, 62 ; calcaneum, 21.

" Skull : Basal length, 52 mm. ; greatest breadth, 30 ; supra-orbital foramen to tip of nasals, 24·5 ; interorbital breadth, 6·5 ; intertemporal breadth, 5·0 ; breadth from tip to tip of postorbital processes, 19·1 ; palate, length 32, breadth outside first molar 16·0 ; length of first molar 5·0.

" It is unfortunate that of this new species the only specimens of any use for description are females, since it might happen that, as is sometimes the case in *Pt. nicobaricus,* while the females are wholly black, the males have the usual yellow or orange tippet. It is therefore much to be hoped that male specimens will soon be obtained and the point settled. In any case, however, *Pt. natalis* is a very well-marked species. From *Pt. nicobaricus* it may be distinguished by its much smaller size and smaller, shorter molars, and especially by its much shorter and feebler canines, the latter character, in fact, distinguishing it from all the other allied species except *Pt. lombocensis. Pt. pselaphon,* another woolly-black species of about the same size, a native of Bonin, may be separated at once by its hairy legs, the hind limbs being closely haired right down to the feet. *Pt. gouldi,* also generally black, has a forearm 165 mm. long, and has also large teeth and long canines bearing no resemblance to those of the present species.

" On the whole *Pt. natalis* seems to be most nearly allied to *Pt. lombocensis,* Dobs.,[1] as yet only known from Lombock, which

---

[1] Cat. Chir. B.M., p. 34 (1878).

also has similarly short canines, and is of about the same size. That animal, however, is of a dull light-brown colour, with the neck pale yellow. Its teeth, especially the anterior molar, are narrower and lighter than those of *Pt. melas* ; the first lower pre-molar and the last molars both above and below are much smaller, and the basal ledges to the canines are decidedly narrower than in *Pt. natalis*. In the skull, again, *Pt. lombocensis* has a shorter, broader muzzle, greater spread of zygomata, broader interorbital space, and larger postorbital processes than the present species. Of course, in comparing the colours of these two species the question of sex again arises, as the only known specimens of *Pt. lombocensis* are both males ; but considering not only the differences in the skull and teeth, but also the fact that even if the male of *Pt. natalis* have a yellow tippet, it would in all probability have at least its head and body jet-black, like the female, I should certainly not be justified in assigning the Christmas Island specimens to *Pt. lombocensis*. It should also be noticed that the little hair that has appeared on the crown and between the shoulders of specimen *c*, a newborn male, is woolly black ; its neck is unfortunately still entirely naked."

The above description was founded upon female specimens. In some males, probably old individuals, there is a distinct trace of the tippet, in the shape of a band of brownish fur most conspicuous on the sides of the neck and narrowing towards the middle of the back, where it is interrupted by a strip of black fur like that covering the rest of the body. Scattered through the fur there are a few white hairs or white banded with brown. The fur of the lumbar region is smooth and straight.

This species is very common all over the island, and at the settlement causes great destruction of fruit, particularly of papaias and bananas. When the wild fruits are ripe comparatively few of these bats visit the gardens, but great numbers may be seen feeding in the forest. The wild fruits to which they are most destructive seem to be those of the 'Saoh' (*Sideroxylon*) and the 'Gatet' (*Inocarpus*).

One remarkable point about this species is, that it has to a very great extent abandoned the nocturnal habits usual in the group. Several might often be seen sailing and circling high in the air in the hot sunlight, sometimes even at midday, and I have also frequently seen them feeding in the daytime.[1] The cry is a very loud, harsh screech, apparently uttered both during the inspiration as well as the expiration of the breath. At the end of July I shot

---

[1] Macgillivray has recorded that on Fitzroy Island he saw great numbers of *Pteropus conspicillatus* flying in bright daylight. (Voyage of the " Rattlesnake," vol. i, p. 96.)

a female carrying a well-grown young one, but was never able to
obtain another specimen in this condition. Towards the end of
December several fœtal specimens, some near the term, were
obtained. At this season most of the females seem to live in the
deeper parts of the forest, and nine out of ten of the specimens
killed near the settlement were males. Shortly afterwards these
also began to disappear, and it was not till March that they again
became numerous in the clearings. At this time a dead tree near
the east coast was seen covered with hundreds of these bats, but
a week or two afterwards they had completely forsaken it.

Measurements of specimens in the present collection are given
below :—

		Head and Body.		Hind-foot.		Ear.
♂	...	190 mm.	...	37 mm.	...	28 mm.
♂	...	198 ,,	...	38 ,,	...	22 ,,
♂	...	180 ,,	...	36 ,,	...	27 ,,
♀	...	170 ,,	...	40 ,,	...	28 ,,
♀	...	187 ,,	...	35 ,,	...	26 ,,
♀	...	180 ,,	...	32 ,,	...	25 ,,
♀	...	167 ,,	...	36 ,,	...	25 ,,
♀	...	193 ,,	...	35 ,,	...	25 ,,
♀	...	180 ,,	...	35 ,,	...	26 ,,

2. Pipistrellus murrayi, sp.n.

Muzzle obtuse, but less so than in *P. abramus*; the glandular
prominences rather well marked.

Ears triangular, with broadly rounded tips, relatively longer and
narrower than in *P. abramus*; outer border somewhat concave.
Tragus with parallel borders and rounded tip; anterior border
straight, posterior convex.

Feet small; wing membrane attached just below base of toes.
Distinct post-calcaral lobe. Last caudal vertebra (2 mm.) free.
Fur covers about the upper third of the humerus and half the
femur; it extends very slightly on to the body membrane. On
the ventral surface the fur scarcely extends below anus, but sparse
hairs clothe the interfemoral membrane nearly to the tip of
the tail.

Colour, a dark brown with yellowish tips to the hairs, but some
specimens are a distinctly reddish brown. Fur on dorsal surface
long and thick. In front of ear and round eye the skin is nearly
bare, and the same is the case with the tip of the muzzle.

The outer incisor is rather longer than the outer cusp of the
inner, and on its postero - external surface the cingulum bears
a small but distinct cusp.

The lower incisors slightly crowded. The point of the first
premolar is visible through space between the canine and p.m. 2.

This species is considerably smaller than *P. abramus* and the
common Pipistrelle. It is larger and much darker in colour than

P. pachypus, and in point of size comes very near to *P. tenuis*, which, however, is distinguished from it by its much blacker tint, and the complete absence of the rufous tinge which is noticeable to a greater or less extent in all the specimens of the present species. In *P. tenuis* also the outer incisor is stouter than the outer cusp of the inner. *P. indicus* is brighter-coloured and somewhat larger.

The measurements of this species are as follows :—

Type Specimen.	Head and Body.	Tail.	Ear.	Hind-foot.	Forearm.
♂ ...	36·5 mm. ...	29·5 mm. ...	10 mm. ...	7 mm. ...	31 mm.
b. ♂ ...	35 ,, ...	29 ,, ...	9·5 ,, ..	6·5 ,, ...	30 ,,
a. ♀ ...	36 ,, ...	29 ,, ...	10·5 ,, ...	7 ,, ...	32 ,,
c. ♀ ...	34 ,, ...	29 ,, ...	8·5 ,, ...	6 ,, ...	32·5 ,,
d. ♀ ...	36 ,, ...	30·5 ,, ...	9·5 ,, ...	6·5 ,, ...	31·5 ,,
e. ♀ ...	36 ,, ...	30 ,, ...	9 ,, ...	6·5 ,, ...	31·5 ,,

The above measurements are taken from spirit specimens. The length of the tail is given approximately only.

The following measurements are from freshly-killed specimens :—

	Head and Body.	Tail.	Ear.	Hind-foot.	Forearm.
♂	... 35 mm. ...	? mm. ...	9 mm. ...	6 mm. ...	31 mm.
♂	... 40 ,, ...	? ,, ...	10 ,, ...	7 ,, ...	32 ,,
♀	... 38 ,, ...	30 ,, ...	11 ,, ...	6 ,, ...	30·5 ,,
♀	... 38 ,, ...	31 ,, ...	10 ,, ...	8 ,, ...	31 ,,
♀	... 35 ,, ...	? ,, ...	9 ,, ...	6 ,, ...	31 ,,

3. Crocidura fuliginosa, Blyth, var. trichura, Dobson.

Sorex fuliginosus, Blyth : Journ. Roy. Asiatic Soc. Bengal, xxiv, p. 362.
Crocidura fuliginosa, var. *trichura*, Dobson : P.Z.S., 1888, p. 532.

The Christmas Island shrew was described by Dobson as a local variety of *Crocidura fuliginosa* (Blyth), a species occurring in the Eastern Himalayas, Assam, and Tenasserim. His description is as follows :—

" This variety differs from the typical form in the much greater length of the tail, which also, unlike most specimens of that species, is beset with long fine hairs.

" In the shape of the skull and teeth and in all other characters it so closely resembles typical examples of *C. fuliginosa* that I hesitate to consider it more than a local variety of that species."

The specimen which Dobson took as type seems to have possessed an exceptionally long tail, some 10 mm. longer than the head and body. In most of my specimens measured in the flesh the tail is shorter (in one case by 10 mm.) than the head and body, and in one or two specimens only is it slightly longer. Nevertheless, since in all the specimens from the island the tail differs from that of the typical form in being thickly covered with fine hairs, it will be best to retain Dobson's varietal name *trichura*.

Measurements of the specimens obtained are given below :—

	Head and Body.		Tail.		Ear.		Hind-foot.
♂ ...	72 mm.	...	75 mm.	...	7 mm.	...	15 mm.
♂ ...	65 ,,	...	68 ,,	...	7 ,,	...	16 ,,
♂ ...	76 ,,	...	72 ,,	...	10 ,,	...	17 ,,
♂ ...	73 ,,	...	74 ,,	...	10 ,,	...	16 ,,
♂ ...	79 ,,	...	73 ,,	...	8 ,,	...	15 ,,
♂ ...	70 ,,	...	65 ,,	...	9 ,,	...	15 ,,
♀ ...	67 ,,	...	63 ,,	...	7 ,,	...	14 ,,
♀ ...	78 ,,	...	70 ,,	...	8 ,,	...	13 ,,
♀ ...	82 ,,	...	72 ,,	...	11 ,,	...	16 ,,
♀ ...	70 ,,	...	63 ,,	...	9 ,,	...	15 ,,

The measurements of Dobson's type are—

Head and body, 70 mm. ; tail, 80 mm. ; hind-foot, 16 mm.

This little animal is extremely common all over the island, and at night its shrill squeak, like the cry of a bat, can be heard on all sides. It lives in holes in rocks and roots of trees, and seems to feed mainly on small beetles.

4. Mus nativitatis, Thomas. (Plate II.)

P.Z.S., 1888, pp. 533–4.

Mr. Thomas's description of this species is given below :—

	Head and Body.	Tail.	Hind-foot.	Forearm and Hand.	Ear.	Heel to front of last footpad.
	mm.	mm.	mm.	mm.	mm.	mm.
a. ♂ (type) .	254	176	54	66	20 × 17	26·6
b. ♂ . . .	264	175	54	65	18 × 17	27·3

"Skull : Basal length 46·8, greatest breadth 24·8 ; nasals, length 20·5 ; interorbital breadth, 8·7 ; interparietal, length 7·1, breadth 12·5 ; infraorbital foramina, length of outer wall 4·1, breadth from outer corner of one to that of the other 13·4 ; palate, length 26·7, breadth outside m.[1] 9·0, inside m.[1] 4·5 ; diastema, 15·5 ; length of anterior palatine foramina, 9·3 ; length of upper molar series, 7·6. Lower jaw, length (bone only) 30, (to incisor-tips) 34·6 ; greatest height, obliquely, from coronoid to angle, 15.

"Size large ; form thick and clumsy, the limbs and tail stout and heavy, but the head peculiarly small, slender, and delicate. General colour dark umber-brown all over, the belly not or scarcely lighter than the back. Ears small, laid forward they barely reach to the posterior canthus of the eye. Fur of back, long, thick, and

coarse, but without the extremely long piles so characteristic of
M. macleari, the longest hairs being about 40 or 45 mm. in length.
Hands and feet very thick and heavy; the claws, especially on
the fore feet, enormously broad and strong, not compressed, more
than twice the size of those of *M. macleari*, and evidently modified
for burrowing. Palms and soles naked, smooth; the pads broad,
low, and rounded, unusually little prominent; last hind foot pad
elongate. Tail shorter than the body without the head, very
thick, evenly tapering, nearly or quite naked; its scales triangular,
very large, the rings averaging about seven or eight to the
centimetre;[1] its colour uniform blackish brown throughout, above
and below, the white skin, however, showing to a certain extent
between the scales.

"Skull[2] disproportionally small, light, and delicate; compared
with that of *M. macleari* it is slightly shorter and very considerably
narrower. Supraorbital edges evenly divergent, slightly beaded,
but without any marked postorbital thickening. Outer plate of
anterior zygoma-root short and weak, scarcely projected forwards.
Anterior palatine foramina long, reaching backwards just to the
level of the front of m., Bullæ rather larger than in *M. macleari*,
but far smaller than in *M. everetti*. Lower jaw very thin and
slender, contrasting very markedly with *M. macleari* in this respect.

"Teeth[2] small and weak, their structure as usual. Front of
incisors orange above, yellow below.

"This fine rat cannot possibly be confounded with any other
known species of the genus.[3] Its size, peculiarly small and delicate head, short unicolor tail, large hands and feet, and powerful
digging claws, separate it at once from any of its congeners. In
some respects it agrees with the description given long ago by
Hermann of his *Mus javanus*,[4] but its brown under-side and naked
tail prove that it is not really the same, and it is probable that
Hermann's description was merely founded on an unusually large
specimen of *Mus decumanus*.

"The presence of a second large rat in such a small island as
Christmas Island is a very noteworthy fact, and recalls the state
of things existing in Guadalcanar, Solomon Islands, where two
still larger rats, *Mus imperator* and *M. rex*, one terrestrial and
fossorial and the other arboreal, live side by side in the same
locality."[5]

---

[1] Ten to twelve in *M. macleari*.
[2] For figures of the skull and teeth see Plate II (*bis*), figs. 2, 4, 5, 9, 10.
[3] *Mus infraluteus*, a species from Mount Kina Balu, North Borneo, described
by Mr. Thomas (Ann. and Mag. N. H. (6), ii, p. 409) since the above was
written, has a considerable superficial resemblance to *M. nativitatis*. Its tail,
however, is longer, and its skull is large and heavy, in due proportion to the size
of the body.
[4] Obs. Zool., p. 63 (1804).
[5] See *suprà*, pp. 479–481.

To the above account it need only be added that some specimens are of a much warmer brown than others, a difference that occurs irrespective of sex. In some individuals there is a small irregular patch of white fur on the belly. In very young specimens the fur is a bluish black. The mammary formula is $0 - 3 = 6$.

This rat, though very numerous in places, especially on the hills, e.g. Phosphate Hill, is very much less common than *M. macleari*. I never saw one in Flying Fish Cove, though they certainly have been killed there. They seem to live in small colonies in burrows, often among the roots of a tree, and occasionally several may be found living in the long, hollow trunk of a fallen and half-decayed sago-palm (*Arenga listeri*). The food consists of wild fruits, young shoots, and, I believe, the bark of some trees. *M. nativitatis* is a much more sluggish animal than *M. macleari*, and, unlike it, never climbs trees; and it is difficult to avoid the belief that the former species is being supplanted by the latter in spite of the abundance of food. Both animals are strictly nocturnal, and *M. nativitatis*, when exposed to bright daylight, seems to be in a half-dazed condition. The Ross family in Christmas Island have given this species the name "Bull-dog Rat," and this has been adopted by the Malays.

Measurements of the specimens in the present collection are given below :—

		Head and Body.		Tail.		Ear.		Hind-foot.
♂	(figured)	275 mm.	...	182 mm.	...	24 mm.	...	50 mm.
♂	... ...	273 ,,	...	159 ,,	...	23 ,,	...	52 ,,
♂	... ...	265 ,,	...	170 ,,	...	23 ,,	...	53 ,,
♂	... ...	260 ,,	...	170 ,,	...	25 ,,	...	54 ,,
♀	... ...	253 ,,	...	170 ,,	...	22 ,,	...	53 ,,
♀	... ...	250 ,,	...	168 ,,	...	25 ,,	...	52 ,,
♀	... ...	235 ,,	...	160 ,,	...	23 ,,	...	55 ,,
♀	... ...	228 ,,	...	183 ,,	...	21 ,,	...	55 ,,
♀	... ...	202 ,,	...	140 ,,	...	21 ,,	...	50 ,,

5. Mus macleari, Thomas.

P.Z.S., 1887, p. 513.

Mr. Thomas's description of this species is as follows :—

"Fur very long, thick, and coarse, but not or very slightly spinous, thickly intermixed on the back with enormously long piles from 2 to $2\frac{1}{4}$ inches in length. General colour grizzled rufous-brown, belly but little lighter pale-rufous. Shorter hairs everywhere, pale slaty-grey at base, shining red at tip; longer piles uniformly black; the general tint of the dorsal surface not unlike that of *Arvicola amphibius*, except that the median line is a good deal darker owing to the great number of the longer black piles there present. Whiskers very long, many of them more than three inches in length, mostly black. Ears naked, black, broad, short, and rounded, their breadth about equal to their length; laid forward they fall short of the eye by about a quarter of an inch. Limbs coloured externally like back, internally dull grey; upper sides of hands and feet uniform dark-brown; solepads six, very broad, flat, and rounded, evidently adapted for climbing; pad at the base of the fifth toe with a secondary pad at its postero‑external angle. Claws, both anterior and posterior, short, stout, curved, and sharply pointed, brown horn‑colour, that of the hallux markedly shorter than the rest; pollex with a broad nail as usual; fifth hind‑toe without claw reaching just to the end of the first phalanx of the fourth.

"Tail very long, its posterior half black all round, its distal half white or yellow, thinly and finely haired with short grey hairs, not hiding the scales; the scales large, the rings averaging just ten to the centimetre.

"Palate‑ridges 3–5. Mammæ 4, one axillary and one inguinal pair.

"Skull [1] large and strong. Nasals extending to about a millimetre past the level of the anterior edge of the orbit. Supraorbital edges beaded, but the beading not continued so far forward as in *M. everetti*. Interparietal large. Front edge of the anterior zygoma‑root very prominent, projecting forwards. Palatal foramina very long, their posterior end about one millimetre in front of the level of m.$_1$ Bullæ small and flattened.

"Incisors thick and strong, much bevelled externally, their faces dull orange‑yellow above and yellow below, but apparently the colour has been more or less affected by spirit. Molars of medium size.

"Measurements of the type, an adult female in spirit:—Head and body, 222 mm.; tail, 248; hind‑foot, 48·5; ear, 13; head, 64; forearm and hand, 66; last hind footpad, 10·5; heel to front of last footpad, 26.

"Skull: [1] Basal length, 47·5; greatest breadth, 26·2; nasals, length 19·5, greatest breadth 5·7; interorbital constriction, least breadth 7·0; interparietal, length 6·6, breadth 11·5; length of base of anterior zygoma‑root, 6·0; palate, length 30·0; breadth outside m.$_1$ 10·3, inside 4·4; palatal foramina, length 10·1; back of incisors to m.$_1$ (alveoli), 15·7; upper molar series, 9·0.

"This fine new rat belongs to a small group of species inhabiting the East Indian Archipelago, all of which agree with *Mus macleari* in being of large size, with very long tails tipped with yellow, and with small rounded ears. Their differential characters as compared to *M. macleari* are best put in tabular form:—

M. macleari. Mammæ 1—1 = 4. Dorsal piles present. Front edge of anterior zygoma‑root projecting, very convex. Palatal foramina long. Bullæ very small. Christmas Island.

[1] For figures of the skull and teeth see Plate II (*bis*), figs. 1, 3, 6, 7, 8. This species has been figured in P.Z.S., 1887, pl. xlii.

M. celebensis, Gray.[1] Mammæ 1—2 = 6. No dorsal piles.
Front edge of anterior zygoma - root not projecting.
Palatal foramina short.
Celebes.

M. xanthurus, Gray.[2] Mammæ 1 — 2 = 6. Long dorsal piles
present. Front of zygoma - root but little projecting.
Palatal foramina long.
Celebes.

M. everetti, Günth.[3] Fur long, but the piles not enormously
lengthened. Front of zygoma - root convex. Palatal
foramina long. Bullæ very large.
Philippines.

M. meyeri, Jent.[4] Fur without lengthened piles. Supra-
orbital edges much developed. Front of zygoma-root
slightly convex. Palatal foramina short. Teeth very
large.
Celebes.

M. muelleri, Jent.[5] Mammæ 2 — 2 = 8. No dorsal piles.
Tail unicolor. Front edge of zygoma convex. Palatal
foramina short. Teeth rather small. Bullæ medium.
Sumatra and Borneo.

"This last does not properly belong to the present group of
species, but is only introduced to complete the list of those of
which it is necessary to mention the distinguishing characters
when describing *M. macleari* as new. All these species also differ
from *M. macleari* in having the general colour grey or yellow
instead of rufous. No other described species could possibly be
confounded with the present most interesting new form, with which
I have much pleasure in connecting the name of Captain Maclear,
of H.M.S. 'Flying Fish,' to whom the Museum is indebted for
the Christmas Island specimens."

To this description it may be added that in the young the under
surface is much lighter coloured, and in one specimen is quite
white, the inner side of the fore and hind limbs being nearly so.
In the young, moreover, the long piles are not fully developed,
though they are visible among the fur.

There is considerable variation in colour in this species. In
some specimens the back is darker and less rufous and the long
piles are less developed than in the typical form.

---

[1] P.Z.S., 1867, p. 598.
[2] Loc. cit.
[3] P.Z.S., 1879, p. 75.
[4] Notes Leyd. Mus., i, p. 12 (1878).
[5] Op. cit., ii, p. 16 (1879).

This species is by far the commonest of the mammals found in the island; in every part I visited, it occurred in swarms. During the day nothing is to be seen of it, but soon after sunset numbers may be seen running about in all directions, and the whole forest is filled with its peculiar querulous squeaking and the noise of frequent fights. These animals, like most of those found in the island, are almost completely devoid of fear, and in the bush if a lantern be held out they will approach to examine the new phenomenon. As may be imagined, they are a great nuisance, entering the tents or shelters, running over the sleepers, and upsetting everything in their search for food. They seem to eat anything, and destroy any boots or skins incautiously left within their reach. Their natural food appears to be mainly fruits and young shoots, and to obtain the former they ascend trees to a great height. I have often seen them run up the trailing stems of the lianas, and, in fact, they can climb as well as a squirrel. In the settlement they utterly destroy all the fruit they can get at, and frequently come into conflict with the fruit-bats on the tops of the papaia - trees. A number of dogs is kept to keep them in check, and near the settlement they are certainly already less numerous than elsewhere.

In the daytime these rats live in holes among the roots of trees, in decaying logs, and shallow burrows. They seem to breed all the year round.

In the bush beaten tracks a few inches broad may often be seen, and Mr. Ross informs me that these are made by rats travelling in great numbers in search of food. I never had an opportunity of observing this, and am not sure whether it is this species or *Mus nativitatis* which makes the paths.

The measurements of the specimens of this species in the present collection are given below:—

	Head and Body.		Tail.		Ear.		Hind-foot.
♂	... 238 mm.	...	260 mm.	...	24 mm.	...	49 mm.
♂	... 234 ,,	...	265 ,,	...	25 ,,	...	50 ,,
♂	... 228 ,,	...	240 ,,	...	25 ,,	...	48 ,,
♂	... 210 ,,	...	240 ,,	...	22 ,,	...	45 ,,
♂	... 210 ,,	...	240 ,,	...	23 ,,	...	50 ,,
♂	... 208 ,,	...	218 ,,	...	23 ,,	...	47 ,,
♂	... 200 ,,	...	245 ,,	...	23 ,,	...	50 ,,
♂	... 187 ,,	...	207 ,,	...	25 ,,	...	46 ,,
♂	... 184 ,,	...	196 ,,	...	23 ,,	...	42 ,,
♂	... 152 ,,	...	170 ,,	...	19 ,,	...	40 ,,
♀	... 255 ,,	...	235 ,,	...	25 ,,	...	45 ,,
♀	... ? ,,	...	260 ,,	...	25 ,,	...	50 ,,
♀	... 240 ,,	...	255 ,,	...	23 ,,	...	46 ,,
♀	... 210 ,,	...	260 ,,	...	24 ,,	...	47 ,,

NOTES ON THE OSTEOLOGY OF *MUS NATIVITATIS* AND *MUS MACLEARI.*

By Dr. C. I. FORSYTH MAJOR, F.Z.S.

(PLATE II, *bis.*)

EVEN if it were not known that *Mus nativitatis* is terrestrial and burrowing, while *Mus macleari* is arboreal, the examination of the manus of both species would reveal this fact at once. The bones of the antebrachium, the carpals, metacarpals, and proximal phalanges

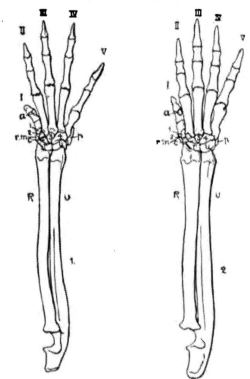

FIG. 1.—Antebrachium and carpus of *Mus macleari.*
FIG. 2.—Antebrachium and carpus of *Mus nativitatis.*

R, radius; *U*, ulna; *r*, radiale; *u*, ulnare; *rm*, radiale marginale;
p, pisiforme; *c*, centrale; 1–4, first to fourth carpale; *a*, dorsal
phalange of first digit; i–v, first to fifth digit.

are all slenderer and more elongate in the latter species, stouter and broader in the former, the longitudinal dimensions of the fore-limb as a whole being about the same in both.

The above remark does not, however, apply to the ungual phalanges, which in *M. nativitatis* are longer, stronger, and less curved than in the other species; the difference in length is the more striking, as with regard to the proximal phalanges and metapodials the proportions are reversed, these being more elongate in *M. macleari*, as already pointed out.

The ungual phalange of the first digit of *M. nativitatis* is not different in character from those of the other digits. In *M. macleari* the whole of the thumb, including the Metac. i, is more reduced than in the former species; and its ungual phalange has a rounded, nail-like form, absolutely different from the claw-like, curved ungual phalanges in the other fingers, and resembling somewhat the same element in Primates. A still more appropriate comparison of the digits of the arboreal *M. macleari* is with that of *Sciurus* (e.g. *S. vulgaris*), where we find the same curved, claw-like, ungual phalanges of digits ii–v, and the same rounded, nail-like, ungual phalange of the first digit. The reduction of the thumb has, however, in the squirrel, proceeded further than in *M. macleari*; whilst the third and fourth digits have further proceeded in the opposite sense, being disproportionately long.

In both *M. nativitatis* and *M. macleari*, an ossicle overlies, dorsally, the interphalangeal articulation of the thumb. I have, on a recent occasion, P.Z.S. London, 1899, p. 430, suggested that this ossicle, which, although never mentioned before, is of quite common occurrence in Rodentia and Insectivora, may be the second phalange of the thumb, having been thrust out on the dorsal surface.

In the same place, quoted before, I have treated at length of the distal pisiform of Muridæ, etc.; this bone forms, so to say, a 'pendant' to the distal 'præpollex' (see below); it occurs in both the species. See Text-fig. 5, op. cit.

The ossicle, which in the figures given in the above quoted paper is marked *x*, is equally present in both species from Christmas Island, situated on the volar side, between the latero-distal angle of the radius and the pisiform; in old specimens it becomes fused with the former, but it is quite possible that it often vanishes.

In *M. nativitatis* it is much smaller than in the other species.

Marginal radials.—The only writer, to my knowledge, who has made mention of the 'præpollex' in the genus *Mus*, is Emery, who describes it in *M. decumanus*. In this species there is in connection with the distal extremity of the bone in question a lamina of tendinous connective tissue having cartilaginous consistence ("eine knorpelharte Platte von schnigem Bindegewebe"), and acting as a support to the very prominent and compact radial pad. The single bone of *Mus decumanus* is considered to be the homologue of the proximal of the two bones occurring in *Pedetes*; to the distal bone of the latter would correspond the 'tendinous lamina' of *Mus decumanus*. The character of a cartilage being denied to the latter structure, the inference drawn from this is that its homologue in *Pedetes* is a dermal bone of secondary origin. In the latter genus the radial pad of other Rodents has been transformed into the volar prominence sheathed with a horny cap; in other words, the structure which in most Rodents is an organ of touch has been adapted to fossorial functions in *Pedetes*.[1]

It is not clear to me on what grounds Emery here denies a cartilaginous condition to the distal element of *Mus decumanus*. In a subsequent memoir[2] he seems disposed to adopt a different view. After having shown that in Marsupialia the ' præpollex ' is ' typically ' composed of two elements, he adds : " It will be of particular interest to investigate whether in other mammals, provided with a compound præpollex, the distal element has a cartilaginous Anlage ('knorpelig angelegt wird '), and is the homologue of the distal portion of the marsupial præpollex."

Like all Muridæ which have come under my observation, both *Mus nativitatis* and *Mus macleari* have a large-sized marginal radiale, articulating with the ' scapholunar ' and the Metac. i on their median and volar side, and thence extending obliquely across the vola in the direction of the distal pisiform bone. In both the species there is attached to the distal and ulnar margin of the marginal radiale, what appears to be a laminar cartilaginous appendix, incompletely ossified on the ulnar side. Neither of the two specimens—one from each species—is adult. I expect that in adult specimens the ossification will be found to extend over the whole of the distal part also. This condition I find to be the case in an individual of a genus closely allied with *Mus*, viz. in *Arvicanthis* (*A. niloticus*), although the specimen is not perfectly adult.

The principal differences in the skulls of the two specimens have been pointed out by O. Thomas (P.Z.S., 1888, pp. 533, 534), and are borne out by the figures of Plate II (*bis*). The skull of *M. nativitatis* is weaker, more slender, and narrower than that of the other species ; the outer wall of the infraorbital foramen is shorter and projects less forward ; the incisive foramina extend farther backwards. The molars of this species likewise are weaker and less complicated with secondary cusps. In *M. macleari*, the outer cusps of the upper and the inner cusps of the lower molars are much stronger than the corresponding parts in *M. nativitatis*. In several specimens of the latter the teeth present a diseased appearance, which is not the case in any of the specimens of *M. macleari*. I append the measurements in millimetres of some of the skulls collected by Mr. Andrews, three of *M. macleari* and two of *M. nativitatis*.

---

[1] C. Emery, " Zur Morphologie des Hand- und Fuss-skelets " : Anat. Anz., v, pp. 288–291 (1890).

[2] C. Emery, " Beiträge z. Entwicklungsgesch. und Morphologie des Hand- und Fuss-skelets der Marsupialier " : Semon's Forschungsreisen, ii, p. 394 (1897).

	M. macleari, 32	*M. macleari,* 35	*M. macleari,* 37	*M. natividatis,* 30	*M. natividatis* (from skel.),
Basilar length (Henselion) ...	47·4	40·5	42	42·5	42·5
Greatest breadth of skull ...	26·1	22·5	23·5	23·5	23·5
Length of nasals	19·6	18	18·5	19·5	19
Greatest breadth of nasals ...	5·8	5·0	5·0	5·7	5·5
Least breadth in interorbital constriction	6·9	6·5	8·0	7·5	7·5
Least length of outer wall of infraorb. foramen .	6·1	5·5	5·5	4·5	4·0
Length of palate	30·1	24·0	24·0	22·5	23
Breadth outside m. 1	10·2	9·0	8·5	9	—
Back of incisor to m. 1 ..	17·5	14·5	14	16	15·5
Length of upper molar series.	8·0	8·0	8·0	7	6·5
Length of lower molar series.	8·2	8·0	8·0	6·8	6·5

AVES.

By R. Bowdler Sharpe, LL.D., F.L.S., F.Z.S.

(PLATES III-VI.)

When the "Flying Fish" under Captain Maclear first visited Christmas Island in January, 1887, two new species of birds were discovered by the expedition, viz., *Carpophaga whartoni* and *Turdus erythropleurus.* The "Egeria" shortly afterwards paid a visit to the island, and Mr. J. J. Lister, who was naturalist to the expedition, made a good collection of birds and discovered several new species. His notes on his collection were also of great interest.

Mr. Andrews obtained series of all the species found on Christmas Island by Mr. Lister, and he was able to add several migratory species which the other expeditions had not met with, while the number of birds and eggs which he has obtained evince great energy on his part. In the following pages his field notes are accompanied by his initials 'C. W. A.'

Order COLUMBIFORMES.

1. Carpophaga whartoni.

Carpophaga whartoni, Sharpe, P.Z.S., 1887, p. 515, pl. xliii; Lister, P.Z.S., 1888, p. 520; Salvad., Cat. B. Brit. Mus., xxi, p. 184 (1893); Sharpe, Handl. B., i, p. 64 (1899).

No. 6, ♂ ad. Flying Fish Cove, August 8, 1897.
No. 57, ♀ ad. Flying Fish Cove, October 21, 1897.

No. 61, ♂ ad. Flying Fish Cove, October 22, 1897.
a, b, ♀ juv. Phosphate Hill, October 24, 1897.
c, d, e, ♂ ad. et imm. Flying Fish Cove, November 29, 1897.
No. 72, ♂ imm. Flying Fish Cove, November 21, 1897.
♂ ad. Phosphate Hill, November 3, 1897.
♂ ad. Flying Fish Cove, November 28, 1897.
No. 71, ♀ imm. Flying Fish Cove, November 24, 1897.
♂ imm. Flying Fish Cove, November 16, 1897.

Of this fine and peculiar Fruit-Pigeon Mr. Andrews procured a good series. There does not seem to be any appreciable difference in the colour of the sexes, but the young birds are more reddish underneath, and the first feathers of the throat and breast are of a dull grey, without any purplish or vinous tint whatever.

[The large Fruit-Pigeon, called by the Malays 'Pergám,' is very common over the whole island, but is much more often heard than seen, since it lives among the thick foliage of the tops of the lofty forest trees, where to the unpractised eye it is extremely difficult to discover. In addition to the ordinary cooing note, the male utters a deep booming cry which is the most striking of the forest sounds during the daytime. This note is said to resemble closely the noise made by tigers, and Mr. Ross told me that an old Bantamese wood-cutter who came to the island was at first afraid to enter the forest, and was with much difficulty persuaded that a bird was responsible for the sound. These birds are very tame, and when a number were feeding in a tree it was generally possible to shoot several, one after the other, without disturbing the rest. The boys in the island used to catch them with a noose of string at the end of a long stick, and the birds would sit quietly while the instrument of their destruction was prepared, and the boy climbed into a convenient position for using it. On one occasion I caught one with my hands while it was drinking at a puddle on a tree trunk.

The food is the fruit and leaf-buds of the various forest trees, and the birds gather in great numbers in trees of which the fruit is just ripening. The feet are very powerful, prehensile organs, and, while feeding, this Pigeon clambers about among the branches like a Parrot. The nest is a very scanty structure of sticks placed high up in a tree. The eggs are two in number, white, and elongated, with both ends alike. I saw a pair building on December 24th, and obtained an egg on January 6th; many young birds were shot in April. There seem to be two broods a year, for in the middle of November there were also great numbers of young birds, characterized by their looser, duller plumage and grey legs; in the adult the legs are a bright red. I have counted between fifty and sixty on the bushes round the small waterfall on the east coast. The year before I visited the island was a very dry one, and Mr. Ross informed me that great numbers of these Pigeons had died of thirst.—C. W. A.]

2. Chalcophaps natalis.

Chalcophaps natalis, Lister, P.Z.S., 1888, p. 522 ; Salvad., Cat. B. Brit. Mus.,
    xxi, p. 520 (1893) ; Sharpe, Handl. B., i, p. 84 (1899).

Nos. 24, 26, ♂ ad. ; No. 25, ♀ ad. Flying Fish Cove, August 6,
1897.
  ♂ ♀ ad. Flying Fish Cove, October 21, 1897.
No. 54, ♀ ad. Flying Fish Cove, October 21, 1897.
No. 55, ♂ juv. Flying Fish Cove, October 21, 1897.
♀ ad. Flying Fish Cove, November 15, 1897.

Young birds have the greater wing-coverts for the most part
rufous, and the under parts irregularly mottled with dusky bars.
As Count Salvadori points out, the male is not to be distinguished
from some of the males of *C. indica*, but the female differs considerably from the female of that species.
[The Ground-Pigeon is by far the most brightly coloured of the
birds of Christmas Island. It usually feeds on the ground, and
can run rapidly. Though generally seen in pairs, small flocks
sometimes occur, particularly near water. The food consists of
small fruits. The nest is said to be placed in thickets of screw-pine
(*Pandanus*), but I never saw either it or the eggs. At pairing-
time the males fight fiercely, and are said to kill one another
occasionally. Young birds are seen in April. In spite of the
brightness of its colouring, this bird is difficult to see, the green
of the back and chestnut brown of the breast matching very closely
the colours of the leaves and soil.—C. W. A.]

Order RALLIFORMES.

3. Limnobænus fuscus.

Limnobænus fuscus (Linn.), Sharpe, Cat. Brit. Mus., xxiii, p. 146 (1894).

No. 40, ♀ ad. Flying Fish Cove, August 29, 1897.
Iris brownish red, lightest round the pupil ; legs reddish brown.
This is an interesting addition to the list. The species may
visit the island regularly on migration, but Mr. Andrews only
obtained one specimen.

Order LARIFORMES.

4. Anous stolidus.

Anous stolidus (Linn.), Saunders, Cat. B. Brit. Mus., xx, p. 136 (1896).

a, ♂ ad. Rocky Point, November 15, 1897.
b, ♀ ad. Flying Fish Cove, November 16, 1897.

This species has not been obtained on Christmas Island before, but it was met with by Dr. H. O. Forbes on the Cocos-Keeling Islands in February.

[Breeds round the coast, the eggs being deposited on small shelves of the sea cliff.—C. W. A.]

Order CHARADRIIFORMES.

5. Glareola orientalis.

Glareola orientalis, Leach: Sharpe, Cat. B. Brit. Mus., xxiv, p. 58 (1896).

No. 48, ♀ imm. Flying Fish Cove, October 3, 1897.
Not previously noted from the island, but certain to be a regular visitor on migration.

6. Charadrius dominicus.

Charadrius dominicus, P. L. S. Müll.: Sharpe, Cat. B. Brit. Mus., xxiv, p. 195 (1896); id., Handl. B., i, p. 152 (1899).

♂ imm. Flying Fish Cove, November 14, 1897.
Not met with by Mr. Lister, but certainly a regular visitor on migration.

7. Ochthodromus geoffroyi.

Charadrius geoffroyi, Wagl.: Lister, P.Z.S., 1888, p. 528.
Ochthodromus geoffroyi, Sharpe, Cat. B. Brit. Mus., xxiv, p. 217 (1896); id., Handl. B., i, p. 153 (1899).

♀ ad. Flying Fish Cove, November 14, 1897.
An adult female in full winter plumage. It is evidently a regular visitor to Christmas Island on migration.

8. Numenius variegatus.

Numenius variegatus (Scop.), Sharpe, Cat. B. Brit. Mus., xxiv, p. 361 (1896).

a, b, ♂ ♀ ad. Flying Fish Cove, November 17, 1897.
c, ♀ ad. Flying Fish Cove, December 26, 1897.
New to the Avifauna of Christmas Island, but doubtless a more or less regular visitor on migration. Mr. Andrews only saw one small flock of four, out of which three specimens were killed.

9. Tringoides hypoleucus.

Tringoides hypoleucus (Linn.), Lister, P.Z.S., 1888, p. 528; Sharpe, Cat. B. Brit. Mus., xxiv, p. 456 (1896); id., Handl. B., i, p. 161 (1899).

No. 62, ♀ imm. Flying Fish Cove, October 22, 1897.
This is also apparently a regular visitor on migration, as it was likewise obtained by Mr. Lister.

10. Calidris arenaria.

Calidris arenaria (L.), Sharpe, Cat. B. Brit. Mus., xxiv, p. 526 (1896).

An adult bird in moult, still retaining a few of the feathers of the summer plumage on the back. This is an interesting addition to the Avifauna of Christmas Island, and increases our knowledge of the line of migration pursued by the Sanderling, which has in recent years been discovered in North Australia and in the Malay Archipelago.

11. Limonites ruficollis.

Limonites ruficollis (Pall.), Sharpe, Cat. B. Brit. Mus., xxiv, p. 545 (1896); id., Handl. B., i, p. 163 (1899).

a, b, ♂ juv., *♀* juv. Flying Fish Cove, September 20, 1897.

Both these specimens are immature birds in their first winter plumage. The male has the wing 4·15 inches and the female 4·0. The species has not been met with before on Christmas Island, but is doubtless a regular visitor on migration.

12. Gallinago stenura.

Gallinago stenura, Bp.: Sharpe, Cat. B. Brit. Mus., xxiv, p. 619 (1896); id., Handl. B., i, p. 165 (1899).

a, ♂ ad. Flying Fish Cove, December 1, 1897.

Not previously recorded from Christmas Island.

Order ARDEIFORMES.

13. Demiegretta sacra.

Ardea jugularis, Wagl.: Sharpe, P.Z.S., 1889, p. 516; Lister, P.Z.S., 1888, p. 138.
Demiegretta sacra (Gm.), Sharpe, Cat. B. Brit. Mus., xxvi, p. 138 (1898); id., Handl. B., i, p. 198 (1899).

No. 5 { ad. Flying Fish Cove, July, 1897.
{ ad. [white phase].
Nos. 2, 4, ♂ imm. Flying Fish Cove, August, 1897.
No. 3, ad. [white phase].
a, ♂ ad. Flying Fish Cove. November 18, 1897.

The bird in the white phase of plumage has very little crest, but the long ornamental breast-plumes are fully developed. Two of the outer scapulars are grey externally, and another grey plume is concealed by the long ornamental feathers of the lower back.

Order PELECANIFORMES.

Sub-Order FREGATI.

14. Fregata aquila.

Fregata aquila (Linn.), Sharpe, P.Z.S., 1887, p. 516; Lister, P.Z.S., 1888, p. 529; Ogilvie Grant, Cat. B. Brit. Mus., xxvi, p. 443 (1898); Sharpe, Handl. B., i, p. 237 (1899).

a, b, ♂ ♀. Flying Fish Cove, November 13, 1897.
c, d, ♂ ♀ juv. Flying Fish Cove, November 4, 18, 1897.

According to Mr. Andrews, who shot some breeding birds, the male of the large Frigate Bird is almost entirely black, being white only from the lower breast down to the vent, including the lower flanks and upper part of the thighs. The female is black above, and has the throat black, but is white from the lower throat downwards; the sides of the body black, with a large white patch on the flanks. The young birds have a rusty-coloured head and throat.

[Perhaps the most interesting of the birds of Christmas Island are the Frigate-birds, two species of which occur. Numbers of these birds could nearly always be seen sailing and circling in the air at all heights; in calm weather they often soar till scarcely visible. The flight is wonderfully graceful, and it is a pleasure to watch a group moving along the coast in a succession of sweeping circles, rising against the wind, or descending with it. In flight the head is carried close to the body, so that the bird seems to have no neck, and the tip of the beak is about on a level with the anterior angle of the outstretched wings. The feathers are often cleaned during flight, and occasionally the bird shakes itself like a dog that has just left the water, dropping through the air meanwhile. The young birds seem to be able to fly perfectly well as soon as they leave the nest, and groups of them could often be seen near the coast stooping to the water, one after the other, to pick up leaves and other floating objects, and then dropping them, apparently practising the method by which their parents obtain their food, which consists of surface fish and cephalopods. I never saw a Frigate-bird dive.

The old birds by no means depend for food on the fish they catch themselves, but systematically rob the Gannets, which breed in great numbers on the island. Towards sunset many Frigate-birds may be seen sailing along the coast, watching for the return of the Gannets, full-fed from the fishing grounds. The birds being well aware of what is in store for them, and knowing that if they can reach the shelter of the trees they are safe, approach the island at a great speed, flying as low down as possible. Usually, while they are still at some distance, two or three Frigate-birds give chase, and hunt the Gannet backwards and forwards, continually trying to get beneath it and to cut off its retreat to the trees. The chase may last several minutes, but at length the exhausted bird disgorges some of the fish it had swallowed, and this is immediately caught in mid - air by one of the pursuers. Mr. Ross told me that occasionally two Frigate-birds would come into collision and break their wings, but this I never saw. The twigs for building the nests are obtained on the same system of robbery, and although these birds will pick up twigs floating in the sea and lying on the beach, I never saw one attempt to break them off the dead branches as the Gannets do. If, when a nest is partly built, the bird in charge of it is killed, dozens of its neighbours come round and steal the material thus conveniently collected for them. The nest consists merely of a few handfuls of twigs placed on the fork of a small branch, and it seems wonderful how the egg remains on it. When the young has been hatched a few days the nest becomes converted into a hard, nearly flat cake of twigs and excrement. Old nests, and those of Gannets, are often utilized.

About the beginning of January the adult males begin to acquire the remarkable pouch of scarlet skin beneath their throat. This they can inflate till it is nearly as large as the rest of the body, and a dozen or more of these birds sitting in a tree with outstretched drooping wings and this great scarlet bladder under their heads are a most remarkable sight. When a hen bird approaches the tree the males utter a peculiar cry, a sort of ' wow-wow-wow-wow,' and clatter their beaks like castanets, at the same time shaking the wings. When they take to flight the air is allowed to escape from the pouch, but occasionally they might be seen flying with it partly inflated.

The pairing season extended from January till April; eggs were found in February, and in August there were still many young birds in white down, but by October all had flown. The young continue to get a certain amount of food from their parents even after the latter have begun to build again.

In the neighbourhood of Flying Fish Cove the large species builds near the sea, the small one on the higher part of the island farther inland. The cry of the male in the small species is quite different from, and much more musical than that of the large one.

At present Frigate-birds are one of the chief articles of food of the inhabitants of Christmas Island, and they are very good indeed. The usual way of obtaining them is for a man to climb into the topmost branches of a high tree near the coast, armed with a pole eight or ten feet long and a red handkerchief. The latter he waves about, at the same time yelling as loudly as possible. The birds attracted by the noise and the red colour swoop round in large numbers, when they are knocked down with the long pole. In this way sufficient birds to supply the small colony with food can usually be obtained in an hour or two; occasionally, however, in unfavourable states of the wind, they are difficult to procure.

Young. Brownish on back, head fawn brown, whiter on back and upper part of neck. The brown of the front of the neck passes on breast into a band of brownish-black feathers. Breast and belly white. Beak greyish pinkish - white ; throat and eyelid greyish white. Feet ditto. Some white feathers on sides of breast. Secondary-coverts blackish brown, axillaries white, edged with white. Rectrices slightly tipped with brownish white.— C. W. A.]

15. Fregata ariel.

Fregata ariel (Gould). Ogilvie Grant, Cat. B. Brit. Mus., xxvi, p. 447 (1898).

No. 18, ♂. Flying Fish Cove, August, 1897.
No. 45, ♀. Flying Fish Cove, August, 1897.

According to Mr. Andrews, the male is entirely black below, but the female is white on the throat, breast, and sides of body. The centre of the lower breast, abdomen, and lower flanks are black.

Sub-Order SULÆ.

16. Sula sula.

Sula sula (Linn.), Ogilvie Grant, Cat. B. Brit. Mus., xxvi, p. 436 (1898) ; Sharpe, Handl. B., i, p. 236 (1899).

Nos. 7, 9, ♀ ad. Flying Fish Cove, August 4, 5, 1897.
No. 10, ♀ pull. Flying Fish Cove, August 4, 1897.
No. 94, ♀ imm. Flying Fish Cove, November 16, 1897.

The young bird was obtained by Mr. Andrews on the 4th of August, with its mother (No. 9). It is still covered with white down, though more than half-grown.
[*Sula sula* (Booby) breeds near the coast. Nest of sticks on ground, usually near edge of sea cliff, but sometimes on the high inland cliffs at some distance from the sea. One or two eggs.— C. W. A.]

17. Sula abbotti.

Sula abbotti, Ridgw., Proc. U.S. Nat. Mus., xvi, p. 599 (1893) ; Sharpe, Handl. B., i, p. 237 (1899).

a, ♂ ad. East coast, October, 1897.

This species was hitherto known only from Assumption Island in the Indian Ocean. Mr. Ogilvie Grant united it to *Sula cyanops,* but it is certainly quite distinct.
[Builds nests of sticks near the tops of the highest trees, usually on the high land round the plateau. Shot young in September. This bird is rarely seen on the north coast of the island, but on the south it seems largely to take the place of *S. piscatrix.*— C. W. A.]

18. Sula piscatrix.

Sula piscatrix (Linn.), Sharpe, P.Z.S., 1887, p. 516; Ogilvie Grant, Cat. B.
Brit. Mus. xxvi, p. 432 (1898); Sharpe, Handl. B., i, p. 237.

No. 94, ♀ imm. Flying Fish Cove.

[*Sula piscatrix* is very common all round the coast. Builds nest
of sticks in high trees. Begins to breed about January, and there
are great numbers of young birds in grey plumage in October.—
C. W. A.]

Sub-Order PHAETHONTES.

19. Phaethon rubricauda.

Phaethon phœnicurus, Gm.: Lister, P.Z.S., 1888, p. 529.
Phaethon rubricauda, Bodd.: Ogilvie Grant, Cat. B. Brit. Mus., xxvi, p. 451
(1898); Sharpe, Handl. B., i, p. 238 (1899).

No. 14, ♂ ad. Flying Fish Cove, August, 1897.
a, b, ♂ ♀ ad. Flying Fish Cove.
No. 15, ♀ juv. Flying Fish Cove, August, 1897.
c, ♀ ad. Flying Fish Cove, August, 1897. "Taken on nest
with No. 15."
d, ♂ ad. Flying Fish Cove, March 21, 1898. Taken from nest
in hole of cliff.

[The habits of the white Tropic Bird are much like those of
the yellow one, but it seems to nest almost exclusively in holes
in the cliffs, and I never saw it flying among the trees. The
colour of the young bird is exactly like that of the other species.—
C. W. A.]

20. Phaethon fulvus. (Plate III.)

Phaethon flavirostris (nec Brandt), Lister, P.Z.S., 1888, p. 528.
Phaethon fulvus, Brandt: Grant, Cat. B. Brit. Mus., xxvi, p. 455 (1898).

No. 38, ♂ ad. Flying Fish Cove, August 28, 1897.
No. 41, ♀ ad. Flying Fish Cove, August 30, 1897.
No. 47, ♀ juv. Flying Fish Cove, September 20, 1897. "Just
beginning to fly."
Nos. 67, 69, ♀ ad. Flying Fish Cove, November 19, 1897.
No. 68, ♂ ad. Flying Fish Cove, November 19, 1897.
a, b, ♂ ♀ ad. Flying Fish Cove. December 26, 1897.

There appears to be no difference in the colour of the sexes, and
the orange tint is equally well developed in both the male and
female. The young bird, however, shows no orange in the
plumage, but is white, spotted on the head and barred on the back
with black; the inner secondaries with black longitudinal markings
of irregular shape on the outer web; the primaries and a few of

the secondaries black-shafted, the outer primaries with more or less black along the outer web ; tail-feathers white, with a sub-terminal black spot; a circular spot of black in front of the eye, extending below backwards in a line under the latter, and with a black line above the ear-coverts ; flanks with a tuft of chequered black feathers with white notches and spots.   These latter feathers, and also many on the back and secondaries, seem to indicate by the variation of their pattern that the latter changes a great deal, so that the aspect of the feather becomes gradually whiter and whiter.

[The most beautiful of the sea-birds is the yellow Tropic Bird, which, though much less numerous than the Frigate-birds, is still fairly common.   The flight of these birds is swift, though, owing to the rapidity of the strokes of the wing, it often seems as if they were labouring.   I never saw them sail except for a short distance when wheeling round.   On hot days they may be seen in twos and threes, flying rapidly up and down above and among the tree tops, continually uttering their peculiar crackling cry, and pausing now and then to hover before holes in the trees which seem to offer an eligible position for a nest.   It can hardly be said, however, that they make a nest, for the single dark-brown mottled egg is merely placed in a slight hollow on the floor of a hole in a tree or in the sea cliff.   The young bird, when nearly full-grown, is white, barred with black, and since I never saw one in this plumage out of the nest, it seems that the yellow colour is acquired before it flies.   The only distinguishing mark of the youngest bird I ever saw flying was the presence of a few black bars on the back just above the root of the tail.   Eggs and young were obtained in August and September; the breeding season seems to be less definite than in the case of the other birds.—C. W. A.]

Order ACCIPITRIFORMES.

21. Astur natalis. (Plate V.)

Urospizias natalis, Lister, P.Z.S., 1888, p. 523.
Astur natalis, Sharpe, Handl. B., i, p. 251 (1899).

♂ juv. Flying Fish Cove, August 14, 1897.
Nos. 30–33, ♂ ♀ juv. Flying Fish Cove, August 13, 1897.
No. 36, ♀ ad. Flying Fish Cove, August 20, 1897.
Nos. 43–44, ♀ ad. } Flying Fish Cove, August 22, 1897.
      ♂ juv. }
♂ juv. Flying Fish Cove, September, 1897.
♂ juv. Flying Fish Cove, October, 1897.
♀ juv. Phosphate Hill, November 28, 1897.
No. 35, ♂ ♀ ad. } South-east coast, August 20, 1897.
      ♂ juv. }

Mr. Lister has given a very good description of this species, and has pointed out its similarity to *A. griseigularis*. It differs from the latter species, however, in its much darker slaty-grey head, slaty-grey bars on the chest, and in the lighter underwing- and tail-coverts, which are barred with white and vinous rufous, and are not so uniform vinous as in *A. griseigularis*.

[The Goshawk is common all over the island, and is very destructive to young poultry in Flying Fish Cove. Its food consists of the White-eyes, Ground-Thrushes, and Ground-Pigeons, and it is said to kill the large Fruit-Pigeon also, but this I never saw. In the crop of one there were remains of numerous locusts. The nest is made of twigs and pieces of creepers, and is placed near the top of a high tree. A nest with one young was found on January 24th. The cry is a sharp 'tweet-tweet-tweet,' and when shooting Fruit-Pigeons in the high trees a rough imitation of this call was often employed to cause them to thrust out their head, so that they could be more easily seen, and would present a better mark.—C. W. A.]

22. Ninox natalis. (Plate IV.)

Ninox natalis, Lister, P.Z.S., 1888, p. 525.

No. 37, ♂ ad. Flying Fish Cove, August 8, 1897.
No. 65, ♀ ad. Flying Fish Cove, October 24, 1897.
No. 66, ♂ ad. Flying Fish Cove, November 9, 1897.
No. 70, ♂ ad. Flying Fish Cove, November 24, 1897.
♀ ad. Flying Fish Cove, December 24, 1897. Iris and feet bright lemon-yellow.

The sexes do not differ in colour, and there is scarcely any variation in size, as the males have the wing 7·6–7·8 inches and the females 7·4–7·8.

[The Owl is most often seen in thickets of screw-pine and in the denser parts of the forest. Its food consists of lizards, locusts, white-eyes. and perhaps rats. The nest I never found, but Mr. Hugh Ross told me it is usually placed in a screw-pine and made of twigs. The peculiar cry, resembling very closely the bark of a small dog, has been described by Mr. Lister. In the forest after sun-down several of these birds could be heard barking in answer to one another. They usually begin with a scarcely audible 'chuk-chuk,' which is repeated crescendo till they break out into a regular bark, which may be repeated a considerable number of times ; this may stop suddenly or die away gradually as it began.—C. W. A.]

Order CORACIIFORMES.

Sub-Order CYPSELI.

23. Collocalia natalis.

Collocalia natalis, Lister, P.Z.S., 1888, p. 520 ; Hartert, Cat. B. Brit. Mus., xvi, p. 511 (1892) ; id., Tierreich, Lief. i, Aves, Macropt., p. 70 (1897).

No. 28, ad.　Flying Fish Cove, August, 1897.
♀ ad.　Flying Fish Cove, November 24, 1897.
♂ ♂ ♀ ad.　Flying Fish Cove, November 25, 1897.
♀ ad.　Flying Fish Cove, December 28, 1897.
ad.　Flying Fish Cove, February 15, 1898.
♂ ♀ ♀ ad.　Flying Fish Cove, March 4, 1898.
♂ ♂ ♀ ♀ ♀ ad.　Flying Fish Cove, March 7, 1898.
The series brought home by Mr. Andrews confirmed the characters of the species, but the differences between *C. natalis* and *C. neglecta* are not very strongly pronounced.

Order COCCYGES.

Sub-Order CUCULI.

24. Chalcococcyx basalis.

Chalcococcyx basalis (Horsf.), Shelley, Cat. B. Brit. Mus., xix, p. 294 (1891).

A single immature female in full moult.　This species has not before been obtained on Christmas Island.

Order PASSERIFORMES.

Family MOTACILLIDÆ.

25. Motacilla melanope.

Motacilla melanope, Pall. : Sharpe, Cat. B. Brit. Mus., x, p. 497 (1885).

♂ ad.　Flying Fish Cove, October 7, 1897.
Iris blue-black.　On the shore.　Stomach contained small marine worms.
Also not recorded from Christmas Island previously.

26. Motacilla flava.

Motacilla flava, Linn. : Sharpe, Cat. B. Brit. Mus., x, p. 515, pl. vi, figs. 3–5 (1885).

No. 49, ♂ imm.　Flying Fish Cove, October, 1897.
a, b, imm.　Flying Fish Cove.
Three young birds, evidently procured on migration.

Family ZOSTEROPIDÆ.

27. Zosterops natalis. (Plate VI.)

Zosterops natalis, Lister, P.Z.S., 1888, p. 518, pl. xxvii.

No. 21, ♂ ad. Flying Fish Cove, August 5, 1897.
a, ♂ ad. Flying Fish Cove, August 10, 1897.
b, c, ♂ ad. Flying Fish Cove, November 29, 1897.
d, ♂ ad. Flying Fish Cove, November 24, 1897.
e, ♀ ad. Flying Fish Cove, December 3, 1897.
f, g, ♂ ♀ ad. Flying Fish Cove, March 4, 1898.

The White-eye of Christmas Island is a large species, and easily recognized by its colour. I can see no difference in the plumage of specimens killed in various months, and the young resemble the adults. The yellow at the base of the bill scarcely amounts to more than a small loral patch and does not form a frontal band. N.B.—In Mr. Lister's diagnosis of the species (p. 519) the first character, viz., that the crown becomes paler "towards the base of the *tail*," must be a misprint for 'bill.'

The nest is a pretty little structure—a shallow cup suspended between the forks of a twig, to which it is attached. The nest consists of vegetable fibre, with wool as a basis, and it is lined with the same black fibre of the sago-palm as that used by the Thrush for its nest. A second nest is deeper in the cup, contains more cotton, and has a few white feathers interlaced in the outside. The two eggs,. obtained by Mr. Andrews in November, are uniform bluish white. Axis 0·7 ; diam. 0·5.

[The little Zosterops (Burung Waringin) swarm everywhere, even in the middle of the forest. They seem to form small flocks, and behave much like Titmice, climbing about among the foliage and often hanging head downwards under a leaf or branch in their search for insects. They also eat a good deal of fruit, and destroy many papaias, custard-apples, and bananas, of which they are so fond that they often come on to the dinner-table to get them. They have only a twittering note, but when a Hawk is in the neighbourhood the noise made by a flock of them is considerable. The nest is usually placed between two twigs or in the fork of small branches of bushes, and is made of fibres of the sago-palm, or any other vegetable fibre they can get. They seem to breed nearly all the year round.—C. W. A.]

Family TURDIDÆ.

28. Merula erythropleura.

Turdus erythropleurus, Sharpe, P.Z.S., 1887, p. 515.
Merula erythropleura, Lister, P.Z.S., 1888, p. 517.

No. 23, ad. Flying Fish Cove, August, 1897.
Nos. 52, 53, ♂ ♀ ad. Flying Fish Cove, October 20, 1897.

E

No. 60, ♂ ad.   Flying Fish Cove, October 22, 1897.
♂ ♀ ad.   Flying Fish Cove, November 4, 1897.
♂ ad.   Flying Fish Cove, November 12, 1897.
♂ ad.   Flying Fish Cove, November 21, 1897.
♂ ♀ ad.   Flying Fish Cove, December 29, 1897.
♂ juv.   Flying Fish Cove, February 14, 1898.
♀ ad.   Flying Fish Cove, February 20, 1898.
♀ ad.   Flying Fish Cove, March 7, 1898.
♀ juv.   North Coast, March 17, 1898.
♀ ad.   Phosphate Hill, November 3, 1897.

This species is of the group of *Merula javanica*, but is especially remarkable for the size of its bill, which is very large in proportion to the bird. The sexes are alike in colour, and the young birds are more dusky brown, with pale shaft-lines to the feathers of the upper surface. In the young the bill is horn brown, not yellow, and the under surface of the body is mottled with dusky-brown edges to the feathers.

[The Ground-Thrush is common everywhere, but is most numerous near the coast. Like the other birds of the island, it is very tame, and when I was breaking up rotten wood searching for beetles, several of them would stand quite close by in readiness to pick up any grubs that were uncovered. Its food consists of insects, seeds, and any carrion it can find, and I have seen one kill a small brown lizard, though it seemed to have some difficulty in doing so. When hunting for insects among the dead leaves, the colours of the plumage harmonize so exactly with the surroundings that, were it not for the bright yellow beak and eye-lids the bird would be almost invisible. The alarm cry is much like that of the European Blackbird, and in the pairing season (December–January) the male has a song something like that of the English Thrush, but harsher and less varied. The nest is made of fibres of the wild sago-palm (*Arenga listeri*), skeleton leaves, and other vegetable fibre; it is not mud-lined. One nest was taken from the crown of a screw-pine (*Pandanus*), another from the hollow top of a broken tree trunk, some fifteen feet from the ground. Eggs were found in December, and in the following month young birds just able to fly were numerous, and continued to be so till April.—C. W. A.]

Family HIRUNDINIDÆ.

29. Hirundo gutturalis.

Hirundo gutturalis, Scop.: Sharpe, Cat. B. Brit. Mus., x, p. 134 (1885).

♀ juv.   Flying Fish Cove, October 16, 1897.
A young female of the Eastern Chimney Swallow, in moult from the first plumage to the glossy dress of the adult.

REPTILIA.

By G. A. BOULENGER, F.R.S.

(PLATE VII.)

THE first collection made on Christmas Island by the officers of H.M.S. "Flying Fish" yielded examples of three species — *Gymnodactylus marmoratus*, Kuhl, *Lygosoma naticitatis* (n sp.), and *Typhlops exocœti* (n.sp.). Mr. Lister's visit to the island in 1888 resulted in the discovery of two further new species—*Gecko listeri* and *Ablepharus egeriæ*. To these five species Mr. Andrews has added a sixth, the widely distributed *Lygosoma atrocostatum*.

LACERTILIA.

Family GECKONIDÆ.

1. Gymnodactylus marmoratus, Kuhl.

Gymnodactylus marmoratus, Boulenger, Cat. Liz., i, p. 44 (1885).

Known from Java, Sumatra, and Borneo; also from the mountains of Perak, in the Malay Peninsula, whence I have recently received a specimen.

2. Gecko listeri. (Pl. VII, Fig. 1.)

Gecko listeri, Boulenger, P.Z.S., 1888, p. 535.

Head moderate, snout once and one-third the diameter of the orbit, which equals its distance from the very small round ear-opening; forehead scarcely concave. Head covered with small granules, which are considerably larger on the snout; rostral quadrangular, more than twice as broad as deep, without cleft; nostril pierced between the rostral, the first labial, and three nasals; twelve upper and ten lower labials; three transverse rows of small hexagonal chin-shields. Dorsal scales uniform, minutely granular; ventrals much larger, roundish hexagonal, subimbricate. Digits with a very slight rudiment of web; seven or eight angularly curved lamellæ under the median toes. A short angular series of twelve præanal pores. Tail cylindrical, covered with uniform small flat scales, which are largest inferiorly. Pale grey-brown above, with a few rather indistinct brown spots and scattered white dots; a brown streak from the nostril to the eye; lower parts white, with small brown spots.

Total length	... ...	79 mm.	Fore limb	12 mm.
Head	... ...	12 ,,	Hind limb	15 ,,
Width of head	...	8·5 ,,	Tail	38 ,,
Body	... ...	29 ,,		

This small *Gecko*, of which a single male specimen was obtained
by Mr. Lister, is closely allied to *G. pumilus*, Blgr., from Papua
(Port Moresby and Torres Straits), from which it is at once
distinguished by its nearly free toes.

Family SCINCIDÆ.

3. Lygosoma atrocostatum, Less.

Lygosoma atrocostatum, Boulenger, Cat. Liz., iii, p. 295 (1887).

Mr. Andrews has brought home two specimens of this species,
which is widely distributed, being known from the Philippines,
Celebes, the Moluccas, New Guinea, Cape York, the Caroline and
Santa Cruz Islands. I may also add to its known habitat Pulo
Tikos, Penang, where it was found by Mr. S. S. Flower, and
whence it had been described by Stoliczka under the name of
Mabouya jerdoniana.

Lives among rocks on beach at Flying Fish Cove.

4. Lygosoma nativitatis. (Pl. VII, Fig. 2.)

Lygosoma nativitatis, Boulenger, P.Z.S., 1887, p. 516, and 1888, p. 536.

Section *Emoa*. Habit lacertiform; the distance between the end
of the snout and the fore limb is contained once and one-third to
once and a half in the distance between axilla and groin. Snout
long, obtuse. Lower eyelid with an undivided transparent disk.
Nostril pierced between a nasal, a postnasal, and a supranasal;
frontonasal broader than long, forming a suture with the rostral
and with the frontal; latter shield nearly as long as the frontoparietal, in contact with the first and second supraoculars; four
supraoculars; seven or eight supraciliaries; frontoparietals united
into a single large shield; a small interparietal, behind which the
parietals form a suture; a pair of nuchals and a pair of temporals
border the parietals; four or five labials anterior to the large
subocular. Ear-opening oval, a little larger than the transparent
palpebral disk, with three or four very small lobules on its anterior
border. Thirty to thirty-four scales round the middle of the body,
all smooth in the adult, quinquecarinate in the young, laterals
a little smaller than dorsals and ventrals. No enlarged præanals.
The hind limb reaches the elbow. Digits moderately elongate,
a little flattened at the base, compressed at the end; subdigital
lamellæ smooth, thirty-one to thirty-four under the fourth toe.
Tail two-thirds of the total length. Brown above, strongly
iridescent, with small golden and blackish spots, most numerous
on the sides and limbs; lower surfaces white.

Head...	...	...	...	15	mm.
Width of head		...	...	9·5	,,
Body ...	...	...	...	56	,,
Fore limb	...	...	...	22	,,
Hind limb	...	...	...	31	,,

This species was originally described from a single specimen; numerous examples have since been obtained by Mr. Lister and Mr. Andrews.

5. Ablepharus egeriæ. (Pl. VII, Fig. 3.)

Ablepharus egeriæ, Boulenger, P.Z.S., 1888, p. 535.

Snout pointed, rostral not projecting. Eye entirely surrounded with granules; upper eyelid represented by three or four larger scales. Rostral largely in contact with the frontonasal; præfrontals forming a long suture; frontal small, in contact with the first and second supraoculars; five supraoculars, second largest, fifth smallest; seven supraciliaries; interparietal distinct from the very large, single frontoparietal; a pair of large nuchals. Ear-opening rather small, oval. Scales smooth or feebly striated, two vertebral rows largest; 26 or 28 scales round the middle of the body. Limbs well developed, pentadactyle; the hind limb reaches the axilla in the male, the elbow in the female; digits long and slender, smooth inferiorly. Tail once and a half the length of head and body. Bronzy above, with blackish and pale greenish spots; a light, dark-edged dorso-lateral band; end of tail blue; lower parts greenish white.

Total length	... ...	113 mm.	Fore limb	... ...	17 mm.
Head	...	10 ,,	Hind limb	... ...	21 ,,
Width of head ...	...	6 ,,	Tail	... ...	68 ,,
Body	...	35 ,,			

Numerous specimens were obtained by Messrs. Lister and Andrews.

Closely allied to the widely distributed *A. boutonii*, Desj., from which it differs in the distinct interparietal shield. I have, however, recently noticed (Ann. Mus. Genova [2], xviii, 1898, p. 719) the presence of a distinct interparietal in a specimen of that species from Lugh, Somaliland. *A. egeriæ* should therefore perhaps be regarded as a race of *A. boutonii*.

OPHIDIA.

Family TYPHLOPIDÆ.

6. Typhlops exocœti.

Typhlops exocœti, Boulenger, P.Z.S., 1887, p. 517, and Cat. Sn., i, p. 36, pl. iii, fig. 2.

Snout depressed, rounded, strongly projecting; nostrils inferior. Rostral broad, upper portion broadest anteriorly, about half the width of the head, extending to the level of the eyes; nasal incompletely divided, the cleft proceeding from the second labial; a præocular, of about the same size as the ocular, in contact with the second and third labials; eyes distinguishable; upper head-scales a little larger than the scales on the body; four upper labials. Diameter of body 50 to 66 times in the total length; tail nearly twice as long as broad, ending in a spine. Twenty scales round the body. Pale brownish, each scale with a brown spot; these spots largest and darkest on the dorsal surface, where they form longitudinal lines.

Total length, 480 mm.

Two specimens were captured on the occasion of the visit of the "Flying Fish." Several more were brought home by Mr. Andrews, who found them in damp places, under rocks and fallen trees. Only seen out on dark rainy days.

[Turtles are often seen round the coasts of the island, and they occasionally come up on to the white beaches to deposit their eggs in the coral sand—one nest on the West White Beach contained 142 eggs. There are probably three species—*Thalassochelys caretta*, *Chelone imbricata*, and *C. mydas*. In January, a small specimen of the last was speared in shallow water near North-East Point.—C. W. A.]

MOLLUSCA.

By E. A. Smith, F.Z.S.

(PLATE VIII.)

The land-shells of Christmas Island are insignificant both in size and the number of species. Eleven different forms were enumerated by the writer in 1888,[1] nine of which were collected by Mr. Andrews, besides single specimens of three additional species, namely, *Opeas subula*, *Melampus castaneus*, and *Assiminea andrewsiana*. These, however, do not throw any additional light on the relationship of the fauna with that of other parts of the world. Although seven of the fourteen species recorded are, so far as we know, peculiar to the island, it must be pointed out that they belong to genera the species of which have no very striking characters. The three forms of *Lamprocystis* are very much alike, and approximate very closely to certain species from the Philippines and the Malay Archipelago. The Succineas also present no marked features, and might have been found anywhere. *Opeas*, too, is a genus notorious for the sameness of its species and the wide

---

[1] Proc. Zool. Soc., 1888, p. 536.

distribution of several of them. The other genera represented at Christmas Island — *Pythia*, *Melampus*, *Truncatella*, *Assiminea*, and *Leptopoma*—are also recognized as containing species which are very widely distributed.

In conclusion, therefore, it may be stated that the fauna, as represented by the terrestrial Mollusca, does not show any special affinity with that of any other particular locality; and that the same species, or others very similar, might be expected to occur not only at adjacent localities, such as Sumatra or Java, but also further eastward in New Guinea and some of the Pacific Islands.

Family ZONITIDÆ.

1. Lamprocystis normani (Smith). (Pl. VIII, Figs. 1–3.)

Ariophanta (Microcystis) normani, Smith, P.Z.S., 1888, p. 537.

Testa parva, plus minus depressa, anguste perforata, tenuissima, nitida, vel pellucida et dilute fusco-cornea, vel magis opaca, fusca, infra suturam et ad basim pallida, supra et infra microscopice spiraliter striata; spira brevissime conoidea; anfractus 5–6, lente accrescentes, convexiusculi, ad suturam anguste marginati, ultimus ad peripheriam acute rotundatus aut vix angulatus; apertura oblique lunata; peristoma tenue, marginibus distantibus, columellari ad insertionem breviter expanso et reflexo. Diam. maj. 6½, min. 6 mm.; alt. 4½ mm. Exemplum majus : diam. maj. 7½, min. 7 mm.; alt. 5½ mm.

This species is variable in size, form, and colour. The typical specimens were uniformly pellucid, horny, and thin in texture, whilst some of those obtained by Mr. Andrews are more solid, larger, and of a brownish or reddish brown colour, but pale beneath the suture and upon the base of the body-whorl. Sometimes the upper surface, with the exception of the apex, which is palish, is of a uniform reddish brown tint. The spiral striæ are only visible under the microscope, and are less conspicuous on the under surface than above.

2. Lamprocystis mabelæ (Smith). (Pl. VIII, Fig. 4.)

Ariophanta (Microcystis) mabelæ, Smith, P.Z.S., 1888, p. 537.

Testa *L. normani* simillima, sed magis depressa, anfractibus minus convexis, distinctius striatis, ultimo ad peripheriam subacute angulato. Diam. maj. 6, min. 5½ mm.; alt. 3¼ mm.

Collected by Mr. J. J. Lister.

This species, if the specimens upon which it was founded be adult, is a little smaller than the preceding. It is similarly perforated, of the same texture and glossy appearance, but more depressed, and has flatter whorls which are a trifle more distinctly spirally striated; the body-whorl is quite angular, and consequently the form of the aperture is rather different.

3. Lamprocystis mildredæ (Smith).   (Pl. VIII, Figs. 5–7.)

Ariophanta (Microcystis) mildredæ, Smith, P.Z.S., 1888, p. 537.

Testa *L. normani* similis, sed minor, latius perforata, anfractibus magis convexis, utrinque distinctius spiraliter striatis. Diam. maj. 5, min. 4¾ mm.; alt. 3 mm.
Collected by Mr. J. J. Lister.
This species is smaller than either of the preceding, and also is more distinctly striated both above and below, and more widely umbilicated. The whorls are rounder and the suture deeper.

Family SUCCINEIDÆ.

4. Succinea solidula, Pfeiffer.   (Pl. VIII, Figs. 8, 9.)

Succinea solidula, Pfeiffer, P.Z.S., 1849, p. 134 ; Monog. Helic., vol. iii, p. 22 ; Smith, P.Z.S., 1887, p. 578, figs. 1, 2.

Testa ovata, pallide flavescens vel dilute rufescens, subpellucida, incrementi lineis fortibus obliquis curvatis sculpta, undique minute subgranulata ; anfractus 3, rapide accrescentes, perconvexi, sutura obliqua sejuncti, ultimus magnus ; apertura inverse auriformis, intus nitens ; peristoma tenue, vel interdum intus leviter incrassatum, margine columellari paulo incrassato, callo tenuissimo labro juncto. Long. 13 mm., diam. maj. 10 mm. ; apertura 9 mm. longa, 6 lata.
Another small but adult specimen is 9 mm. in length and 7¼ in diameter.
Hab.—Flying Fish Cove (Andrews).
There are two principal characters which distinguish this species, namely, the thickened peristome and the peculiar sculpture. The former is not, however, observable in all specimens, but its absence may be due to their immature condition. It is only slight in any of the specimens, and internal; hence Pfeiffer's expression "perist. submarginatum." The sculpture has the appearance (under a strong lens) of the texture of very fine linen, or minute crisscross lines, rather than minute granulations. Besides this excessively fine ornamentation the surface exhibits rather strong lines of growth or subplications.

5. Succinea solitaria, Smith.   (Pl. VIII, Figs. 10, 11.)

Succinea solitaria, Smith, P.Z.S., 1887, p. 518, figs. 3, 4.

Testa suboblique ovata, supra acuminata, solidiuscula, vel albida, versus apicem rufescens, vel omnino rubescens, lineis incrementi validis, valde obliquis, curvatis, striisque spiralibus, fortibus, plus minus distinctis, sculpta ; anfractus 3, rapide crescentes, duo superiores perconvexi, ultimus supra declivis, antice descendens; apertura rotunde ovata, superne acuminata, intus pallida vel rubescens; peristoma tenue, intus interdum subincrassatum, margine columcllari plus minus incrassato et reflexo, superne callo tenui labro juncto. Long. 9½, diam. 5½ mm.; apertura 5 mm. longa, 4½ lata.

Only a single specimen of this species has hitherto been known. The few examples obtained by Mr. Andrews differ in being of a very rich reddish colour. The solidity, the strong lines of growth, and the spiral striæ are the principal distinguishing features of the species. The transverse striæ are rather coarse, and more conspicuous in some specimens than others.

6. Succinea listeri, Smith. (Pl. VIII, Figs. 12, 13.)

Succinea listeri, Smith, P.Z.S., 1888, p. 537.

Testa elongato-ovata, superne acuminata, tenuis, cornea, rubescens; anfractus 3, rapide crescentes, ultimus permagnus, incrementi lineis tenuibus striatus; apertura elongata, ovata, superne acuminata; peristoma tenue, marginibus callo tenuissimo junctis. Long. 13½ mm., diam. maj. 8 mm.; apertura 10½ mm. longa, 7 lata.

This species differs in form and sculpture from both the other species from the island. It is smoother, and has a shorter spire and a longer body-whorl.

Family STENOGYRIDÆ.

7. Opeas subula (Pfeiffer). (Pl. VIII, Fig. 14.)

Achatina subula, Pfeiffer, Wiegmann's Arch. Naturg., 1839, vol. i, p. 352.
Bulimus subula, Reeve, Conch. Icon., vol. v, pl. lxix, fig. 494.
Stenogyra (Opeas) subula, Binney & Bland, Land and Fresh-water Shells of North America, pt. i, p. 230, fig. 392.
Bulimus oparanus, Pfeiffer, P.Z.S., 1846, p. 34.

Hab. — Many islands in the West Indies, Florida, Mexico, Venezuela, Fernando Noronha, Borneo, Cochin China, Island of Opara or Rapa, etc.

A single specimen obtained by Mr. Andrews is inseparable from this species, which, as will be seen from the above localities, has a very wide range. I am unable to find any characters which will distinguish this species from *O. oparanus* (Pfr.), the sculpture being precisely similar in both. The crenulation at the suture, especially in the upper whorls, a feature not noticed in the descriptions, is very peculiar, and, although visible under a simple lens, is best seen under a compound microscope.

Binney and Bland account for the wide distribution of this species by its transplantation with the banana and plantain throughout the Tropics. These trees have been introduced into Christmas Island from Java, and possibly the *Opeas* along with them, although at present I am not aware of its having been recorded from that island.

Family AURICULIDÆ.

8. Pythia scarabæus (Linn.). (Pl. VIII, Fig. 15.)

Pythia scarabæus, Pfeiffer, Mon. Auric., p. 82.

Hab.—Flying Fish Cove.   Widely distributed in the islands
of the Malay Archipelago and Oceania.

The specimens from Christmas Island are much smaller than
usual, the largest having a length of only 20 mm.

9. Melampus luteus (Quoy & Gaimard).   (Pl. VIII, Fig. 16.)

Melampus luteus, Pfeiffer, Mon. Auric., p. 36.

Hab.—Same as preceding.
Also rather smaller than usual.   Length, 14 mm.

10. Melampus fasciatus (Deshayes).   (Pl. VIII, Fig. 17.)

Melampus fasciatus, Desh.: Pfeiffer, Mon. Auric., p. 38.

Hab.—Same as preceding.
Again the examples are small, only 11½ mm. in length.   Some
are red-banded, whilst others are of a livid greyish tint without
bands, the spire being slate-blue in all.

11. Melampus castaneus (Mühlfeldt).   (Pl. VIII, Fig. 18.)

Melampus castaneus, Pfeiffer, Mon. Auric., p. 30.

Hab.—Sandwich and Samoa Islands.
Only a single young specimen was obtained by Mr. Andrews.
It agrees in every respect with examples from the Hawaiian
Islands.

Family CYCLOPHORIDÆ.

12. Leptopoma mouhoti, Pfeiffer, var.   (Pl. VIII, Figs. 19, 20.)

Leptopoma mouhoti, Pfeiffer, P.Z.S., 1861, p. 185; Monog. Pneumon., vol. iii,.
          p. 82; Reeve, Conch. Icon., vol. xiii, pl. v, fig. 25.

Testa breviter conica, umbilicata, tenuiuscula, subpellucida,.
sordide albida, epidermide tenuissima lutescente induta, interdum
infra peripheriam fusco maculata; spira conoidea, ad apicem haud
acuta; anfractus 5, convexi, liris spiralibus filiformibus (in anfr.
ultimo circiter 6) striisque inter liras spiralibus tenuibus, incrementi lineis obliquis ornati, ultimus in medio vix angulatus, liris
circa 12 (mediana ad peripheriam cæteris paulo-fortiori), succinctus;
apertura fere circularis, long. totius ½ paulo superans; peristoma
anguste expansum, haud duplicatum, marginibus callo tenui junctis,.
columellari sinuato.   Long. 11½ mm., diam. maj. 11½ mm.

Hab.—Found on mossy trunks of trees in the upper part of the island (J. J. Lister); north coast (Andrews).

The type of *L. mouhoti* was described from Camboja, and differs slightly in being a trifle more elevated than the specimens from Christmas Island. Its peristome also is slightly broader. At present I have seen only two specimens, so am unable to judge of the constancy of these differences.

Family TRUNCATELLIDÆ.

13. Truncatella valida, Pfeiffer. (Pl. VIII, Figs. 21, 22.)

Truncatella valida, Pfeiffer, Mon. Auric., p. 184; Küster, Conch.-Cab., p. 11, pl. ii, figs. 19–21, 23.

Hab.—Philippine Islands, New Caledonia, Samoa, etc.

The two or three apical volutions, constituting the protoconch, are very convex, and although apparently smooth under a simple lens, under the microscope are seen to be very finely, regularly, longitudinally striated.

Family ASSIMINEIDÆ.

14 Assiminea andrewsiana, n.sp. (Pl. VIII, Fig. 23.)

Testa elongata, conica, imperforata, rufescenti - cornea, vix pellucida; anfractus 7, convexiusculi, lente accrescentes, infra suturam linea pellucida marginati, læves, nitentes, ultimus brevis, rotundatus; apertura obliqua, inverse auriformis, longit. totius ⅓ fere adæquans; peristoma marginibus callo tenui junctis, externo acuto, tenue, columellari valde incrassato et reflexo. Long. 4, diam. 2⅓ mm.

Only a single specimen was obtained of this pretty little species. It is closely allied to *A. woodmasoniana*, Nevill,[1] from Port Canning, near Calcutta. It is similar in colour, but has more convex whorls, and wants the keel which surrounds the umbilical region, also a fine thread-like line which winds up the spire round the middle of the whorls. This character, present in all four specimens of *A. woodmasoniana* obtained by the Museum from Dr. Hungerford's collection, is not noticed in Mr. Nevill's description.

---

[1] Journ. As. Soc. Bengal, 1880, vol. xlix, pt. 2, p. 163; 1891, vol. L, p. 158, pl. vii, fig. 1.

INSECTA.

(PLATES IX-XV.)

Order 1.—LEPIDOPTERA.

LEPIDOPTERA RHOPALOCERA.

By Arthur G. Butler, Ph.D., F.L.S., F.Z.S., etc.

(PLATE IX, Fig. 8.)

In the Proceedings of the Zoological Society for 1888 I gave an account of a collection of Lepidoptera obtained by Mr. J. J. Lister on Christmas Island in 1887; this collection contained five species of Butterflies, two of which I had described in the Proceedings of the preceding year in a Report on a Zoological Collection made by the Officers of H.M.S. "Flying Fish."

Previous to Mr. Andrews' visit, therefore, the following species were recorded as occurring on the island: — *Vadebra macleari*, *Hypolimnas listeri*, *Nacaduba aluta*, *Terias amplexa*, and *Terias patruelis*; but, as the last of these turns out to be quite distinct from Moore's species, and the ordinary female of *T. amplexa*, only four distinct species were known to exist on the island. To these Mr. Andrews has added five others, one of which, however, was evidently blown across from Java, to the species of which island those of Christmas Island show some affinity, although less than to those of North Australia.

The following is a list of the species :—

Family NYMPHALIDÆ.

EUPLŒINÆ.

1. Limnas petilia.

Papilio petilia, Stoll, Suppl. Cramer's Pap. Exot., pl. xxviii, fig. 3 (1787–91).

Three males and four females were obtained near Rocky Point in September and November.

Hitherto this species has only been known as purely Australian; its occurrence on Christmas Island, therefore, is the more remarkable. If *L. petilia* reached this island from Australia there seems no reason why it should not have passed northwards to Java; it would therefore appear more probable that it has travelled in a south-easterly direction to Australia, but that it should have crossed such a vast tract of sea is indeed extraordinary; nevertheless, the forms of *Hypolimnas nerina* occurring in Australia and Java are almost identical.

2. Vadebra macleari.

Vadebra macleari, Butler, Proc. Zool. Soc., 1887, p. 522, fig. 1.

Flying Fish Cove; August to November, 1897; March, 1898.

One nearly perfect female was obtained, which (in the character of its primaries) shows rather more resemblance to the female of *P. sepulchralis* of Java than do the males; seventeen males were secured.

SATYRINÆ.

3. Melanitis ismene, var. determinata.

Melanitis determinata, Butler, Proc. Ent. Soc., 1885, p. vi.

One female of the wet-season phase (not dated).

This species has an enormous range, and may have reached the island from Java; it is the Indo-Malayan insect, and does not show the characteristics of *M. leda* (which occurs in no part of India, Burma, Ceylon, or Malaysia).

NYMPHALINÆ.

4. Charaxes andrewsi, sp.n. (Pl. IX, Fig. 8.)

More nearly related to *C. pyrrhus* from Amboina than to any other species of the genus, but altogether a far more smoky-coloured insect on the upper surface; all the white markings on the primaries of *C. pyrrhus* are here represented by more or less buff-coloured spots; the internal patch, bounded above by the second median branch, diffused, and more or less heavily irrorated with black scales; the secondaries are much darker than in *C. pyrrhus*, the central whitish band more sharply defined, and almost always abruptly abbreviated, so that it rarely descends below the second subcostal branch; the greyish-lavender markings of *C. pyrrhus* entirely wanting; the black outer border extended inwards, so as to cover nearly half the wing-surface; a submarginal ochreous band, broken by grey-greenish streaks, bordering the extremities of the nervures.

The pattern and colouring of the under-surface is much more like that of *C. jupiter* (from Duke of York Island, the Solomon Islands, and New Guinea); it differs, however, in the slenderness of all the black markings, the much smaller patch across the end of the discoidal cell of the primaries, and the much reduced, or wholly obliterated, patch below the cell; on the secondaries, the red patches are brighter and somewhat broader; the white submarginal spots are bordered externally with bluish-lavender, and the interrupted ochreous band is brighter and better defined; expanse of wings, ♂ 87–92 mm., ♀ 106–112 mm.

West of Flying Fish Cove in August and September; at and near Rocky Point, November and December, 1897; Flying Fish Cove, April, 1898.

One perfect female and a dozen more or less broken examples (of both sexes) were collected. As usual with the species of this genus, *C. andrewsi* has an extremely rapid flight and is difficult to catch.

5. Junonia villida.

Papilio villida, Fabricius, Mant. Ins., ii, p. 35 (1787); Donovan, Ins. New Holl., pl. xxv, fig. 3 (1805).

Five specimens, not dated.

This is the typical Australian form of the species, differing from that occurring on the islands of the South Pacific in the narrower and less brilliantly red-tinted fulvous markings. Dr. Horsfield obtained the same form in Java.

6. Hypolimnas misippus.

Papilio misippus, Linnæus, Mus. Lud. Ulr., p. 264 (1764).

♀ Flying Fish Cove, March, 1898.

The single example obtained is much rubbed and shattered; it was the only specimen seen, and appeared immediately after north-easterly gales, so that there can be little doubt that it was blown over from Java.

7. Hypolimnas nerina, var. listeri.

Hypolimnas listeri, Butler, P.Z.S., 1888, p. 542.

Typical *H. listeri* is the prevalent form in Christmas Island, but it proves to vary more than the eight examples obtained by Mr. Lister led me to believe, though certainly far less than the race occurring at Suva (Viti Levu). In the wet season it is represented by a form the male of which is like *H. nerina* on both surfaces, but the female differs in having the tawny patch on the primaries small, as in *H. iphigenia*; a second form agrees exactly with *H. iphigenia* on both surfaces; a third form nearly approaches *H. proserpina,* but has much smaller tawny patches on the female, and the white belt on the under-surface of the secondaries represented in both sexes by a whitish haze; this variety occurs in both large and small phases. Then follows typical *H. listeri,* and finally a form near *H. alcmene,* but with only a spot of tawny on the primaries and none on the secondaries. It will be necessary to consider these varieties separately.

Var. 1 (wet phase). Three very much shattered examples, not dated, but probably collected in February or March, 1898.

Var. 2 = *H. iphigenia,* ♀ 24th December; ♂ Flying Fish Cove, 29th December, 1897.

Var. 3, near *H. proserpina*, ♀ November; ♂, ♀ ♀ Flying Fish Cove, December, 1897.

Var. 4, similar, but much smaller, five males and two females, not dated.

Var. 5, *H. listeri.* West of Flying Fish Cove, August; North-East Point, 23rd December; the remaining specimens were probably all taken at Flying Fish Cove, and are dated October, November, and December, 1897.

Var. 6, near *H. alomene.* ♂, ♀ Flying Fish Cove, in December. Unfortunately, most of the specimens of this species are so much broken as to be hardly fit for the cabinet.

8. Nacaduba aluta.

Cupido aluta. Druce, P.Z.S., 1873, p. 349, pl. xxxii, fig. 8.

Flying Fish Cove, 20th October, 28th, 29th, and 30th December, 1897; March, 1898; north coast, March, 1898.

A good series of this species was obtained; it varies considerably in size.

9. Terias amplexa.

♂ *Terias amplexa*, Butler, P.Z.S., 1887, p. 523, fig. 5.
♀ *Terias patruelis*, Butler (not Moore), P.Z.S., 1888, p. 545.

♂ Flying Fish Cove, August; ♀ September; ♂♂ November; ♂♂, ♀♀ 24th, 25th, 28th, and 29th December, 1897; ♂ north coast, December, 1897; ♀ February; ♂ Rocky Point, March, 1898.

There is no distinctive seasonal characteristic in this species; all the males show a wet type of coloration, and the females a dry one. It was the dry characteristic of the latter sex which led me to suppose it might be a variety of *T. patruelis.* There can be little doubt now that *T. amplexa* is an endemic form, and the only *Terias* in the island.

- - - - - - - -

LEPIDOPTERA PHALÆNÆ.

By Sir George F. Hampson, Bart.

The number of species of Moths taken (exclusive of Pterophoridæ and Tineidæ) was 65, among which are all the five species taken by Mr. Lister, and described in the P.Z.S. for 1888, pp. 542–546, by Mr. Butler.

The most interesting point in working out the fauna and flora of an oceanic island is the distribution of its species. I have therefore given the full distribution of each species as far as they are known to me. The distribution of Christmas Island Moths seems to show very clearly that it has no connection with the Malayan sub-region, but is very intimately related to the Ceylonese sub-region, with a less strong relationship to the Australasian fauna found in Queensland, New Guinea, and the Pacific groups. In the collection hardly any of the numerous species confined to the Malayan sub-region occur; and where there are closely allied species in the Ceylonese and Malayan faunas, it is the species of the former region that occur in Christmas Island, not of the latter, and this holds with regard to large conspicuous species whose distribution is well known, and not only small and obscure species which might be supposed to have been overlooked in the Malayan sub-region.

Family SYNTOMIDÆ.

1. **Euchromia horsfieldi,** Moore: P.Z.S., 1859, p. 200, pl. lx, fig. 13.

4 ♂, 5 ♀; January, February.
Distrib.—Borneo, Java, Bali, Sumbawa.

Family ARCTIADÆ.

NOLINÆ.

2. **Nola distributa,** Wlk.: Journ. Linn. Soc., Zool., vi, p. 113(1862).

East coast, 1 ♀.
Distrib.—Madagascar, China, India, Burma, Borneo, Bali.

ARCTIANÆ.

3. **Deiopeia pulchella,** Linn.: Syst. Nat., 10th ed., p. 534 (1758).

6 ♂, 5 ♀; October. All of the pale form *candida*, Butl.
Distrib.—Almost universal in Old World.

4. **Argina cribraria,** Clerck: Icones Ins., ii, pl. liv, fig. 4 (1759).

1 ♀. Both wings extremely pale.
Distrib.—Madagascar, Mauritius, China, Malayan sub-region to New Hebrides.

Family AGARISTIDÆ.

5. **Mimeusemia econia,** n.sp. (Pl. IX, Fig. 7.)

Head yellowish white; palpi with the second and third joints banded with black; a short black streak above the frontal prominence; antennæ and patches above and behind eyes black; thorax black, with white stripes on dorsum and patagia; pectus and legs orange yellow, tarsi banded with black ; abdomen orange yellow, with dorsal fuscous bands. Fore wing chocolate red, with sub-basal yellowish-white spot ; an oblique triangular antemedial spot from subcostal nervure to submedian fold ; a small medial spot below costa, and a large spot from above median nervure to submedian fold ; a spot beyond the cell from below costa to below vein 3 ; the costal area black, with silvery-blue spot near base ; a silvery-blue streak on basal half of vein 1 ; antemedial spots in and below cell, with a streak of scales above them on costa ; the discocellulars silvery blue ; the postmedial line silvery blue, oblique from costa to vein 4, then recurved to below end of cell ; the area from just beyond it strongly irrorated with whitish scales ; cilia white near apex and tornus. Hind wing black, with basal white patch extending on inner area to middle, its outer edge slightly angled at subcostal and median nervures ; an elliptical spot beyond the cell ; cilia white near apex and towards tornus.

3 ♂, 1 ♀ ; Flying Fish Cove, October. *Exp.* ♂ 40, ♀ 42 mm. Allied to *Perakana*, Roths.

Family NOCTUIDÆ.

CARADRININÆ.

6. Dipterygia vagivitta, Wlk.: Journ. Linn. Soc., Zool., vi, p. 185.

2 ♀ ; February, March.
Distrib.—Sikhim, Borneo.

7. Amyna selenampha, Guen.: Noct., i, p. 406.

5 ♂ ; March.
Distrib.—Natal, Madagascar, China, India, Ceylon, Andamans, Philippines, Borneo, Java.

8. Amyna octo, Guen.: Noct., i, p. 233.

5 ♂, 4 ♀ ; December–February. Of these six belong to the form *axis*, with the white discoidal spot on fore wing.

There are also 1 ♂, 1 ♀, of a very dark form, fore wing with some orange on the white discoidal spot, and a prominent white spot on costa close to apex ; this is also found in Pulo Laut and Fergusson Island, New Guinea.
Distrib.—Throughout the Tropical Zone.

9. Prodenia littoralis, Boisd.: Faun. Ent. Madag. Lép., p. 91, pl. xiii, fig. 8.

8 ♂, 4 ♀ ; September–March.
Distrib.—Mediterranean sub-region, and throughout the Tropical and sub-Tropical Zones of the Old World.

F

10. Leocyma tibialis, Fabr.: Syst. Ent., p. 578.

1 ♀.
Distrib.—India, Formosa, New Caledonia, Tonga, Tahiti.

NOCTUINÆ.

11. Armactia columbina, Wlk., xxxiii, 808.

6 ♂, 6 ♀; December–March.
Distrib.—Queensland.

12. Brana calopasa, Wlk., xiii, 1100.

15 ♂, 8 ♀; September–January. Found on several occasions in dense masses measuring about 2 × 1 ft. × 6 in., or in long narrow masses on trees or rocks; probably due to a single female attracting a large number of males.
Distrib.—Ceylon, New Guinea.

13. Ophiusa honesta, Hübn.: Samml. Exot. Schmett., ii, p. 4, pl. 203, figs. 1, 2.

14 ♂, 8 ♀; February–March.
Distrib.—India, Ceylon, Burma, Andamans, Philippines.

14. Ophiusa coronata, Fabr.: Syst. Ent., p. 596.

2 ♂, 7 ♀; September.
Distrib.—India, Ceylon, Burma, Andamans, Java, Queensland.

15. Ophiusa serva, Fabr.: Syst. Ent., p. 593.

5 ♂, 18 ♀; December–March.
Distrib.—India, Ceylon, Burma, Borneo, Java, Celebes, Queensland, New Hebrides.

16. Bocula limbata, Butl.: P.Z.S., 1888, p. 545. (Pl. IX, Fig. 1.)

2 ♂, 8 ♀; December–March. The genus *Eudragana* was described by Mr. Butler from the single female collected by Mr. Lister, which had remained unique in the collection. It will form a section of the genus *Bocula*, Guen.: antennæ of male with long bristles and cilia; patagia short, ending in tufts of hair; abdomen with large lateral, oval tufts; hind wing with slight costal fold and subcostal fringe of very long scales on upper side.

17. Acantholipes similis, Moore : Lép. Atk., p. 174, pl. vi, fig. 5.

1 ♀. Small, like specimens from Borneo.
Distrib.—India, Borneo.

18. Thermesia rubricans, Boisd.; Faun. Ent. Madag. Lép., p. 106, pl. xvi, fig. 1.

1 ♀.
Distrib.—Africa, Madagascar, throughout the Oriental region to the Pacific groups.

19. Ophideres salaminia, Fabr.: Ent. Syst., iii, 2, p. 17.

1 ♀.
Distrib.—Madagascar, Formosa, throughout the Oriental region to Queensland and Fiji.

20. Ophideres ancilla, Cram.: Pap. Exot., ii, pl. 149, F.

4 ♂, 4 ♀ ; August-February.
Distrib.—India, Ceylon, Burma.

21. Ophideres fullonica, Linn.: Syst. Nat., i, 2, p. 812.

6 ♂, 8 ♀ ; September, October.
Distrib.—Africa, and throughout the Oriental region to New Guinea and Queensland.

22. Ophideres materna, Linn.: Syst. Nat., i, 2, p. 840.

7 ♂, 5 ♀ ; September.
Distrib.—Tropical Africa, India, Ceylon, Burma, Andamans, Java, North Australia.

23. Cosmophila erosa, Hübn.: Zutr. Samml. Exot. Schnutt., ii, 19, figs. 287, 288.

1 ♂, 2 ♀ ; March. The male belongs to the form with pectinated antennæ.
Distrib. — United States, West Indies, Africa, Madagascar, Mauritius, throughout the Oriental region to Queensland and Fiji.

24. Cosmophila vitiensis, Butl.: Trans. Ent. Soc., 1886, p. 408. (Pl. IX, Fig. 12.)

4 ♂, 5 ♀ ; March. The antennæ of males have short branches on outer side, and are fasciculate on the inner; the postmedian line

of fore wing has its excurved portions rounded or straight, not
angled; the usual colour variations occur.

Distrib.—New Hebrides, Fiji, Tahiti.

25. Eutelia delatrix, Guen. : Noct., ii, p. 304.

3 ♂, 3 ♀.

Distrib.—India, Ceylon, Burma, Singapore, Java, Queensland.

26. Stictoptera describens, Wlk., xiii, 1139.

1 ♀ ; December.

Distrib.—South India, Ceylon, Singapore.

27. Hydrillodes vexillifera, sp.n.   (Pl. IX, Fig. 6.)

♂. Palpi recurved over head, the first joint angled with scales
in front; the second largely tufted with hair at the extremity, the
third bent downwards and tufted with hair; fore tibiæ and femora
with large tufts of hair; fore wing with slight costal fold on
under-side fringed with large scales; hind wing with the basal area
on under-side clothed with fulvous androconia.

Fuscous brown; the tufts on fore legs and at extremity of
abdomen tinged with ochreous. Fore wing with faint traces of an
antemedial line; a black point at middle of cell; the postmedial
line arising from a white point on costa, then indistinct, waved,
and incurved from vein 3 to submedian fold; the subterminal line
indistinct, curved and angled inwards in submedian fold; hind
wing with discoidal lunule. Under-side of hind wing paler, with
distinct discoidal spot and waved postmedial line; the fulvous
scales in male extending on inner area to near tornus.

1 ♂, 4 ♀; December–March. *Exp.* 26 mm.; also from the
Louisiades, St. Aignan (Meek).

28. Maliattha signifera, Wlk., xii, 793.

12 ♂, 18 ♀; August–March.

Distrib. — Japan, China, India, Ceylon, Burma, Andamans,
Penang, Queensland.

29. Erastria griseomixta, sp.n.   (Pl. IX, Fig. 5.)

♀. Head and thorax grey, slightly mixed with brown scales ;
abdomen fuscous brown. Fore wing grey, irrorated with brown
scales ; an indistinct sub-basal line oblique from costa to median
nervure, where it is angled, obsolete below submedian fold; the
antemedial line indistinct, slightly waved, oblique from costa to
median nervure, then nearly erect; a slight rufous point at lower
angle of cell ; the postmedial line indistinct, bent outwards below

costa, where there is an obscure brownish spot on it, then minutely
dentate and slightly defined by white scales, the area between it
and the slightly waved subterminal line browner. Hind wing dark
brown, paler towards base; cilia greyish.

1 ♀; February. *Exp.* 22 mm.

30. Tarache olivacea, Hmpsn.: Ill. Het. B.M., viii, p. 63, pl. 142, fig. 9.

1 ♂; February.
Distrib.—Shanghai, Nága Hills, Nilgiris; a closely allied species
in Abyssinia.

31. Earias chromataria, Wlk., xxvii, 204.

1 ♀. Fore wing with the dark terminal band very broad; hind
wing tinged with fuscous.
Distrib. — Africa, Japan, India, Ceylon, Burma, Andamans,
Sula, Java.

Family LYMANTRIADÆ.

32. Porthesia pulverea, sp.n. (Pl. IX, Fig. 9.)

♂. White; head and thorax strongly or slightly tinged with
yellow brown; antennæ with the branches brownish; abdomen
with the anal tuft orange. Fore wing strongly òr slightly irrorated
with large yellow-brown scales; more or less prominent brown
medial and postmedial lines excurved from costa to median
nervure. Hind wing white, the termen and cilia often tinged
with brown.
♀. The anal tuft pale yellow or brownish; fore wing much
less irrorated with brown, the lines hardly traceable, or quite
obsolete.
20 ♂, 8 ♀; December–March. Allied to *P. irrorata*, Moore,
from Java.

33. Orgyia postica, Wlk., iv, 803.

1 ♂; January.
Distrib.—Formosa, India, Ceylon, Burma, Borneo, Java, New
Guinea, Queensland.

Family SPHINGIDÆ.

CHÆROCAMPINÆ.

34. Chærocampa erotus, Cram.: Pap. Exot., ii, pl. 104 ʙ.

10 ♂, 4 ♀; July–January.
Distrib.—Andamans, Queensland, Solomons, Tonga.

35. Chærocampa vigil, Guér.: Deless. Voy., ii, p. 80, pl. xxiii, fig. 1.

13 ♂, 7 ♀ ; August–January.
Distrib.—India, Ceylon, Andamans, Philippines, Java, Queensland, New Hebrides.

36. Theretra lucasi, Wlk., viii, 141.

1 ♀ ; December.
Distrib.—Oriental region to North Australia.

SPHINGINÆ.

37. Pseudosphinx discistriga, Wlk., viii, 209.

4 ♀ ; December, January.
Distrib.—Japan, China, India, Ceylon, Andamans, Borneo, Java, Queensland.

MACROGLOSSINÆ.

38. Cephonodes hylas, Linn.: Mant. Ins., p. 539.

9 ♂, 6 ♀ ; September–March.
Distrib.—West and South Africa, Oriental region to Australia, and Gilbert Islands.
All the specimens belong to the form *confinis*, Boisd., previously recorded from South Africa only.

Family GEOMETRIDÆ.

BOARMIANÆ.

39. Hyperythra lutea, Cram.: Pap. Exot., iv, p. 157, pl. 370 c, D.

2 ♂, 2 ♀ ; January.
A small form of the species, with the male extremely dark, similar to a specimen from Claremont Island, North Australia.
Distrib.—Oriental region to North Australia.

40. Boarmia acaciaria, Boisd.: Faun. Ent. Madag. Lép., 116, pl. xvi, fig. 4.

4 ♂, 1 ♀ ; October–February. Showing the usual large amount of variation, but all belonging to the dark form *cornaria*, Guen.

Distrib.—West and South Africa, Madagascar, Oriental region to Australia and North Caledonia.

41. Boarmia scotozonea, sp.n. (Pl. IX, Figs. 4, 15.)

♂. Pale olive-brown, irrorated with black scales; palpi at sides and frons black; forelegs streaked with black; abdomen dorsally suffused with black from second to subterminal segment. Fore wing with obscure, slightly curved, antemedial series of points and indistinct oblique medial line; a postmedial series of points, with dark spots on it between veins 6 and 4, with a diffused blackish patch beyond it extending nearly to termen; a pale subterminal line dentate towards costa; some black points on termen. Hind wing with obscure antemedial line; a more prominent, minutely dentate, medial line followed by a rust-red line; an ill-defined, pale, subterminal line, somewhat dentate towards costa, and with rust-red line on its inner side, the area beyond it pale from vein 4 to tornus; two terminal black lunules towards apex and one towards tornus. Under-side, with the terminal area of both wings, black, with subterminal series of pale spots becoming a line towards inner margin of hind wing. Antennæ ciliated; fore wing with small fovea.

♀. The area beyond the postmedial line of fore wing and medial line of hind wing suffused with black, except the costal area of fore wing.

24 ♂, 3 ♀; September–March. The only close ally of this species is *B. cessaria*, Wlk., from India and Ceylon.

LARENTIANÆ.

42. Sauris hirudinata, Guen.: Phal., ii, p. 362.

1 ♂, 3 ♀; December–March.
Distrib.—South Africa, India, Ceylon, Burma, Sumatra, Java, Queensland, Fiji.

GEOMETRINÆ.

43. Thalassodes veraria, Guen.: Phal., i, p. 360.

One ♀ in bad condition, which is bright yellow-green instead of blue-green, and may belong to a closely allied species.
Distrib.—India, Ceylon, Java.

ACIDALIANÆ.

44. Craspedia optivata, Wlk., xxiii, 780.

5 ♂, 16 ♀; December–March. The females agree very well with the Australian form, but the males have the discoidal spots and terminal points larger.

Distrib.— North Australia, Queensland, New South Wales, Tasmania.

45. Craspedia, sp.

One ♀ in too bad condition to identify, apparently allied to *C. eulomata*, Snell.

Family URANIADÆ.

EPIPLEMINÆ.

46. Epiplema inhians, Warr.: A.M.N.H. (6), xvii, 214.
(Pl. IX, Fig. 2.)

6 ♂, 3 ♀; December–March. Agrees exactly with specimens from Sikhim and the Khásis, from which it has been previously recorded only; one female is browner, with a black medial band to both wings.

Family PYRALIDÆ.

GALLERIANÆ.

47. Dolöessa castanella, Hmpsn.: Moths Ind., iv, p. 4.

1 ♂; February.
Distrib.—Ceylon.

48. Corcyra cephalonica, Stt.: Ann., 1866, p. 147.

1 ♂, 4 ♀; March.
Distrib.—Europe, West Indies, Ceylon. Probably introduced.

PHYCITINÆ.

49. Homœosoma nimbella, Zell.: Isis, 1839, p. 178.

1 ♂.
Distrib.—United States of America, Europe, Syria, Cape Colony.

50. Ephestia scotella, sp.n. (Pl. IX, Fig. 13.)

♀. Dark purplish-brown slightly suffused with grey. Fore wing without trace of antemedial line or discoidal points; a very indistinct pale subterminal line excurved from below costa to vein 2; a terminal series of indistinct black points. Hind wing fuscous; veins 3 and 5 stalked.

2 ♀; December, January. *Exp.* 16 mm.

51. Heterographis singhalella, Rag.: Ann. Soc. Ent. Fr., 1888, p. 283.

1 ♀; January. In bad condition, which may belong to a closely allied species.
Distrib.—Ceylon.

52. Eusophera cinerosella, Zell.: Stett. Ent. Zeit., 1867, p. 380.

2 ♀; January.
Distrib.—Europe. Probably introduced.

53. Epicrocis œgnusalis, Wlk., xix, 905.

3 ♀; January–March.
Distrib.—Madagascar, China, India, Ceylon and Burma, Sumatra, Australia.

ENDOTRICHINÆ.

54. Endotricha listeri, Butl.: P.Z.S., 1888, p. 546.
(Pl. IX, Fig. 3.)

28 ♂, 81 ♀; August–March.

PYRALINÆ.

55. Herculia nannodes, Butl.: Ill. Het. B.M., iii, p. 71, pl. lviii, fig. 5.

1 ♂, 10 ♀; December–February.
Distrib.—Japan, China, Borneo.

PYRAUSTINÆ.

56. Zinckenia nigerrimalis, sp.n. (Pl. IX, Fig. 10.)

Antennæ of male, with the tuft of scales from basal joint very large, convolute, and enclosing the base of the shaft, which is greatly thickened by scales on inner side after the excision. Deep dull black; palpi with the second joint banded with white; pectus and legs partly white; abdomen with slight dorsal segmental lines on upper sides and broad bands on ventral surface. Fore wing with medial white spots in cell, below the cell and on inner margin; a trifid spot beyond the cell above vein 5, and two spots nearer the termen between veins 3 and 5; cilia white above middle and tornus. Hind wing with oblique, slightly curved, white medial band not reaching costa or inner margin; cilia white below apex, and tipped with white near middle.

4 ♂, 8 ♀; December–March.

57. Zinckenia fascialis, Cram. : Pap. Exot., iv, pl. 398 c.

4 ♂, 7 ♀; August.

Distrib. — Neotropical, Nearctic, South Palæarctic, Ethiopian, Oriental, and Australian regions.

58. Dichocrocis surusalis, Wlk., xviii, 695.

1 ♀.

Distrib.—Japan, Ceylon, Sumatra, Borneo, Bali, Celebes.

59. Sylepta lunalis, Guen. : Delt & Pyr., p. 352.

1 ♀.

Distrib. — Formosa, India, Ceylon, Burma, Borneo, Celebes, Sumbawa, Venezuela.

**60. Dichocrocis auritincta, Butl. : Trans. Ent. Soc., 1886, p. 431.
(Pl. IX, Fig. 14.)**

1 ♀.

Distrib.—Bali, Tenimber, Australia.

61. Glyphodes (Phacellura) holophæalis, sp.n.　(Pl. IX, Fig. 11.)

Fuscous; palpi below, pectus and ventral surface of abdomen white; the anal tuft fulvous, with black tips; wings fuscous brown, with a purplish tinge; an oblique opalescent shade on medial area of both wings.

7 ♂, 8 ♀; September–March.　The only near allies of this species are Neotropical.

62. Glyphodes indica, Saund. : Trans. Ent. Soc., 1851, p. 163.

4 ♂, 1 ♀.

Distrib.—Ethiopian, Oriental, and Australian regions.

**63. Glyphodes suralis, Led. : Wien Ent. Mov., 1863, p. 405,
pl. xiv, fig. 7.**

3 ♂, 6 ♀; August–March.

Distrib.—Nicobars, Amboina, New Guinea, Solomons, and Pacific groups.

64. Hellula undalis, Fabr. : Ent. Syst., iii, 2, p. 226.

1 ♀.

Distrib.—United States of America, Mediterranean sub-region, Ethiopian and Oriental regions.

MICRO-LEPIDOPTERA.

By the Rt. Hon. Lord WALSINGHAM, M.A., LL.D., F.R.S.,
Trustee Brit. Mus.

PYRALIDINA.

Family OXYCHIROTIDÆ, Meyr.

1. Oxychirota paradoxa, Meyr.

Oxychirota paradoxa, Meyr.: Tr. Ent. Soc. Lond., 1884, 438–9.[1]

Hab.—N.S. Wales : Sydney, June.[1]
Christmas Island; Jan.-Mar., 1898; seven specimens. (C. W.
Andrews.)
I find a specimen in my collection, apparently belonging to this
genus, collected at Paradeniya in Ceylon by Dr. G. H. K. Thwaites,
which is quite distinct from Meyrick's species.

Family PTEROPHORIDÆ.

2. Cosmoclostis quadriquadra, Wlsm., sp.n.

Antennæ white. Palpi scarcely projecting beyond the head;
white. Head pale rust-brown above, face white. Thorax yellowish
white anteriorly, rust-brown posteriorly; under-side shining white,
tinged with yellowish at the sides. Fore wings cleft to beyond
middle; yellowish white, the costa and dorsum narrowly pale rust-
brown; a few rust-brown scales crossing the wing at one-fourth
are succeeded by a rust-brown patch at the base of the fissure,
wider on the tornal than on the apical lobe; before the middle of
the apical lobe is another transverse oblique rust-brown patch,
joined along the dorsum of the lobe to an ante-apical patch of the
same colour which overflows the dorsal but not the costal cilia; on
the tornal lobe there is also a broad straight transverse rust-brown
patch beyond its middle, colouring the cilia above and below it, the
cilia (except where so coloured) are whitish. *Exp. al.* 11–13 mm.
Hind wings and cilia bronzy grey, the cilia of the dorsal lobe paler.
Abdomen rich rust-brown, with four quadrate whitish patches
above—one basal, one ante-median, one post-median, and one on
the anal segment; under-side shining white, tinged with yellowish

at the sides. Hind legs white, smeared above on the tibiæ and banded on the tarsi with pale rust-brown; spurs white, tinged with rust-brown before their extremities, the scales at the base of the spurs not conspicuously raised, rust-brown mixed with white.

Co-types (3), Mus. Br.

Hab.—Christmas Island; Dec., 1897 — Jan., 1898; fourteen specimens. (C. W. Andrews.)

The specimens are in poor condition, but show that the species is distinct from *C. aglaodesma*, Meyr., not only from its smaller size but from the different arrangement of the abdominal spots and the tint of the hind wings, besides minor differences in the arrangement of the markings. It is obviously an insular form allied to the New South Wales species, which, however, also occurs in the Solomon Islands.

TINEINA.

Family HYPONOMEUTIDÆ.

3. Brenthia elachista, Wlsm., sp.n.

Antennæ annulate with bronzy fuscous and whitish towards the base, becoming blackish above on their outer half. Palpi porrect; white, annulate, with bronzy fuscous—two annulations on each joint. Head and thorax bronzy brownish. Fore wings cinereous, profusely speckled with bronzy brownish, forming transverse sinuate strigulæ across the outer half; a short, bronzy brown, basal patch, wider on the costa than on the dorsum, this is outwardly bounded by a band of the pale ground-colour, beyond which the wing is again shaded with bronzy brownish; a minute patch of fuscous speckling at the outer end of the cell, with a white spot on the costa above it, this is succeeded by a blue and lilac metallic spot; the apex and termen are broadly ornamented with velvet-black, alternating on its inner margin with golden brown and speckled on its outer margin with lustrous shining metallic iridescent spots— the first two slightly below the apex, silvery white set in black, the others more or less coalescing in a narrow band about the middle of the termen, with some scattered metallic scales again below them; cilia shining, greenish grey on their basal half, pale bronzy brownish externally. *Exp. al.* 6 mm. Hind wings bronzy brownish grey, with an oblique transverse white band from the costa to below the middle at one-third from the base, with some shining metallic lilac spots towards the apex and termen; cilia brownish grey, streaked with white through their middle below the apex. Abdomen bronzy brownish. Legs white, spotted with bronzy brownish above on the tibiæ and tarsi.

Co-types (2), Mus. Br.

Hab. — Christmas Island ; Jan.-Mar., 1898 ; six specimens. (C. W. Andrews.)

Smaller than any previously described species of this genus, greatly resembling *B. pavonacella*, Clem., and the larger *quadriflorella*, Z., from North and South America respectively.

4. Simaethis ornaticornis, Wlsm., sp.n.

Antennæ with the basal joint enlarged, obtuse ; brownish ochreous, the stem white, conspicuously annulated with black. Palpi whitish, barred with brownish ochreous on the outer sides. Head brownish ochreous, mixed with pale cinereous. Thorax brownish ochreous, becoming dark brownish grey posteriorly. Fore wings with the costa much arched, widening outward from the base, apex rounded, termen obliquely convex ; olivaceous brownish, with two narrow transverse bands of pale cinereous speckling between base and middle, the outer one terminating in a whitish costal spot, beyond which is another reduplicated whitish costal spot, the space between them dark brownish fuscous, another small white spot lies in the costal cilia immediately above the apex ; some blackish patches around the outer end of the cell are succeeded by some paler transverse strigulæ and accompanied by brownish cinereous scaling, the ante-apical and ante-terminal portion of the wing being irregularly clouded with fuscous, the termen olivaceous brown, with a dark brown line along the base of the bronzy greyish cilia. *Exp. al.* 11 mm. Hind wings dark bronzy brownish, with some faint pale curved streaks running through them before the margin ; under-side with two speckled pale cinereous bands. Abdomen bronzy brownish. Legs fuscous, tarsi with three white bands.

Co-types (2), Mus. Br.

Hab. — Christmas Island ; Feb.-Mar., 1898 ; ten specimens. (C. W. Andrews.)

This species resembles in shape, colouring, and markings the typical forms of *Simaethis*, and is apparently nearer to the European *oxyacanthella*, L., than to any other well-known species.

5. Phycodes adjectella, Wkr.

Nigilgia adjectella, Wlk.: Cat. Lp. Ins. B.M., XXVIII, 512 (1863).[1]
Phycodes adjectella, Wlsm.: Tr. Ent. Soc. Lond., 1891, 80.[2]

Hab.—Sierra Leone.[1] East Africa: Tangani, Kolumbi Creek, Aug.[2]

Christmas Island ; Dec., 1897 — Jan., 1898 ; two specimens. (C. W. Andrews.)

Apparently a small form (*exp. al.* 11 mm.) of Walker's African species.

6. Tortricomorpha chlorolepis, Wlsm., sp.n.

Antennæ dark brown. Palpi dark brown externally, brownish cinereous on their inner sides; terminal joint short, not rising above the level of the head. Head greyish brown. Thorax dark brown, sprinkled with greenish and pale cinereous scales. Fore wings dark brown, profusely sprinkled with pale yellowish green scales, the greenish scaling is somewhat thicker on the basal half, on a transverse band passing the end of the cell, and about the apical and terminal portion of the wing, leaving a brown band less thickly scaled across the middle; cilia brownish grey, a narrow brownish ochreous marginal line preceding them. *Exp. al.* ♂ 28, ♀ 23 mm. Hind wings greyish brown, the outer two-thirds of the cilia whitish cinereous. Abdomen greyish brown. Legs greyish brown, the end of the hind tibiæ and the last four tarsal joints brownish ochreous.

Type.—♂ ♀ Mus. Br.
Hab.—Christmas Island; Feb., 1898; three specimens. (C. W. Andrews.)

Family TORTRICIDÆ.

[EPAGOGE, Hb. = DICHELIA, Gn. = HASTULA, Mül.]

7. Epagoge halysideta, Wlsm., sp.n.

Antennæ greyish cinereous. Palpi triangular; pale brownish ochreous. Thorax greenish olivaceous, with two scarlet longitudinal streaks. Fore wings dull olive-green to two-thirds from the base; on the green portion are three lines of scarlet streaks—the first, from the base below the costa, broken beyond its middle, the basal half tending to join the outer half of a similarly broken median streak; the third, also from the base, is broken into three spots below the middle and outer half of the fold; three small scarlet spots and a transverse elongate one precede the darkened outer third of the wing, which, after a narrow margin of metallic pinkish ochreous, becomes rich yellowish brown, with obscure greyish fuscous semi-metallic shading and reticulations; along the costa, commencing near the base, is a series of minute pale ochreous spots, gradually increasing and becoming oblique geminated streaks, continuing to the apex; these, beyond the middle, are joined in pairs at their lower extremities, giving the appearance of links of a chain; cilia pale ochreous, with fuscous streaklets running through them. *Exp. al.* 9 mm. Hind wings dark greyish. Abdomen bronzy grey; anal tuft ochreous. Legs pale ochreous.

Type.—♂ Mus. Br.
Hab.—Christmas Island; Jan., 1898; unique. (C. W. Andrews.)
A single specimen, adding to the somewhat curious tropical distribution of this conspicuous form, allied species occurring on the west coast of Africa, Malaysia, Queensland, and extending northwards to Shanghai.

CÆNOGNOSIS, Wlsm., gen. nov.

(καινός = 'new'; γνῶσις = 'knowledge.')

Type: *Cænognosis incisa*, Wlsm.

Antennæ (♀) simple. Palpi porrect, median joint clothed with loose hair-scales beneath; terminal joint nearly half the length of the median, slightly drooping, smooth. Head rather rough above. Thorax smooth. Fore wings narrow at the base, slightly widening outward, costa moderately straight, apex obtusely falcate, termen deeply sinuate, not oblique, tornus rounded: neuration, 12 veins—2 from scarcely beyond middle of cell; 3 from before angle of cell, much recurved, approximating to 4 on termen; 4 and 5 separate, 4 recurved, 5 to sub-apical sinus; 6 to lower extremity of the falcate apex; 7 to above apex, 8 and 9 out of 7; 10 nearer to 7 than to 11; 11 from outer third of cell. Hind wings as broad as the fore wings, scarcely sinuate below the rounded apex: neuration, 8 veins—3 and 4 connate; 5 parallel to 4; 6 and 7 stalked. Abdomen normal. Legs smooth; a slight projecting tuft of scales at the end of the hind tibiæ.
Apparently allied to the New Zealand genus *Epalxiphora*, Meyr., which is also represented in New South Wales.

8. Cænognosis incisa, Wlsm., sp.n.

Antennæ pale brownish. Palpi white, a brownish streak on the outer side of the median joint reaching to half its length, terminal joint tinged with brownish. Head dark rust-brown. Thorax white, with a brownish tinge. Fore wings sericeous white, costa narrowly tinged with rust-brown, through which run short oblique white streaklets commencing before the middle and continuing nearly to the apex; apex obtusely caudate, rich ferruginous, a silvery streak running through the lower half of the ferruginous patch, joined at its base by a similar slender streak from the costa and at its apex by another curving around the base of the apical cilia; this patch is preceded by a dark fuscous quadrate spot a little beyond the upper angle of the cell with smaller patches of fuscous scales on either side of it; along the middle of the termen are three or four patches of similar fuscous scales between the veins, and a few, less noticeable, are distributed along the dorsum below the fold; cilia at the apex ferruginous, below it white tipped with fuscous, around the tornus plain white. *Exp. al.* 17 mm. Hind wings pale yellowish brown with a roseate gloss; cilia pale brownish, tipped with dirty whitish towards their apex. Abdomen pale yellowish brown. Legs pale yellowish brown, the terminal four joints of the hind tarsi darker brownish above, with whitish spot at the joints.

Type.—♀ Mus. Br.

Hab. — Christmas Island; March, 1898; unique. (C. W. Andrews.)

Family TINEIDÆ.

9. Dendroneura punctata, Wlsm., sp.n.

Antennæ olivaceous ochreous. Palpi divergent; whitish ochreous beneath, streaked with fuscous along their upper side. Head pale olivaceous grey; face flattened, slightly paler. Thorax and fore wings shining pale olivaceous grey, with a greenish iridescent gloss; a small fuscous spot lies a little below the costa at three-fourths from the base, and is preceded by a similar small spot on the dorsum; cilia pale olivaceous greyish. *Exp. al.* 11–12 mm. Hind wings widened near the base, becoming rapidly attenuate beyond the middle to the acute apex; tawny olivaceous greyish, cilia scarcely paler. Abdomen pale cinereous. Legs with the usual flattened femora characteristic of this genus; hind tibiæ very hairy above; pale cinereous.

Co-types (2), Mus. Br.

Hab. — Christmas Island; Dec., 1897; Jan.–Feb., 1898; ten specimens. (C. W. Andrews.)

The species of this genus are said to be attached to sugar-cane and the banana. One has been recorded from the West Indies; others occur in Hawaiia and the Society and Marquesas Islands.

Order 2.—HYMENOPTERA.

By W. F. Kirby, F.L.S., F.E.S., etc.

(PLATE XIV, Figs. 5-9.)

I HAVE been able to identify eleven species of *Hymenoptera*, obtained by Mr. Andrews on Christmas Island, all but two of which are, as far as yet known, peculiar to the island. Of these, I have described six as new, one of which I have made the type of a new genus. There are also single specimens of three species of Ichneumonidæ, which it is not desirable to describe until more specimens are obtained. I have added the descriptions of new species, and any notes of importance from my former paper on the *Hymenoptera* collected by Mr. Lister (P.Z.S., 1888, pp. 551, 552).

LIST OF SPECIES.

TEREBRANTIA.

ENTOMOPHAGA.

PROCTOTRYPIDÆ.
  DRYININÆ (?).
    Mantibaria, g.n.
      anomala, sp.n.

ICHNEUMONIDÆ.
  OPHIONINÆ.
    Ophion, Fabr.
      flavocephalus, sp.n.

ACULEATA.

HETEROGYNA.

FORMICIDÆ.
  PONERINÆ.
    Lobopelta, Mayr.
      diminuta, Smith.

  FORMICINÆ.
    Camponotus, Mayr.
      melichloros, Kirb.

FOSSORES.

CRABRONIDÆ.
  LARRINÆ.
    Notogonia, Costa.
      alecto, Smith (?).

DIPLOPTERA.

EUMENIDÆ.
  Odynerus, Latr.
    polyphemus, Kirb.
VESPIDÆ.
  Polistes, Latr.
    balder, Kirb.

ANTHOPHILA.

APIDÆ.
  ANDRENINÆ.
    Halictus, Latr.
      andrewsi, sp.n.
      binghami, sp.n.

  MEGACHILINÆ.
    Megachile, Latr.
      rotundipennis, sp.n.
      nivescens, sp.n.

G

MANTIBARIA, Kirby, gen. nov.

Head very large, oval, as broad as the thorax, and broader than long; ocelli arranged in an equilateral triangle, antennæ inserted close together between the eyes, and set with short hairs, scape slightly curved, about four times as long as broad, second joint rather longer than broad, slightly narrowed at the base and truncated at the extremity; flagellum nine-jointed. the joints transverse, closely appressed, a little broader than long, except at the extremities, the last as long us the preceding three, and ending in a fine point; pronotum nearly square, a little rounded in front; scutellum forming an obtuse-angled triangle, truncated behind, and with a slight central carina; abdomen moderately broad, with six dorsal segments visible, of about equal length; legs short, stout, clothed with short hairs, but destitute of spines; tarsi five-jointed, the first joint rather longer than broad, the second, third, and fourth transverse, the fifth as long as all the rest put together, greatly swollen, and followed by large claws, which are, however, more or less damaged in all the specimens before me, and hence cannot be further described. Rudimentary wings visible under the microscope.

Affinities uncertain; I am inclined to refer the species to the *Dryininæ*, but without feeling at all sure that this is its real position.

1. Mantibaria anomala, sp.n. (Pl. XIV, Figs. 5, 5a.)

Long. corp. 2·5 mm.

Black above, very finely punctured; antennæ, legs, face, and sometimes a ring round the eyes, testaceous or rufo-testaceous; tip of abdomen and sometimes the incisions more or less reddish.

Five specimens from Flying Fish Cove, August, 1897. Parasitic on *Mantis*, etc.

2. Ophion flavocephalus, sp.n.

Long. corp. 14 mm.; exp. al. 22 mm.

Male and Female.—Testaceous, head yellow, except the antennæ and mouth-parts, which are testaceous, and the very large ocelli, which are black. Thorax, in the male, with three longitudinal brown stripes. Abdomen: first segment with its apical third rather suddenly enlarged; second segment fusiform, thickest beyond the middle, but before the extremity; the abdomen is thickly clothed with short hair, especially towards the extremity, which is brownish, darkest in the male. Wings iridescent hyaline, with piceous nervures; costa of fore wings blackish as far as the stigma, and, including the latter, yellow beyond. Stigma slightly indented at its base by the cubito-discoidal cell, below which point are two testaceous specks, enclosed by a curved water-line; the outer extremity of the cubito-discoidal cell is unusually broad, about two-thirds as broad as its lower extremity; costa of hind wings edged with a blackish line.

Described from one pair, taken near Flying Fish Cove.

3. Lobopelta diminuta. (Pl. XIV, Fig. 6, ♀.)

Ponera diminuta, Smith: Cat. Hym. B.M., vi, p. 89, n. 23 (1860).

Nine workers; north part of island, March, 1898. One female (?) without locality; described below.

A common East Indian species, previously recorded from Christmas Island, as well as from Calcutta, Borneo, etc.

Mr. Lister's collection contained four workers from a nest found near the summit of the island, on October 4, 1887.

Lobopelta diminuta, ♀ (?). (Pl. XIV, Fig. 7.)

Long. corp. 6 mm.; exp. al. 12 mm.

Dull black, clothed with short grey hairs, especially conspicuous on the abdomen. Antennæ dull reddish, clothed with a very fine pile. Mouth-parts, tegulæ, and the last two segments and under-surface of the abdomen, and a narrow border to the segments; the trochanters, base and tip of femora, and the tibiæ and tarsi rufous; the hind tibiæ brown in the middle. Front coxæ much thickened, front tibiæ cultrate, with a very large oblique terminal spine. Petiole large, erect, sloping in front, and truncated behind. Wings fusco-hyaline, with fuscous nervures; stigma blackish; neuration nearly that of *Ponera*.

4. Camponotus melichloros.

Camponotus melichloros, Kirb.: P.Z.S., 1888, p. 551.

"Long. corp. 7–8 mm.

"Worker. Structure nearly that of *C. ligniperdus*, Latr. Thoracic sutures fairly well defined; node of petiole forming a rounded plate. Smooth and shining, sparingly clothed with erect white hairs; thorax honey-yellow; head and tarsi reddish; flagellum paler; abdomen black, with pale sutures; eyes and extreme tips of mandibles black, the latter sexdentate.

"The following label was attached to the bottle: 'Two forms from same nest in rotten wood, Flying Fish Cove, October 2'

[1887]. The specimens differ little, except that some are rather smaller and paler than others, and with conspicuously smaller head."

A large series of the various forms of this species from Flying Fish Cove, August–October, 1897, and February, 1898; from north coast, December, 1897; and from north part of island, January, 1898. The workers vary from 3–9 mm. in length. The females are 10–11 mm. long and 22–25 mm. in expanse. They are of a rather darker chestnut red than the workers, and the abdomen is black, clothed with short grey hairs. The wings are yellowish hyaline, with yellowish nervures. The males are 7 mm. long and 14 mm. in expanse; the upper part of the head is black, the antennæ and front of the head and face reddish. The thorax is reddish, with brown or black markings, and the abdomen is black, with the sutures light reddish. The legs are reddish, with black femora. Workers found in a rotten stump.

5. Notogonia alecto (?).

? Larrada alecto, Smith: Journ. Linn. Soc., Zool., ii, p. 103, n. 6 (1858).

Long. corp., ♂ 7, ♀ 10 mm.; exp. al., ♂ 11, ♀ 17 mm.

Black, head and thorax thickly and finely punctured, clothed with a very fine silvery pile, especially on the face, scutellum, and abdomen; middle and hind tarsi more or less reddish in the female, and hind tibiæ edged within with silvery pile; scutellum oval, much longer than broad, thickly, coarsely, and very irregularly rugose-punctate, wings brownish hyaline, with brown nervures.

Nine specimens, from Flying Fish Cove, August–October, 1897; east coast, September, 1897; north coast, 1898.

Apparently identical with a specimen marked " *Larrada alecto*, Smith," from Celebes; but as we have no authentic specimens of that species from Singapore, the original locality, I am not certain that the Christmas Island insect is the true *alecto*.

6. Odynerus polyphemus.

Odynerus polyphemus, Kirb.: P.Z.S., 1888, p. 551.

"Long. corp. 10 mm.; exp. al. 17 mm.

" Black, thickly and closely punctured; head with a yellow spot between the antennæ; the orbits opposite the antennæ very narrowly edged with yellow; a yellow streak on each side of the base of the clypeus, just below the antennæ, and a yellow streak behind each eye, above the middle. Prothorax edged in front with a broad yellow stripe, tapering and interrupted in the middle, and cut squarely off on each side. Tegulæ pitchy, with a very small yellow dot in the middle, a triangular yellow spot above, and another, sub-rotund, on the mesopleura. Scutellum with a broad longitudinal yellow stripe on each side; post-scutellum yellow, metathorax with a broad curved yellow stripe on each side. Abdomen with the first segment yellow above, except in front, a black line, interrupted behind, on the median line above; second segment yellow above, except at the base, and on a wide conical space which extends to three-quarters of its length; on the hinder edge of the segment the yellow colour is continued on the lower surface, but does not form a complete ring, being widely interrupted in the middle; the third segment bordered behind on the upper surface. Wings dirty hyaline, smoky along the costa, and in the radial cell.

"Allied to *O. confluentus*, Smith, from Sumatra, but differing much in colour from any described species."

Thirteen specimens, from Flying Fish Cove, August, 1897; west coast, October, 1897; north part of island, December, 1897, and January, 1898; central part of island, February, 1898.

7. Polistes balder.

Polistes balder, Kirb.: P.Z.S., 1888, p. 552.

"Exp. al. 28 mm.; long. corp. 13 mm.

"Ochreous-yellow, with linear black markings. Head with a black line just above the antennæ, the ends of which run upwards on each side, and slightly diverge; below the antennæ the clypeal suture is black, and this curve is sometimes connected with the upper one by a black line on each side within the antennæ; a black line crosses the head just behind the ocelli, over which extends a continuous black spot; the tips of the mandibles are also black, as well as the basal parts of the head and prothorax. Thorax with all the sutures more or less black, sometimes not continuously; the central black line is frequently incomplete behind. Pectus and pleura black, the latter marked with four or five large and small yellow spots. Scutellum, post-scutellum, and metathorax yellow; the sutures rather broadly black; groove of the metathorax black. Legs almost entirely yellow, or reddish yellow; the trochanters and the extreme tips of the coxæ and base of the femora black. Abdomen inclining to reddish yellow, but with no distinct markings, except a black spot above at the base of the first segment, and the suture between the first and second segment, which is generally black. Wings smoky hyaline, with brown nervures; costal nervure and costal region yellowish.

"Allied to *P. hebræus*, Fabr., but smaller and differently coloured. The first segment of the abdomen, too, appears to be a little longer and more gradually widened.

"Two nests accompanied these wasps. They are round, and the smaller one is considerably raised in the middle. The upper surface is grey; the outer portion is inky black towards the base, and whitish on the sides above.

"One of the wasps was taken on October 1, at Flying Fish Cove; a nest, with eggs, larvæ, and cocoons, was found on the under-side of a branch at the same place on October 2; and another nest, with wasps flying round it, on October 5."

Six specimens. from Flying Fish Cove, August, 1897; and north part of island, December, 1897, and January, 1898.

Makes small hanging nests on trees and bushes, and stings severely.

8. Halictus andrewsi, sp.n. (Pl. XIV, Fig. 8.)

Long. corp. 6 mm; exp. al. 10 mm.

Female.—Face forming a long oval between the eyes, clothed with bronzy-green pile, back of head bronzy green, rarely purplish black, cheeks clothed with long grey hair; antennæ rufo-testaceous. with the scape and following joint black; mesonotum and scutellum bronzy green, the borders of the former sometimes purplish black; post-scutellum broad, depressed, more strongly punctured than the rest of the thorax, and of a darker bronzy-green; it is bordered behind and on the sides with long whitish hairs. Abdomen shining bronzy-green, very finely punctured, with the sutures narrowly testaceous. Under-surface mottly bronzy green, but paler than above; legs testaceous, frequently more or less bronzed, especially on the femora; wings iridescent hyaline, with brown nervures; centre of stigma yellow.

Probably allied to *H. buccinus* and *vicinus*, Vachal.

Eleven specimens, those with localities marked "North part of island," January, 1898.

9. Halictus binghami, sp.n. (Pl. XIV, Fig. 9.)

? *Halictus proteus*, Bingham: Faun. Brit. Ind., Hym. i, p. 428, n. 737 (1897); *nec* Vachal.

Long. corp. 5·5 mm.; exp. al. 10–11 mm.

Female.—Head and thorax black, sometimes with a very faint, greenish tint, very finely punctured, an impressed vertical line from between the bases of the antennæ to half the distance from thence to the anterior ocellus; lower part of the face clothed with grey pubescence; tongue testaceous; metanotum longitudinally striated, and bordered with grey pubescence. Abdomen more shining black, the segments not constricted, basal segment polished, smooth, rufous, the segments narrowly bordered behind with testaceous, and fringed with yellowish - grey pubescence. Legs dark reddish-brown, sometimes with a darker line above, and clothed with long yellowish-grey pubescence. Wings iridescent hyaline, with yellowish-brown neuration.

Four specimens, from north part of island, January, 1898. This insect agrees very well with Lieut. - Col. Bingham's description of the female from Tenasserim, which he doubtfully refers to *H. proteus*, Vachal; but I cannot regard it as Vachal's species, which is described as having the "metanotum (post-scutellum) tomento croceato tectum." It is black in the Christmas Island specimens, bordered with grey pubescence. But it is possible that the male, which Bingham doubtfully refers to the same species, may be Vachal's insect. However, as I have no specimens of these *Halicti* to compare, and as the Christmas Island species would in any case require to be renamed, I have named it after my friend Lieut.-Col. Bingham, whose book on the Aculeate Hymenoptera of India is so useful to all who have occasion to study foreign Hymenoptera.

10. Megachile rotundipennis, sp.n.

♂ long. corp. 9 mm.; exp. al. 17 mm. ♀ long. corp. 12 mm.; exp. al. 21 mm.

Male.—Head transverse, very finely punctured, fully as wide as thorax; mandibles and lower part of head black; mouth-parts more or less ferruginous in rubbed specimens, but in fresh specimens the face, like the greater part of the head and thorax, is clothed with pale fulvous pubescence. Eyes with their inner orbits obliquely approximating below; abdomen black, the segments banded behind with brighter fulvous pubescence, and the two apical segments densely clothed with the same above. Legs black, clothed with long grey hair, with a slight fulvous shine: front tarsi beneath, and at the tips, ferruginous; middle and hind tarsi thickly clothed with fulvous pubescence beneath, darkest in the latter. Wings hyaline, slightly clouded towards the margins; nervures brown; wings rather broad, and the fore wings obtusely rounded at the tips.

Female similar, with the abraded thorax much more coarsely punctured than the head, and the abdomen clothed with fine golden-grey pubescence; the last segment above clothed with thick fulvous pubescence; the abdomen beneath coarsely punctured, and clothed, especially towards the extremity, with long, recumbent, fulvous hair; the greater part of all the tarsi likewise thickly clothed with bright fulvous hair.

Described from five males and one female, from Flying Fish Cove, August and September, 1897, and West Coast, October, 1897. On the flowers of forest trees (especially *Grewia*); rather scarce.

This species resembles *M. buddæ*, Dalla Torre (*rufipes*, Smith),
more than any other species in the Nat. Hist. Mus. Collection ;
but the latter species is more brightly coloured, and the costal
nervure is fulvous instead of brown.

11. Megachile nivescens, sp n.

♂ long. corp. 10, exp. al. 19 mm.; ♀ long. corp. 14, exp. al.
23 mm.

Much resembles the last species, but the face, except the
ferruginous proboscis, is entirely black, and the head, face, thorax,
and bands on the abdomen above are clothed with dense silvery-
white pubescence. The bands towards the tip of the abdomen are
slightly bordered behind with fulvous in very fresh specimens, and
the terminal segment is clothed above with rich fulvous ; beneath,
the abdomen is banded with silvery white, as above, in the male,
and clothed with long, recumbent, fulvous hair in the female. The
legs are clothed with yellowish-grey hair, the hair on the tarsi
being bright fulvous beneath, and more or less above, at least on
the middle tarsi.

Twelve specimens, mostly worn females, from Flying Fish Cove,
August–October, 1897 ; west coast, October, 1897 ; north part of
island, December, 1897, and January, 1898. Very common on
sea-cliffs, frequenting flowers of *Pemphis* and *Scævola*.

Order 3.—DIPTERA.

[The Diptera unfortunately have not yet been determined. The
specimens collected are roughly as follows:—*Tipulidæ*, 3 or 4 species;
Culicidæ, 2 species ; *Mycetophilidæ*, 1 species ; *Stratiomyidæ*,
2 species; *Asilidæ*, 4 species; *Bombylidæ*, 1 species; *Dolichopodidæ*,
probably 2 species; *Syrpindæ*, 1 species; *Muscidæ*, at least 7 or 8
species; *Micropezidæ*, 1 species; *Ortalidæ*, 1 species; *Ochthiphilidæ*,
1 species; *Hippoboscidæ*, 2 species. There are also several other
specimens, and the collection probably includes between thirty
and forty species in all.—C. W. A.]

Order 4.—COLEOPTERA.

By C. O. WATERHOUSE, F.E.S., C. J. GAHAN, M.A., F.E.S.,
and G. J. ARROW, F.E.S.

(PLATES X AND XI.)

Family CARABIDÆ.

1. Morio orientalis, Dej.

Common in rotten wood.
In the Museum there are specimens from Java, Penang, Andaman
and Nicobar Islands.

2. Harpalus, sp.

Two specimens, which at present are undetermined.

3. Trechus (?).

A small species apparently referable to this genus.

Family STAPHYLINIDÆ.

4. Gyrophæna, sp.

This and the following we are at present unable to determine.

5. Philonthus, sp.

6. Lithocharis, sp.

7. Pæderus listeri, Gahan, sp.n. (Pl. X, Fig. 1.)

Niger, articulis duobus primis et duobus ultimis antennarum
fulvis ; elytris chalybeato - cyaneis, dense fortiterque punctatis,
quam prothorace vix brevioribus ; tarsis fulvo-testaceis, interdum
leviter infuscatis. Long. 8-9 mm.

Head and prothorax black and glossy. Antennæ with the first
two and the last two joints fulvous or testaceous, the intermediate
joints dark brown. Elytra very slightly shorter than the prothorax ; steel blue or sometimes greenish blue in colour ; thickly
and rather strongly punctured. Abdomen pitchy black ; the legs
of the same colour, with the tibiæ less dark towards the extremity,

and the tarsi fulvous or testaceous, sometimes shaded with dark brown.

Phosphate Hill, November, 1897 ; North Coast, December, 1897. This species was obtained also by Mr. Lister in Christmas Island. Dr Sharp informs me that he has in his collection an allied but distinct species from Java.

8. Lispinus castaneus, Fauv.

One example only of this species was obtained by Mr. Andrews. Through Dr. D. Sharp's kindness I have been enabled to compare it with a typical specimen of *L. castan-us*, from New Guinea. It is somewhat smaller in size, and its elytra, instead of being reddish chestnut, are dark brown in colour.

Family HYDROPHILIDÆ.

9. Daotylosternum abdominalis, Fabr.

Flying Fish Cove, in August and October.
Specimens in the Museum are from Brazil, Fernando Neronha, Madeira, Canaries, Cape Verdes, St. Helena, Rodriguez, Mauritius, Sierra Leone, Angola, Natal, Ceylon, Penang, Andamans, Sandwich Islands, etc.

Family HISTERIDÆ.

10. Hololepta malleata, Lewis, sp.n.

Oblongo-ovata, subdepressa, nigra, nitida; fronte plana; thorace impunctato, stria marginali tenui ; elytris striis dorsalibus, 1ª brevi, 2ª brevissima, appendice brevi curvato, subhumerali haud lata utrinque abbreviata ; propygidio lateribus anguste punctato ; pygidio sparse punctato postice lævi; prosterno lato ; mesosterno sinuato utrinque angulariter marginato ; tibiis anticis 4-dentatis.

Long. (absque mandibulis) 8–9 mm.

Oblong oval, rather depressed, black, shining ; the head, surface flat, smooth, and impunctate, mentum in both sexes agrees with that of *H. indica*, Er. ; the thorax is arched at the sides, bisinuous before the scutellum, very feebly angulate behind the middle of the lateral edge, marginal stria fine and ceasing at the anterior angle; the elytra, lateral fossa rather narrow, not very deep, and shortened at both ends ; striæ, first dorsal short and a little oblique, second very short, the apical appendage is short and slightly incurved at the apical tip; the propygidium is smooth except for a few lateral punctures before the middle; the pygidium ♂ is smooth, with a few punctures scattered transversely and irregularly along its base, ♀ punctures similarly placed, but more numerous and less scattered; the prosternum is rather broad and dilated at the base; the mesosternum is sinuous anteriorly and distinctly angulate on either side, and the short marginal striæ follow the course of the angles; the anterior tibiæ are 4-dentate.

The species is in many respects similar to *H. indica*, Er., but in Erichson's species the pygidium is densely punctured and the mesosternum is not so conspicuously angulate laterally.

Hab.—Northern part of the island, January, 1898.

11. Platysoma lignarium, Lewis, sp.n.

Oblongum, subparallelum, parum convexum; fronte concava, labis transversa, stria transversa integra sed tenuiter impressa; pronoto stria laterali haud interrupta, valida: elytria, striis dorsalibus 1–3 integris, 4–5 et suturali apicalibus; propygidio transversim punctato; pygidio parum dense ocellato - punctato, margine postice elevato; prosterno haud striato; mesosterno, sinuato, marginato; tibiis anticis 4-dentalis.

Long. ♂ 4·5–5 mm.

Oblong. somewhat parallel, little convex, black, shining, legs and tarsi reddish brown; the head, forehead concave, labrum transverse, stria complete but fine; the thorax transver-e, rounded off at the anterior angles only, marginal stria very fine and ceasing near the eye, lateral stria strong, with the interstice uniform in width, not narrowing at the base, and distinctly wider than that of *P. birmanum*, Mars.; scutellar puncture linear; the elytra, striæ. inner humeral fine, basal, and oblique, outer humeral wanting. 1–3 dorsal strong, parallel, and complete, 4 apical, and not reaching the middle, 5 shorter, not half the length of the fourth, and with a wider space between it and the apex; sutural commences behind the middle of the dorsum, and reaches only to a point on a line with the anterior part of the fifth; the propygidium has ocellate punctures transversely arranged, which leave a smooth margin along its edges both before and behind; the pygidium is closely punctured, punctures ocellate, hinder margin strongly elevated; the tibiæ, anterior 4-dentate, intermediate 4–5, posterior 3-spinose.

This species belongs to the same group as *Platysoma odiosum*, Mars., and in its oblong, rather parallel form, it resembles *P. suturale*, Lew.

Hab.—Found in rotting wood on the coast and in the central part of the island.

12. Paromalus, sp.

There is a single example in this collection of an apparently undescribed species; it has a large and deep round fovea in the centre of the pygidium, and is therefore probably a male.

Hab.—In rotting wood.

Family NITIDULIDÆ.

13. Prometopia quadrimaculata, Motsch.

This is evidently a widely distributed species, as it was described
by Motschulsky from Ceylon, and there is a specimen in the British
Museum from the Philippine Islands. A long series was collected
by Mr. Andrews, showing that the species varies considerably, and
little importance need therefore be attached to its failure to
correspond in every respect with the description. Motschulsky
mentions an impressed median line on the thorax, of which I can
find no trace; and Reitter, in a table of the Oriental species of
this genus, characterizes *P. quadrimaculata* as having the basal spot
of the elytron "peu developpée transversalement," whereas the
development of this spot differs greatly in different specimens,
sometimes extending transversely to the suture and sometimes
upwards to the base of the elytron.

14. Stelidota orientalis, Arrow, sp.n.

Elongato-ovalis, convexa, fusco-niger; capite prothoraceque
punctato-rugosis, fulvo-setosis, prothoracis lateribus arcuatis, rufo-
flavis, angulis anticis obtusis, posticis acutis, disco prope basin
leviter bifoveolato; elytris costatis, costis setosis, interstitiis grosse
seriato-punctatis, punctis setiferis, marginibus maculisque rufo-flavis.
Long. 3 mm.

The colour is a deep brownish-black, with the margins of thorax
and elytra and markings on the latter reddish yellow. The pattern
on each elytron consists of a spot bordering the scutellum, another
beneath near the suture, a wavy fascia beyond this extending
nearly across the elytron, and another between the first and second
spots reaching the external but not the internal margin. There
are two large but not deep impressions near the base of the
prothorax.

The British Museum collection contains a specimen of this species
from Macassar. Another, from Mr. Andrew Murray's collection,
bears the unpublished name of *Stelidota orientalis*, Motsch.

Family TROGOSITIDÆ.

15. Shoguna polita, Arrow, sp.n.

Cylindrica, nitida, castanea; capite prothoraceque subtiliter parce
punctatis, illo antice ustulato, arcuatim emarginato, oculis promi-
nulis; antennæ clava 3-articulata; prothorace convexo, medio postice

subsulcato, lateribus concavis; elytris indistincte seriato-punctatis, prope suturam linea impressa, apicis subtruncatis.

Long. 5 mm.

This closely resembles the typical species *S. rufotestac·a*, Lewis (Ann. & Mag. Nat. Hist., iv, 1889, p. 274), but is darker in colour, with the emargination of the head arcuate and not angular. The head and thorax are sparsely punctured, and the latter furrowed along its posterior half. The elytra have indistinct rows of punctures and a single pair of striæ bordering the suture. The pygidium is furnished with long, erect fulvous setæ.

A single specimen was obtained on the north coast of the island.

16. Shoguna striata, Arrow, sp.n.

Cylindrica, subdepressa, nitida, rufo-castanea; capite prothoraceque parcissime sat distincte punctatis, capitis fronte arcuatim emarginato, oculis minutis, antennæ clava 2-articulata, articulo nono vix precedentibus majore; prothoracis dorso subplano, medio postice subsulcato, lateribus concavis; elytris fortiter strigatis, utrisque ad apicem rotundatis.

Long. 4 mm.

Rather smaller and more depressed than the preceding species; the head and thorax with large scattered punctures, the latter longitudinally furrowed posteriorly. The eyes are very small, and the ninth joint of the antennæ is hardly larger than those preceding it. The elytra are deeply striated, and the pygidium is fringed with yellow hairs.

Only a single specimen was found.

The previously described species of the genus *Shoguna* inhabit Madagascar, Burma, Japan, and New Britain respectively. Mr. Lewis mentions species from the New World, which he does not think can be generically separated, but an examination of these convinces me that they constitute a closely allied but distinct genus.

ONISCOMORPHA, Arrow, gen. nov.

Caput elongatum, exsertum, emarginatum, oculi integri, ovales remoti, antennæ 11-articulatæ, clava elongata triarticulata; prothorax transversus, antice non capitis ad marginem attingens, angulis anticis valde rotundatis, posticis emarginatis; scutellum transversum; elytra parallela, postice parum attenuata, subacuminata.

Allied to *Narcisa*, and of similar appearance, but the head is not sunk into the prothorax, and the eyes are entire, and situated on the sides of the head, the upper and lower divisions being equal, but without constriction or emargination. The facets are very large. The antennal club is compact, and twice as long as broad, with the last joint sphæroidal. The prothorax is deeply emarginated for the head, but the lateral lobes do not extend beyond the front of the eyes; the hind margin is lobed in the middle, and has a blunt right-angled tooth on each side fitting into a corresponding notch in the elytron. The elytra are parallel - sided, slightly acuminate towards the apex, with the margins entire, and, together with the rest of the upper surface of the body, are clothed with flat oval scales.

17. Oniscomorpha marmorata, Arrow, sp.n. (Pl. X, Fig. 2.)

Oblonga, subdepressa, fusca, squamis albidis supra tecta, ore antennis pedibusque ferrugineis; clypeo late emarginato-truncato; prothorace elytrorum latitudine, lateribus valde rotundatis, crenatis, subtus squamulis albis parce vestito; elytris costatis, lateribus parallelis, integris, costis tuberculiferis, interstitiis albo-squamosis, fusco-marmoratis.
Long. 6 mm.

Family COLYDIIDÆ.

18. Xuthia maura, Pascoe: Journ. Ent., ii (1863), p. 128.

A single example from rotting wood. The specimen is, perhaps, a trifle narrower than the type from Morty, but this is probably a sexual difference.

19. Bothrideres strigatus, Arrow, sp.n. (Pl. X, Fig. 3.)

Angustatus, piceus, subnitidus, capite prothoraceque dense et profunde strigoso-punctatis, hujus medio linea lævi, ante medium impressione haud profunda, post medium spatio impunctato circulari fossa profunda postice incluso, striis duabus ad basin connexa; marginibus leviter sinuatis, postice valde contractis, angulis posticis rectis; elytris disco striatis, partibus exterioribus carinatis, intervallis 1 et 3 paullo punctatis.
Long. 8 mm.
The colour is black, with the antennæ and legs a very dark red. The head and thorax are coarsely punctured, and there are a few scattered punctures on the first and third interstices of each elytron. The third interstice is also angularly elevated, and beyond it the striæ are replaced by three sharp costæ. Near the base of the thorax is a U-shaped impressed line enclosing a smooth area, and in front of this is a shallow depression.
The species is represented only by a single specimen.

Family CUCUJIDÆ.

20. Psammœous concinnula, Walker.

There are two specimens of this species, originally described from Ceylon. Others in the Museum collection are from Java and China, and a single example from Sierra Leone.

Family DERMESTIDÆ.

21. Dermestes felinus, Fabr.

This species, like many others of its genus, occurs in all parts of the world. Several specimens were taken.

D. subcostatus, Murr., the type of which is now in the British Museum, belongs to this species.

Family CRYPTOPHAGIDÆ.

A single example of a minute species, taken on the east coast in September, apparently allied to *Paramecosoma,* and closely resembling *P. serrata* in general form and colour, but with differently formed tarsi.

Family COCCINELLIDÆ.

22. Epilachna indica, Muls.: Spec. Col. Trim., p. 776.

Numerous specimens of this widely distributed Asiatic species were taken, together with their larvæ, near Flying Fish Cove.

23. Epilachna nativitatis, Arrow, sp.n. (Pl. X, Fig. 6.)

Lata, subdepressa, flava, parce pubescens, oculis magnis, prothoraceque angusto, basi fortiter arcuato, immaculato; elytrorum marginibus late explanatis, ad humeros valde rotundatis, deinde fere ad apicem recte angustatis, singulo grosse sex-punctato, punctis tribus prope suturam, uno ad callum humeralem et duobus prope marginem, punctis quatuor basalibus linea recta, quatuor intermediis equidistantibus linea arcuata ordinatis.

Long. 7·5 mm

This species is of a pale tawny colour, and is not very thickly clothed with hair. The prothorax is much narrower than in the preceding species, and is strongly arcuate at the base, so that its length in the middle is almost equal to half its breadth. The elytra are broadly margined, and the size and position of the spots recall the common European *E. chrysomelina* rather than any of the Oriental species. The four basal spots are arranged in a straight line, and the inner spots of the middle row are scarcely farther removed from the suture than those above and below them.

Three specimens were brought by Mr. Andrews from the north coast of the island. This species was also found both by Mr. Lister and the officers of the " Flying Fish."

24. Scymnus, sp.

A single specimen of a small species, probably new.

Family PSEUDOCORYLOPHIDÆ.

25. Aphanocephalus, sp.n.

A single specimen, which it seems inadvisable to describe.

Family EROTYLIDÆ.

26. Euxestus parki, Woll. : Ann. & Mag. Nat. Hist., iii (1858), p. 411.

Of this insect, originally described from Madeira, three examples were found in the north part of the Island in January. It has been recorded from Rodriguez Island and Damma Island.

Family LUCANIDÆ.

27. Paraegus listeri, Gahan : P.Z.S., 1888, p. 539. (Pl. XI, Figs. 1, 2.)

A good series of examples, including both sexes, of this species was obtained by Mr. Andrews. Mr. Lister's collection, on which my previous paper was based, contained only male specimens, though I was able to describe the female from a single specimen of this sex previously obtained by the officers of H.M.S. " Flying Fish."

28. Figulus rossi, Gahan, sp.n.

Niger nitidus; capite supra paullo concavo, sparse minuteque punctato, utrinque prope oculos tuberculato, clypeo inviso, canthis oculorum late rotundatis; mandibulis bidentatis, mento sat profunde concavo, valde punctato; pronoto antice in medio leviter tuberculato, disco fovea media punctis 15 ad 20 impressa, versus latera subtilissime vel haud punctato; elytris regulariter punctato-striatis,

punctis magnis rotundatis in latitudine interstitiis lævibus costatis
fere æqualibus, utroque elytro prope angulum apicalem reticulato-
punctato ; lateribus prosterni, metasternique, et abdominis processu
intercoxale fortiter punctatis, ceteris abdominis fere impunctatis.
Long. (mandib. exclusis) 9–11·5 ; lat. 3–4 mm.

Head sparsely and very feebly punctured, slightly concave in the
the middle above, and having on each side an obtuse tubercle,
which is separated from the eye by a short longitudinal ridge;
anterior margin straight in the middle, and very slightly projecting
forwards in a short obtusely rounded process at each side ; ocular
canthi regularly rounded both in front and at the sides, slightly
oblique behind ; mandibles each with two teeth on the inner side,
those of the right mandible being placed, one just in front of the
middle, the other near the base, those of the left, which are shorter,
between the middle and the apex. Prothorax very minutely or
not at all punctured above, except in the median fovea (which is
impressed with from about 15 to 20 strong punctures) and also at
the anterior margin close to the lateral angles, where there are
a few irregular rows of moderate-sized punctures. Elytra strongly
punctate-striate, the punctures being large, broadly elliptical, or
nearly circular in outline, and almost equal in width to the smooth
subcostate intervals between the rows ; near the apical angle each
elytron is somewhat reticulately punctured. Sides of the prosternum and metasternum, and the intercoxal process of the
abdomen strongly punctured ; sides of the first segment with a few
large punctures, and the rest of the abdomen with some minute
sparsely scattered punctures. Anterior tibiæ with four or five, the
middle and hind tibiæ with two or three teeth on the outer border.

Five specimens collected in the north part of the island.

In general form and structure this species approaches *F. sulcicollis*,
Hope, from which it is chiefly to be distinguished by its smaller
size, less punctured prothorax, and the relatively much larger size
of the punctures of the elytra.

Family PASSALIDÆ.

29. Leptaulax, sp.

Mr. Andrews obtained a number of specimens of this genus at
Flying Fish Cove in October. They closely resemble *L. timoriensis*,
but will probably prove to be one of the many allied species recently
described by Herr Kuwert.

Family APHODIIDÆ.

30. Rhyssemus inscitus, Wlk.

One example, taken in the north part of the island, which does
not seem to be specifically distinct from Walker's type from Ceylon.

31. Trichyerhyssemus (gen. nov.) **hirsutus**, C. de P., sp.n.

A specimen sent to M. L. Clouët des Pesruches was kindly examined by him and returned with this name, which will be published in his forthcoming monograph.

CETONIIDÆ.

32. Protætia andrewsi, Gahan, sp.n. (Pl. X, Fig. 5.)

Nigra, nitida, interdum viride vel purpureo tincta, supra sparse setosa, thorace subtus pedibusque sparse sat longeque villosis; clypeo transverso, margine antico late rotundato (fere truncato) et fortiter elevato: capite pronotoque sat dense fortiterque punctatis, longitudinaliter in medio obtuse leviterque carinatis; elytris dense punctatis, squamis luteis sparse guttatis, depressionibus posticis haud vel obsolete striatis, marginibus suturalibus postice elevatis et ad angulos apicales paullo productis.

Long. 12–15, lat. 6·5–8·5 mm.

Colour black, but in some specimens tinged with metallic green or purple. Head strongly and rather thickly punctured, clypeus transverse, broadly rounded or almost truncate in front, with the margin strongly raised. Pronotum with an obtuse and very feebly raised carina along the middle; this carina, a median space at the base in front of the scutellum, and one or two smaller areas towards the sides, smooth, the rest of the surface strongly and rather thickly punctured. Elytra somewhat strongly punctured, the punctures being less thickly placed in the neighbourhood of the scutellum than over the rest of the surface; the broad depression on each side of the sutural carina on the posterior half of the elytra is rather thickly punctured and usually destitute of striæ (in one or two specimens among those examined traces of striæ in the form of one or two broken lines are to be seen). Antennæ varying in colour from light mahogany-brown to dark chestnut-brown; the inner lamella of club almost as long as the whole of the proximal part of the antenna. Legs and under-side of the body with a long sparse pubescence; metasternum with an impressed line along the middle.

This species seems to come nearest to *P. acuminata*, Fab., from which, however, it is very distinct. It differs not only in colour and sculpture, but in being more pubescent above and below and in having the anterior margin of the clypeus more strongly raised, the apices of the elytra less produced at the sutural angles, the metasternum impressed with a median line, and the hair-fringe of the intermediate and hind tibiæ much longer and more sparse.

Family BUPRESTIDÆ.

33. Chrysodema simplex, Waterh. : P.Z.S., 1881, p. 520.

Mr. Andrews met with this species in abundance at Flying Fish Cove in October.

34. Chrysobothris andrewsi, Waterh., sp.n. (Pl. X, Fig. 8.)

Obscure brunneo-cuprea, parum nitida, creberrime sat fortiter punctata; elytris maculis sex marginibusque aureo-viridibus.
Long. 10 mm.

Head in front green, circularly impressed, closely and rather coarsely punctured; the forehead more finely and very closely punctured. Thorax transverse, rather strongly punctured, the punctures on the disk widely separated from each other, becoming gradually closer together, till they are crowded at the sides, the intervals on each side of the disk forming transverse shining rugæ. The sides are nearly parallel posteriorly, strongly sinuate in front of the middle, so that there is a well-marked rectangular projection before the anterior angle. Elytra gently convex, without costæ, brownish coppery, with a slight purple tint in some lights, rather strongly, evenly, and very thickly punctured, the punctures green. The base and margins are tinted with golden green; and each elytron has a transverse, oval, golden-green impression on the disk, before the middle, and two contiguous impressions behind the middle, the inner one oblique. The margins are denticulate from behind the middle. The anterior femora are much thickened in the middle, and furnished with a rather small acute tooth. The under-side of the body is green, tinted with coppery, especially on the abdomen, the terminal segment of which has a well-marked median carina, and is deeply emarginate at the apex.

This species is quite isolated. I know of no species at all resembling it either in colour or markings. The thorax has not the posterior angles turned in, as is generally the case, and the angular projection at the sides is very marked.

Family EUCNEMIDÆ.

35. Fornax, sp. (?).

A single example, apparently referable to this genus, taken at Flying Fish Cove in October.

Family ELATERIDÆ.

36. Tetrigus murrayi, Waterh., sp.n.

Elongatus, parallelus, brunneus, fulvo - pubescens. Thorace creberrime punctato; elytris striatis, striis sat fortiter punctatis, interstitiis crebre punctatis.

Long. 22 mm. ♂.

The thorax has the punctuation very close, and considerably stronger than in *T. parryi* or *flabellatus*, and the pubescence is rather coarser. The elytra are striated, the punctures in the striæ are much stronger than in *T. flabellatus* about the same as in *T. lewisi*, but closer together; the dorsal striæ are nearly as strongly marked as the lateral ones. The interstices are closely and more strongly punctured than in *T. flabellatus*, and there is a slight tendency of the punctures to be asperate. The apex of each elytron is angular, the angle nearly a right angle, not at the suture (as in *T. parryi*) but between the second and third striæ. The prosternum is rather closely and very strongly punctured, but there is a smooth median line posteriorly. The apex of the abdomen is arcuately rounded, not emarginate.

37. Anchastus discoidalis, Waterh., sp.n.

Sordide testaceus; capitis vertice, thoracis disco, elytrisque (basi excepto) fuscis.

Long. 6–6·5 mm.

This insect has much the appearance of *Dolopius marginatus*, but it is rather more elongate, the thorax is rather longer and more narrowed in front, and the elytra are a little narrower and more acuminate. The clypeal carina is very sharp and prominent. The antennæ have the third joint distinctly longer than the second, a little shorter that the fourth. The thorax is shining, moderately strongly punctured, the punctures distinctly separated on the disk, close together at the sides; the posterior angles are prolonged and very acute, the inner carina is fine, and not very sharply defined, so that it is only visible in certain positions. The base is testaceous, the sides and anterior angles light brownish-testaceous, the disk dark brown, with a trace of a lighter median line. The elytra are strongly striated, the striæ closely and strongly punctured, the interstices slightly convex, rather closely, finely, but distinctly asperate-punctate; the dorsal surface is dark brown, the extreme base testaceous, the sides light brown, the prosternum is very dark brown, shining; the under flanks of the pronotum testaceous, with a broad dark-brown stripe. The rest of the underside is rather dark, the segments bordered with lighter colour.

Two examples in rotting wood. A single specimen was also taken by Mr. J. J. Lister.

This species is very like *A. infumatus*, Cdz., from Ceylon, but is larger, the thorax is much less closely and more strongly punctured, and the brown on the elytra is much more extended.

38. Megapenthes andrewsi, Waterh., sp.n. (Pl. X, Fig. 7.)

Piceo-flavus, parum nitidus; capitis vertice thoraceque infuscatis, elytris fortiter striatis, fusco variegatis, striis confertim sat fortiter punctatis, interstitiis parum convexis, crebre asperato-punctatis. Long. 14–17 mm.

This species is one of those that resemble *Agrotis* in general form, and must be placed near *M. agrotus*, Cdz.

Head convex, very closely and rather coarsely punctured; dark fuscous, the anterior margin obscure yellow, this colour ascending a little on each side. Thorax a little longer than broad, convex, rather straight at the sides, very slightly narrowed before the posterior angles, which are very slightly diverging, acute, with the inner carina so near to the outer one that it is scarcely distinguishable viewed from above. The punctuation is densely and moderately fine. There is an impressed line at the posterior part of the disk. The fully-coloured specimen has the thorax entirely dark fuscous, except the posterior angles. Scutellum fuscous. Elytra deeply striated, the striæ strongly and very closely punctured; the interstices moderately closely and rather strongly asperate-punctate, giving the surface an uneven appearance. The colour is sordid yellow, with a spot on the shoulder, and the suture fuscous, the fuscous colour dilating behind the middle. The under-side fuscous, except the margins of the segments and the prosternum.

Varieties.—(1) Elytra with the dark colour extended at the base, and the dilated portion behind the middle joined to the humeral spot on the seventh interstice. (2) Thorax with the margins and a median line light brown. (3) Almost entirely pitchy yellow, with a spot on the forehead, two discoidal spots on the thorax, the shoulders and suture of the elytra rather darker.

Taken in September and October, December and January, at Flying Fish Cove.

39. Melanoxanthus dolosus, Cdz.

Candèze, Elatérides Nouv.: Mém. Ac. Sci. Bruxelles, xvii, 1865. Two specimens which seem to be referable to the species from Ceylon, found on the north coast in December, 1897, and March, 1898.

40. Melanoxanthus litura, Cdz. (?).

Candèze, Elat. Nouv.: Mém. Ac. Sci. Bruxelles, xvii (1865), p. 34.

Three examples. One taken by Mr. Lister. Two by Mr. Andrews in the central part of the island in February, and near Flying Fish Cove.

The specimens vary in colour, two having the thorax black, with the hind angles only yellow; the third has the whole of the sides .yellow. The extent of the yellow markings on the elytra also varies considerably. Of the numerous allied described species, this seems to be nearest to *M. litura*, Cdz., from Ceylon, but it may be distinct. The material at disposal is not sufficient to determine the question.

Family MELYRIDÆ.

41. Laius tibialis, Gahan, sp.n. (Pl. X, Fig. 4.)

Cyaneus aut viridi-cyaneus, ore et antennarum articulis duobus primis flavo-testaceis.

♂. Articulo 1° antennarum curvato et compresso, secundo crasso parum oblongo, haud excavato; tibiis anticis intus ad basim rufo-callosis.

Long. 5, lat. 2 mm.

Dark blue or greenish blue, with the first two joints of the antennæ, the epistome, labium, and maxillæ (last joints of palpi excepted) yellowish testaceous. In the male the first two joints of the antennæ are enlarged; the first joint is curved, and is compressed from side to side, so that it appears narrow looked at from above, but is as broad as the second when seen from the front; the second joint is thick, somewhat oblong in form, and is not compressed nor excavated. Each of the anterior tibiæ of the male has a small reddish callosity close to the base on the anterior (inner) side, with a small pit placed just below the callosity. In some of the allied species there is a deep oblique groove occupying the same position.

Family PTINIDÆ.

42. Lasioderma testacea, Duft.

A single example of this species, which is found almost everywhere.

NEOPTINUS, Gahan, gen. nov.

(♀?) Antennæ inserted on the front, nine-jointed, with the ninth joint as long as the two preceding joints taken together. Prothorax with distinct lateral margins. Middle coxæ moderately distant from one another; hind coxæ widely separated, the intercoxal process of the abdomen being broad, and obtusely rounded in front. First three abdominal sternites more or less fused together, the sutures between them being apparent only towards the sides ; fourth sternite very narrow, with its hind margin, like that of the third, arcuate behind. Tarsi five-jointed, of equal width throughout their whole length, ciliated on each side below, even on the claw-joint.

This genus seems best placed in the group *Ptinidæ* of the family Ptinidæ, although it does not agree in some important particulars with Lacordaire's definition of that group.

43. Neoptinus parvus, Gahan, sp.n. (Pl. X, Fig. 10.)

Nigro-piceus, supra sub-erecte setosis, pedibus et antennarum apice testaceis ; antennis basin prothoracis paullo superantibus, articulis 2° ad 8ᵘᵐ inter se subæqualibus, articulo 9° duobus precedentibus unitis æquilongo, paullo crassiore ; prothorace trans-verso, lateribus marginatis, postice cum basi rotundatis ; elytris late ovatis, humeris nullis ; striato-punctatis, breviter sub-erecte setosis.

Long. 1·5, lat. 1 mm.

Pitchy black, with the legs and the last joint of the antennæ testaceous. Eyes small ; antennæ inserted upon the front at a short distance in advance of the eyes, nine-jointed, with the first joint thick, and nearly twice as long as the second, joints second to eighth sub-equal in length, the ninth thicker than the seventh or eighth and a little longer than these two united. Pronotum trans-verse, convex above, deflexed towards the sides, basal margin rounded, and forming with the lateral margins a continuous curve ; so that, looked at from above, the pronotum has somewhat the form of a segment of a circle, the anterior margin being, however, not straight, but slightly bowed forwards in the middle ; the surface sparsely setose. Elytra broadly oval, without shoulders, convex above, and the surface of each marked with eight rows of rather large and closely approximated punctures, each of which is slightly transverse in direction, and carries a greyish-white seta springing from its anterior margin ; on the deflexed (and slightly inflexed) side of each elytron there are two or three less regular rows of punctures. Prosternum much shorter than the pronotum ; narrow in the middle, and scarcely separating the anterior coxæ from one another ; metasternum short, its sides, as well as the sides of the abdomen, thickly impressed with large shallow punctures ; these punctures extend also on to the middle of the intermediate sternites, but are absent from the intercoxal process and from the fifth sternite ; the latter is narrow, and is rounded at the apex.

Taken on the east coast of the island, September, 1897.

44. Paranobium posticum, Gahan, gen. et sp. n.
(Pl. X, Fig. 9.)

(♀) Fuscum, pube fulvo-grisea sat dense vestitum; antennis
11-articulatis, fortiter serratis, articulis 4° ad 10um inter se subæqualibus, 11° quam 10° paullo longiore; prothorace dense
punctulato, ad latera sub-obliquiter gibboso sed non marginato,
disco postice valde gibboso, fere in cristam elevato; elytris dense
sat fortiterque punctatis, fusco - brunneis, utroque elytro lineis
quatuor pallidioribus, paullo elevatis, instructo.

Long. 7·5, lat. 3 mm.

Head and prothorax dark brown, with a rather dense tawny-grey
pubescence. Antennæ reddish brown, about half as long again as
the head and prothorax together, 11-jointed, with the joints from
the third to the tenth sub-equal in length, the third feebly angular
a little before its apex, the fourth to tenth each produced antero-
distally into a sharply angular process, eleventh a little longer than
the tenth. Prothorax with an oblique projection, passing forwards
from the basal margin, on each side; the disk raised in the middle,
so as to form a blunt crest or tubercle behind; surface closely
punctulate, but with the punctures more or less concealed by the
pubescence. Elytra nearly half as broad again as the prothorax,
closely and somewhat strongly punctured, reddish brown in colour,
and clothed with a fulvous - grey pubescence, which is somewhat
paler along four slightly raised lines running from the base to the
posterior declivous part of each elytron, these lines being connected
together behind by means of one or two oblique branches. First
joint of each of the tarsi as long as the three succeeding joints
taken together, slightly narrowed towards the base; the second
joint a little longer than either the third or fourth.

One example, taken near Flying Fish Cove, December, 1897.

As this species does not fit well into any of the described genera
of Anobiides, I have given to it the generic name of *Paranobium.*
Two very closely allied species are represented in the British
Museum collection, one by a single unnamed specimen from Natal,
the other by a specimen from Siam. In the Natal specimen, which
probably is a male, the antennæ are longer than in the specimen
described above, and the joints from the fourth to the tenth are
furnished with longer processes.

45. Aspidiphorus orbiculatus, Gyll.

Examples of this species have been obtained with a fungus—
Stemonitis splendens, Rost., collected by Mr. Andrews in Christmas
Island. This species is found in England, though rarely, and also
on the Continent. An example from Java in the British Museum
collection, in which the prothorax and elytra are of a reddish-brown

colour, appears to be an immature specimen of the same species, which hitherto has not been recorded from any locality outside of Europe.

Family BOSTRICHIDÆ.

46. Dinoderus minutus, Fabr.

Of this species, which occurs throughout the Malay Archipelago and in many other parts of the world, three specimens were found.

Family CIOIDÆ.

47. Minthea rugicollis, Walker.

Ditoma rugicollis, Walker: Ann. & Mag. Nat. Hist., ii (1858), p. 206 (Ceylon).
Minthea simidata, Pascoe: Journ. Ent., ii (1863), p. 141 (Saylee).

A single example of this species, taken on the north coast in October.

Family TENEBRIONIDÆ.

48. Opatrum dubium, Arrow, sp.n.

Breve, latum, rufo-fuscum, undique breviter erecte setosum; capite granulato-punctato, clypeo triangulariter emarginato, a fronte sulca obsoleta separato; prothorace elytrorum latitudinis, lateribus regulariter arcuatis, minutissime ciliatis, antice paullo contracto, disco utrinque oblique sulcato; elytris brevibus, convexis, punctato-striatis, interstitiis convexis, granulatis; antennis brevibus, articulis 9° et 10° transversis, 8° et 11° globosis; tarsis rufo-piceis.
Long. 9–11 mm.

This species, which was found in considerable numbers, exhibits a wide range of variation. Small specimens are narrow, with the thorax hardly margined, and the foveæ on each side of its disk obsolete. The colour varies from a deep reddish-chocolate in fresh specimens to a dull black, the whole upper surface, with the legs, being clothed with short, nearly erect bristles. The clypeus is very deeply emarginate, and meets the anteocular lobes in a deep notch on the sides of the head. The prothorax is strongly curved, and more or less flattened at the lateral margins, and has a slightly oblique longitudinal groove on each side of the middle. There are eight striæ on each elytron, and the interstices are studded with somewhat regularly arranged tubercles, each of which gives rise to a stout hair.

49. Bradymerus seminitidus, Arrow, sp.n.

Elongatus, fuscus, opacus, palpis, antennis basi tarsisque rufis; capite, cum prothorace punctato rugoso, clypeo crebrius punctato, truncato, antennis clava nigra 6-articulata ; prothoracis medio fortiter sulcato, lateribus integris leviter arcuatis, basi quam humeros minus lato, antice vix contracto, angulis omnibus acutis, elytris pallidioribus, nitidis, punctato-striatis, interstitiis carinatis ; corpore subtus dense punctato.
Long. 7–9 mm.
Allied to *B. clathratus*, Schauf., and *semiasperatus*, Fairm., but differing from all closely related species by the almost metallic gloss of the elytra.
This species was found in large numbers all over the island, although it did not occur in either of the two previous collections.

50. Alphitobius piceus, Oliv.: Ent., iii, No. 58, p. 17.

A single specimen was obtained of this species, which is of world-wide distribution.

51. Palorus depressus, Fab.: Ent. Syst., i, 2, p. 501.

This insect is also very generally distributed. Two specimens were found.

52. Toxicum antilope, Arrow, sp.n.

Parvum, angustum, ♂ capite cornubus 4 retro-curvatis armato, posterioribus fere parallelis sed paullo bisinuatis apice divergentibus antice crinitis, antennæ clava 4-articulata, articulis vix transversis ; prothorace subtiliter punctato, ♂ valde transverso, ♀ subquadrato ; elytris striato-punctatis ; pedibus fuscis.
Long. 12 mm.
Allied to *T. quadricorne*, Fab., but rather smaller, and readily distinguishable from this and all other species hitherto described by the curvature of the posterior horns, which converge from the base, and slightly diverge towards the tip.
Several specimens of both sexes were collected.

53. Nyctobates carbonaria, Arrow, sp.n.

Parva, nigra, nitida ; capite subtiliter inter oculos minus dense punctato, sutura clypeali distincta, semicirculari ; prothorace parvo transverso, crebre punctato, margine anteriore quam posteriorem angustiore, angulis anticis valde rotundatis, posticis acutis, disco

leviter sulcato ; elytris sulcatis, sulcis grosse interstitiis subtilissime
punctatis; pedibus sat brevibus, ♀ tibiis anterioribus quam inter-
medias non longioribus.
Long. 18 mm.

The thorax is small, with the median groove lightly impressed,
and the anterior angles rounded. The anterior tibiæ show no trace
of the usual elongation.

A single female specimen was brought by Mr. Andrews. The
British Museum contains a second specimen, also a female, captured
by Mr. Lister in 1888.

54. Amarygmus funebris, Arrow, sp.n.

Elongato-ovalis, indigaceo-niger, antennis tarsisque ferrugineis;
capite prothoraceque obscure purpureo vel viridi, clypeo crebre
punctato, sutura clypeali distincta, anguste ab oculis separata,
antennis brevibus paullo ultra humeros attingentibus; prothorace
brevi, subtiliter punctato ; elytris striatis, striis minutissime
punctatis.
Long. 9 mm.

This species apparently resembles *A. inornatus*, Macl. The colour
is black, tinged with a deep purplish or greenish hue, especially
upon the head, thorax, and anterior part of the elytra. Some
specimens present a slightly sericeous bloom upon the upper
surface. Underneath it is a shining black, with the abdominal
segments striated longitudinally.

Nine specimens from various parts of the island.

Family ŒDEMERIDÆ.

55. Sessinia andrewsi, Arrow, sp.n.

Flavo-testacea vel fusco-testacea, sericea, immaculata, distincte
punctata; prothorace elongato flavo, margine basali vix reflexo;
elytris flavis vel fusco-testaceis, margine laterali pallidiore, margine
suturali elevato et costis duabus disco tertiaque ab callo humerali
incipiente prope marginem lateralem.
Long. 8–12 mm.

The colour of the elytra and under-side varies from a pale
testaceous to a smoky brown, that of the prothorax being fairly
constant. The average size of the males is larger than that of the
females, and the antennæ are shorter, with the rudimentary 12th
joint very apparent.

This species was also obtained by Mr. Lister. It is stated by
Mr. Andrews, who found it exceedingly abundant, to exude an
oily liquid, which is considered by residents to have most injurious
properties, and which no doubt serves as a protection from insectivorous animals.

The following species was obtained by Mr. Lister, and is represented only by a single female :—

58. Sessinia listeri, Arrow, sp.n.

Flavo-testacea, nitida, sericea, sat grosse punctata; palpis maxillaribus gracilibus latere apicali articuli ultimi latere interiori subequali, ut lato quam longi, parum dense punctato, margine basali valde reflexo; elytris nitidis, distincte punctatis, ecostatis, parce sericeis.

Long. 13 mm.

This species closely resembles the typical species *S. livida*, Fab., but the silky covering is less fine and dense, and the punctuation coarser. The prothorax is shorter, and the terminal joint of the maxillary palpus, which in *S. livida* is almost cylindrical, is distinctly triangular.

Family CURCULIONIDÆ.

Sub-Family OTIORRHYNCHINÆ.

RHYNCHOLOBUS, Gahan, gen. nov.

Apterous; corbels of posterior tibiæ open; claws of tarsi connate at the base. Rostrum rather broad, strongly dilated at the apex in the male, so as to have a very distinct lateral process on each side just below, and in front of, the insertion of the antennæ; gradually and slightly dilated towards the apex in the female, and without distinct lateral processes; marked off from the head by a slight transverse impression; scrobes deep, extending to the eyes and almost as wide as them behind, narrowed in front. Scape of the antennæ reaching to, or a little beyond, the anterior margin of the prothorax; funiculus of seven joints, the second joint longer than the first and almost or quite equal to the third and fourth united; club short, ovate, three-jointed. Prothorax broadest in front of the middle, slightly narrowed towards the base, more strongly towards the apex. Elytra somewhat oval in shape; broader and less convex above in the male; very little or not at all broader than the prothorax at the base. Second sternite of the abdomen almost as long as the post-coxal part of the first, and marked off from it by a straight suture; much longer than the third sternite, but not quite equal to the third and fourth taken together. Femora stout, thick in the middle; the hinder pair flattened, or sometimes even slightly concave, on the posterior (or inner) face; hind tibiæ obliquely truncate at the extremity.

57. Rhyncholobus rossi, Gahan, sp.n.   (Pl. XI, Figs. 7, 8.)

Niger, squamis viridibus (interdum cœrulescentibus) dense vestitus; prothorace supra granulis, nigris, nitidis, setigeris instructo; elytris punctato-striatis, interstitiis nigro-granulatis, granulis setigeris; sutura interdum fere omnino nigra; articulo 3° funiculi quam 4° vix longiore; tibiis posticis ad apicem sat late truncatis.

♂. Rostro ad apicem late sat abrupteque dilatato (vel lobato); elytris supra minus convexis; inter discum lateraque anguste convexis; femoribus crassioribus, tibiis intus denticulatis.

♀. Rostro versus apicem gradatim leviterque dilatato; elytris supra valde convexis.

Long. 7–12, lat. 3–6 mm.

Black; closely covered with scales, which are mostly of a bright green colour (sometimes bluish) mixed with a few of a golden or coppery tint. On the sides of the thorax and elytra, as well as on the legs and under-side of the body, the scales are often of a paler and more silvery colour. The setæ or hairs, which are present on nearly all parts of the body, are somewhat longer and denser on the legs and the posterior part of the elytra; those on the prothorax and elytra mostly arise from punctures situated each at the summit or on the hinder face of a little black granule. Head and rostrum together about equal in length to the pronotum. Rostrum flattened above, with a feeble carina along the middle, ending in front at the apex of a triangular space, of which the base, forming part of the anterior margin of the rostrum, has a small angular notch in the middle. Prothorax almost equal in length to its greatest width, which lies a little in front of the middle; distinctly narrower at the apex than at the base; disk with scattered and very slightly raised, shining - black setigerous granules. Exposed part of the scutellum triangular and very small. Elytra punctate-striate; the interstices in no wise costiform, furnished with feebly raised, shining-black setigerous granules; the punctures along the striæ rather deep and oblong, but those at the sides much smaller and less conspicuous. (In a few examples, not otherwise distinct, the punctures on the disk are narrower and less conspicuous, and the setigerous granules a little more raised.)

Scape of the antennæ only just reaching to the anterior margin of the prothorax; second joint of the funiculus equal in length to the third and fourth united, the third joint very little longer than broad, and scarcely longer than the fourth joint. Posterior (or inner) face of hind femora flat and smooth; hind tibiæ rather broadly truncated at the end. In the male there is a row of small teeth along the lower margin of all the tibiæ; in the female these teeth are obsolete or wanting.

58. Rhyncholobus discoidalis, Waterh.

Pissonotus discoidalis, Waterh. : P.Z.S., 1887, p. 521, fig. 3.

This species, to which a female example obtained by Mr. Andrews may possibly belong, was described from a single male specimen from Christmas Island. It differs from the preceding species in having a somewhat broader prothorax, which is more densely and sharply granulate above, and marked with a broad black band along the middle; the elytra also are somewhat more granulate, and the punctures along the striæ less distinct; the third joint of the funiculus is distinctly longer than the fourth. The female specimen referred to differs from the male type in having a line of green scales along the middle of the pronotum, dividing the longitudinal black band into two; as well as by those characters which, in the generic description, I have indicated as being sexual.

59. Rhyncholobus vittatus, Gahan, sp.n.   (Pl. XI, Fig. 6.)

♂. Viridi-squamosus ; vitta lata longitudinali prothoracis, vitta suturali et vitta utrinque medio disco elytrorum, nigris; prothorace quam longiore sat distincte latiore ; antice posticeque sat fortiter angustato, basi quam apice paullo latiore ; elytris punctato-striatis, interstitiis disco elevatis, seriatim regulariterque granulatis ; scapo antennarum apicem prothoracis paullo superante, articulis 3° 4° que funiculi unitis quam articulo 2° distincte longioribus ; rostro ad apicem lobato.

Long. 9, lat. 4 mm.

With a broad black band along the middle of the pronotum ; with a sutural vitta and a broad band along the middle of each elytron, also black; the rest of the upper surface covered with green scales. Antennæ a little longer and more slender than in the other species of the genus ; third and fourth joints of the funiculus each much longer than broad, and taken together distinctly longer than the second joint. Prothorax somewhat hexagonal in form, being obtusely angular on each side just in front of the middle, with the sides converging strongly both before and behind; a little broader across the base than at the apex; upper side distinctly and rather densely granulate, especially along the black band. Elytra slightly convex above; punctate-striate, with the interstices between the striæ on the disk sub-costate and carrying each a single row of granules; those between the striæ on the sides being flattened, and less strongly and less regularly granulate. Inner margins of the tibiæ obsoletely denticulate. Posterior (or inside) face of the hind femora flat and smooth, shining black. Truncated end of hind tibiæ moderately broad.

One male example of this very distinct species was taken near Flying Fish Cove. The female sex is still unknown.

60. Rhyncholobus andrewsi, Gahan, sp.n.

♂. Piceus, viridi - squamosus (interdum coeruleo - squamosus); prothorace quam longiore evidenter latiore, sat dense nigro-granulato ; supra in medio minus dense squamoso ; elytris punctato-striatis, interstitiis convexis, sat dense irregulariterque granulatis; disco paullo convexo, lateribus abrupte deflexis; facie postica femorum posticorum planata vel leviter concava, sat fortiter transversim rugosa; tibiis omnibus subtus denticulatis.

Long. 9–11, lat. 4–5 mm.

♀. Piceo-fuscus (interdum brunneus); prothorace supra versus latera luteo-viridi-squamoso; elytris punctato-sulcatis, interstitiis subcostiformibus, disco sat fortiter convexo, versus latera et apicem luteo-viridi-squamoso.

Long. 8–10, lat. 4–5 mm.

Male.—Pitchy-black, covered with bright green or with bluish scales, which are more thinly placed or entirely wanting along the middle of the pronotum. Prothorax distinctly broader than long, its greatest width being in front of the middle, where the sides also are most rounded. Disk of the elytra only slightly convex, and the sides abruptly deflexed, so as to form with the disk a rather acute angle ; the interstices between the punctured striæ are slightly convex, and rather thickly and irregularly granulate. Posterior (or inner) face of the hind tibiæ flattened, or perhaps slightly concave, and distinctly wrinkled in a transverse direction. Lower margin of all the tibiæ denticulate.

Female.—Dark brown, varying to reddish brown, in colour. The scales are almost entirely confined to the sides of the pronotum and to the lateral and apical parts of the disk of the elytra, and are, moreover, of a yellowish- or greenish - grey colour. Pronotum relatively shorter than in the male. Elytra strongly enough convex above, punctate-striate, with the interstices raised, convex, and somewhat costiform. Posterior flattened face of hind femora feebly wrinkled towards the margins, but not in the middle. Tibiæ very faintly denticulate along the lower margin.

Although the sexes here described are so remarkably different in many characters, there can be little or no doubt that they belong to the same species. Mr. Andrews collected a fair series of each sex on the same day and at the same place on the island—viz., North-East Point, December 23, 1897.

Mr. J. Faust, who has kindly examined some specimens sent to him, points out that while this new genus has a general resemblance to *Elytrogonus*, Guér., it agrees in the connate claws of the tarsi with Lacordaire's group *Oosomides*, and might be placed near *Embrithes*, Sch., and *Dicastious*, Pasc.

61. Acionemis andrewsi, Gahan, sp.n.

Minor, angustior, nigro - picea, ochraceo - brunneo - squamosa et
sparse albo-setosa, supra albido fuscoque variegata; rostro arcuato,
piceo, quam femoribus anticis vix longiore, basi confertim punctato;
antennis ferrugineis, ad medium rostri insertis, articulo 2° quam 1°
sesqui-longiore, clava fusiforme, sub-solida; prothorace confertim
punctato, antice constricto, supra sparse irregulariterque nigro-
granulato, disco medio squamis brunnascentibus, lateribus squamis
albidis vestito; elytris quam prothorace latioribus, punctato-striatis,
interstitiis antice remote nigro - granulatis, ochraceo - brunneo -
squamosis, fascia parva transversa ad medium albida, fasciis duabus
obliquis nigris literam V formantibus paullo pone hanc fasciam;
maculis parvis nigris et albidis inter hanc fasciam et basin, dispersis;
tibiis omnibus annulo lato fusco supra medium notatis.

Long. 3·5–5·5, lat. 1·5–2 mm.

Densely covered with scales, which are mostly of an ochreous-
brown colour, but mixed with others forming small bands and
spots of a whitish and dark-brown colour; the most distinct of
these being a short sinuately transverse white band at the middle
of the elytra, and a V-shaped fuscous band placed a little posterior
to it. Rostrum scarcely longer than the anterior femora, dark
brown, closely punctured, and more or less squamous at the base.
Antennæ inserted at the middle of the rostrum, reddish brown,
second joint of the funiculus very little more than half the length
of the third, club fusiform, with two articular sutures faintly
visible; prothorax constricted at the apex, very closely punctured
and densely squamose, ochreous-brown on the middle of the disk,
dirty-white, with brownish patches on the sides; with sparsely
scattered black granules on the disk. Elytra punctate-striate,
interstices with rather widely separated black granules. Proximal
half of each tibia almost entirely dark brown in colour, distal half
whitish; femora covered with luteous scales, sparsely mixed with
short flattened white setæ like those present also on the prothorax
and elytra.

62. Camptorhinus crinipes, Gahan, sp.n.

Squamis ochraceo - brunneis et griseis dense vestitus, capite
rostrique basi confertim punctulatis; prothorace confertim sat
fortiterque punctato, antice in medio leviter carinato; dense
squamoso, squamis ad latera et in medio disco (præsertim prope
basin) pallidioribus; elytris seriatim fortiterque punctatis, interstitiis alternis magis elevatis et breviter setosis; pedibus elongatis,
femoribus anticis intermediisque subtus dente parva, femoribus
posticis dente validiore, armatis; tibiis omnibus intus longe
fulvo-pilosis, articulis duobus primis tarsorum quoque pilis fulvis
longis fimbriatis.

Long. 9·5, lat. 2·2 mm.

This species is somewhat stouter than *C. doriæ*, Pasc., to which it has a pretty close resemblance in colour and sculpture. The scales with which it is covered are, however, darker in colour, being mostly of an ochreous-brown tint, with grey patches on the sides of the prothorax, on the middle of the disk close to the base, along the median third of the elytral suture, and behind the middle of each elytron. The species differs further from *C. doriæ* in having longer and straighter posterior tibiæ, the inner face of which is furnished along the distal half with long tawny-brown hairs, similar to but less dense than those which are present also along nearly the whole length of the inner (or lower) face of the anterior and middle tibiæ; the first two joints of the anterior and middle tarsi are thickly, those of the posterior tarsi sparsely, fringed on each side with similar long hairs.

One male example, taken on the north coast; March, 1898.

63. Mecopus bispinosus, Web., var.

This is a variable species, and widely distributed throughout the Eastern Archipelago.

64. Trochorhopalus strangulatus, Gyll.

Sphenophorus strangulatus, Gyll.: in Schoen. Gen. Curculion., iv, p. 963.

The examples from Christmas Island, while agreeing in most respects with others which I have seen, are somewhat narrower in form, and may possibly be distinct. Mr. J. Faust, who has been good enough to examine some specimens I sent to him, considers them to belong to this species, which is a widely distributed one, having been recorded from Siam, Malacca, the Philippines, Java, Borneo, and other islands of the Malay Archipelago as far as New Guinea.

65. Rhabdocnemis fausti, Gahan, sp.n.

R. obscuro (Boisd.) sat similis sed prothorace angustiore, elytris plus oblongis, densius tomentosis et fortius punctatis.

Long. 12–13, lat. 42–45 mm.

Rostrum not very strongly curved, tuberculate underneath in the male, unarmed in the female. Prothorax almost one-half longer than broad, scarcely narrowed towards the base, the sides converging from the middle up to the tubulate apex; disk naked along the middle, but marked with sericeous grey punctures. Elytra covered with a dense silky tomentum; punctate-striate, the punctures being large and distinct, and wider than the striæ along which they are placed.

I

This species has a somewhat close resemblance to *R. obscurus*, Boisd., but is relatively longer and narrower; the elytra are more oblong and more densely tomentose, and the punctures along the striæ are very much larger and more distinct.

Family COSSONIDÆ.

66. Cossonus variipennis, Gahan, sp.n.

Niger, nitidus, elytris medio plus minusve testaceis, lateribus sutura et apice nigris; prothorace antice constricto et transversim sulcato, lateribus punctatis a basi versus apicem curvatim paullo convergentibus, disco lævi, utrinque medio seriebus duobus irregularibus punctorum impresso; elytris punctato-striatis, interstitiis paullo convexis.

Long. 4–4·25, lat. 1–1·25 mm.

Black and glossy, with the elytra testaceous to a greater or less extent along the middle of each, the sides, suture, and apex being black. Head impressed in the middle between the eyes with a small round pit, from which a shallow groove extends forwards along the rostrum as far as to a point in a line with the insertion of the antennæ. Prothorax constricted, and marked with a deep transverse groove a little behind the apex; its sides punctured, and converging slightly from the base up to the anterior constriction; the disk smooth, with two irregular rows of well-marked punctures along each side of the middle from the base to the anterior groove; the space on each side between these rows of punctures and the side of the prothorax is sparsely and very minutely punctate, the narrow space along the middle between the rows of punctures being wholly impunctate. Elytra punctate-striate, five equidistant rows of punctures being visible from above on each elytron, while four closely approximated rows, in addition to a short marginal row along the anterior third, are present on each side; the interspaces between the rows of the punctures on the disk are slightly convex. The colour of the elytra is variable; in some specimens the middle of the disk of each elytron from the base up to the posterior fourth or fifth is testaceous; in others there is but a narrow testaceous strip extending a short distance from the base; while in one example the elytra are wholly black.

This species resembles *C. suturalis*, Boh., but is flatter on the disk of the prothorax and elytra, and much less strongly punctured on the sides of the prothorax and on the middle of the breast and abdomen.

67. Phlœophagosoma dubium, Gahan, sp.n.

Sub-fusiforme, nigro-piceum aut fuscum; rostro longiusculo, sub-parallelo, antice vix latiore, minute punctulato: oculis prominentibus; antennis ante medium rostri insertis; prothorace sub-ovato, quam latitudine maxima (paullo ante basin) vix longiore, prope apicem nec constricto nec sulcato, disco (linea media brevi excepta) dense sat fortiterque punctato; scutello sat conspicuo, sub-semicirculare, nitido; elytris quam pronoto duplo longioribus et paullulo latioribus, fortiter punctato - striatis, interstitiis minutissime uniseriatim punctulatis.

Long. 4, lat. 1·35 mm.

Rostrum and front of head finely punctured; the rostrum longer than the head, slightly curved, with its sides sub-parallel or very slightly and scarcely perceptibly diverging anteriorly; with the antennæ inserted a little in front of the middle of its length. Eyes strongly convex and prominent, but not large. Prothorax scarcely longer than its greatest width, which is about midway between the base and the middle; sides curved, slightly constricted at the base, converging gradually towards the apex, where there is neither a constriction nor transverse groove; disk slightly convex, thickly and rather strongly punctured, except on a short linear space along the middle. Scutellum distinct, smooth and glossy, somewhat semicircular in form. Elytra about twice as long as the pronotum, and a little wider than the latter at its widest part, strongly punctate-striate, with the intervals between the rows slightly convex, and marked each with a single series of rather distant and very minute punctures. Intercoxal part of the prosternum about half as broad as one of the anterior coxæ; that of the mesosternum equal in width to one of the middle coxæ. Third joint of the tarsi broader than the other joints.

In its relatively short form this species resembles the true *Rhyncoli* rather than the species placed by Wollaston in *Phlœophagosoma*; but it differs essentially from the former by its broader sternal processes, its more conspicuous scutellum, and less convex prothorax.

68. Pachyops (?) incertus, Gahan, sp.n.

Angustus, parallelus, convexiusculus, cylindricus, piceo-niger, nitidus; capite rostroque sat dense minute punctulatis, prothorace conico-cylindrico, dense punctulato; elytris sat fortiter punctato-striatis, interstitiis paullulo convexis, uniseriatim minutissime punctulatis; coxis anticis sat late distantibus; scapo clavoque antennarum piceo-rufescentibus, clavo anguste ovato, haud compresso.

Long. 4, lat. 1 mm.

This species resembles *Pachyops cylindricus*, Woll., in general form, but is smaller, and differs in the following points of structure: The space between the anterior coxæ is as wide as one of the coxæ; the club of the antennæ is narrowly ovate, and not compressed; the elytra are less strongly punctured than in *cylindricus*, Woll., and the intervals between the rows of punctures are wider, very slightly convex, and not in the least costiform, with the exception, however, of the interval between the two outermost rows of punctures on the posterior half of the side of each elytron, this interval being narrow and somewhat cariniform; the antennæ are inserted a little behind the middle of rostrum, and nearer to the eyes than in *P. cylindricus.* In *Pachyops cylindricus* the space between the anterior coxæ is scarcely half the width of one of the coxæ; and the club of the antennæ is compressed, and is broadly oval or almost rounded in outline.

The differences between the two species are therefore pretty considerable, and such as might perhaps be regarded as of generic importance. But unless a new genus be formed for its reception, the present species cannot be better placed than in the genus *Pachyops.*

69. Dryophthorus assimilis, Gahan, sp.n.

D. lymexyloni similis sed minor, elytris brevioribus, utrinque ad apicem minus fortiter carinatis.

Long. (rostro excl.) 3, lat. 1 mm.

Resembling the European *D. lymexylon*, Fab., in colour and sculpture, but smaller in size, with the elytra relatively shorter, being rather less than, instead of more than, twice as long as the prothorax, and with the sub-apical carina, which is continuous with the sixth interstice of each elytron, much less prominent.

It also presents a somewhat close resemblance to *D. modestus*, Sharp, a species from the Sandwich Islands, but differs by its proportionately narrower prothorax, and the narrower and more acutely raised intervals between the rows of punctures on the elytra.

Family SCOLYTIDÆ.

70. Platypus solidus, Walk.

Platypus solidus, Walker: Ann. & Mag. Nat. Hist. (3), ii, p. 286 (1858).

Specimens found in "rotting wood." They agree well with the type from Ceylon.

71. Xyleborus perforans, Woll.

Tomicus perforans, Woll.: Cat. Col. Mad., p. 96 (1857).
Bostrichus testaceus, Walker: Ann. & Mag. Nat. Hist. (3), iii, p. 260 (1859).
Xyleborus perforans, Blandf.: Kew Bull., 67, 68, 1892, p. 157; Report on the Destruction of Beer Casks in India by the attacks of a Boring Beetle, 1893.

Found in "rotting wood."

72. Xyleborus parvulus, Eichhoff: Berl. Ent. Zeit., 1868, p. 152; Mém. de la Soc. Roy. de Liége (2), viii, p. 392 (1878).

Found in "rotting wood."
This species was described from specimens from Siam and Ceylon. It probably is widely distributed throughout the Oriental region. There are in the British Museum collection examples from China and New Guinea which agree with those found in Christmas Island.

Family BRENTHIDÆ.

73. Orychodes andrewsi, Gahan, sp.n.

♂. Rostro supra basi sulcato ; capite postice bituberculato, utrinque vix pone oculum dentato, dente sat recte transversa, ultra oculum paullo projiciente ; prothorace rufo-castaneo, polito, quam latitudine maximo fere duplo longiore, apice quam basi latiore, ad basin transversim bisulcato, et ante sulcos linea mediana leviter impresso ; elytris quam pronoto quarta parte longioribus, rufo-brunneis, lineis flavis interruptis, ornatis, longitudinaliter striatis, striis intermediis versus medium plus minusve obsoletis.
♀. Capite breviore, postice haud tuberculato, rostro simplice, nec dentato nec ad apicem dilatato ; prothorace quam latiore dimidio parte longiore.
Long. (rostro incl.) 13–21 mm.
♂. Rostrum grooved above at the base ; anterior part with two rows of teeth ; head with two backwardly projecting and slightly diverging tubercles behind, and at each of the post-ocular angles with a rather sharp tooth which projects outwards to a level with or even a little beyond the outermost portion of the eye. Antennæ, when turned forwards, reaching beyond the apex of the rostrum by less than half their length. When they are pressed close to the rostrum it will be seen that the sixth joint does not extend beyond the apex of the rostrum. Prothorax about three-quarters of the length of the elytra, and nearly twice as long as its own greatest breadth ; it is a little broader across the apex than at the base ; at the base it is constricted and marked with two transverse grooves, from the anterior of which a faintly impressed median line extends as far as the middle. Elytra reddish-brown, marked with interrupted yellow lines, these lines, which do not offer so strong a contrast with the general colour of the elytra as in allied species, being arranged as follows :—One on the second interstice, which is yellow at the base and on the posterior declivity ; one on the third interstice, which is yellow at the base and in front of and behind the middle, as well as on the posterior declivity ; fourth interstice similar to the third, but with the yellow parts shorter and less distinct ; fifth yellow at base, behind the middle, and near the

apex; ninth interstice yellow from the base almost up to the apex; the anterior part of this interstice is common to it with the tenth, and the latter is yellow for a short distance back from the point of junction with the ninth.

♀. Head obsoletely or not at all tuberculate behind; prothorax scarcely longer by one-half than its greatest breadth, and rather less than two-thirds of the length of the elytra. Differs also from the male in the shape of the head, the unarmed anterior tibiæ, etc.

Dr. Angelo Senna, who has a considerable acquaintance with the beetles of this family, has very kindly examined some specimens of this species, and has told me that they are quite new to him, and the species distinct from any other described. I have to thank him also for pointing out some of the most important characters detailed above. The new species must be placed in the group of *O. serrirostris*, Fab.

Family ANTHRIBIDÆ.

74. Xenocerus nativitatis, Gahan, sp.n.

X. flagellato affinis sed differt capite supra inter oculos, pygidio, et utriusque elytri interstitio nono fulvescentibus, elytris magis fortiter punctatis, antennis omnino nigris.

Long. 13, lat. 4 mm.

This species comes nearest to *X. flagellatus*, Fähr., and *X. enganensis*, Jordan, from both of which it differs in having the upper part of the head between the eyes, the pygidium, and the ninth interstice of each elytron of a tawny colour: the two lateral vittæ on the pronotum also have a tendency to be of the same tawny colour; the elytra are a little more strongly punctured, and the white markings somewhat different. The latter consist of (1) a narrow sutural band reaching from the base to the middle, behind which it joins two short diverging bands placed one on each elytron between the suture and the third row of punctures; (2) a basal spot just within the shoulder, and continued behind as a narrow vitta, which runs slightly inwards to end in the fourth interspace a short distance before the middle; (3) a spot on the seventh interspace and a narrow spot on the tenth at about one-third of the length of each elytron from the apex; and (4) a spot close to the apex.

Xenocerus flagellatus, Fähr., to which *X. enganensis*, Jord., is very closely allied, is, according to Dr. Jordan, very widely distributed in the Indo-Australian Archipelago.

75. Litocerus jordani, Gahan, sp.n.

L. plagiato (Jordan) affinis sed differt: prothorace breviore, vitta mediana pronoti in medio angustata, area luteo-ochraceo-tomentosa elytrorum minus extensa, sed striis elytrorum etiam luteis.

Black. Head with a dull ochraceous tomentum, which extends between the eyes on to the vertex as far as in a line with the posterior border of the eyes; behind this, the head is dark brown. Prothorax dark brown, with a broad median vitta, three small spots on each side between this vitta and the lateral margin, and a larger spot on each side just within the lateral margin, luteous, the part of the median vitta which lies between the transverse sulcus and carina is narrower than either the part in front of the groove or the part between the carina and the base. Elytra dark brown, with the striæ and a large common plaga, reaching from the base to a little beyond the middle, luteous; the plaga is broad at the base, constricted as it approaches the middle of the elytra, and again widened out just behind the middle. Under-side and femora with a greyish tomentum; tibiæ and tarsi dark brown, with the base of the first joint, a spot at the base of the second, and the whole of the third joint of each tarsus, as well as a ring above the middle of each tibia, fulvo-testaceous.

One female specimen, taken in April, 1898.

I am indebted to Dr. Jordan for his kindness in pointing out the chief differences between this species and *L. plagiatus,* Jordan, which, among those described, is the species most nearly allied to it. *L. plagiatus* was described from North Luzon, Philippine Islands.

76. Apatenia apioalis, Gahan, sp. n.

♂. Capite fulvo-pubescente, in vertice fusco-plagiato; rostro quam spatio interoculare plus duplo latiore; prothorace supra pube luteo-grisea obtecto, macula ante scutellum fulva, disco medio utrinque leviter tuberculato et antice fusco-notato, angulo inter carinam ante-basalem et carinam lateralem acuto, retrorsum leviter producto; elytris griseo-fumosis, ad apicem fulvo-albido-plagiatis, utroque elytro tuberculis 9 vel 10 instructo; corpore subtus griseo, pedibus testaceis, femoribus tibiisque medio fuscis; segmento primo abdominis tuberculis duobus prope medium instructo.

Long. 8, lat. 3¼ mm.

Head clothed with a somewhat sparse tawny pubescence, which is interrupted on the vertex by two dark-brown plagæ or vittæ; eyes somewhat approximate in front, the space between them being rather less than half the width of the rostrum. Prothorax with a luteous-grey pubescence; with a distinct pale tawny spot in front of the scutellum; the disk with a small, feebly raised tubercle on each side of the middle, and two fuscous spots between the middle and the anterior border; ante-basal carina forming with the lateral carina of each side a rather acute angle, which is slightly produced backwards. Elytra with a dingy grey pubescence, but with a pale fulvous patch on the declivous apical portion, similar in colour to the pygidium; each with about nine or ten unequal-sized tubercles, the three largest of which are placed—

one a little behind the middle of the base, the second behind the middle of the disk, and the third at the beginning of the posterior declivity. Under-side with a greyish pubescence; legs reddish testaceous, with the thickened part of the femora and the lower half of the tibiæ more or less fuscous. First abdominal segment of the male with a tubercle on each side of the middle.

One male example, taken April, 1898.

77. Aræocerus, sp.

This is one of the forms closely allied to *Aræocerus coffeæ*, Fab.

Family PRIONIDÆ.

78. Prinobius coxalis, Gahan, sp.n. (Pl. XI, Fig. 3.)

Brunneo-testacea, elytris plus minusve fulvescentibus, coriaceis, basi prope suturam sub-asperatis, utrisque lineis quatuor paullo elevatis, instructis.

♂. Prothorace transverso, supra subtusque confertissime punctulato, disco antice plagis duabus triangularibus, sub - nitidis, impresso; lateribus breviter dentatis postice subparallelis, antice rotundatim paullo convergentibus; antennis apicem elytrorum paullo superantibus, articulo 3° quam 1° plus duplo longiori, et articulis 4°, 5°, 6°que conjunctis fere æquali; articulis 3° 4°que subtus breviter spinosis, articulis 1° ad 4um supra fortiter sat dense punctatis, articulis 5° ad 9um sparsius punctatis, 10° 11° et apice noni longitudinaliter striatis et opacis; mesosterno, metasternique lateribus et coxis posterioribus nudis, confertissime punctulatis et opacis; plaga triangulari mediana metasterni nitida sparse punctulata et hirsuta, fortiter depressa.

♀. Antennis quam corpore multo brevioribus; prothoracis lateribus a basi antice convergentibus, sat fortiter dentatis vel spinosis; disco medio sparse, versus latera dense et rugose, punctato.

Long. 35–50, lat. 10–14 mm.

The females of this species offer no very prominent characters by which they may be distinguished from those of several other species of the genus. The third joint of the antennæ is relatively long, being nearly equal in length to the three following joints taken together, and is also comparatively slender, as it is not so distinctly thicker than the fourth joint as it is in nearly all the other species.

The male is readily distinguished by the following characters:—Prothorax transverse, furnished at the sides with very short teeth, and very closely punctured and opaque over almost the whole surface excepting two small triangular sub-nitid and impressed areas placed between the middle and anterior part of the disk. Hind coxæ, as well as the prosternum, mesosternum, and sides of

the metasternum, very closely punctured, opaque, and destitute of
pubescence. Median triangular area of the metasternum deeply
depressed and very sharply marked off from the closely punctured
lateral areas. Antennæ reaching a little beyond the apex of the
elytron, with the third joint almost equal in length to the three
following joints taken together, and distinctly thicker than any of
those joints. Anterior tibiæ nearly straight, scarcely curved
towards the apex; first joint of anterior tarsi not quite so long as
the two succeeding joints taken together.

Prinobius ceramensis, Lansb. (Notes Leyden Mus., vol. vi, p. 148),
seems to have many characters in common with the present species,
but as the author in his description states that the antennæ are
shorter than the body, and has not called attention to the relative
proportions of the joints, nor has pointed to any unusual character
in the hind coxæ, it is safe to assume that the species is quite
distinct.

Zooblax elateroides, Thoms., from the Andaman Islands, also has
certain affinities with the present species.

Family CERAMBYCIDÆ.

79. Ceresium quadrimaculatum, Gahan, sp.n.

Nigrum, antennis pedibusque (clavis femorum nigris, prætermissis)
ferrugineis; pronoto fortiter subrugoso-punctato, maculis quatuor
fulvis ornato; elytris sat sparse punctatis et albo-setosis.

Long. 11–13, lat. 3–4 mm.

Black, with the antennæ, tibiæ, tarsi, and the bases of the
femora reddish brown. Head coarsely punctured; antennæ more
than half as long again as the body, with the third joint a little
longer than the first or fourth, but distinctly shorter than the fifth;
fifth and following joints as far as the tenth sub-equal in length to
one another, the eleventh longer than the tenth. Prothorax nearly
one-third longer than broad, strongly and thickly punctured, and
somewhat rugose, especially towards the sides; with a faint patch
of fulvous pubescence on each side, and with four distinct fulvous
spots above, two of which are near the anterior, two near the
posterior, margin. Elytra black, glossy, not very closely punctured,
with the punctures diminishing in size towards the apex, and each
bearing a short, decumbent yellowish-white seta.

Taken in the central part of the island, and also near Flying
Fish Cove.

In colour this species resembles *C. nigrum*, Gah., though
differing in having the thickened portion of the femora black,
and in having four distinct tawny spots on the pronotum. It is,
however, easily to be distinguished by structural differences. In
C. nigrum the pronotum is as broad as it is long, and is scarcely
punctured towards the sides; the femora, especially those of the

anterior and middle pairs, are much stouter than in the present species; and the antennæ are only a little longer than the body, with the eleventh joint distinctly shorter than the tenth.

80. Ceresium nigrum, Gahan.

P.Z.S., 1888, p. 540.

81. Examnes affinis, Gahan, sp.n.

Brunneo-testaceus, setis albo-fulvescentibus sat dense obtectus; abdomine piceo-nigro ; scutello, capitis fronte verticeque et pro-thoracis maculis quatuor fulvo - pubescentibus, prothorace quam longiore paullo latiore, fortiter sub-rugosoque punctato ; elytris sat dense punctatis, punctis setigeris et versus apicem gradatim decrescentibus ; antennis ($\male$) quam corpore duplo longioribus, ($\female$) quam corpore haud sesqui-longioribus.
Long. 9–20, lat. 2·5–5·5 mm.
Several examples of this species were captured, exhibiting almost every gradation in size within the limits of the measurements given above.
The species is closely allied to *Examnes philippensis*, Newm., from which it differs chiefly in having the prothorax broader, more rounded at the sides, and marked above with four distinct tawny-coloured pubescent spots, placed two on each side, one near the base, the other close to the apex.
In the Munich Catalogue, *Examnes philippensis*, Newm., is placed as a synonym of *Ceresium simplex*, Gyll. It is, however, quite distinct from that species, and appears to me to be identical with *Examnes longicornis*, Pasc., a species which, in its turn, is not to be distinguished from *Examnes idoneus*, Pasc.

Family LAMIIDÆ.

82. Monohammus nativitatis, Gahan.

P.Z.S., 1888, p. 540.

83. Olenecamptus basalis, Gahan, sp.n.

O. bilobo (Fab.) affinis, sed differt, capite supra usque ad occiput sparse fusco-punctato, elytris basi albo-cinereo-pubescentibus deinde luteo-pubescentibus, utrisque macula oblonga irregulari nivea infra humerum, et macula parva nivea limbo piceo glabro circumcincta, ultra medium, ornatis, apicibus paullo nigrescentibus.
Long. 19, lat. 4·5 mm.
Allied to *O. bilobus*, Fab. (a widely distributed species, ranging from China to North Australia), but differing from it by the following

characters :—Head speckled above with a number of small glabrous brown spots, each of which surrounds a puncture. Pubescence of elytra ashy white in colour at base, yellowish grey over the rest of their surface ; each elytron with two snow-white spots—one under the shoulder, similar to that in *bilobus*, the other, which is very small, and surrounded with a naked brownish-testaceous border, being placed on the disk beyond the middle. The two snow-white spots, which in *O. bilobus* are present on the disk near the base, are in the new species wanting, their place being taken by two glabrous spots, not very regular in outline, and therefore, possibly, due to accidental rubbing.

One male specimen, taken in the north part of the island.

84. Pterolophia perplexa, Gahan. (Pl. XI, Fig. 5.)

Praonetha perplexa, Gahan : P.Z.S., 1888, p. 541.

85. Prosoplus banksi, Fab.

Two specimens of this species were taken at Flying Fish Cove.

I have already recorded the species from Christmas Island under the name of *Micracantha*.

86. Apomecyna nigritarsis, Gahan, sp.n.

Pube fulvescente sat dense obtecta ; tarsis et antennarum articulis septem ultimis nigris ; prothorace immaculato ; elytris, albo-maculatis, maculis in seriebus obliquis tribus vel quatuor ordinatis, spatiis inter series macularum plus minusve fusco-variis ; apicibus elytrorum fortiter obliquis et paullo emarginatis.

Long. 8-9·5, lat. 2·25-2·5 mm.

Covered with a dense yellowish-tawny pubescence. Head and prothorax without spots, and rather thickly punctured ; antennæ with the last seven joints and the apex of the fourth joint black ; these seven joints together not longer than the third and fourth taken together. Elytra with white spots arranged in three or four oblique rows on each side, the first row consisting of two or three spots, the second of four, the third of three, and the fourth, which is sometimes wanting, made up of two or three distinct spots ; between the third and fourth rows is a single white spot placed near the lateral margin ; the interspaces on the elytra between the rows of spots are rather strongly punctured, and more or less mottled with dark brown ; the apices of the elytra are strongly oblique and slightly emarginate. Tarsi and extreme tip of the tibiæ black, with a faint grey pubescence ; the rest of the legs covered like the under-side of the body with a yellowish-tawny pubescence.

87. Ægocidnus exiguus, Gahan, sp.n. (Pl. XI, Fig. 4.)

Parvus, capite testaceo vel fusco pube grisea tenuiter vestito; prothorace griseo - pubescente, fusco - maculato, lateraliter paullo pone medium spina brevi antice obliqua armato; elytris sat fortiter punctatis, rufo - brunneis, pube grisea, plagis fuscis interrupta, vestitis; antennis testaceis, quam corpore sesqui-longioribus, articulo 4º quam 3º vel 5º distincte longiori, articulo 3º quam 1º vix longiori, articulis 6º et sequentibus gradatim brevioribus.

Long. 3·5–4, lat. 1·25–1·5 mm.

Head dark brown or reddish brown in colour, covered with a thin greyish pubescence. Antennæ about half as long again as the body, with the fourth joint, which is the longest, distinctly longer than the third or fifth, and the third joint scarcely longer than the first. Prothorax armed a little behind the middle of each side with a short spine, the posterior face of which stands out almost at right angles, while the anterior face is oblique and continuous with the side of the prothorax in front of it. Elytra rather strongly punctured, with the punctures for the most part irregularly placed. but towards the sides of the disk, having a tendency to be arranged in longitudinal rows; reddish brown in colour, with a covering of grey pubescence, which is interrupted by a number of dark-brown patches. (In one of two specimens there is a large and conspicuous dark-brown patch placed towards the side on the middle of each elytron). Legs pale testaceous, with the thickened part of the femora more or less infuscate.

Two examples taken on the north coast of the island; one in March, the other in December.

This species resembles *Ægocidnus ignarus*, Pasc., in colour, but it is smaller in size, and differs from it also in the shape of the lateral spine of its prothorax, and in the relative proportions of the first, third, and fifth joints of the antennæ.

Family EUMOLPIDÆ.

88. Rhyparida rossi, Gahan, sp.n.

Testacea, elytris antennis pedibus et abdomine pallidioribus; capite subtilissime granuloso et opaco, sparse minutissime punctulato; prothorace transverso, lateraliter rotundato, angulis anticis posticisque minute dentato, disco sub - opaco sparse minuteque punctulato; elytris nitidis fortiter seriatimque punctatis; antennis articulo 3º quam 2º fere triplo longiore, articulo 4º quam 3º paullo breviore, ceteris gradatim decrescentibus.

Long. 7, lat. 3·5 mm.

Reddish testaceous in colour, with the elytra, legs, antennæ, and abdomen somewhat paler or more fulvous. Head very minutely granular and opaque, sparsely and very finely punctulate; clypeus somewhat in the form of a triangle, with curvilinear sides and a slightly sinuate base; vertex impressed between the eyes with three lines, one short median, and one on each side passing outwards from the apex of the clypeus, and then curved round the inner and posterior border of the eye. Thorax rounded at the sides, and broadest across the middle; upper surface dull, finely, and rather sparsely punctured. Elytra glossy, distinctly punctured, with the punctures arranged in definite rows which, counted across the middle, are to the number of eleven on each elytron; the first or sutural row becomes double at the base, the sixth, seventh, and tenth stop short at the shoulder, and the eighth and ninth a little further back, the eleventh or marginal row, before reaching the base, sends off a short inner branch as far as to the shoulder; posteriorly the eleventh row also becomes double, its outer branch joining the first or sutural row at the apex, its inner branch joining the second row, the tenth row and the third being similarly united behind; the punctures of the remaining rows are somewhat closely crowded and confused behind; the interstice between the short eighth and ninth rows is raised and sub-costate. Femora unarmed.

89. Rhyparida modesta, Gahan, sp.n.

Fusca, violaceo-tincta, corpore subtus fere nigro, antennis pedibusque testaceis; capite dense sat fortiter punctato; prothorace transverso, lateraliter ante medium, rotundato, deinde versus apicem basimque angustato, angulis anticis posticisque leviter dentatis; elytris sat fortiter seriatimque punctatis; antennis articulo 1° quam 2° duplo longiore.

Long. 8–9, lat. 4·5 mm.

Colour varying from brownish testaceous to a darker brown, with a more or less distinct violaceous tint and metallic lustre; the under-side, except at the apex of the abdomen and the sides of the prothorax, almost quite black; the legs and antennæ testaceous. Head distinctly and rather thickly punctured, especially on the clypeus; the latter with curvilinear sides, from each of which an impressed line passes to the inner and posterior border of the eye, its basal margin very slightly sinuate in the middle. Prothorax nearly twice as broad as long; rounded at the sides; broadest a little in front of the middle, and thence narrowed towards the base and apex; distinctly and rather thickly punctured above. Elytra rather strongly punctured, the punctures being arranged in regular rows on the disk and close to the lateral margins, more irregularly on the intervening space at each side; interstices between the rows of punctures very minutely and sparsely punctulate. Antennæ reaching to a little beyond the base of the elytra; second joint less than half the length of the first or third; fourth joint a little longer than the third; fifth and following joints sub-equal to one another in length, with the last three or four somewhat thicker than those preceding them. Femora unarmed.

This species and the preceding one differ from nearly all the Australian species of *Rhyparida* in having the second joint of the antennæ less than half as long as the third. In this respect they resemble certain Indo-Malayan species, and agree with those of the genus *Lindinia*, Lefev.

90. Demotina lateralis, Gahan, sp.n.

Parva, testacea, setis decumbentibus fulvis sat dense vestita; capite supra linea media glabra a clypeo ad occiput extensa, clypeo glabro transverso sub-semilunare; prothorace transverso, lateribus rotundatis, margine omnino deleta; elytris crebre sat fortiter punctatis, disco paullo convexo, lateribus valde deflexis, costa utrinque inter discum latusque; antennis basin elytrorum vix superantibus, articulis 1°, 2° que crassis, subovalibus, 3° angusto, cylindrico, quam 2° haud longiore, articulis 7° ad 11um paullo dilatatis.

Long. 2·5 mm.

Colour testaceous, with the middle of thoracic disk and spots on the elytra dark brown; the whole rather thickly covered with decumbent tawny setæ. Prothorax broader than long, slightly rounded at the sides, which are wholly without a sharp carinate margin. Elytra thickly and rather strongly punctured, abruptly deflexed at the sides; the latter being vertical and marked off each from the disk by a slightly projecting costa or line.

In the abruptly deflexed and vertical sides of the elytra this species differs from all others belonging to the genus *Demotina*.

In general appearance it most resembles *D. bowringi*, Baly, a species occurring in Hongkong, Formosa, and Chusan; and it is, perhaps, more nearly allied to this than to any other described species. The genus *Demotina* has a distribution ranging from China and Japan to New Guinea.

91. Scelodonta nitidula, Baly, var. ?

One example, taken on Phosphate Hill; November, 1897.

This example may possibly represent a distinct species; it differs from *nitidula* in having the elytra of a uniform dark coppery-brown colour, slightly tinged with metallic green; smoother on the middle of the disk; and furnished with shorter setæ. *S. nitidula*, Baly, occurs in Borneo, Sumatra, Java, Malacca, and in North and South India. In every example I have seen there are two or more spots of a purplish or steel-blue colour on each elytron; but these spots are sometimes very small and faint.

Family HALTICIDÆ.

92. Psylliodes tenuepunctata, Gahan, sp.n.

Nigro-cœrulea, nitida, antennis pedibusque (femoribus posticis exceptis) testaceis ; pronoto subtilissime irregulariterque punctulato ; elytris seriatim subtilissime punctulatis ; articulo secundo antennarum primo æquilongo, quam tertio paullo longiore.

Long. 3 mm.

Dark blue and very glossy, with the antennæ and the legs (posterior femora excepted) testaceous. Prothorax and elytra very finely punctured, with the punctures on the elytra arranged in regular rows, the interspaces between the rows being quite impunctate, or with the punctures so minute as not to be visible under a strong lens. Antennæ with the first, second, and fourth joints sub-equal in length, each being a little longer than the third, with the joints from the fifth to the tenth becoming gradually and slightly thicker.

This species is distinguished from all other species of the genus known to me by the much finer punctuation of its prothorax and elytra. In the relative proportion of the basal joints of the antennæ it agrees with *P. gracilis*, Boh., *balyi*, Jac., and other Oriental species.

Order 5.—HEMIPTERA.

By W. F. KIRBY, F.L.S., F.E.S.

(PLATE XV.)

IN the following Report, I have only included the more easily determined species taken by Mr. Andrews, postponing any notice of the remainder until the Museum collection of the families to which they belong has been rearranged. There are about twice as many species represented as are here noticed.

Family CYDNIDÆ.

1. Æthus nitens, sp.n. (Pl. XV, Fig. 1.)

Long. corp. 4 mm. ; lat. 3 mm.

Black, very shining, antennæ rufo-testaceous ; pronotum and base of scutellum not punctured ; the rest of the scutellum (which is rather long, and narrowed towards the extremity) with large punctures ; tegmina with the punctures arranged in regular rows, converging in front; membrane brownish hyaline. Legs with a slightly ferruginous shade.

Three specimens (one immature), North Coast, December, 1897, and April, 1898. On plants.

Family PENTATOMIDÆ.

2. Pentatoma grossepunctatum, sp.n. (Pl. XV, Fig. 2.)

Long. corp. 7-10 mm.; lat. thor. 5 mm.

Head with the central lobe about as long as the greatest width of the head, and traversed by a double row of punctures; the lateral lobes slightly waved before the eyes, but curving inwards, and more thickly punctured than the central lobe; front and back of head obtusely convex. General colour of the upper surface reddish brown, with numerous large black punctures on the head, thorax, scutellum, and tegmina; they are largest and most numerous on the thorax, where they run in irregular transverse curves. Thoracic lobes obtusely prominent, and more or less blackish; corium black, with the costal border broadly testaceous: membrane brownish hyaline; extremity of scutellum rather broad and rounded, nearly smooth, and testaceous; abdomen and under-surface testaceous; rostrum (which extends a little beyond the base of the hind femora), tarsi, and tip of the antennæ brown.

Five specimens, from Flying Fish Cove (no date), and North Coast, December, 1897. Not common, but came to lamp in evening.

Not closely allied to any other species in the Museum.

Family LYGÆIDÆ.

3. Lygæus subrufescens. (Pl. XV, Fig. 3.)

Lygæus subrufescens, Kirb.; P.Z.S., 1888, p. 553.

"Long. corp. 11-13 mm.

"Pitchy brown above; the head, pronotum, and base of the tegmina bordered with dull red; the ocelli, and the space between each eye, brighter red; antennæ and legs pitchy brown above and below; head and body dull red beneath (in the female the abdomen is shaded with brown on the sides, and towards the extremity, and the legs are of a redder brown beneath than above). Proboscis pitchy, extending to the middle of the third segment of the abdomen.

"Allied to *L. longiusculus*, Wlk., from Celebes."

Flying Fish Cove (Lister).

Two specimens, Flying Fish Cove, August, 1897, and West Coast, October 15th, 1897. Also ten immature specimens, one from East Coast, September 28th, 1897; the others marked "April, 1898."

Family BRACHYRHYNCHIDÆ.

4. Brachyrhynchus lignicolus, sp.n. (Pl. XV, Fig. 4.)

Long. corp. 6 mm. ; lat. 2·5 mm.

Dull red, the upper part of the head, the middle of the pronotum, the scutellum, the corium, and the membrane black ; the clavus testaceous ; and the segments of the connexicum often with large dusky markings. Head square, obliquely sloping outwards, with a projecting point laterally behind the eyes, and another projecting on each side in front of the antennæ, between which it is triangularly narrowed as far as the broad frontal process, which extends beyond this point for about one-third of the total length of the head; it is slightly denticulated at the sides, and slightly bifid at the extremity. Antennæ with the four joints all of nearly equal length. Pronotum slightly contracted in front, where it is rounded, and slightly concave in the middle, with slight denticulations on the sides in front ; on each side of the median line of the front half is a black, irregularly-shaped space. The greater part of the insect is moderately coarsely punctured ; the spaces between the veins of the membrane look like large depressed pits. Femora thickened and, as well as the tibiæ, very finely denticulated. Undersurface varied with black and red.

A large number of specimens found under bark in rotting wood. Nearest allied to some specimens of *B. rubrescens*, Walker (which probably includes more than one species), but with the markings more clearly defined.

Family HALOBATIDÆ.

5. Halobates princeps.

Halobates princeps, Buchanan White : Rep. Pelagic Hemipt. (Challenger Rep., xix), p. 44, pl. i. fig. 3 (1883).

Three specimens, Flying Fish Cove, August, 1897.

The type, now in the British Museum (Natural History), was brought from the Celebes Sea.

6. Halobates proavus.

Halobates proavus, Buchanan White : Rep. Pelagic Hemipt. (Challenger Rep., xix), p. 54, pl. ii, fig. 1 (1883).

Two specimens, Flying Fish Cove, August, 1897.
Originally described from Gilolo.

Order 6.—HOMOPTERA.

By W. F. Kirby, F.L.S., F.E.S., etc.

(PLATE XV.)

Of this Order eleven species are enumerated in the following list, all of which, so far as is known, are peculiar to the island. Of these, seven are now described as new, one being considered to represent a new genus, the other four having been described by me in 1888 from Mr. Lister's collection; of these the descriptions are here reprinted. It is curious that six species out of the eleven belong to a single family, the Ricaniidæ.

Cicadidæ.
  Pæcilopsaltria, Stål.
    calypso, Kirb.

Ricaniidæ.
  Ricania, Germ.
    flavifrontalis, sp.n.
  Paurostauria, g.n.
    delicata, sp.n.
  Varcia, Stål.
    flavicostalis, Kirb.
  Nogodina, Stål.
    affinis, Kirb.
    hyalina, Kirb.
    subviridis, sp.n.

Delphacidæ.
  Bidis, Walk.
    aristella, sp.n.

Aphrophoridæ.
  Clovia, Stål.
    eximia, sp.n.

Issidæ.
  Issus, Fabr.
    andrewsi, sp.n.

Jassidæ.
  Idiocerus, Lewis.
    punctatus, sp.n.

Family CICADIDÆ.

1. Pœcilopsaltria calypso.

Oxypleura calypso, Kirb. : P.Z.S., 1888, p. 553.
Pæcilopsaltria calypso, Dist. : Mon. Oriental Cicadidæ, p. 6, tab. x, figs. 3*a*, *b*
    (1889).

"*Male.*—Black, with testaceous markings. Head black; front of vertex with a wide testaceous stripe on each side, extending from the inside of the eye to the striated portion of the face. Longitudinal sulcation broad, rather deep black, surmounted by a trapeziform ochreous spot; the transverse striations, except the upper ones, are marked with ochreous, ending in a continuous ochreous stripe, not striated, on each side of the extremity of the longitudinal sulcation. Sides of face clothed with thick yellowish-grey hair; labrum with a longitudinal testaceous stripe, expanded above and below, proboscis testaceous, black towards the extremity, and reaching as far as the hinder trochanters; antennæ black. Pronotum testaceous, entirely so behind; a dumb-bell shaped black mark in front of this, extending to the front edge, and the central sutures blackish; sides not greatly expanded, with irregular black markings, and dotted with grey hair; mesonotum black, with two short, thick, tawny stripes on each side, not reaching the front edge, and a spear-headed, tawny mark, filled with black in the middle, directed forwards; scutellum with the hinder half and lateral ridges testaceous. Abdomen black, sutures narrowly edged with testaceous, especially on the sides; segment 7 with two testaceous dots in the middle, and a larger spot on each side. Sternum mostly black, clothed with greyish hair; legs testaceous; coxæ, four front femora, and tarsi streaked with black above; opercula testaceous, extending nearly to the end of the first segment of the abdomen. Abdomen beneath testaceous; basal segment entirely black, the following segments triangularly blackish on each side at the base, the last two lateral lobes spotted with black. Tegulæ and wings hyaline, with brown nervures; costal nervures and inner marginal nervure testaceous.

"Allied to *O. bufo* and *O. polita,* Walk., but differently marked.

"An extremely hairy pupa, marked 'Dug up, earth, October 8,' accompanied the specimen, besides an empty pupa-skin, both probably belonging to the same species."

Three males, one from the west coast, October, 1897, and another from Flying Fish Cove, August, 1897. Also three pupæ, one darker than the others, found in April, 1898.

Besides these, there is a female specimen from the east coast, October, 1897. It differs little from the male, except in the paler colour of the light markings.

Family RICANIIDÆ.

2. Ricania flavifrontalis, sp.n. (Pl. XV, Fig. 5.)

Long. corp. 3·25 mm.; exp. al. 11–13 mm.

Head brown above; pronotum blackish on the back; abdomen blackish in the middle, otherwise rufo-testaceous; face and under-surface dull yellow, clypeus slightly broader than long, nearly square, but with the lower angles slightly rounded off; a slight vertical carina. Tegmina brown, costa with a white or yellowish-white basal stripe, sometimes extending to two-fifths of the length of the tegmen. Beyond this the costa is marked with pale spots as far as a large white band on the costa at about two-thirds of its length; this band is subinterrupted below, and then turns obliquely outwards. This lower part extends for about half the length of the upper, and is much narrower, and rather pointed at the end. Within this is a broad white band, outwardly concave on its upper portion, and extending to the inner margin.

The basal portion of the corium is much mottled with white. The lower part of the hind margin is dotted with white, and the marginal portion of the tegmen is marked off on the inside in one specimen by a row of hardly indicated white dots. Wings hyaline, with broad pale-brown borders. The fringes of both the tegmina and wings consist of very short, straight, isolated bristles, only visible under the microscope. Before the tip of the tegmina is a slightly oval black spot, rather large for the size of the insect.

Two specimens, North Coast, January, 1898.

The white markings and well-marked subapical black dots will easily distinguish this interesting little species.

PAUROSTAURIA, Kirby, gen. nov.

Front quadrangular, broader than long, slightly expanded below, and with a central carina. Vertex transverse, about three times as broad as long, and gradually concave behind. Pronotum curved, transverse, mesonotum oval, tricarinate, rather long. Tegmina hyaline, very broad at the extremity, the costa slightly arched, much longer than the inner margin, which is a little shorter than the hind margin. Apex much rounded, and hind margin curving obliquely to the hinder angle, which is obtusely rounded; inner margin convex. Costal cell with oblique transverse nervules; subcostal cell free; basal cell oval, broader than long. Three longitudinal nervures running from the basal cell, the upper one forked close to its base, and the branches again forking at about half their length, and ultimately throwing off long forks to the hind margin. The middle nervure forks a little further from the base, and once or twice more before or near the middle of its length; the lower nervure forks only once, at about half its length. An obsolete nervure curves round inwards from the costa at three-fourths of its length to the base of the first fork of the lower branch of the middle longitudinal nervure. Before the apex of the tegmen is a large black stigma, and the marginal area, which is rather broad, is marked off by a row of pale nervules between the nervures. The clavus throws off a vein of about half the rest of its length near the base, which curves to the inner margin; between and beyond are several transverse nervules. Wings hyaline, much shorter than the tegmina, the three upper longitudinal nervures variously forked, and connected by two oblique transverse nervures. Hind tibiæ bispinose.

Allied to *Ricanoptera*, Melichar; but it does not appear to be congeneric with the species of that genus before me. *Inter alia*, the subapical spot seems to be always absent in *Ricanoptera*. The name *Paurostauria* has been suggested by the paucity of cross-nervures in this insect.

3. Paurostauria delicata, sp.n. (Pl. XV, Fig. 6.)

Long. corp. 3 mm.; exp. tegm. 10 mm.; lat. tegm. 3 mm.

Male.—Testaceous (probably green when living, as the abdomen is still green in one of the specimens); eyes and vertex brown. Tegmina hyaline, with most of the nervures yellow, except in the dark portions. Marginal area brown, broadest at the apex. An oval, subapical black spot, below which a hyaline curved stripe runs down to the inner margin; the brown band within this is bisected by the light cross-nervules marking off the marginal area. Costa with a black line, commencing at about half the length of the costal cell, and curving round the end of the subcostal cell; it also throws off an expanding pear-shaped black spot, running downwards to half the width of the tegmen, beside the marginal markings. Between these black markings, the costa, and the subapical spot, the wing is brown, with hyaline markings. The subcostal nervure is broadly black above, narrowly edged with yellow below, and the upper longitudinal nervure is marked with a large black spot in the middle. The curved dividing-line in the middle of the tegmen is edged outside with black, and a series of irregular black markings is continued to the inner margin. Nearer the base are two or three more small black spots, and the greater part of the lower vein of the clavus is broadly black.

Described from three specimens, without special locality.

4. Varcia flavicostalis. (Pl. XV, Fig. 7.)

Ricania flavicostalis, Kirb.: P.Z.S.. 1888, p. 554.
Varcia flavicostalis, Melichar: Ann. Nat. Hofmuseums, xiii, p. 319 (1899).

" Exp. al. 20 mm.; long. corp. 7 mm.

" *Male.* — Head yellow, with four keels ; vertex depressed, brown, except at the sides and on the median line; front quadricarinate, the angles of the outer carinæ very prominent, the middle ones hardly projecting on the frontal edge; all the carinæ black, and with a short dark line on the clypeus between them, the middle ones rather wide apart, and meeting in a point at the extremity of the clypeus. Thorax and abdomen blackish brown above, the thorax tricarinate, varied with ferruginous on the sides and along the outer edges of the two outer carinæ; abdomen with the second segment greenish, and the base of the three following segments ferruginous. Undersurface of the body and legs yellowish ; the four front tibiæ brownish above ; abdominal segments edged behind with a green line; the last two segments reddish brown. Wings hyaline; fore wings with the costal space yellow as far as the black stigma, beyond which is a hyaline space ; hind margin broadly purplish brown, intersected by a curved line nearly parallel to the hind margin; within the middle of this runs a narrow vitreous stripe covering the outer half of seven cells; one or two very irregular series of transverse cells beyond the middle of the wing, not even uniform on both sides; inner marginal region tinged with yellow, but less strongly than the costa; costal cross-nervures not forked, but most of the apical nervures beyond the stigma and on the hind margin are forked. Hind wings hyaline, brown along the hind margin, the first six or seven marginal nervures from the tip furcate or bifurcate.

"The neuration of this and the two following species somewhat resembles that of *R. panorpæformis*, Guér. No dates of capture are attached to any of the specimens."

Two specimens: Flying Fish Cove, August, 1897, and East Coast, October, 1897.

5. Nogodina affinis. (Pl. XV, Fig. 8.)

Ricania affinis, Kirb.: P.Z.S., 1888, p. 554.
Nogodina affinis, Melichar: Ann. Nat. Hofmuseums, xiii, p. 309 (1899).

"Exp. al. 22 mm.; long. corp. 9 mm.

"*Male.*—Very similar to the last species, but darker above, the brown bands on the clypeus beyond the inner carina darker; undersurface of body yellow, with irregular black markings beneath the wings, and a large spot on the pectus between the two first pairs of legs; abdomen not banded with green above, but with a row of yellow spots on the sides. Wings hyaline, not tinged with yellow on the costa or inner margin, but with a yellow spot on the costa (likewise edged with black within) before the black stigma; below the stigma are some small brown blotches along the line of the inner row of transverse cells; there are also two small brown spots nearer the base on the lower half of the wing; hind margin brown for about one-sixth of the width of the wing, and marked with two irregular hyaline spaces, each covering several cells; close to the hind margin runs an interrupted row of small hyaline dots. Hind wings hyaline, edged with brown, except towards the anal angle. Neuration nearly as in the last species, but the outer row of transverse cells less numerous."

6. Nogodina hyalina. (Pl. XV, Fig. 9.)

Ricania hyalina, Kirb.: P.Z.S., 1888, p. 555; Melichar, Ann. Nat. Hofmuseums, xiii, p. 337 (1899).

"Exp. al. 15 mm.; long. corp. 5 mm.

"*Male.*—Head yellowish; the carinæ black, the clypeus marked with brown lines between them; the middle carinæ not projecting on the vertex, which is deeply and triangularly depressed in the middle ; thorax reddish above, the middle carinæ yellow ; abdomen brown above, the sides marked with yellow, and the segments bordered with green behind. Undersurface of the body yellow, the femora, the extremities of the five first segments of the abdomen, and a large spot at each side at its extremity green ; the base of the five first abdominal segments rich cream-colour.

"Allied to *R. pellucida* and *R. panorpæformis*, Guér."

Twenty-eight specimens, all those specially labelled taken in January, 1898, on the North Coast. An abundant and very variable species, both in colour and neuration ; but without exhibiting well-marked differences which appear to be of specific or even varietal importance. Some of the specimens are of a pale testaceous yellow, others are of a darker yellowish brown, with the abdomen more or less green, with a black dorsal band, and black sutures. The number of nervures in the costal cell before the stigma varies from 8 to 11; the stigma covers about five cross-nervures, and is generally but slightly browned, but in the darker specimens (which are usually those with most cross-nervules in the basal cell and elsewhere) it is blackish. The subcostal space is always (?) empty; but the two following longitudinal spaces are sometimes free, almost as far as the first fork of the second longitudinal nervure, which is usually preceded by a cross-nervure in each space; or there may be one, two, or three cross-nervules in each of these spaces, preceding the fork. Sometimes the marginal third of the tegmen is mapped out into three fairly regular areas; but sometimes the neuration of this portion is much more irregular. The shape, too, of the various cells differs considerably.

7. Nogodina subviridis, sp.n. (Pl. XV, Figs. 10, 11.)

Long. corp. 7 mm. ; exp. al. 20 mm.

Female.—Testaceous ; abdomen, except at tip, green, with black sutures, expanding in front, and connected ; front long, with black lateral and central carinæ, the latter crossing, and between their upper part is a brown line. Sutures of pronotum more or less black. Tegmina yellowish hyaline, with yellowish-brown nervures ; costal area with 11 or 12 cross-nervures before the stigma, which is very large, extending between six or seven cross-nervures, those towards its base being more or less yellow. Subcostal area free. The three upper longitudinal nervures rising together from the upper angle of the basal cell ; the second forking at three-fifths of its length, the third at one-fourth. The fourth is widely separated from the others at its base. It is parallel with and closely approximating to the upper vein of the clavus, and it throws off a branch upwards at two-fifths of its length. The middle vein of the clavus unites with the lower one at half its length ; lower branch of the clavus broadly brown, and united with the upper by from four to six cross-nervules. Wings hyaline, with brown nervures. (Fig. 10.)

Variety (?). *Female.*—Differs in the body being mostly black, except the front, the sides of the thorax, and the base of the abdomen, which are testaceous. The black central carinæ are merely indicated in brown, below the point where they cross; the stigma on the tegmina is almost wholly black, and there are one or two cross-nervures in the subcostal area. I can hardly consider these differences specific, having only single specimens to compare. (Fig. 11.)

The type is from the East Coast, and the variety from the North Coast, January, 1898.

Allied to *N. plena*, Wlk., and *N. affinis*, Kirb.

Family DELPHACIDÆ.

8. Bidis aristella, sp.n. (Pl. XV, Figs. 12, 13.)

Long. corp. 4 mm.; exp. al. 12 mm.

Testaceous, the two joints of the antennæ long, cylindrical, of equal length, and set with very short brown bristles; the second joint slightly thicker than the first, subannulated, and with two long brown bands, not extending to either extremity; it is followed by a bulb bearing a very fine bristle, longer than the two joints together. Vertex and front quadricarinate, the carinæ brown, and the centre of the front and the narrowest space between the central carinæ, on the vertex, brown. Beyond this point, the central carinæ unite with the outer ones, and run backwards parallel to the eyes, the space between which is very deeply concave behind; there is also a brown spot between the carinæ, where they diverge.

Pronotum with three black carinæ, one central, the others starting from it in front, curving round each eye. Mesonotum with five longitudinal black carinæ, the two outer ones slightly diverging, and followed by a brown line on the sides of the pronotum. Both the pronotum and mesonotum have very prominent lateral angles, before which is a brown line. Abdomen testaceous, with red central and terminal carinæ, the latter preceded by broad brown bands; the two terminal segments are blackish, bordered behind with testaceous. Ovipositor of the female blackish, up-curved; above it is a long, broad, blackish process, set with rather long bristles, and bifid at the extremity. Tegmina yellowish hyaline, the nervures and fringes set with short bristles, and alternately brown and yellow for rather long spaces. There is a large brown spot in the middle of the clavus, and in the female the space between this and the base is also brown. There is also a brown curved nervure marking the apical area, and the space between this and the apex is much clouded with brown, especially in the female; and nearer the base the dark portions of the nervures are more or less clouded with brown. Wings hyaline, mostly with brown nervures. Legs testaceous, end of tibiæ, and the tarsi mostly brown.

† Four specimens: East Coast, September, 1897, and Flying Fish Cove, 1898.

Allied to *B. pictula* and *B. punctifrons*, Wlk., but with the nervures running to the costa yellow and unspotted; in the other species they are brown, and terminate in brown spots on the costa.

Stål notes *Bidis*, Wlk., as = *Ugyops*, Guér.; but as some of the characters disagree, I retain Walker's name for the present.

Family APHROPHORIDÆ.

9. Clovia eximia, sp.n. (Pl. XV, Fig. 14.)

Exp. al. 14 mm.; long. corp. 5 mm.

Head and thorax black, dull above, shining beneath, upper part of front with seven transverse testaceous bands, the uppermost widely interrupted, and those below the second more or less irregular and indented in the middle; below them is a trace of an eighth; proboscis and a triangular spot just above its base also testaceous. Vertex and thorax hardly separated, front yellow, narrowly edged with black from eye to eye, and with a short waved transverse black stripe in the middle. Behind this is another, longer, curving from eye to eye in front, and there is again a broader black band between the eyes, followed by two yellow ones. The thorax may be described as black, with three broad transverse yellow lines, and the scutellum is marked with three yellow lines, converging behind, and joined by a yellow curve in front. Sides of metathorax and extremity of the rufous-brown abdomen varied with testaceous. Tegmina rufous brown, with testaceous yellow markings, those towards the extremity tinged with golden. An oblique long oval spot at one-third of the length of the costa, a short slightly curved spot on the costa at two-thirds of its length, and three pale stripes on the lower part of the hind margin. The outer portion of these is brown, but does not touch the hind margin, and the two lower ones contain a longitudinal brown dash on the outer part. There is a bifid yellow stripe, traversing the clavus parallel with the inner margin, from the base; the outer branch is narrow; the inner one is broader, and curves up to meet a corresponding spot on the inner margin of the corium. Legs testaceous, longitudinally striped with brown, the hind legs darkest.

Eleven specimens: from East Coast, September 28, and October, 1897; and North Coast, January, 1898.

Not closely allied to any other species at present in the British Museum (Natural History); but appears to approach *C. lemniscatus*, Stål, described from Java.

Family ISSIDÆ.

10. Issus (?) andrewsi, sp.n. (Pl. XV, Fig. 15.)

Long. corp. cum tegm. 6 mm.; long. tegm. 5 mm.; lat. tegm. 2·5 mm.

Testaceous, front black, tricarinate in the middle, the lateral carinæ meeting above in an acute angle; the sides are dotted with testaceous, and the summit of the angle is of the same colour. There are also outer carinæ, raised at the summit within the eyes; vertex and lower mouth-parts testaceous. Legs testaceous, the femora and tibiæ more or less black in the middle. Tegmina coriaceous, greenish grey, a little mottled with brown or reddish brown, especially on the clavus and along the borders, wings brownish hyaline.

One specimen, without special locality. Allied to some unnamed Indian species in the collection of the Museum.

Family JASSIDÆ.

11. Idiocerus (?) punctatus, sp.n. (Pl. XV, Fig. 16.)

Long. corp. cum tegm. 5 mm.; long. tegm. 3·5 mm.

Almost uniform testaceous, darkest on the thorax, which is sculptured with transverse striæ. The front of the thorax is sometimes speckled with brown, and the hinder part and base of the scutellum are marked with four rather indistinct brownish bands. Ocelli in the middle of the front, about twice as far apart as each is distant from the margin of the eye. Tegmina with longitudinal rows of brown setiferous punctures, and with a brown spot on the inner margin towards the end of the vein of the clavus. Hind tibiæ long, whitish, strongly ciliated.

Five specimens: from East Coast, August, 1897; Flying Fish Cove, October, 1897; and North Coast, January, 1898.

Somewhat resembles *Bythoscopus testaceus*, Wlk., from Sarawak, but much smaller, paler, and with the ocelli much further from the eyes. It is still nearer *B. unicolor*, Wlk., from Makian (Celebes); but the latter species has a brown spot at the end of the tegmina, and the front is less rounded above.

Order 7.—MALLOPHAGA.

By W. F. Kirby, F.L.S., F.E.S., etc.

A single specimen (East Coast, September, 1897), probably from some marine bird, but closely resembling, except in its much greater size, *Nirmus attenuatus*, Nitsch, as figured by Giebel (Insecta Epizoa, Tab. vi, fig. 1). The latter species is found on the corncrake.

Order 8.—NEUROPTERA.

By W. F. KIRBY, F.L.S., F.E.S., etc.

(PLATE XIV.)

In this Order, Mr. Andrews collected a *Termes*, two Ant-lions, and three wide-ranging species of Dragon-flies. One of the latter is the ubiquitous *Pantala flavescens*, which inhabits almost all the warmer parts of the world, from Egypt to Natal, from Kamtchatka to Ceylon and Australia and Tahiti, and from Georgia to Brazil; it is even said to have been once taken many years ago in the English Fens. It is almost certainly a migratory species, and Mr. Andrews informs me that enormous swarms of dragon-flies appear suddenly in Christmas Island from Java when the wind is in the north and north-east, and disappear again in a few days.

ODONATA.

Family LIBELLULIDÆ.

Sub-Family LIBELLULINÆ.

1. Pantala flavescens.

Libellula flavescens, Fabricius: Ent. Syst., Suppl., p. 285 (1798).

Nineteen specimens: from Flying Fish Cove, September 2 to October 20, 1897; West Coast, October, 1897, and March 28, 1898.

2. Trithemis trivialis.

Libellula trivialis, Ramb.: Ins. Névr., p. 115 (1842).

Four specimens. North Coast, on sea-cliffs.

Family ÆSCHNIDÆ.

Sub-Family ÆSCHNINÆ.

3. Anax guttatus.

Æschna guttata, Burmeister: Handb. Ent., ii, p. 840, n. 14 (1839).

Flying Fish Cove.
One male specimen only. Rare; only two or three specimens seen. Called 'Rajah' by the natives.

PLANIPENNIA.

Family MYRMELEONIDÆ.

4. Formicalæo morpheus, sp.n. (Pl. XIV, Fig. 3.)

Exp. al. 55–60 mm.; long. corp. 25–29 mm.

Male and Female.—Dark brown, varied with testaceous; antennæ ringed with black and testaceous, much thickened before the tip in the male; face testaceous, the tips of the mandibles, a narrow transverse band below the antennæ, and a broad band above black, the latter indented in the middle beneath. Above this is a testaceous stripe, followed by a black one, and then by two lateral ones, curving backwards in the middle; the vertex is black, with two short longitudinal testaceous lines, with a testaceous spot between in front, and three large testaceous spots behind, followed, on the occiput, by two lateral testaceous spots and a central line. Thorax black, pro- and mesothorax with a testaceous middle line, and a broader longitudinal stripe on each side; metathorax with a Y-shaped testaceous mark on the sutures, and the base and extremity of the front lobe also marked with testaceous. Abdomen black, with about two longitudinal spots on the back of each segment, and two oval ones on the sides of several segments at least. Legs testaceous, front femora thickened, striped longitudinally with black; front tibiæ with two black rings, hinder ones with indications of the same; joints of the tarsi ringed with black; all the legs set with very long, fine bristles. Wings rather long, moderately pointed, most of the nervures varied alternately with fuscous and yellowish; pterostigma yellowish; wings towards the extremity with about four irregular rows of blackish stippling, most distinct on the fore wings, and the innermost row largest.

Four specimens: Flying Fish Cove (900 feet), August and November, 1897; East Coast, September 2, 1897; near water, in forest.

Allied to *Myrmeleon insomnis*, Wlk., from an unknown locality, but differently marked. The specimens are not in first-rate condition, but it is hoped that the description will be sufficient for identification.

5. Myrmeleon iridescens, sp.n. (Pl. XIV, Fig. 4.)

Long. corp. 25 mm.; exp. al. 59 mm.

Female black, head with the lower mouth-parts testaceous, a short testaceous line below the base of each antenna, two testaceous dots on the middle of the vertex, and the upper and hinder orbits very narrowly testaceous. Thorax narrowly bordered in front, at the sides, and behind with testaceous; base of the wings with testaceous callosities above and beneath. Legs testaceous, with dark rings towards the end of the femora, and obsoletely on the tibiæ; tarsi mostly black. Wings very iridescent hyaline, without markings; neuration black, except the subcostal nervures and those of the pseudostigmatal space of the fore wings, which are yellowish.

Described from a single specimen, without special locality.

This species much resembles *M. lethifer*, Wlk., from Natal, but has somewhat narrower wings.

ISOPTERA.

Family TERMITIDÆ.

6. Termes, Linn.

Many specimens of a species allied to *T. sarawakensis*, Haviland.

Abundant everywhere. Nests formed of a dark-brown papier-maché, on stumps, or plastered against trunks of trees.

Order 9.—ORTHOPTERA.

By W. F. KIRBY, F.L.S., F.E.S., etc.

(PLATES XII-XIV.)

THE principal feature of the collection of Orthoptera is in the comparatively large number of Forficulidæ obtained. This, however, is probably more apparent than real, for although in a few countries, such as England and, still more, the United States, the family is very poorly represented, there are probably a very large number of existing species, which only require to be collected, for, as a rule, they are passed over entirely by collectors.

As regards the other Orthoptera, it is remarkable how many important groups appear to be represented in Christmas Island only by a single conspicuous species, generally peculiar to the island, as far as is at present known. Most of the species in the following list which have been previously described from other countries, are wide-ranging species of Blattidæ. Want of sufficient material renders it somewhat doubtful whether other specimens provisionally referred to known species may not ultimately prove to be distinct.

Twenty-three species, obtained by Mr. Andrews, are enumerated
in the following list, of which seven are described as new. Of the
remaining species, at least seven appear to be peculiar to the island.
I have reprinted the descriptions of these from my previous paper.

ORTHOPTERA.

FORFICULIDÆ.
Labidura, Leach.
nigricornis, Kirb.
Platylabia, Dohrn.
dimidiata, Dohrn.
Anisolabis, Fieb.
ståli, Dohrn.
Labia, Leach.
Murrayi, sp.n.
incerta, sp.n.
indistincta, sp.n.
subarmata, sp.n.
Anechura, Scudd.
sp.

BLATTIDÆ.
Temnopteryx, Brunn.
fulva, Brunn.
Phyllodromia, Serv.
supellectilium, Serv.
Periplanata, Burm.
americana, L.
Leucophœa, Brunn.
surinamensis, L.
Panesthia, Serv.
javanica, Serv.

MANTIDÆ.
Hierodula, Burm.
dispar, sp.n.

PHASMIDÆ.
Clitumnus, Stål.
stilpnoides, Kirb.

GRYLLIDÆ.
Ectadoderus, Guér.
flavipalpis, sp.n.

GRYLLACRIDÆ.
Gryllacris, Serv.
rufovaria, Kirb.

CONOCEPHALIDÆ.
Pseudorhynchus, Serv.
lessonii, Serv.

LISTROCELIDÆ.
Phisis, Stål.
listeri, Kirb.

PHANEROPTERIDÆ.
Psyra, Stål.
pomona, sp.n.

LOCUSTIDÆ.
Oxya, Serv.
orientalis, Kirb.
Cyrtacanthacris, Walk.
disparilis, Kirb.
Epacromia, Fisch.
rufostriata, Kirb.

Family FORFICULIDÆ.

1. Labidura nigricornis, Kirb.: P.Z.S., 1888, p. 546.
(Pl. XII, Fig. 2 ♂, Fig. 3 ♀.)

"Long. corp. 18–20 mm.
"Black, head smooth, not much raised, broad behind, and narrowed
and enlarged in front; lower mouth-parts sometimes testaceous;
antennæ seventeen-jointed, sometimes inclined to pitchy beneath,
but with none of the joints white or yellow; pronotum smooth in

front and very finely reticulate behind, nearly quadrate, the hinder edge rounded; a central groove on the front half, on each side of which is a slight elevation; tegmina nearly smooth, broader than the thorax, and 1½ times as long as broad; projecting portion of the wings rather narrow, sparingly punctate, about one-third as long as the tegmina, and very slightly tipped with pale testaceous; femora slightly thickened; tarsi, and sometimes the extreme tips of the tibiæ, ferruginous; abdomen thickly and finely punctured, the hinder margins of the segments appearing as if milled. Under-surface more inclining to pitchy. Forceps nearly as long as the abdomen, moderately broad, more or less punctured, and incurved at the extremity; in the male with a tooth at the base, and another, preceded by two or three small denticulations, at two-thirds of the length.

"Several specimens obtained October 3rd, 1887 (Lister). This species appears to be the common earwig of the island. It has considerable external resemblance to *Chelisoches morio*, Fabr., from which the structure of its legs and the unicolorous antennæ will at once distinguish it."

Three males, one from North Coast, December, 1897, and one female, April, 1898 (Andrews).

2. Platylabia dimidiata (†).

Platylabia dimidiata, Dohrn: Stett. ent. Zeit., xxviii, p. 348 (1867).

A single damaged specimen, agreeing approximately with the description of *P. dimidiata*; but in the absence of specimens of the latter from Luzon (from whence the types were received), it is impossible to be sure of the identification.

3. Anisolabis ståli.

Forcinella ståli, Dohrn: Stett. ent. Zeit., xxv, p. 286 (1864).

Three specimens (from "North Coast, Dec., 1897"), apparently belonging to this Javanese species.

4. Labia murrayi, sp.n. (Pl. XII, Fig. 6, ♂; Pl. XIII, Fig. 5, ♀.)

Long. corp. cum forcip. 9 mm.; segm. ult. cum forcip. 3 mm.; long. tegm. 1¼ mm.

Male.—Rufo - testaceous, very shining, head convex, shining black, face testaceous, antennæ testaceous, rather darker above than below, antennæ pubescent, thirteen-jointed (?), second joint narrower than the scape, and short, the rest cylindrical, abdomen finely punctured, terminal segment smooth, but coarsely punctured towards the base of the forceps; legs pale testaceous, femora

darker, forceps separated at the base by a space about equalling
their breadth, gradually tapering, and curved inwards to the tips,
which are crossed, and not very acute; a large tooth on the inner
edge at about one-quarter of their length, followed by two or more
smaller ones; tegmina short, obliquely truncated (no wings), and
one or two of the following segments of the abdomen marked
with blackish at the sides; pygidium short, broad, transversely
oblong; pliciferous tubercles obsolete.

Described from two males. An hermaphrodite specimen is paler,
and has the tegmen on the left side longer than the other, and
subacute, and the right branch of the forceps is considerably shorter
and slenderer than the other; waved, unarmed, and more acute at
the extremity.

The last specimen is from North Coast, March, 1898; the others
are without special locality.

5. Labia incerta, sp.n. (Pl. XII, Fig. 5.)

Female.—Resembles the last species, but the head, pronotum, and
tegmina are purplish brown. Abdomen fulvous, with purplish-
brown markings at the base and sides. Forceps rather slender,
waved, with the tips pointed and approximating; the inner edge
finely serrated.

A single specimen.

6. Labia indistincta, sp.n. (Pl. XII, Fig. 4.)

Male.—Rufo-castaneous, antennæ thirteen-jointed, head above,
hinder part of pronotum, and tegmina varied with brownish;
tegmina rather narrow, subtruncated; abdomen beneath them,
with a transverse blackish band, but the rest of its upper surface
uniformly reddish. Forceps nearly straight, incurved at the tips,
and set with long, fine, grey hairs; the inner edge with a cultrate
projection at the base, about twice as broad as the short transverse
pygidium, which is rounded off towards the extremity; beneath
this is a quadrangular projection.

A single specimen obtained.

Much resembles the two last species. In all these small *Labiæ*
the pliciferous tubercles on the abdomen are almost, if not quite,
obsolete.

7. Labia (?) subarmata, sp.n. (Pl. XII, Fig. 7.)

Long. corp. cum forcip. circà 5 mm.

Male.—Dark chestnut-brown, thickly and very finely punctured
on the tegmina and abdomen, and covered with a very close pile.
Head black above, nearly quadrate, but with the hinder angles
obtusely rounded off. Antennæ eight-jointed (?), pilose, rufo-
testaceous, the scape oblong, at least three times as long as broad,

second joint small, the others oval, much longer than broad. Head below the antennæ pale testaceous. Pronotum narrower than the head, longer than broad, subquadrate, with the hinder angles slightly rounded off, and the front angles very obtuse, sides slightly bordered with pale testaceous. Tegmina and exposed part of wings long, subacute, thickly dotted with grey pile, as is also the abdomen. Terminal segment red; forceps red, about half as long again as the terminal segment, unarmed, widely apart, and slightly thickened at the base, regularly incurved, and crossing at the extremity. Pygidium short, obtusely angulated. Legs testaceous, paler at the joints. No pliciferous folds visible on abdomen. Under-surface brownish testaceous, abdomen and forceps reddish.

Female.—Similar to the male, but with the pronotum and abdomen of a lighter brown, head reddish. Legs testaceous, brownish towards the base of the femora. Forceps approximate, stout, subcontiguous, triquetral, with the inner ridges very strongly marked ; tips incurved. Antennæ ten-jointed. Under-surface of body more uniformly reddish in the male.

The apparent absence of pliciferous folds makes me doubt whether this species is a true *Labia.* It much resembles some American species, such as *L. rotundata* and *L. brunnea*, Scudder.

8. Anechura, sp.

An immature female, probably belonging to an undescribed species. " North Coast, March, 1898."

Family BLATTIDÆ.

9. Temnopteryx fulva (?).

Temnopteryx fulva, Brunner: Syst. Blatt., p. 85 (1865).

One specimen, considerably smaller than the Javanese type described by Brunner, but possibly belonging to the same species.

10. Phyllodromia supellectilium (?).

Blatta supellectilium, Serv.: Ins. Orth., p. 114 (1839).
Phyllodromia supellectilium, Brunn.: Syst. Blatt., p. 98 (1865).

One specimen, north part of island, January, 1898, belonging to this or to an allied species.

11. Periplaneta americana.

Blatta americana, Linn.: Syst. Nat., 10th ed., i, p. 424, n. 4 (1758).
Periplaneta americana, Brunn.: Syst. Blatt., p. 232, Tab. v, fig. 24 (1865).

. One specimen only, December, 1897.

12. Leucophœa surinamensis.

Blatta surinamensis, Linn.: Syst. Nat., 10th ed., i, p. 424, n. 3 (1758).
Panchlora (Leucophœa) surinamensis, Brunn.: Syst. Blatt., p. 278, Tab. vii,
    fig. 32 (1865).

Flying Fish Cove, August, 1897.
A single specimen of this cosmopolitan species was found in
rotting wood.

13. Panesthia javanica.

Panesthia javanica, Serv.: Ann. Sci. Nat., xxii, p. 38 (1832); Brunn., Syst.
    Blatt, p. 393, Tab. viii, fig. 58 (1865); Kirb., P.Z.S., 1888,
    p. 547.

These insects abound under rotten wood, and in large holes in
it, which they seem to make. In various stages of development.
West End, Christmas Island, October 1. 4, 5, 1887 (Lister).
Ten specimens in various stages. Flying Fish Cove, August,
1897; also December, 1897. They appropriate the burrows of
wood-boring beetles. (Andrews.)

Family MANTIDÆ.

14. Hierodula dispar, sp.n.

Dimensions.				♂		♀
Long. corp.	...	...	...	55–65 mm.	...	63–74 mm.
Long. partis anticæ pronoti	...		6 ,,		...	7–9 ,,
Long. partis posticæ pronoti	...		14 ,,		...	13–16 ,,
Long. pronoti toti	...	...		20 ,,	...	20–27 ,,
Long. tegminarum		...		45–55 ,,	...	50–65 ,,
Lat. pronoti	...	...	...	7 ,,	...	9–11 ,,

Male.—Body probably green when living; afterwards yellowish
or brown; pronotum often with some brown or purplish markings.
Pronotum broadest in front, and serrated at the sides. Front coxæ
beneath, with a dentated ridge at the base, generally rising in two
large, flat, triangular projections (sometimes three larger projections)
followed by a few smaller ones, irregular in number and position.
Front tibiæ with four strong teeth on the outer edge, and many on
the inner, mostly tipped with black; front tarsi black on the inside.
Wings and tegmina vitreous, with green nervures, which are very
numerous towards the apex; costal area of tegmina green (or
yellow, as well as the nervures, in faded (?) specimens); stigma
large, oval, yellowish white.
Female.—Green, or purplish grey (rarely olive yellow); tegmina
nearly opaque, mottled with purplish grey, and in the costal area
with yellowish; front coxæ and femora beneath white; tibiæ
mostly yellowish. Coxæ with two large, flat, round plates on the

inside at the base, ending in triangular dentated points; beyond and above these are numerous small teeth. Femora with four white spines on the outer edge, ringed, tipped, and lined with black; a row of alternately large and small black spines, streaked with white inside, on the inner carina, and four large median oblique basal spines, black, standing in black rings, and white only on the inside. Tibial spines tipped with black; tarsi streaked with black on the inside. Propectus with two broad black bands; mesopectus with one. (In the males, the colours beneath are not sufficiently well preserved to be described.)

A very distinct species, but most nearly related to *H. patellifera*, Serv.

Described from four males (two labelled "Flying Fish Cove, Aug., 1897," and another, "West Coast, Oct., 1897"), and six females (three from Flying Fish Cove or neighbourhood), September 20 to October 20, 1897. There is also a pupa and an empty pupa-skin from the same locality.

Family PHASMIDÆ.

15. Clitumnus stilpnoides. (Pl. XII, Fig. 1.)

Clitumnus stilpnoides, Kirb.: P.Z.S., 1888, p. 547.

"Long. corp. 100 mm.

"*Male.*—Uniform brown; head and pronotum somewhat more grey; antennæ about two-thirds as long as the mesonotum; pronotum hardly longer than the head; mesonotum one-fourth longer than the metanotum; two small horns between the eyes; legs long, slender, unarmed, clothed with very fine oblique bristles; outer anal appendages longer and less incurved than in *C. stilpnus*.

"Taken October, 1887 (Lister). Also two immature specimens, apparently belonging to the same species. Closely allied to *C. stilpnus*, Westwood."

Four specimens: from Flying Fish Cove, August, 1897; and East Coast, November, 1897. (Andrews.)

There are two other Phasmidæ in Mr. Andrews' collection, apparently belonging to the allied genus *Entoria*, Stål, but hardly in sufficiently good condition to describe, though probably new.

Family GRYLLIDÆ.

16. Ectadoderus flavipalpis, sp.n. (Pl. XIII, Fig. 3 ♂, Fig. 4 ♀.)

♂. Long. corp. 6–8 mm.; long. pron. 2½–3 mm.; long. elytr. 2–2½ mm.

♀. Long. corp. 8–9 mm.; cum ovip. 15 mm.; long. pron. 2½ mm.

Male.--Testaceous or rufo-testaceous, in the darkest specimens inclining to reddish on the head, pronotum, and the raised border of the tegmina; mouth blackish, palpi and femora yellow, abdomen black above and below; knees, tibiæ, and tarsi more or less varied with blackish.

Female.--Apterous, the abdomen more or less testaceous above.

Four specimens, East Coast, August and September, 1897, and Flying Fish Cove; also four specimens from Mr. Lister's collection. Nearest allied to *E. xanthopterus*, Guér.

Family GRYLLACRIDÆ.

17. Gryllacris rufovaria. (Pl. XIV, Fig. 1.)

Gryllacris rufovaria, Kirb.: P.Z.S., 1888, p. 548.

"Long. corp. 32 mm.; ovipositoris ♀ 12 mm.; exp. al. 65 mm.; long. antennarum circâ 110 mm.

"Yellowish brown; the head, especially the face, red; the vertex, the neighbourhood of the eyes and of the antennæ, the space between the latter, the lower mouth-parts, and the palpi more or less varied with yellowish, prothorax and sides of abdomen beneath varied with red; spines of the hind legs tipped with black; tegmina yellowish, with yellowish veins. Wings ample, pale grey; the longitudinal nervures yellowish brown; the cross-nervures blackish, bordered with dusky on each side, except the two or three outer rows, the outermost of all being varied with yellowish.

"Moderately stout, smooth and shining; face with a few shallow punctures; head and thorax of equal breadth; antennæ, legs, and anal appendages (except ovipositor) sparingly clothed with fine, short woolly hairs; hind femora with from nine to eleven short spines, hardly arranged in pairs, on each side; hind tibiæ with six irregular pairs, without counting the apical ones. In the male the last segment of the abdomen terminates in two short, stout, conical projections; the upper anal appendages are long, tapering, divergent in the middle, and slightly incurved at the tips; the lower appendages are only half the length of the upper ones, and are simply divergent. In the female the upper appendages are stouter at the base and more incurved at the tips than in the male, but are of nearly equal length.

"Belongs to the same group as *Gryllacris tessellata*, Drury, but readily distinguished by the total absence of black markings on the head and thorax, and by the colour of the tegmina and wings. It is probably more closely allied to *G. variabilis*, Brunner (Verh. Zool. bot. Ges. Wien., xxxviii, p. 353, fig. 40) than to any other described species.

"Appears to be a common species in Christmas Island, as one male and four females were obtained." (Lister.)

Taken on leaves on a tall tree-top, October 9th (Lister) ; Forest, East Coast, September, 1897.

Three specimens, a male and two females. (Andrews.)

Also two larval forms, from Flying Fish Cove, August, 1897. They are in spirit, and the present colours are as follows :—The larger specimen has the head and thorax light rufo - testaceous above, with the lower mouth-parts, and three spots between the eyes, whitish ; of these, the middle spot is rather long, and is deeply concave above, ending in a point on each side ; the lateral spots are nearly round, and each contains two black dots. The short wing-cases are black, and the back of the abdomen dark reddish-brown ; the under-surface of the body and legs are white, the coxæ and trochanters being marked with pale reddish ; the knees (except for a white spot on the hind tibiæ just in the joint) and the spines are black ; the four front tibiæ and their spines are reddish brown. The smaller specimen differs in being black above, except the three spots and the labrum and labium, which are white. In both specimens the middle of the abdomen is banded with black beneath.

Family CONOCEPHALIDÆ.

18. Pseudorhynchus lessonii.

Pseudorhynchus lessonii, Serv. : Ins. Orth., p. 511 (1839).
Conocephalus alienus, Wlk. : Cat. Derm. Salt., ii, p. 324, n. 14 (1869).

Flying Fish Cove, August, 1897.
Three male specimens. Originally described from Java.

Family LISTROCELIDÆ.

19. Phisis listeri. (Pl. XIII, Fig. 6.)

Phisis listeri, Kirb. : P.Z.S., 1888, p. 547.

" Long. corp. 15 mm.

" *Male.*—Pale green ; head and pronotum darker, with two conspicuous yellow lines, slightly convergent, running from the back of the eyes to the base of the pronotum ; suture of the tegmina yellowish, and the antennæ, legs, and under-surface of body likewise inclining to yellow ; four front femora and tibiæ armed with long slender spines ; hind femora considerably thickened before the middle ; hind femora and tibiæ with very numerous short spines.

" Three specimens, two immature (Lister). The adult specimen above described shows only three spines on the intermediate femora, but one of the others has four, showing that this is not a constant character. One of the immature specimens bears a label : ' Christmas Island, October 3. Colour grass-green.' The colour is now much mixed with yellow.

"Allied to *P. pectinata,* Guér., but considerably smaller than any of our specimens of that species."

One specimen, East Coast, September, 1897. (Andrews.)

Family PHANEROPTERIDÆ.

20. Psyra pomona, sp.n.

Long. corp. (absque ovip.) 26 mm.; cum ovip. 35 mm.; exp. tegm. 93 mm.; lat. tegm. 11 mm.

Female.—Body testaceous, more or less tinged with green (doubtless greener when alive); head whitish, almost ivory-white under the eyes and on the labrum; last joint of palpi green; antennæ green, becoming brown towards the extremity; scape testaceous. Thorax with the hinder third dark green, edged behind by a lighter carina, and in front, in the middle, somewhat blackish. Ovipositor green, about twice as long as the thorax, upcurved, and reddish brown on the upper and lower edges, towards the extremity, which are crenulated. Legs pubescent, with slender green spines, tipped with blackish. Tegmina unicolorous, bright apple-green; wings greenish hyaline, with green nervures, and tipped with green.

Two females came to lamp at night: Flying Fish Cove.

Allied to *P. ensis,* De Haan, but the antennæ are not banded, the tegmina are not spotted, and there are no dark markings on the legs, except that there is a darker green spot at the base of the front tibiæ. It is evident that Brunner's descriptions of the species of this genus are taken from more or less discoloured specimens.

Family LOCUSTIDÆ.

21. Oxya orientalis.

(Pl. XIII, Fig. 1, dark form; Pl. XIV, Fig. 2, typical form.)

Primnia (?) *orientalis,* Kirb.: P.Z.S., 1888, p. 549.

"♂ Exp. al. 44 mm.; long. corp. 26 mm.

"Grass-green; antennæ about twice as long as the head and pronotum, yellowish (faded?), the tips brownish; tips of mandibles and palpi dark green; vertex with four dusky lines approximating in front; the inner ones much nearer together than the space between these and the others, the transverse grooves on the pronotum black, the first shorter than the others, and ending in a dusky spot on each side, behind which is another dusky spot (between the second and third grooves); the second groove is angulated forwards at its extremities, ending in blackish spots; before the first groove runs a transverse reddish line, only distinct on the sides. Abdomen blackish above, green on the sides and beneath; a large dark-green spot beneath, towards the extremity of the eighth segment. Tegmina green, with many of the longitudinal nervures yellowish; the intermediate spaces inclining to hyaline beyond the middle. Wings smoky hyaline, with brown nervures; costal nervure yellow, and the nervures at the base and along the inner margin grass-green. Spines short, tipped with black, as well as the claws."

"Flew into light in tent (October 9th)." (Lister.)

Seven specimens: from Flying Fish Cove, October, 1897, and February, 1898; and East Coast, January, 1897. Common on herbage, especially near coast. The same remark applies to the two following species. (Andrews.)

These specimens apparently represent a duller form of the species than the type. Mr. Andrews informs me that they were brownish green when alive; they are now testaceous brown, with only the tips of the spines of the hind tibiæ black. The two females are larger and darker than the males, expanding 55–60 mm. They have some obscure brown markings on the back of the thorax, and the middle of the tegmina is longitudinally varied with light brown and yellowish for the basal third, and with light brown and pale testaceous beyond. The abdomen is black at the base for two-thirds of its length, and the hind femora are marked with two large brown patches, interrupted by the striæ on the outside, one near the middle, and the other towards the extremity.

22. Cyrtacanthacris disparilis.

Cyrtacanthacris disparilis, Kirb.: P.Z.S., 1888, p. 549.
C. fusilinea, Kirb. (*nec* Wlk.), l.c., 1888.

"Exp. al. ♂ 90 mm., ♀ 115 mm.; long. corp. ♂ 54 mm., ♀ 80 mm.

"*Male.* — Head and body yellow, inclining to reddish above; antennæ with the first two joints yellow, the remainder black above, beneath pitchy or yellowish; tegmina longer than the abdomen, yellow; the longitudinal veins darker; towards the tip the membrane becomes nearly hyaline, and many of the nervures are brown. Wings smoky hyaline, the nervures towards the base and costa yellow, the remainder brown; the nervures immediately at the base incline to reddish. Legs yellow, darker above; tarsi inclining to reddish, the joints sometimes marked with green; claws black at the tips; hind femora with three carinæ above, with short and distant serrations; these and the lower lateral carina are irregularly marked with black; the intermediate space above is slightly reddish, more so at two points than in others, which gives the appearance of two interrupted lines. Sutures of the knee-joint black. Hind tibiæ with a green spot at the base above, otherwise dull green; the under-surface yellow. Spines yellow, tipped with black; hind tarsi yellowish or reddish.

"*Female.*—Reddish brown, inclining to black on the upper part of the head and thorax; antennæ black (including the two basal joints), and pitchy towards the extremity; face reddish. The frontal concavity is black on the sides, but is filled up with yellow, which forms the front of a broad yellow stripe which runs to the extremity of the prothorax, of which the borders, and especially the lower hinder angles, are more or less yellow; the borders of this streak above, the facial carinæ, and a stripe under each eye are darker than the surrounding parts. Four front legs dirty green, varied with yellow; the arolia reddish; middle femora with a double row of yellow spots on the outside. Hind femora brown above and reddish beneath, with two blackish transverse bands above; the space between the lateral carinæ with oblique or oval whitish or pale-yellow marks, and a continuous yellow stripe on the under-surface. Hind tibiæ black above, with a yellow spot at the base, and brownish yellow beneath; spines yellow, tipped with black. Hind tarsi reddish, with a black carina above; tegmina brown, the interspaces more hyaline towards the tips. Wings as in the male.

"Allied to *C. melanocerus*, Serv. (*nigricorne*, Burm.), from Java and Malacca.

"I should not have ventured to place these insects together but for a memorandum which accompanied them, stating that they were found *in coitû* by Lieutenant Richardson near the shore of Christmas Island on October 1, 1887. Another specimen of the male was met with on October 2 at Flying Fish Cove."

Besides the above specimens contained in Mr. Lister's collection, I am now inclined to refer the insect which I formerly regarded as possibly *C. fusilinea*, Wlk., to *C. disparilis*.

Four specimens, one marked Flying Fish Cove, August, 1897, and another, December, 1897, were in Mr. Andrews' collection, as well as two dark female specimens, with the pale band on the pronotum entirely absent. They may represent a variety of this species, but do not appear to be specifically distinct.

23. Epacromia rufostriata.　(Pl. XIII, Fig. 2.)

Epacromia rufostriata, Kirb.: P.Z.S., 1888, p. 550.

"Exp. al. ♂ 43 mm., ♀ 40 mm.; long. corp. ♂ 20 mm., ♀ 22 mm.

"*Male.*—Testaceous, speckled with reddish and black; a small black spot beneath each eye; a black 'stripe (bordered above by a pale line, and suffused below) runs behind each eye to the extremity of the pronotum; it is intersected at the third groove of the pronotum by the pale line which runs below instead of above the hinder part of the black stripe, which is conical and more sharply defined than the rest; hind femora on the inside black for half their length, followed by a long black spot; the inside sutures of the knees are also black, hind tibiæ beneath black at the base and for the last three-quarters of their length; spines whitish, tipped with black. Tegmina testaceous, sub-hyaline beyond the middle, with reddish nervures; the basal half of the principal nervure black; wings clear hyaline, with pale nervures; several of the longitudinal nervures before the middle of the wing black for at least part of their length.

" *Female* similar to the male, but much redder, and hardly speckled; edges of the frontal concavity blackish, and from this run two slightly diverging blackish lines between the eyes and as far as the occiput. Markings of the head and pronotum nearly as in the male; sides of pronotum varied with yellowish. Hind femora red (very bright red beneath), and marked as in the male; hind tibiæ black at the base on the inside and beneath; the basal third otherwise yellow, the middle third black, and the apical third red. Spines white, tipped with black; extreme tip of hind tibiæ, including the base of the terminal spines, and hind tarsi, yellow. Tegmina and wings nearly as in the male, but the tegmina, and especially most of the longitudinal nervures, darker; many of the cross nervules, a short stripe before the middle above the principal nervure, and most of the nervures on the inner marginal region, are red.

"In both sexes the costa is moderately arched at one-fourth of its length.

"Not very closely related to any species previously represented in the British Museum." Captured October 1st. (Lister.)

One taken at Flying Fish Cove, October, 1897. (Andrews.)

CHILOPODA, DIPLOPODA, AND ARACHNIDA.

By R. I. Pocock.

(PLATE XVI.)

INTRODUCTORY REMARKS.

Up to the present time our knowledge of the Arachnid and Myriopod fauna of Christmas Island rested upon two collections. The first was made in January, 1887, by the officers of H.M. surveying vessel "Flying Fish"; the second in the autumn of the same year by Mr. J. J. Lister, when acting as naturalist on board H.M. surveying vessel "Egeria." The reports upon these collections, published in the Proceedings of the Zoological Society for 1887, p. 520, and 1888, pp. 556–561, contain references to one species of Scorpion, three species of Spiders, three of Centipedes, and two of Millipedes.

With the exception of the two species of *Cryptops* obtained by Mr. Lister, Mr. Andrews, during his stay on the island, rediscovered all the species that had been collected by his predecessors, and, in addition, supplemented the list by procuring one fresh species of Millipede, three species of Pseudoscorpions, one of which appears to be undescribed, and adult and identifiable representatives of six species of Spiders, as well as several other examples of this order unfortunately too immature for determination.

Quite sufficient material, however, has been procured to show that the fauna of the island bears unmistakable signs of derivation from that of the area of the Oriental region, represented especially by Burma and Java, lying to the north.

There is no evidence that any of the species have been introduced artificially. Indeed, the absence of such forms as the Spider *Heteropoda venatoria*, the Scorpion *Isometrus europæus* (= *maculatus*, De Geer.), and the Centipede *Scolopendra morsicans*, which accompany man in all his wanderings and establish themselves wherever the conditions of existence are favourable, seems to indicate that the species or their ancestors now found in the island crossed the sea that separates it from Malaysia by purely natural means—the Scorpions and the Myriopods and possibly some of the Spiders in connection, in all probability, with floating tree trunks or other vegetation; the majority of the Spiders, especially the web-spinning, bush-living species, on their so-called gossamer webs in the early days of their existence; and the Pseudoscorpions by clinging to the legs of flies or bees, or lurking beneath the elytra of beetles.

Class CHILOPODA.

Family CRYPTOPIDÆ.

1. Cryptops hortensis, Leach.

One specimen apparently identical with the typically Palæarctic species *C. hortensis*, collected by Mr. J. J. Lister. Mr. Andrews did not find this species.

2. Cryptops inermipes, Poc.

Pocock: P.Z.S., 1888, p. 556, fig. 1; Ann. Mus. Genova (2), x, p. 422, 1891.

This species was based upon specimens obtained in Christmas Island by Mr. J. J. Lister. It has subsequently been found by Sig. L. Fea upon Mount Mooleyit, in Tenasserim.

Mr. Andrews did not rediscover this species.

Family GEOPHILIDÆ.

3. Mecistocephalus castaneiceps, Haase.

Abh. Museum, Dresden : Chilopoden, p. 102, pl. vi, fig. 109.

Specimens taken by both Mr. Lister and Mr. Andrews. Originally recorded from Pulo Edam, off the north coast of Java ; also occurring in Table Island, Andamans (*E. W. Oates*), and in Rotuma (*S. Gardiner*).

Class DIPLOPODA.

Family STRONGYLOSOMIDÆ.

1. Orthomorpha coarctata (Sauss.).

Paradesmus coarctatus, Sauss.: Mém. Soc. Phys. Genève, 1860, p. 298.
Paradesmus vicarius, Karsch: Anz. f. Naturg., 1881, p. 38, pl. iii, fig. 8.
Strongylosoma poeyi, Bollman: Ent. Amer., iii, p. 81.

Not previously recorded from Christmas Island.
Universally distributed, and of common occurrence in conservatories in various parts of Europe.

Family CYLINDRODESMIDÆ.

CYLINDRODESMUS, Poc.

Cylindrodesmus, Pocock: P.Z.S., 1888, p. 558; Ann. Mag. Nat. Hist. (7), 1898, i, p. 329.
Haplosoma, Verhoeff: Zool. Anz., 1894, xvii, p. 8 (*nom preoc* .).
Haplodesmus, Cook: Ann. N. York Acad., ix, p. 4.

2. Cylindrodesmus hirsutus, Poc.

P.Z.S., 1888, p. 558, fig. 2 ; Ann. Mag. Nat. Hist. (7), 1898, i, p. 329.

Taken by Mr. Lister and by Mr. Andrews in various parts of the island.

The specimens of this Millipede collected by Mr. Lister were the only representatives of the genus known at that time. Within the last six years, however, two fresh species have been discovered. One of these was met with in Amboina, and was named *Haplosoma strubelli* by Verhoeff; the other, described by myself as *Cylindrodesmus villosus*, was obtained by Mr. Stanley Gardiner in the island of Rotuma. The specific features of the three are tabulated in my above cited paper in the "Annals" for last year.

Family CAMBALIDÆ.

3. Iulomorpha exocœti (Poc.).

Spirostreptus (Nodopyge) exocœti, Pocock: P.Z.S., 1858, p. 560. ·

Many specimens taken in and above Flying Fish Cove by Mr. Lister and Mr. Andrews.

The anterior legs in the ♂ of this species are five-jointed, not four-jointed, as in the species described by Porat.

Class ARACHNIDA.

Order SCORPIONES.

Family ISCHNURIDÆ.

1. Hormurus australasiæ (Fabr.).

Scorpio australasiæ, Fabr.: Syst. Ent., p. 309.

Collected by Captain Maclear and Mr. Andrews. "Always found under the bark of fallen tree trunks."

Abundantly distributed from Burma and Siam to the Polynesian Islands.

Order PSEUDOSCORPIONES.

Family CHELIFERIDÆ.

2. Trachychernes claviger (Thor.).

Chelifer claviger, Thorell: Ann. Mus. Genova, 1889, xxvii, p. 591, pl. v, figs. 5a, b.

A single example of this or of a closely allied species taken under the bark of a decaying tree above Flying Fish Cove.

C. claviger was originally recorded from Bhamo in Burma.

3. Chelifer javanus, Thorell.

Ann. Mus. Genova, 1882, xviii, p. 37, pl. v, figs. 20–22.

A single specimen, apparently identical with *C. javanus,* Thorell, taken on the north coast of the island.

4. Chelifer murrayi, sp.n. (Pl. XVI, Figs. 1, 1a.)

Colour tolerably uniform chestnut-brown, with paler legs.

Carapace entirely covered with fine granulation; sides of its posterior portion nearly straight and parallel, of its anterior portion somewhat abruptly converging in front; cephalic or anterior portion subglobose posteriorly, defined by a deep transverse sulcus, the external edges of which curve forwards above the lateral margin; ocelliform spots large and distinct, a row of six simple bristles along the anterior border between them. *Tergal plates* finely and closely covered with squamiform granules, each half transversely oblong and about four times as wide as long, a row of setiferous tubercles along the posterior margin, and two close together, one on each side of the middle line, and a few smaller scattered about; the whole abdomen narrow, nearly parallel-sided, posteriorly rounded. *Sterna* at most coriaceous; coxæ and maxillæ smooth.

Chelæ with humerus and brachium finely granular, sparsely setose; humerus subcylindrical, about three times as long as wide; brachium elliptical, elongate, also about three times as long as wide, scarcely longer and only a little thicker than the humerus; hand smooth, much wider than brachium, an elongate oval, nearly twice as long as broad, and about as long on the brachium; considerably longer than the movable digit. Process on tip of movable digit of *mandible* straight and cylindrical at base, curved slightly outwards towards the apex, where it ends in three short finger-like processes and a short thumb-like projection, the whole structure much resembling a four-fingered human hand.

Total length of body, 3 mm.

Our knowledge of the Oriental species of this group is still in its infancy, and the species here described will very likely be rediscovered in Burma, Sumatra, or Java, but it apparently differs from all the Indo-Malayan species described by Thorell (Ann. Mus. Genova, xxvii, pp. 591–606). For example, *C. birmanicus* has no trace of eyes and is quite smooth. *C. orites*, also from Burma, is allied to *C. javanus* in being smooth and in having the carapace entire. *C. sumatranus* has a different flagellum; and, lastly, both *C. hansenii* and *C. bisulcus* from Burma have the eyes very distinct, and not mere pale integumental patches, *bisulcus* in addition being smooth. *C. hansenii*, on the contrary, except so far as the eyes are concerned, is certainly nearly allied to *C. murrayi*, but differs also in the structure of the setæ and of the mandibular flagellum (see Thorell's figures, op. cit., pl. v, fig. 8).

The three species of Cheliferidæ obtained in Christmas Island may be determined as follows:—

    a. Carapace without eyes, but with two very strong transverse grooves; integument of dorsal surface coarsely granular, the bristles short and thickly clavate; coxæ of posterior legs enlarged; abdomen very broad . . *claviger*, Thor.

    b. Carapace with a pair of pale ocelliform patches, and at most one transverse groove; integument smooth, or at most very finely granular; bristles simple; coxæ of fourth leg not enlarged; abdomen narrow.

        a¹. Integument shining, smooth; carapace without transverse sulcus; chelæ much stouter . *javanus*, Thor.

        b¹. Integument finely and closely granular; carapace with a strong transverse groove defining the cephalic area; chelæ much thinner . . . . . *murrayi*, sp.n.

Order ARANEÆ.

Family DYSDERIDÆ.

5. Ariadna natalis, sp.n.

Colour.—Carapace castaneous, becoming gradually blacker in the -cephalic region; mandibles black; legs and palpi clear reddish-yellow, with the protarsi and tarsi of the first and second legs and the tibia and tarsus of the palpi blackish; abdomen a pale greyish-olive tint throughout.

Carapace slightly longer than patella and tibia of first leg, smooth, sparsely hairy; eyes of posterior line straight when viewed from above, slightly procurved from the front.

Legs.—Femur of first armed apically with six spines, three of which are longer and serially arranged on the inner (anterior) side; tibia armed below with seven to eight anterior and nine or ten posterior spines, mostly long, but a few quite short; protarsi armed with eight pairs of strong spines, some long, some short; tibia of third with two median inferior, protarsus with two median and two apical inferior spines. Patellæ of legs unarmed; fourth leg unarmed.

Measurement (in millimetres).—Total length, 8·5; length of carapace 4, of first and second leg about 8, of third 6, of fourth 7·5.

"Above Flying Fish Cove; on the ground under decaying tree trunks. In holes in limestone blocks, top of cliff, N.E. Point, about 600 feet."

Recognizable from its nearest geographical allies, the Sumatran *A. snellemanii*, Van Hasselt ("Midden Sumatra, etc., Araneæ," 1882, p. 37; see also Thorell, Ann. Mus. Genova (2), 1889-90, viii, p. 388), and from the Burmese *A. monticola*, Thorell (Ann. Mus. Genova (2), 1897, xvii, p. 190), in the following particulars:—

a. Carapace and abdomen black, tibia of legs of first pair armed with only 7-9 spines, six of which are arranged in three inferior pairs.

　　a¹. Protarsus of first with seven pairs, of second with five
　　　　　pairs of spines . . . . . *snellemanii*, V. H.
　　b¹. Protarsus of first armed beneath with only four spines,
　　　　　arranged 1, 1, 2, of second with five, arranged 2, 1, 2
　　　　　beneath and 1 in front . . . . . *monticola*, Thor.

b. Carapace ferruginous, with blackish head; abdomen olive grey, with silky lustre; tibia of first leg armed beneath with from fourteen to seventeen spines, biserially arranged; protarsi of first and second with eight pairs of inferior spines . . . . *natalis*, sp.n.

Family SCYTODIDÆ.

6. Scytodes (Dictis) venusta, Thor.

Dictis venusta, Thorell: Ann. Mus. Genova (2), 1889-90, viii, p. 301.

Several specimens apparently identical with *D. venusta*, Thorell, which has hitherto been recorded only from Sumatra.

Family PHOLCIDÆ.

7. Smeringopus elongatus (Vinson).

Pholcus elongatus, Vinson: Aran. des îles . . . Réunion, Maurice, et Madagascar, 1863, p. 135, pl. iii, fig. 5.
Pholcus distinctus, O. P. Cambr.: Journ. Linn. Soc., 1869, x, p. 380, pl. xi, figs. 28-30.

"Flying Fish Cove. In houses."

Widely distributed in the tropics of both hemispheres.

Family ARGIOPIDÆ.

8. Argiope reinwardti (Dol.). (Pl. XVI, Fig. 2.)

Epeira trifasciata, Doleschall: Nat. Tijdschrift Nederland. Indie, 1857, xiii (ser. iii, vol. iii), p. 416. Verh. Nat. Vereen. Nederland. Indie, 1858-9, v, pl. i, fig. 3 (*nom. preocc.*).
Epeira reinwardti, id.: loc. cit., p. 31, pl. xv, fig. 5.
Argiope doleschallii, Thorell: Remarks on Syn., 1873, p. 520; Ann. Mus. Genova, 1878, xiii, p. 38.

"Common everywhere; geometrical web in forest. Web furnished with narrow vertical white band of thick silk, crossing centre. Spider rests in form of an X."

Ranges from Java to Amboina.

In the typical Javan form of this species, as figured by Doleschall, the two anterior abdominal stripes are separated by a wider dark space than is observable in any of the Christmas Island specimens. Unfortunately we have scarcely any material from Java wherewith to test the constancy of this character in the typical form. But since in the Christmas Island form the two yellow stripes are sometimes in contact in the middle line, sometimes separated by a narrow space, it is justifiable to assume that Javan specimens will be found to vary in a similar way.

A figure of the species is published on Pl. XVI, as being the most beautiful and one of the most plentiful spiders on the island.

9. Cyrtophora unicolor (Dol.). (Pl. XVI, Fig. 3.)

Epeira unicolor, Doleschall : Nat. Tijdschrift Nederland. Indie, 1857, xiii
(ser. III, vol. iii), p. 149 ; Verh. Nat. Vereen. Nederland. Indie,
1858–9, v, pl. ii, fig. i. Thorell : Ann. Mus. Genova, 1878,
xiii, p. 52.

Abundant on the island.

Ranges from Ceylon to Amboina.

A full figure of this species is also published on Pl. XVI, as
forming a striking feature of the spider fauna of the island.

"Geometrical snare surrounded by mass of irregularly arranged
threads ; sometimes a number of spiders found together in large
compound web. Spiders always found in curled‑up dead leaf
towards outer part of snare."

10. Nephila nigritarsis, L. Koch.

Die Arachniden Australiens, i, p. 152, pl. xii, figs. 4, 4*a*.

Subsp. *insulicola*, nov.

= *N. nigritarsis*, L. Koch : Pocock, P.Z.S., 1888, p. 560.

Recognizable from the typical form which occurs in Queensland,
at least in having the anterior portion of the sternum entirely black
instead of being furnished with a broad yellow border.

Abundant in the island. Many specimens were taken by
Mr. Andrews and previously by Mr. J. J. Lister. "Makes
geometrical webs of yellow silk in the forest among trees and
bushes, sometimes at considerable heights from the ground."

11. Cyclosa mulmeinensis (Thorell).

Epeira mulmeinensis, Thor. : Ann. Mus. Genova, 1887, xxv, p. 221.
Epeira (Cyclosa) mulmeinensis, id. : Descriptive Cat. Spiders of Burma, 1895,
p. 192.
Cyclosa mulmeinensis, Simon : Hist. Nat. Araignées, 1894, i, pt. 3, p. 784.

"East coast. Geometrical web on face of limestone cliffs."

The Christmas Island specimens of this species seem to be
identical with those obtained by Mr. Oates at Tharrawaddy in
Burma, except that the abdominal tubercles are not apparent. The
prominence of the tubercle is probably dependent upon the degree
of distension of the abdomen, as is the case in *Cærostris* and some
other tuberculate spiders. When the spider is full fed and the
abdominal integument at its utmost stretch, the tubercles become
reduced or vanish altogether ; when the spider is killed in a fasting

state, the tubercles project more or less above the general level of the skin. A cluster of the cocoons of this species, strung together in the manner characteristic of the species of *Cyclosa*, was also procured by Mr. Andrews.

According to Simon this species occurs in India, Arabia, and South Africa, as well as in Malaysia.

Family SPARASSIDÆ.

12. Heteropoda listeri, sp.n.   (Pl. XVI, Figs. 4, 4*a–d.*)

Heteropoda venatoria (Linn.), Pocock: P.Z.S., 1888, p. 561 (not *venatoria*, Linn.).

Colour. — Carapace castaneous, with pale posterior transverse band; thickly clothed with hairs of almost a mustard-yellow hue at the sides, more rusty red above; mandibles black or ferruginous, the upper half thickly clothed with long yellow bristles; legs ferruginous, distally infuscate, clothed with yellowish-grey hairs, paler on the femora than on the tibiæ; sternum and coxæ deep reddish-black; upper side of abdomen covered with yellowish or reddish hairs in front, with darker hairs intermixed with blackish patches behind; lower surface darker in the middle than at the sides, the sides yellow, the median area greyish black or pale grey, with a pair of narrow darker lines.

Carapace a little longer than broad, low, longitudinally horizontal above, the ocular region lightly depressed; eyes of posterior line slightly recurved, their anterior edges nearly level, the median a little more than a diameter apart; eyes of anterior line nearly straight, their upper edges in a straight line, the laterals only about one-fourth larger than the medians, the laterals only about half their diameter above the edge of the clypeus; carapace about as long as tibia of first leg, slightly longer than that of fourth, the width just about equal to tibia of third.

Legs 2, 1, 4, 3; the second overlapping first by more than the length of its tarsus, third just surpassing middle of protarsus of second, fourth surpassing third by about half the length of its tarsus.

Vulva (as in Fig. 4*a*).

♂ closely resembling ♀ except in length of legs; carapace about equal to half the length of the patella and tibia of first; third leg not reaching middle of protarsus of second.

Palpus (as in Figs. 4*b, c, d*).

Measurements (in millimetres).—♀ Total length, 19; length of carapace 8·5, width 8, length of first leg 34, of second 38, of third 31, of fourth 32, of palpus 11. ♂ Total length, 16·5; length of carapace 8·5, of first leg 44, of second 52, of third 39, of fourth 38, of palpus 11.

M

"Common on the island. Found under loose bark; also in tent at night and in roof of outbuildings, etc."

A single mutilated female example of this species was brought by Mr. J. J. Lister from Christmas Island in 1888, and wrongly identified by me as *H. venatoria*, L. An examination of well-preserved material, consisting of both young and adults of both sexes, proves the species to be quite distinct from *venatoria*. It differs from all the known species of *Heteropoda*, in having the upper half of the mandibles thickly clothed with long hairs, with the apical half naked, exactly as occurs in the genus *Panaretus*. In this particular it constitutes an intermediate link between *Panaretus* and *Heteropoda*, both of which are represented by several species in the Malaysian area. From the known species of *Panaretus*, *H. listeri* differs in having the posterior portion of the carapace as high and not higher than the anterior.

In addition to the large specimens of this species described above and figured, Mr. Andrews procured a number of small examples of *Heteropoda*, containing both adults and young, which at first sight appear to belong to a distinct species. But since the vulva and palpi are practically identical in structure with those of the larger examples, I conclude that the smaller examples are merely dwarfed representatives of the same species as the larger.

In addition to the spiders above recorded Mr. Andrews brought back—

1. A single sub-adult female trapdoor spider belonging to the family Barychelidæ and possibly referable to the genus *Encyocrypta*. The arrangement of the eyes is less specialized than in that genus, the anterior laterals being further apart. But this primitiveness in the eyes in the Christmas Island specimen is probably to be attributed to immaturity.

2. Several sub-adult specimens of what is probably a new species of *Xysticus*.

3. Immature specimens of a species of *Araneus* — perhaps *A. nauticus*, L. K.

4. A single adult female referable to the genus *Lithyphantes*.

5. A few immature specimens of a species of *Oxyopes*.

6. Several small Attidæ of various kinds, which I refrain from determining.

LAND CRUSTACEA.

By C. W. ANDREWS, B.Sc., F.G.S.

THE land Crustacea are a very important factor in the fauna of the island. They seem to act as the chief scavengers, destroying both animal and vegetable refuse, while the little red crab (*Gecarcinus lagostomus*) to some extent takes the place of earthworms, in loosening the surface soil and incorporating with it the decaying vegetable matter.

I am indebted to Professor Jeffrey Bell and Mr. R. I. Pocock for the determination of the species noticed below.

Family GECARCINIDÆ.

1. Gecarcinus lagostomus, M.-Edw.

Gecarcinus lagostoma, M.-Edw., Hist. nat. Crust., vol. ii (1837), p. 27.
Hylæocarcinus natalis, Pocock, P.Z.S., p. 561, 1888.

In his account of the Crustacea of Christmas Island collected by Mr. J. J. Lister, Mr. R. I. Pocock described as new a small crab, to which he gave the name *Hylæocarcinus natalis*. At the same time he pointed out that the genera *Hylæocarcinus* of Wood-Mason and *Limnocarcinus* of De Man are probably identical, and suggested that the differences between them depend on age.

In the present collection a number of large bright-red crabs, here referred to *Gecarcinus lagostomus*, are undoubtedly the adult of *Hylæocarcinus natalis*.

This is the commonest of the land-crabs inhabiting the island, and is found in great numbers everywhere, even on the higher hills and the more central portion of the plateau. In many places the soil is honeycombed by its burrows, into which it rapidly retreats when alarmed. These crabs seem to feed mainly on dead leaves, which they carry in one claw, held high over the back, and drag down into the burrows. From their enormous numbers they must play a great part in the destruction of decaying vegetable matter and its incorporation into the soil.

Once a year, during the rainy season, they descend to the sea to deposit their eggs, and during this migration hundreds may be seen on every path down steep slopes, and many descend the cliff-face itself. They remain on the beach for a week or two, and deposit their eggs among stones in shallow water inside the reef. Afterwards they gradually make their way back to their accustomed homes. In the year of my visit this migration occurred in January.

2. Cardisoma carnifex (Herbst).

Cancer carnifex, Herbst, Naturgesch. der Krabben und Krebse, vol. ii (1794), p. 163, pl. xli, fig. 1.

This species is now recorded from the island for the first time, the reason why it was not seen by previous collectors being that it occurs only in the neighbourhood of small fresh-water streams which up to the time of my visit had not been explored. In this island, at any rate, this species must be regarded as a fresh-water form, and, in fact, when a specimen was seen it might be taken as an indication that fresh water was not far off. It lives in deep holes in the mud at the sides and bottom of the brooks, and is especially common near the stream about two miles north of Steep Point. (See map.)

Its colour when living is a uniform light slate-grey. This form seems to differ slightly both in colour and in the proportions of its carapace from specimens in the Museum Collection from Tahiti, which have been referred to the same species.

Family OCYPODIDÆ.

3. Ocypoda ceratophthalma (Pallas).

Cancer ceratophthalma, Pallas, Spicilegia Zoologica, 1772, p. 83, pl. v, figs. 7, 8.

This crab is rather common on the shore platform at Flying Fish Cove, where it lives under the blocks of stone, which are strewn at the foot of the cliff.

Family CŒNOBITIDÆ.

4. Birgus latro (Linn.).

Cancer latro, Linn., Syst. Nat., 12th ed., 1766, p. 1049.

This species is found in abundance all over the island, even in the densest parts of the forest on the central plateau. If in any spot none are visible it is only necessary to stand still for a short time before several may be seen approaching rapidly from various directions. As they come near they advance more slowly and with caution, the antennæ continually moving up and down alternately on opposite sides. On the least alarm they scuttle backwards in a succession of ungainly jerks, caused by the thrusts of the long front walking-legs, and as soon as possible they push the unprotected hinder part of their body into any hole or crevice in tree or rock that they can reach.

In defending themselves they seem to rely chiefly on the first pair of walking-legs, which are long and terminate in sharp points; these the crab raises over its back and then strikes downward with both sides at once. The chelæ are extremely powerful, and are used with great effect when an opportunity occurs.

These crabs eat fruits, the pith of the sago-palm and the screw-pines, dead rats and other carrion, and any of their fellows that may have been injured. They frequently ascend trees to a great height in search of food, and occasionally dozens may be seen round a sago-palm of which the fruit is ripening, some ascending and descending the trunk, others eating the fallen fruit.

After dark, as a rule, these crabs cease to wander about, and I found that many of them, particularly the smaller ones, climb a short distance up tree trunks or into low bushes, probably to escape being disturbed by the rats. In moonlight and in the light of the camp-fire they may keep moving all the night.

They are excellent scavengers, and have a curious habit of often dragging their food long distances before attempting to eat it. I have seen a crab laboriously pulling a bird's wing up the first inland cliff, half-a-mile or more from the camp whence it had stolen it.

I never saw one of these crabs voluntarily enter the sea, and they do not appear to migrate to it for the purpose of laying their eggs. At the beginning of the year numerous females carrying large masses of eggs were seen at long distances from the coast and on the highest ground; and about the same time young crabs not more than an inch or two long, but otherwise like the adults, were fairly common. Mr. Andrew Clunies-Ross told me that he believes the eggs are hatched out while the females are buried in holes in the ground. During the wet season both sexes seem to bury themselves temporarily while casting their shell.

5. Cœnobita clypeata (Herbst).

Cancer clypeatus, Herbst, Nat. Krabben und Krebse, ii, 1796, p. 22, pl. xxiii, fig. 2.

This large hermit crab is found in considerable numbers; it is commonest on the lower terraces near the sea, though not unfrequently met with in the higher parts of the island. It usually inhabits large *Trochus* shells, and the occurrence of these on the hills far from the sea was difficult to account for until this circumstance was noticed. These crabs, like *Birgus*, are good climbers; they ascend steep rock faces and get into small trees and bushes in search of food: when disturbed, they let themselves fall at whatever height they may be.

There are several other species of hermit crabs living on the beaches, but since these belong rather to the marine fauna they need not be noticed here.

A small fresh-water Crustacean, apparently an Amphipod, was collected from the mud of a small stream on the East Coast; unfortunately these specimens have been lost.

VERMES.[1]

ON THE EARTHWORMS FROM CHRISTMAS ISLAND.

By DANIEL ROSA, D. Sc.,
Assistant in the Royal Zoological Museum, Turin.

1. Pontodrilus ephippiger, D. Rosa (1898). (Figs. 1, 2.)

D. Rosa: Ann. Mag. Nat. Hist. [7], vol. ii (1898), p. 281, pl. ix, figs. 4, 5.

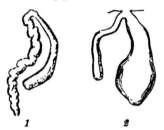

Pontodrilus ephippiger, D. Rosa (1898).

FIG. 1. Prostate.
,, 2. Spermatheca.

Hab.—Christmas Island (near small stream on east coast).

The length of our specimens ranges from 43 to 47 mm., with a diameter of 3 mm.; the number of segments varies from 85 to 100; the colour (in spirit) is an intense yellow.

The prostomium is short, only slightly dovetailed in the peristomium, which is longer than the second segment.

The setæ are distant: behind the clitellum the ventral interval *aa* is twice that between setæ *ab*; the lateral intervals between setæ *ab*, *bc*, *cd* are about equal, though slightly increasing from below upwards; the dorsal middle space *dd* is about three times as wide as *cd*. These distances vary slightly in front of the clitellum; for instance, at the height of the spermathecæ the setæ *bc* are slightly wider apart than setæ *ab* or *cd*, so that the setæ are here paired, though, of course, not very close together.

The clitellum extends over segments 13–17 = 5; it may be termed saddle-shaped, ceasing near the outer ventral seta (*b*): this clitellum is well developed dorsally, where its rings are completely fused together, while on the ventral area the setæ as well as the intersegmental furrows are tolerably visible.

There is a deep transverse fossa on segment 18; the transverse

---

[1] Reprinted, by permission, from Ann. Mag. Nat. Hist. [7], vol. ii (1898), p. 281, pl. ix, figs. 4–7.

margins of this fossa show a slight inward convexity, but are not specially swollen, whereas the longitudinal margins, which overhang the fossa, are in fact the ventral end of a pair of large glandular swellings which are also visible from the dorsal side, where they gradually disappear near the outermost setæ (*d*). The whole has much the appearance figured by Akira Jizuka for *P. matsushimensis*. The male openings are difficult to see, lying in the fovea at the base of the overhanging walls, approximately in a line with the outer ventral seta (*b*).

A deep slit-like sucker, with pale, somewhat raised margins, lies ventrally on the intersegmental furrow between segments 19 and 20, reaching laterally the line of the innermost ventral setæ.

The oviducal openings are two minute pores on the anterior part of segment 14, almost in a line (though a little ventrad) with the innermost ventral setæ (*a*).

The spermathecal pores are on small projecting tubercles between segments 7–8 and 8–9, on a line with the outer ventral setæ (*b*).

There are no dorsal pores. The nephridio-pores lie at the level of the outer ventral setæ, but I could not determine which segment bears the first of them.

Septa 5–6 to 8–9 inclusive are thin; the following, 9–10, 10–11, 11–12, and also, but to a less degree, 12–13, are thickened.

A gizzard is not recognizable, but septum 6–7 is more deeply infundibulate than its neighbours, and we may connect this with the earlier existence of a gizzard in the 6th segment. There are no calciferous glands; the intestine begins behind the 18th segment, perhaps in 16 or 17.

· The hearts occupy segments 11, 12, 13, the last being the largest.

The two pairs of large spermathecæ belong to segments 8 and 9; each spermatheca consists of a pyriform pouch not distinctly marked off from its duct, and of a narrow tubular diverticule which is longer than the main pouch.

The broad grape-like ovaries are readily seen in segment 13, as well as the testes in segments 10 and 11, all these gonads being attached to the anterior septum on each side of the neurochord. In front of the gonads, that is, on the anterior face of septa 10–11, 11–12, and 13–14, the funnels of both pairs of vasa deferentia and of the oviduct are plainly visible.

The small sperm-sacs in segments 11 and 12 have a botryoidal appearance.

The prostates occupy segments 16, 17, and 18, and recall very nearly those of *P. insularis* (Rosa). Their glandular portion has the appearance of a large sausage - like body, formed by the apposition of the several parts of a slightly - coiled lesser duct. The muscular duct which arises from the front end of the glandular tube is moderately bent, with the convexity inwards, and gradually increases in diameter as it proceeds backwards, reaching at last the external openings on the 18th segment.

I could not see exactly where the vas deferens joins the prostate, but I have little doubt that the connection between both structures will be found to be the same as that which has been described by Akira Jizuka for *P. matsushimensis.*

Our species seems to be closely allied to *P. insularis* (Rosa), which I first described from specimens obtained in the Aru Islands,[1] and which has been more recently found also at Ceylon (Michaelsen).[2] Still, a marked difference between the two species exists, as in the spermathecæ of *P. insularis* both Michaelsen and I failed to find any diverticulum. Our specimens were not fully mature, but on the hypothesis of an identity between these two species it seems highly improbable that even in a series of sections no traces could be found of an organ which in the adult reaches so great a development. Moreover, in the descriptions of *P. insularis* no mention is made of a ventral sucker.

Another allied species is undoubtedly *P. matsushimensis,* for a clear description of which we are indebted to Akira Jizuka.[3] However, this Japanese *Pontodrilus* seems to be really different from our species.

First, it is a larger species than ours, as its length ranges from 90 to 110 mm., with a diameter of 3–3·5 mm. ; while our specimens, with a diameter, too, of 3 mm., have only a length of 43–47 mm. Besides, it may be noted that the clitellum of *P. matsushimensis* is described as being well developed all round the body (and the same is shown by the figures), whilst in our species the clitellum is distinctly saddle-shaped. Finally, the appearance of the prostate is (so far as one can judge from the figures) somewhat different.

2. Perichæta brevis, D. Rosa (1898). (Figs. 3, 4.)

D. Rosa: Ann. Mag. Nat. Hist. [7], vol. ii (1898), p. 283, pl. ix, figs. 6, 7.

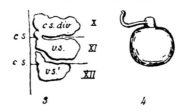

Perichæta brevis, D. Rosa (1898).

Fig. 3. Sperm-sacs (*vs.*), sperm-reservoirs (*cs.*), and diverticulum (*cs.div.*).
  ,,   4. Spermatheca.

---

[1] Ann. d. naturh. Hofmuseum, Wien, Bd. vi, 1895.
[2] Mitth. aus. d. naturhistor. Museum, xiv (Hamburg, 1897).
[3] Annotationes Zoologicæ Japonenses, vol. ii, pars 1 (Tokyo, 1898).

Hab.—Christmas Island (near small stream on east coast).

A very small species, measuring only 15–20 mm. in length by a diameter of 2–2·5 mm.; it consists of about 70–80 segments; the colour (in spirit) is a deep yellow.

The setæ on segment 25 are approximately 50.

The clitellum occupies somites 14, 15, 16.

The male pores are on high conical and almost lateral porophores, which are partially visible from behind. The boundaries of these porophores are laterally indistinct; in front and behind they are marked by the intersegmental furrows 17–18 and 18–19, which are here deflected. Fourteen setæ are visible between the male pores.

The oviducal pore is single and lies in a whitish spot on the 14th segment.

There are three pairs of spermathecal pores between somites 5–6, 6–7, and 7–8, close to the lateral line.

I have not been able to determine the position of the first dorsal pore. There are no copulatory papillæ.

None of the septa are noticeably thick and none are wanting.

The gizzard is between conical and tun-shaped; it is as long as two somites, but is nevertheless comprised between septa 7–8 and 8–9; this last septum is pushed backwards and comes nearly in contact with septum 9–10.

The last heart lies in segment 13.

The spermathecæ lie in segments 6, 7, 8; each consists of a nearly globular sac with a short narrow duct, which is connected at the inner side with a narrow tubular diverticulum; this diverticulum is straight, not enlarged at the end, and extends a little over the middle of the large sac.

The sperm-sacs in segments 11 and 12 are each connected with a minute sperm-reservoir; the sperm-reservoirs of the 10th segment are laterally produced into a large lobe, which looks exactly like another pair of sperm-sacs, but it should be mentioned that the true sperm-sacs lying in segment 10 prove to be connected with the sperm-reservoirs of the 11th, and not with those of the 10th segment.

The prostates extend through six segments; they are very irregular in shape and consist of many lobules, which are only loosely connected; the ejaculatory duct is of moderate length, sigmoid, and does not open into a muscular bulb.

This species somewhat recalls *P. acrophyla*, Rosa,[1] from Sumatra.

---

[1] Ann. Mus. Civ. Genova, vol. xvi, 1896.

3. Perichæta posthuma, Vaill.

Vaillant: Ann. Sci. Nat., 1868, p. 228.

The distribution of this species, according to Beddard, is Celebes, Philippines, India, Bahamas.

4. Megascolex armatus (Bedd.).

Perichæta armata, Beddard: Ann. Mag. Nat. Hist. [5], vol. xii (1883), p. 216.
Megascolex armatus, Rosa: Mus. Civ. Genova, vol. vii (2a), 1889, p. 139.

Hab.—Calcutta, Burmah, Labuan (Borneo), Seychelles, Nias.

BOTANY.

DICOTYLEDONS.

POLYPETALÆ.

By Edmund G. Baker, F.L.S., of the Botanical Department.

(PLATE XVII.)

MENISPERMACEÆ.

1. Tiliacora racemosa, Colebr., forma.

Distrib.—India, Ceylon, Java.

CAPPARIDEÆ.

2. Pedicellaria pentaphylla, Schrank (*Gynandropsis pentaphylla*, DC.).

Settlement No. 84.
Distrib.—Widely spread in tropics.

PITTOSPOREÆ.

3. Pittosporum nativitatis, sp.nov. (Plate XVII.)

Arbor humilis. Ramuli divaricati cortice griseo. Folia apices ramulorum versus subverticillatim disposita ; lamina oblonga vel oblongo-lanceolata utrinque glabra in petiolum attenuata apice acuta penninervia subcoriacea modice petiolata margine integra vel subintegra. Inflorescentia pro genere aliquantulum insignis ; flores ad apices ramulorum subdense capitati-congesti ; pedicellis teretibus brevibus. Sepala lanceolata acuminata petalis breviora. Petala oblanceolata libera. Ovarium subsessile ; stylus brevis, subcrassus petalis brevior, stigmate terminali coronatus. Capsulæ subglobosæ coriaceæ bivalves.

Hab.—Christmas Island Plateau, East Coast. No. 150. In flower and fruit ; March, 1897.

Small tree. Branchlets divaricate. Leaves generally sub-verticillate near the ends of the branches; lamina oblong or oblong-lanceolate, subcoriaceous, penninerved, lateral nerves arching, sub-prominent below, glabrous, margin entire or sub-entire, lamina 3–4 ins. long, often about an inch wide at the broadest part, petiole ± ½ in. long. The flowers are in compact, many-flowered heads terminating branches; pedicels short terete; bracts narrow. Sepals acuminate about two-thirds the length of the petals. Petals free, oblong or oblanceolate, ± 3 lines long, ± ¼ line broad, somewhat hooded at the apex, three-nerved. Stamens five, shorter than the petals; filaments 1 line long or a little longer; anthers ± ¼ line long. Ovary hairy below, gradually tapering to a rather stout style which is less than 1 line long, stigma terminal capitate. Capsule bivalved or sub-trivalved, valves coriaceous; fruiting peduncles about 3 lines long. Seeds reddish-brown, hardly 1 line long.

Noticeable on account of the congested character of the inflorescence.

GUTTIFERÆ.

4. Ochrocarpus ovalifolius, T. And.

East Coast.
Native name: Nyamplon besar.
Distrib.—Malaya, Fiji.

5. Calophyllum inophyllum, Linn.

No. 46.
Native name: Nyamplon.
Distrib.—Widely spread in tropics.

MALVACEÆ.

6. Malvastrum tricuspidatum, A. Gray.

Also in the herbarium from Cocos-Keeling Island. H. O. Forbes, 1879. No. 135.
Distrib.—Widely spread in tropics.

7. Abutilon auritum, Sweet.

Rocky Point. No. 8*a*.
Distrib.—Widely spread in tropics.

8. Abutilon listeri, Baker fil.

Rocky Point. Flowers July and August. Previously collected by Mr. J. J. Lister. No. 8, No. 9.
Distrib.—Endemic.

9. Hibiscus vitifolius, Linn.

Shore terrace, North-East Point. No. 156.
Distrib.—Widely spread in tropics.

10. Hibiscus tiliaceus, Linn.

Nos. 49, 61, 122, 142.
Native name : Waroo.
Distrib.—A common seacoast tree in most tropical countries.

11. Hibiscus (Abelmoschus), sp.

Valley on west coast. Very rare. No. 58.
This may be *H. vriesianus*, Hassk., in Hoev. and De Vriese
Tijdschr. (1838-39), p. 263, a plant which I only know from the
description.

STERCULIACEÆ.

12. Kleinhovia hospita, Linn.

No. 57.
Native name : Laban.
Distrib.—Tropical Asia.

TILIACEÆ.

13. Berria ammonilla, Roxb., forma.

No. 6. North coast. Nos. 72, 153. Most valuable timber tree
on island. Has been called "Teak" in previous reports. The type
is figured in Roxburgh's "Plants of the Coast of Coromandel," iii,
t. 264 (1819). *Espera cordifolia*, Willd., in Ges. Naturf. Freunde
Neue Schr., iii (1801), p. 449, is probably an earlier name for
the above.
Native name : Boognor.
Distrib. (type). — Tropical Asia (var. *rotundifolia*, Bentham),
Cumberland Islands.

14. Grewia lævigata, Vahl.

No. 106.
Native name: Kayu Wangie.
Distrib.—Tropical Africa, India, Malaya.

15. Grewia, sp.

Near *G. oblongifolia*, Blume, but fruit is required. No. 72*a*.

RUTACEÆ.

16. Acronychia andrewsi, sp. nov.

Arbuscula cortice griseo. Folia trifoliolata; foliola oblonga vel -oblanceolata sessilia vel vix petiolulata petiolo longiora e basi acuta apice obtusa vel subemarginata penninervia chartacea glabra pellucido - punctata subtus pallidiora costulis patentibus ante marginem unitis tenuibus; petiolus communis canaliculatus. Paniculæ axillares sub lente pubæ adspersæ; bracteolæ circa basin pedicellorum breves ovatæ. Pedunculi quam petioli breviores. Calyx brevis lobis ovatis. Petala sub anthesi reflexa lanceolata apice apiculata. Filamenta basi ciliolata, antheris dorsifixis ovatis brevibus. Ovarium 4 - loculare globosum, stylo basin versus albo-pubescente.

Hab.—Christmas Island. Small tree, common, especially on the shore terrace. Native name: Kayu djerouk.

Small tree with grey cortex. Branchlets towards extremities pubescent. Leaves trifoliolate; leaflets oblong or oblanceolate, chartaceous, apex obtuse, base cuneate, lateral leaflets slightly smaller than central leaflets (reaching 2 ins. long), central leaflets 2½–2¾ ins. long, but probably longer when older; common petiole rather over an inch, petiolules scarcely any. The flowers are borne below the leaves in short axillary panicles (shorter than the common petioles); pedicels pubescent. Buds oblong - cylindrical. Calyx lobes short. Petals lanceolate ± 1·5 lines long. Filaments ciliolate near the base. Ovary 4-locular, style pubescent, stigma capitate.

Allied to *A. trifoliolata*, Miq., *A. minahassæ*, Miq., and *A. halmaheiræ*, Miq.

MELIACEÆ.

17. Melia azedarach, Linn. ?

In fruit. No. 151.
Native name: Wyndet.
Species uncertain in absence of flowers.

18. Dysoxylum amooroides, Miquel.

Tree reaching 150–200 feet. No. 36.
Native name : Pegou utan.
Distrib.—Java, New Guinea.

CELASTRINEÆ.

19. Celastrus paniculatus, Willd.

Small tree. Shore cliff, Rocky Point. No. 26, No. 75.
Distrib.—India, Malay Archipelago, Philippine Is.

RHAMNACEÆ.

20. Colubrina pedunculata, sp. nov.

Arbor humilis. Ramuli teretes læves apices versus pubescentes.
Folia membranacea ovata vel ovato-lanceolata acuminata vel subacuminata mucronata basi lato-cuneata vel rotundata penninervia
adultiora superne glabra subtus præsertim in costa venisque
strigoso-pubescentia modice petiolata margine integra vel sub-
undulata. Flores in pedunculo longiusculo axillari piloso pedicel-
lati. Calyx externe pilis inspersus; laciniæ ovatæ intus carinatæ.
Petala 5 disci carnosi pentagoni planiusculi ovario adhærentis
margini inserta, oblonga concava quam sepala breviora. Stylus
erectus trifidus; lobis obtusis intus stigmatosis. Capsula haud visa.
Hab.—Christmas Island, north coast, only occurring near settlement. In flower February, 1898.
Easily distinguished from *C. asiatica,* Brongn., and *C. javanica,*
Miq., by having a much longer peduncle.
Small tree. Leaves alternate membranaceous, ovate-acuminate
or subacuminate, margin entire or somewhat undulate, when fully
matured glabrous above and strigose pubescent below, especially
on the veins. Lamina 3–4 ins. long, 1½–2 ins. broad ; petiole
generally about ½ in. long.
Flowers in axillary cymes. Peduncles much longer than in
C. asiatica, Brongn., being from 1¼–1½ in., strigosely hairy, as are
also the pedicels. Calyx pubescent externally, lobes ovate, acute,
with internal keel. Petals shorter than the sepals, nearly 1 line
long, rather remote from each other, concave. Stamens about same
length as petals. Style erect, stigmas 3. Ovary immersed in the
disk semi-inferior. Fruit not seen.
The genus *Marcorella,* Necker, Elem., ii, p. 122 (1790), has been
placed by Mr. Jackson in the Index Kewensis as synonymous with
Colubrina. It is considerably earlier, but I have seen no authentic
material of this.

AMPELIDEÆ.

21. Cissus repens, Lam.

Phosphatc Hill.
Distrib.—Tropical Asia, Queensland.

22. Cissus pedata, Lam.

Nos. 59, 127.
Distrib.—India, Ceylon, Cochin China, Siam, Java.

23. Leea sambucina, Willd.

Native name : Chelenka.
Distrib.—India, China, Philippines, North Australia.
Leea horrida, Teysm., is recorded by Mr. H. N. Ridley.

SAPINDACEÆ.

24. Allophylus cobbe, Blume, forma glaber, Hiern.

No. 119.
Distrib. (type).—India, Indian Archipelago, North Australia, etc.

LEGUMINOSÆ.

25. Erythrina indica, Lam., forma.

Tree on north coast, common in places (one measured 18 feet in circumference); bark smooth, light grey. No. 62.
Native name : Dadup.
This plant approaches so closely in structure to *E. indica*, Lam., that I think it must be considered a form of that species. The calyx of *E. indica* is minutely five-toothed at the very tip, while the Christmas Island plant has three, or sometimes five, bluntish callosities. The standard is about 2 ins. long; the wings and keel are subequal, and ± 1 in. long.
Distrib. (type).—Sea-shores of South-East Asia, from Sunderbuns to Malay Archipelago and Polynesia.

26. Strongylodon ruber, Vogel.

Common near sea. No. 101.
Distrib.—Ceylon, Polynesia.

27. Galactia tenuiflora, W. & A.

Rocky Point. No. 4.
Distrib.—India, Siam, Malaya, Australia, and East Tropical Africa.

28. Canavalia ensiformis, DC.

Shore. No. 132.
Distrib.—Widely spread in tropics.

29. Phaseolus lunatus, Linn.

No. 93.
Distrib.—An American species now widely spread in Old World.

30. Cajanus indicus, Spr.

No. 100.
Distrib.—Cultivated widely in tropics.

31. Pongamia glabra, Vent.

Forest tree, hard wood. No. 31.
Native name : Kayu kwat.
Distrib.—On all coasts from Mascarene Islands to Malaya, North Australia, West Polynesia.

32. Inocarpus edulis, Forst.

Tall forest tree, common everywhere. No. 28.
Native name : Gatet.
Distrib.—Malaya, Polynesia.

33. Guilandina bonducella, Linn.

Distrib.—Widely spread in tropics.

34. Cassia siamea, Lam.

Small tree, flowering in January, near coast. Probably introduced. No. 103.
Distrib.—India, Indo-China, Malay Archipelago.

35. Entada scandens, Benth.

East coast.
Distrib.—Widely distributed in the tropics.

COMBRETACEÆ.

36. Terminalia catappa, Linn.

Large tree. No. 23.
Native name : Katapan.
Distrib.—Widely spread in tropics.

37. Combretum acuminatum, Roxb.

East coast; August. Climber. No. 41.
Distrib.—India, Malaya to Philippines.

38. Gyrocarpus asiaticus, Willd.

Flowering specimens. Also fruit specimens. Common near sea.
Seedlings soon occur in great numbers when clearings are made.
No. 140.
Native name: Buah ba-siap.
Probably synonymous with *G. americanus*, Jacq., Select. Amer.,
p. 282, t. 178 (1763). Comes into leaf January, flowering about
April. As soon as fruit is ripe leaves fall, and tree is bare from
June to December.
Distrib.—Widely spread in tropics.

39. Quisqualis indica, Linn.

Distrib.—India, Malaya, China, Philippine Islands, Tropical
Africa.

MYRTACEÆ.

40. Eugenia, sp.

Large forest tree. Flowers March, April. No. 162.
Native name: Gowok.
This plant requires comparison with some of the Miquelian types
contained in the Dutch Herbaria.

41. Barringtonia racemosa, Blume.

Nos. 13, 27, 38. Also spirit specimens.
Native name: Jamboe passagi.
One of largest and commonest forest trees.
Distrib.—Malaya, Polynesia.

LYTHRACEÆ.

42. Pemphis acidula, Forst.

Forming clumps on sea cliffs. Nos. 65, 116. Also in herbarium
from Cocos-Keeling Island. H. O. Forbes.
Native name: Kayu burung.
Distrib.—Tropical coasts of the Old World.

CUCURBITACEÆ.

43. Momordica charantia, Linn.

Nos. 47, 95, 80.
Distrib.—India, Malaya, China, Tropical Africa.

44. Melothria mucronata, Cogn.

Nos. 2, 59, 67, 70.
Distrib.—India, Malaya, Philippine Islands.

45. Melothria, sp.

Trailing on rocks, east coast. No. 113.

ARALIACEÆ.

46. Heptapleurum ellipticum, Seem. (?).

Climbing on trees. Common. No. 15.
The above species was recorded by Mr. Ridley for Christmas Island. Our specimens are in flower only, and fruit is required for confirmation of this.

GAMOPETALÆ.

By EDMUND G. BAKER, F.L.S., of the Botanical Department.

RUBIACEÆ.

47. Randia densiflora, Benth., laxior, var. nov.

Cymæ quam typi eæ laxiores, sed pedunculis pedicellisque longioribus. Flores majores. Calyx externe glaber dentibus brevibus. Corollæ tubus ± 2 lin. longus, ut in specimine typico interne hirsutus; lobis 4–4·5 lin. longis, antheræ ± 4 lin. longæ.
Hab.—Common everywhere. No. 5.
Native name : Coppee utan.
In the type the corolla tube is scarcely above 1 line long and the lobes 2·5–3 lines. The anthers are about 2 lines long.
Distrib. (type).—India, Hongkong, Malay Archipelago, North Australia.

48. Guettarda speciosa, Linn.

Large forest tree; common. East coast. Sweet-scented flower.
No. 40.
Native name: Melati.
Distrib.—Tropical shores of Old and New World.

49. Morinda citrifolia, Linn.

Small tree in Flying Fish Cove. No. 78.
Native name : Mungkoodoo.
Seems somewhat different from usual form of this plant, leaves
being narrower and flowers occasionally four-merous, but agrees
with a specimen so named in Herb. Banks. from Endeavour River,
New South Wales.
Distrib. (type).—India, Malay Archipelago, Australia, Pacific
Islands.

50. Saprosma nativitatis, sp. nov.

Frutex. Ramuli adultiores glabriusculi, juniores rufo-pubescentes.
Stipulæ interpetiolares opposistæ membranaceæ bicuspidatæ de-
ciduæ. Folia disticha e basi acuta oblonga vel oblongo-lanceolata
vel oblanceolata apice subacuta, breviter petiolata membranacea
subtus pallidiora supra glabra, subtus costulis utrinque 11–13 valde
patentibus ante marginem arcuatis et unitis cum costa prima breviter
rufo-hirsutis. Flores axillares sessiles. Calycis lobi ovati quam
corollæ tubus ± dimidio breviores, persistentes. Corolla infundi-
bularis fauce villosa lobis 4 oblongis vel oblongo-ovatis. Stamina
fauci corollæ inserta; filamentis pro genere aliquantulum longis.
Ovarium 2-loculare; stylus filiformis ramis 2 recurvatis. Semina
plano-convexa.
Hab.—Christmas Island. Above Cove. No. 79.
Small shrub with dark cortex, the younger branchlets covered
with dark rufescent pubescence, the older branches glabrous or
sub-glabrous. Leaves oblong, or oblong lanceolate, or oblanceolate,
lamina often about 1½ in. long and 5–7 lines broad at the widest
part, petiole short (1½–2½ lines long), penninerved, lateral nerves
11–13 arching and uniting before the margin, which is entire.
Flowers axillary, sessile, tetramerous. Calyx lobes reaching about
half the length of the corolla tube. Corolla infundibuliform, lobes
oblong or oblong ovate, tube about 1 line long. Anthers borne on
filaments which are longer than is usual in this genus. Ovary
two-celled; fruiting calyx persistent.

COMPOSITÆ.

51. Ageratum conyzoides, Cass.

Common on shore cliff. No. 48.
Distrib.—All hot countries.

52. Blumea spectabilis, DC.

Common on open spaces where trees have fallen. East coast.
No. 44.
Distrib.—India, Ceylon.

53. Wedelia biflora, DC.

Above East Coast Waterfall, near sea. No. 56.
Distrib.—Tropical shores of Eastern Asia.

54. Synedrella nodiflora, Gærtn.

Common on shore cliff, near Flying Fish Cove. No. 52.
Distrib.—India, Andaman Islands, Tropical America.

GOODENOVIEÆ.

55. Scævola koenigii, Vahl.

On sea cliffs; common near Flying Fish Cove. No. 17.
Native name : Kembang sabla.
Distrib.—Tropical East Asia, Australia, Polynesia.

MYRSINEÆ.

56. Ardisia complanata, Wall.

New South-East Road Plateau. Shrub 6–8 feet. No. 1.
"Small tree." No. 14.
Distrib.—Penang, Malay Peninsula, Java.

SAPOTACEÆ.

57. Sideroxylon sundaicum, Burck., ex descript.

Tall tree; common everywhere. Fruit eatable. Nos. 29 and 73.
Native name : Saoh.
Distrib.—Sunda Islands.

OLEACEÆ.

58. Jasminum sambac, Aiton.

Flowers rather larger than usual.
Distrib.—India, Java, Moluccas.

APOCYNACEÆ.

59. Cerbera odollam, Gærtn., forma.

Small tree, Rocky Point. No. 104.
This plant, as figured by Rheede in the Hort. Mal., i, p. 71,
t. 39, has long lanceolate or oblanceolate leaves. In the Christmas
Island plant the leaves are broader and shorter.
Distrib. (type).—India, Malay Archipelago, China, Australia,
Pacific Islands.

60. Ochrosia ackeringæ, Miquel, angustifolia, var. nov.

Folia quam ea typi longiora et angustiora. Drupæ 2 basi
connatæ divaricatæ conicæ 1½ poll. longæ.
Forest tree. Timber used for building. No. 35.
Native name : Gundra roussa.
Distrib.—Banka Islands.

ASCLEPIADACEÆ.

61. Hoya aldrichii, Hemsley.

Everywhere on trees and rocks ; flowers November–January.
No. 105. Mr. W. B. Hemsley briefly diagnoses this species in
Journ. Linn. Soc., xxv, p. 355. For an amplified description see
Mr. W. P. Hiern in Journ. Bot., 1898, p. 417.
Native name : Kembang jiwa.
Distrib.—Endemic.

BORAGINEÆ.

62. Tournefortia argentea, Linn. fil.

Common on sea cliffs. No. 137.
Distrib.—Ceylon, Australia, Malaya, Mauritius.

63. Cordia subcordata, Lam.

Near sea only. Very hard wood. No. 45.
Native name : Grongan.
Distrib.—South-East Asia to Australia and Sandwich Islands,
Tropical Africa.

64. Ehretia buxifolia, Roxb.

Small shrub, common on the higher parts of the island, where it
forms the worst of the undergrowth. The leaves are rather larger
than usual. No. 68.
Distrib.—Deccan Peninsula, Malaya to Formosa and Philippines.

CONVOLVULACEÆ.

65. Ipomœa pes-capræ, Roth.

This common plant of tropical sea-shores was recorded by Mr. Ridley from the island, but is not in the present collection.

66. Ipomœa (Calonyction) grandiflora, Lamk., forma.

Climbing on trees, north coast. Flowering in April.

This plant approaches very closely to *I. longiflora*, R. Br., the type of which is in the British Museum (Natural History) Herbarium. The leaves and sepals are similar, but the peduncles are longer. Robert Brown's plant came from the Gulf of Carpentaria, and Mr. C. B. Clarke, in Fl. Brit. India, iv, p. 198, unites it with *I. grandiflora*, Lamk.

Distrib. (of *I. grandiflora*, Lamk.).—Widely spread in tropics.

67. Ipomœa peltata, Choisy.

Creeper forming dense masses over low trees, middle of island.
Distrib.—Malaya, Madagascar, Fiji.

68. Ipomœa digitata, Linn.

Distrib.—Widely spread in tropical countries.

69. Convolvulus parviflorus, Vahl.

Trailing herb, White Beach at Settlement No. 33.
Distrib.—Widely spread in tropics of Old World.

SOLANACEÆ.

70. Solanum biflorum, Loureiro.

Middle of island.
Native name : Lombok utan.
Distrib.—Singapore, Malaya, East Ava.

71. Solanum ferox, Linn.

Top of first inland cliff. No. 74.
On road above Flying Fish Cove. No. 97.
Phosphate Hill Road. No. 99.
Native name : Terong glatet.
Distrib.—India, Java.

72. Physalis minima, Linn.

Phosphate Hill. No. 160.
Distrib.—Tropical Asia, Africa, Australia.

73. Datura alba, Nees.

On all coasts.   No. 117.
This species in the Flora of British India is considered a variety of *D. fastuosa*, Linn.
Distrib.—India.

ACANTHACEÆ.

74. Ruellia prostrata, Lamk., var. dejecta, C. B. Clarke.

Dipteracanthus dejectus, Nees.

Common in Flying Fish Cove.   No. 96.
Distrib.—East Africa, India, Ceylon.

75. Asystasia coromandeliana, Nees, forma.

Top of inland cliff, Steep Point.   In flower April 5th, 1898.
No. 154.
Leaves much larger than type, reaching 5½ ins. long at base, gradually narrowing to petiole.
Distrib. (type).—India, Malaya, Africa, Arabia.

76. Dicliptera maclearii, Hemsley.

Common on shore platform.   Nos. 20 and 22.
Distrib.—Endemic.

VERBENACEÆ.

77. Stachytarpheta indica, Vahl.

Settlement, Flying Fish Cove.   No. 29.
Distrib.—Tropical Asia and America.

78. Callicarpa longifolia, Lamk.

Small tree.   East coast, shore cliff, and near Flying Fish Cove.
No. 39.
Native name : Chendana.
Distrib.—India, West Malaya to North Australia.

79. Tectona grandis, Linn. fil.

This tree is recorded by Mr. Hemsley for the island, but it is not in present collection.   The so-called Teak of the island is *Berria*.
[I believe that this record is due to a mistake, and that *Tectona grandis* does not occur in the island.—C. W. A.]

80. Premna lucidula, Miq.

Small tree. First inland cliff. No. 103.
Native name : Kayu durie.
Distrib.—Java.

LABIATÆ.

81. Anisomeles ovata, R. Br.

Common on shore platform. No. 18.
Common on shore cliff. No. 34.
Distrib.—India, Malaya, China.

82. Leucas javanica, Benth., forma.

Shore above the Cove; common. No. 3.
Shore cliff, in clearings. No. 124.
The calyx is smaller and teeth shorter than in Horsfield's Java
specimens of this plant.
Some forms of *L. mollissima,* Benth., seem closely allied to above.
Distrib. (type).—Java, Philippine Islands.

APETALÆ.

By A. B. RENDLE, M.A., D.Sc., F.L.S.,
Of the Botanical Department.

NYCTAGINEÆ.

83. Boerhaavia diffusa, L., var. pubescens, Choisy.

Shore cliff, near Flying Fish Cove. No. 51. Common near
the sea; November. No. 101. On shore cliff; January, 1898.
No. 123.
Distrib.—Tropics generally.

84. Pisonia grandis, R. Br.

Large tree near sea; August to September. No. 19.
Native name: Ampol.
Distrib.—North Australia, Polynesia.

85. P. excelsa, Bl.

A tree, common everywhere, especially in middle of plateau.
No. 96. Flying Fish Cove; April, 1898. No. 159.
Native name: Jamboe.
Distrib.—Malay Islands.

AMARANTACEÆ.

86. Deeringia celosioides, R. Br.

Everywhere near cliffs. Flowering in August. Flowers red.
No. 22. East coast; first inland cliff. No. 114.
Distrib.—India, Malaya, Australia.

87. Celosia argentea, L.

Flying Fish Cove; introduced. No. 21. Flying Fish Cove;
common; December. No. 77.
Native name : Buntoot kuching.
Distrib.—Tropical Asia and Africa.

88. Achyranthes aspera, L.

Rocky point, shore cliffs; common. Three to four feet high.
No. 11.
Distrib.—Tropics.

PIPERACEÆ.

89. Peperomia lævifolia, Miq.

Centre of island ; on fallen trees; February, 1898. No. 145.
Distrib.—Java.

90. P. rossi, Rendle, sp. nov.

Herba parva, carnosula, repens, glabra, foliis oppositis, breviter
petiolatis, ellipticis, obtusis, obscure triplinerviis, frequentissime
et minute atro-punctulatis; spicis terminalibus, crassis, densifloris,
folia duplo excedentibus; bracteolis rotundatis, peltatis; ovario
obtrudente, rotunde-obovoideo, stigmate parvo, punctiformi, sub
apice lateraliter inserto; fructu brunneo, valde exserto, subgloboso,
apiculato, pericarpio punctato.

Shoots 3 to 4 ins. long by about 1¼ line greatest thickness;
leaves ¾ to 1¼ ins. long by 4 to 7 lines broad, on petioles 2 to 3 lines
long. Spikes reaching barely 2 ins. long by 1 line thick; peduncles
less than ¼ in. Bracteoles about ¼ line in diameter, punctulate
like the leaves. Fruit ¾ line long, pericarp scarcely fleshy, covered
with numerous small roundish warts.

The measurements in the above description are taken from a
moistened specimen ; the plants shrink considerably on drying.

Near the Polynesian *P. insularum*, Miq., but distinguished by
its fleshy habit and elliptical leaves.

LAURINEÆ.

91. Cryptocarya nativitatis, Rendle, sp. nov.

Arbor ramulis ferrugine - tomentellis, foliis breviter petiolatis, coriaceis, ovatis vel oblongo - ovatis, interdum lanceolatis vel oblongo - lanceolatis, apice acuminatis, uninerviis, supra glaucis, impresso-costatis, et manifeste reticulatis, subtus glabris cum venis prominentibus et dense prominulo-reticulatis; paniculis floribundis, rhachi ferrugine, ramulis et floribus subfulve-tomentellis, floribus subsessilibus, sesquilineis.

Leaves 4 to 6 ins. long by 1¼ to 2⅜ ins. broad, with 4 to 6 upwardly curving main lateral veins; ultimate meshes of reticulation small, but well marked; petioles ¼ to ⅓ in. long. Terminal panicles spreading, reaching 3 ins. long by 3¼ ins. broad, branches 2 ins. long or less. Perianth - segments oblong - spathulate, blunt, 1 to 1¼ line long; fertile stamens 9, anthers bilocular, the 3 inner extrorse, with a pair of shortly-stalked roundly cordate anther-like glands scarcely ¼ line long, the 3 staminodes (fourth staminal whorl) subsessile, triangular-ovate, acute, base cordate, apex hairy, ¼ line long. Fruit shortly ellipsoidal, about ⅓ in. long.

Approaches the North Australian *B. Cunninghamii*, Meissn., but is distinguished by its larger flowers and ovate leaves.

Phosphate Hill; April 25, 1898. No. 158.

Native name : Jamboo boolut.

92. Hernandia peltata, Meissn.

Large tree; common. No. 146.

Native name : Commendor.

Distrib.—India, Malaya, Polynesia.

Probably the *Hernandia ovigera*, L., of Hemsley's list.

EUPHORBIACEÆ.

93. Euphorbia hypericifolia, L.

Common on the shore and cliff. Nos. 10, 60.

Distrib.—Tropics.

94. E. pilulifera, L.

Shore cliff and terrace, Flying Fish Cove; common. No. 54. Coffee garden ; common. No. 51.

Distrib.—Tropics and subtropics.

95. Phyllanthus niruri, L.

Distrib.—Tropics.

96. Jatropha curcas, L.

Distrib.—Tropics generally.

97. Croton caudatus, Geisel.

Shore terrace, near North-East Point; December, 1897. No. 107. A single specimen, containing unopened male flowers.
Distrib.—India, Malaya.

98. Claoxylon rubescens, Miq.

Rocky Point; December, 1897. No. 112. North coast, February; plateau, March, 1898. Small tree, first inland cliff. No. 53.
Native names: Chundana, Kayu onjay.
Distrib.—Malay Islands to Polynesia.

99. Acalypha wightiana, Muell. Arg.

North-East Point; April, 1898. No. 157.
Distrib.—India, Java.

100. Cleidion javanicum, Bl.

Small tree, east coast, first inland cliff; August, 1897. No. 37.
Distrib.—India, Malaya.

101. Macaranga tanarius, Muell. Arg.

Tall tree; common everywhere. No. 64. Flying Fish Cove; February, 1898.
Native name: Kayu merah.
Distrib.—Malayan islands.

URTICACEÆ.

102. Celtis cinnamomea, Lindl.

Large tree, common everywhere. In fruit, February, 1898. Stinking wood. No. 63.
Native name: Kayu boussouk.
Distrib.—India, Malaya.

103. Sponia amboinensis, Decaisn.

Small tree, Coffee Garden; October, 1897. No. 32.
Distrib.—Tropical Asia, Australia, Polynesia.

104. Ficus retusa, L.

Common everywhere; January, 1898. No. 120.
Native name: Waringin.
Distrib.—India, Malaya to Australia.

105. F. saxophila, Bl., vel aff.

Distrib.—Java, Timor.

106. Cudrania javanensis, Trécul.

Thorny creeper. Plateau near south-east road; August, 1897.
No. 11.
Distrib.—Old World tropics.

107. Fleurya ruderalis, Gaud.

No. 134.
Native name: Pulus.
Distrib.—Malay Archipelago, Polynesia.

108. Laportea crenulata, Gaud.

No. 133.
Native name: Pulus.
Distrib.—India, Malaya.

109. L. murrayana, Rendle, sp. nov.

Arbor dioica(?), ramulis crassis, glabris, foliis petiolatis, paulo supra
basin rotundatam peltatis, late ovatis, acutis, glabratis, venis subtus
sparse stimuloso-pilosis exceptis, marginibus leviter undulatis,
siccis atro-viridibus et membranaceis; inflorescentibus fœmineis
axillaribus petiolos subæquantibus, pedunculis compressis vix alatis,
cum ramis ramulisque sparse stimuloso-retrorso-hispidis, floribus
capitatis; perianthii segmentis 4 inæqualibus, plus minus ovatis
vel ellipticis, acuminatis, dorso puberulis; achænio discoideo,
glabro, cum stigmate subulato terminato.

Leaves 3¼ to 7¼ ins. long by 2½ to 4¼ ins. broad, petioles 2 to 3 ins.
attached about ¼ in. above the base of the leaf, lateral veins about
six each side, subprominent below, curving and anastomosing
below the margin, united by regular scalariform secondary veins;
reticulations minute, obvious; cystoliths numerous, evident;
stipules bluntly ovate, sparsely hispidulous. Inflorescence to 2¾ ins.
long, lateral branches 1¼ in. and less; branchlets subterete; florets
sessile. Perianth-segments brown, ½ line or less; stigmas long,
ferruginously hairy; achenes ¼ line in diameter. Male flowers
absent.

Apparently near the Javanese *L. laxiflora*, Wedd. (from the description in DC. Prodr., xvi, i, 81), which, however, has leaves pubescent beneath, and the female inflorescence larger than the petioles.

Flying Fish Cove. A tree; leaves stinging severely. February, 1898. No. 147.

Native name : Jelaton.

110. Procris pedunculata, Wedd.

A shrub trailing over rocks. First inland cliff, No. 76. Near Flying Fish Cove, No. 91.

Distrib.—Malay Islands, Polynesia, Mascarene Islands.

111. Boehmeria platyphylla, Don.

Small tree, common everywhere. Stinging leaves; wood very soft; in flower all the year. Nos. 18, 60.

Native name : Pulus scrobbo.

Distrib.—India, Malaya, to China and Japan; Polynesia.

MONOCOTYLEDONS.

By A. B. Rendle, M.A., D.Sc., F.L.S.,

Of the Botanical Department.

(PLATE XVIII.

ORCHIDEÆ.

1. Dendrobium crumenatum, Sw.

Common everywhere on trees. No 110.

Distrib.—Malaya.

2. D. macrsei, Lindl.

The flowers are smaller than usual in the species, but I do not think the Christmas Island plant is specifically distinct.

Distrib.—India, Java.

3. Phreatia listeri, Rolfe.

Distrib.—Endemic.

4. P. congesta, Rolfe.

Distrib.—Endemic. A small orchid not found in the present collection.

5. Saccolabium archytas, Ridl.

Doritis, sp.n. (?), Rolfe in Hemsley's list.
February, 1898. On trees everywhere. No. 144.
This is obviously the plant of which fruiting specimens only
were collected, tentatively referred by Mr. Rolfe to *Doritis* in
Mr. Hemsley's list.
Distrib.—Endemic.

6. Sarcochilus carinatifolius, Ridl.

On trees everywhere. No. 143.
Flowering and fruiting specimens. Fruit just before dehiscence
a little over 2 ins. long, tapering regularly from 1¼ line diameter at
the apex; lobes of dehisced capsule 3¼ ins. long.
Distrib.—Endemic.

7. Corymbis veratrifolia, Reichenb. fil.

February, 1898. Common on higher parts of the island.
Distrib.—India, Malaya.

AMARYLLIDACEÆ.

8. Crinum asiaticum, L.

On cliff, North-East Point; March, 1898. No. 142.
Distrib.—Tropical Asia to Japan and North Australia.

PALMÆ.

9. Arenga listeri, Becc.

Didymosperma, sp. of Hemsley's list.
Common everywhere; flowering at all times. No. 109. Some-
times attains a height of 70 feet and a diameter of 13 inches.
Native name : Areng.
Distrib.—Endemic.

PANDANACEÆ.

10. Pandanus, sp.

Male spikes and leaves only. Apparently allied to the common
Indo-Malayan *P. odoratissimus,* Linn. fil.
Mr. Andrews states that there is another species of *Pandanus* of
which he was unable to procure flowers. It forms trees 40 feet high.

AROIDEÆ.

11. Remusatia vivipara, Schott.

Phosphate Hill Road. No. 115. January, 1898.
Distrib.—India, Malaya.

CYPERACEÆ.

12. Fimbristylis cymosa, R. Br.

Distrib. — Malaya, Australia, Polynesia. Not found in the present collection.

GRAMINEÆ.

13. Ischæmum foliosum, var. leiophyllum, Hack.

Flying Fish Cove. Common everywhere round coast. No. 23.
Distrib.—Endemic.
This is the *I. murinum*, Forst., of Hemsley's list; and is probably only a form of the common tropical Asiatic *I. ciliare*, Retz.
I. muticum, L., cited in Mr. Ridley's list, is perhaps a mistake for *I. murinum*, Forst.

14. Digitaria sanguinalis, Scop.

Common on shore cliffs. No. 25 (in part).
Distrib. —Universal.

15. Panicum (Effusæ) andrewsi, Rendle, sp. nov. (Plate XVIII.)

Planta minor culmis tenuibus, basi repentibus tum ascendentibus, usque paniculam foliatis; foliis lanceolatis, acutis vel acuminatis, basi oblique cordatis, sparse pilosis; panicula effusa, glabra, ramis solitariis, tenuibus, inferioribus ascendentibus, superioribus patentibus, ramulis filiformibus; spiculis longe - pedicellatis, ellipsoideis, parvis, glabris, gluma i^a quam gl. iii^a duplo minore, ovata, uninervia, vel obsolete 5-nervia; gl. ii^a obovata, obtusa, 5-nervia; gl. iii^a vix gl. ii^{am} excedente, late elliptica, obtusa, 5-nervia, paleam sterilem includente; gl. fertili coriacea, levi, convexa, elliptica, 5 - nervia, marginibus paleam subæqualem amplectante.
Shoots 6–8 ins. high, internodes short, 6–8 lines long by barely ¼ line or less in diameter, puberulous; sheaths subequal, striate, with pilose margins; ligule very narrow, membranous; blades 1–2 ins. long, 5–7 lines broad, papery, generally seven-nerved;

margins pilose below, becoming glabrous above. Panicle not fully developed, 3 ins. long by 1¼ broad; in Timor specimens 8 ins. long by 4 ins. broad. Spikelets ⅓ line long; barren glumes membranous, green, gl. i less than ¼ line long; gl. ii barely ⅓ line long, very bluntly apiculate, lateral nerves as in gl. iii submarginal; gl. iii ⅓ line, with an empty pale a little more than half its length; fertile gl. barely ⅓ line; grain unripe.

Resembles *P. arborescens*, L. (*P. ovalifolium*, Poir.), in habit, but differs in the much smaller lowest glume, and the shape and size of gls. ii and iii.

Hab.—Christmas Island, 1897. Also collected in Timor by Wallace and Curtis (in Herb. Kew).

16. Oplismenus compositus, Beauv.

Coffee Garden, Flying Fish Cove, and everywhere. Nos. 7, 128. No. 128 is viviparous.

Distrib.—Tropics generally.

17. Eleusine indica, L.

Common on shore cliffs. No. 25 (in part).

Distrib.—Old World tropics.

18. Eragrostis plumosa, Link.

Nos. 26, 138.

Distrib.—Tropical Asia and Africa.

GYMNOSPERMS.

By A. B. RENDLE, M.A., D.Sc., F.L.S.,

Of the Botanical Department.

CYCADEÆ.

Cycas circinalis, L., var. javana, Miq.

Flying Fish Cove, beach.

Grows all round the island; most plentiful on upper terrace (350 feet) at west end of south coast.

Native name : Penawa jambi.

Distrib.—Java, Sumatra, Borneo.

FERNS.

By A. GEPP, M.A., F.L.S., of the Botanical Department.

FILICINÆ.

1. Trichomanes parvulum, Poiret.

On trees, plateau; February, 1898.
Distrib.—East Asia, Malay Archipelago, Oceania, Madagascar.

2. Davallia solida, Swartz.

Common in forest, on trees; November, 1897. No. 82.
Distrib.—Malay Peninsula, Java, Polynesia.

3. Davallia dissecta, J. Sm.

Common on cliffs. No. 81.
Distrib.—Java.

4. Davallia speluncæ, Baker.

One frond.
Distrib.—Tropics and sub-tropics.

5. Asplenium nidus, L.

May, 1898.
Distrib.—Tropics and sub-tropics of the Old World.

6. Asplenium falcatum, Lam.

Common on trees; October, 1897. Nos. 83, 112.
Distrib. — Polynesia, Australasia, Malay Archipelago, India, Africa.

7. Asplenium centrifugale, Baker: in Journ. Linn. Soc., xxv, p. 360 (1890).

Distrib.—Christmas Island (J. J. Lister).

8. Nephrodium syrmaticum, Baker.

Common in forest. No. 87.
Distrib.—India, Malay Archipelago.

9. Nephrodium dissectum, Desv.

Common in forest. No. 88.
Distrib.—India, Malay Archipelago, Oceania, Madagascar.

10. Nephrodium intermedium, Baker.

Distrib.—India, Malay Archipelago, Japan, Christmas Island (J. J. Lister).

11. Nephrodium truncatum, Presl.

Panchoran; January, 1898. No. 121.
Distrib.—India, Malaccas, Australia, Polynesia.

12. Nephrodium polymorphum, Baker.

North-West Point; not common. No. 94.
Distrib.—India, Malay Archipelago.

13. Aspidium membranaceum, Hook.

Plateau, common; No. 12. On trees everywhere; No. 131.
Distrib.—Ceylon, Java, Philippines, West China, Formosa.

14. Nephrolepis exaltata, Schott.

North coast; December, 1897. No. 130.
Distrib.—Tropics.

15. Nephrolepis acuta, Presl.

Common in forest everywhere. No. 85.
Distrib.—Tropics.

16. Nephrolepis ramosa, Moore.

Climbing on trees and shrubs, common. No. 92.
Distrib.—Tropics of the Old World.

17. Polypodium adnascens, Sw.

Distrib.—India and China to Fiji; East and West tropical Africa.

18. Polypodium irioides, Lam.

Common everywhere on trees and rocks. No. 108.
Distrib.—India and China to Fiji and New South Wales; East and West tropical Africa.

19. Vittaria elongata, Sw.

Sine loc. No. 163.
Distrib.—India to Hawaii and New South Wales; East and West tropical Africa.

20. Acrostichum flagelliferum, Wall.

Rare; middle of island; No. 90. Phosphate Hill; January, 1898; No. 126.

Distrib.—Himalayas to Java and the Philippines.

21. Acrostichum listeri, Baker: in Journ. Linn. Soc., xxv, p. 361 (1890).

Common on higher parts of plateau; No. 19. Phosphate Hill; January, 1898; No. 125. *Sine loc.*; No. 129.

Distrib.—Christmas Island.

LYCOPODIACEÆ.

22. Lycopodium phlegmaria, L.

Middle of island; February, 1897.

Distrib.—Tropics of the Old World.

MOSSES.

By A. Gepp, M.A., F.L.S., of the Botanical Department.

1. Leucobryum chlorophyllosum, C. Muell.: Syn. Musc., ii, p. 535 (1851).

Distrib.—Sumbawa, Celebes.

2. Octoblepharum albidum, Hedw.: Musc. frond., iii, p. 15 (1792).

Distrib.—Tropical Zone.

3. Thyridium fasciculatum, Mitt.: in Journ. Linn. Soc., x, p. 189 (1869).

Distrib.—India, Malay Archipelago, Oceania, Chile, Mauritius.

4. Trachymitrium revolutum, Hampe: in Nuov. Giorn. bot. Ital., iv, p. 280 (1872).

Distrib.—Java, Borneo.

5. Neckera lepiniana, Mont.: in Ann. Sci. Nat., ser. III, x, p. 107 (1848).

Distrib.—Malay Archipelago, Oceania, Mauritius.

6. **Thuidium plumulosum,** Doz. et Molk. : Bry. Jav., ii, p. 118, tab. 223 (1865).
Distrib.—Ceylon, Malay Archipelago, Oceania.

7. **Hypnum montagnei,** Lac. : Bry. Jav., ii, p. 181, tab. 279 (1867).
Distrib.—Java.

HEPATIC.

Ptychanthus squarrosus, Mont.
Distrib.—Malay Archipelago.

LICHENS.

By VERNON H. BLACKMAN, M.A., F.L.S.,
Of the Botanical Department.

1. **Parmelia tinctorum,** Despr.
Distrib.—Wide. Asia, Africa, Australia, New Caledonia.

2. **Parmelia appendiculata,** Fée ?
Very poor specimen.
Distrib.—E. Africa.

3. **Physcia picta,** Nyl.
Distrib.—Very wide. Asia, Africa, America, Oceania (Java, Australia).

4. **Pyxine sorediata,** Fr.
Distrib.—Africa, S. America, Japan, Tahiti.

5. **Pannaria rubiginosa,** Del. ?
Poor specimen.
Distrib.—Very wide. Europe, Japan, Africa, America, Australia.

6. Lecanora varia, Ach.

Distrib.—Europe, Siberia, Algeria, Mexico, New Caledonia.

7. Ramalina fraxinea, Ach.

Distrib.—Europe, N. and S. America.

8. Lecidea lutea, Schaer. ?

Distrib.—Europe, Africa, Japan, S. America, Labuan, Sandwich Islands, New Zealand.

9. Leptogium phyllocarpum, Nyl. ?

Distrib.—Asia, Africa, S. America, Oceania (Java, Philippines, etc.).

FUNGI.

By Vernon H. Blackman, M.A., F.L.S.,
Of the Botanical Department.

BASIDIOMYCETES.

1. Schizophyllum commune, Fr.

Distrib.—Cosmopolitan.

2. Polyporus confluens, Fr. ?

Distrib.—Europe, N. America, Australia.

3. Fomes lucidus, Fr.

Distrib.—Of almost universal occurrence.

4. Fomes australis, Fr.

Distrib.—Europe, Borneo, Venezuela, Ceylon, Australia.

5. Polystictus flabelliformis, Kl.

Distrib.—S. America, Cuba, India, Ceylon, Malay Peninsula, Borneo.

6. Polystictus xanthopus, Fr.

Distrib.—In tropics generally.

7. Polystictus luteo-olivaceus, B. & Br.

Distrib.—Australia (Brisbane).

8 Polystictus sanguineus, Mey.

Distrib. — In tropics generally. India, America, Africa, New Zealand, Borneo, Tasmania, Philippines, Java, Pacific Islands.

9. Hexagonia polygramma, Mont.

Distrib.—Central America, Mexico, Cuba, India, Borneo, Ceylon, Australia.

10. Daedalea tenuis, Berk.

Distrib.—Philippines, Australia (Adelaide).

11. Favolus boucheanus, Klotzsch.

Distrib.—Europe, N. America, Australia.

12. Laschia cæspitosa, Berk.

Distrib.—Australia (Clarence River).

13. Hirneola polytricha, Mont.

Distrib.—Mexico, Cuba, India, Ceylon, New Zealand, Java.

14. Hirneola auricula-judæ, Berk.

Distrib.—Europe, N. America, Mexico, Cuba, Tasmania, Borneo.

15. Guepinia sparassoides, Kalchbr.

Distrib.—S. Africa (Kaffraria).

GASTEROMYCETES.

16. Cyathus montagnei, Tul.

Distrib.—Cuba, Brazil, Uruguay, Ceylon, Australia.

17. Geaster andrewsi, Blackm., n sp.

Exoperidium in statu humido subcarneum, in statu sicco coriaceum, multifidum, laciniis (circa 7) acutis, basi integra, extus pallidum, siccitate aspero et veniis instructum, intus leve, cinereum. Endoperidium globoso-depressum, sessile, papyraceum, cinereum; peristomio subconico, minute dentato, in centro areolæ circularis striatæ pallidioris posito; columella persistente, e floccis 3–3·5 μ latis, fuscis; sporis globosis, echinulatis, 3·5–4·5 μ diam., fuligineis.

Exoperidium 20 – 40 mm. latum (expansum), endoperidium 7–12 mm. latum.

This species is characterized chiefly by the nature of the peristomium, but the external veining of the exoperidium and the size of the spores also distinguish it from most of the Geasters.

ASCOMYCETES.

18. Trichoscypha tricholoma, Mont.

Distrib.—Rio de Janeiro, Guiana, Ceylon, Vera Cruz, S. Domingo.

HYPHOMYCETES.

19. Stilbum javanicum, Henn.

Distrib.—Java.

MYCETOZOA.

By Arthur Lister, F.R.S.

1. Stemonitis splendens, Rost., var. *a*, genuina.

Flying Fish Cove and Phosphate Hill.
Distrib.—Europe, America, Australia, Pacific Islands, Java.

2. Arcyria flava, Pers.

Distrib.—Europe, N. America, Java.

3. Lycogala miniatum, Pers.

Distrib.—Europe, N. and S. America, Guiana, Java.

PALÆONTOLOGY

AND

GEOLOGY.

FOSSIL MOLLUSCA FROM THE REEF-LIMESTONES
OF CHRISTMAS ISLAND.

By R. Bullen Newton, F.G.S.

The reef-limestones of Christmas Island have been referred to in
general terms by the few writers who have visited the region, but
we are indebted to Mr. C. W. Andrews, through collections made
in 1897–98, for our first knowledge of the palæontology of this
formation.

Among the specimens brought home from these deposits were
a small number of shells, which, although of rather bad preservation, and many of them not specifically determinable, are more
or less important as a contribution to the Quaternary history of
this area.

The identifications that have been possible appear to prove
conclusively the modern character of these rocks, the species being
inhabitants of the surrounding seas at the present day.

MOLLUSCA : GASTEROPODA.

Genus **TECTUS**, De Montfort, 1810.

Conchyliologie Systématique, 1810, vol. ii, p. 186.

Type.—*Tectus pagodalis*, De Montfort = *Trochus mauritianus*,
Gmelin.

Synonyms.—*Pyramis*, Schumacher, 1817 ; *Pyramidea*, Swainson,
1840.

Tectus pyramis, Born.

G. W. Knorr: Vergnügen Sammlung Muscheln, 1757, vol. i, pl. xii, fig. 4.
Trochus pyramis, Born: Testacea Musei Cæsarei Vindobonensis, 1780, p. 333;
        Chemnitz, Conchylien-Cabinet, 1781, vol. v, pl. 160, figs.
        1510–1512, p. 19.
Trochus obeliscus, Gmelin: Systema Naturæ, 1790, 13th ed., vol. i, pt. 6, p. 3579.
Tectus obeliscus, G. W. Tryon: Manual of Conchology, 1889, vol. xi, p. 19,
        pl. ii, figs. 13, 14.

Description.—Born's original diagnosis of this Trochiform shell expresses very clearly the salient characters of the species. It is as follows: "*Testa conica, acuminata, anfractibus imbricatis, seriatim granulosis, columella torta, imperforata.*"

Remarks.—An undoubted specimen of this species has been obtained from the limestone reefs of Christmas Island. It is a tall, conical form, with about twelve or more somewhat flattened whorls, the upper ones being tuberculate or undulating at the suture. The surface of the whorls is ornamented with a regular series of spiral granulations, which on the last whorl are arranged in eight or nine rows; the periphery is obtusely acute. The base of the shell is flat, wide, and sculptured with concentric lirations, which become obsolete near the outer margin. The shell possesses a shallow, subtriangular aperture and a short twisted columella. No internal characters of the mouth are visible, being hidden by matrix.

Dimensions.—Length 80, diameter 80 mm.

Tryon's illustration (fig. 14, see Synonymy) gives an excellent idea of the specimen from Christmas Island.

Distribution.—Indian and Pacific Oceans; Samoan, Viti, and Philippine Islands, New Caledonia; North Australia, etc.; Singapore. (Tryon.)

Locality.—Flying Fish Cove; found in the lowest raised reef.

Number on specimen: 609.

Examples: 1.

Tectus ?

Remarks.—A fragmentary cast, probably of this genus, occurs embedded in a pink-coloured limestone associated with remains of corals, etc. It is not specifically determinable.

Locality.—Top of first inland cliff, about 300 feet above sea-level.

Number on specimen: 951.

Examples: 1.

Genus TUTUFA, Jousseaume, 1881.

Bull. Soc. Zool. France, 1881, vol. vi, pp. 172, 175.

Type.—*Murex lampas*, Linnæus.

Synonyms.—*Lampas*, Schumacher, 1817, nec Meuschen, 1787 (Brachiopod), nec De Montfort, 1808 (Foraminifer).

Tutufa granifera, Lamarck.

Ranella granifera } Lamarck: Hist. Nat. Anim. sans Vert., 1822, vol. vii,
R. semigranosa }   p. 153.
Lampas granifera } G. W. Tryon: Manual of Conchology, 1881, vol. iii, p. 41,
L. semigranosa }   pl. xxii, figs. 35–37.

Description. — This species is represented by a single cast embedded in a cream-coloured limestone. A thin test is sparingly preserved in places, and the typical high spire is well exposed. The characteristic granulations encircling the whorls are also displayed, each row being separated by a nearly obsolete line of granules. The shell has swollen whorls, and terminates with a short recurved canal. On each side of the specimen is a definite rounded or funiculate varix, which agrees with recent forms in not being regularly continuous.

Dimensions.—Length 35, diameter 20 mm.

Remarks.—Since the present specimen occurs associated with coral structures and other organisms, it is interesting to state that according to Tryon this genus is found at less depth than *Ranella* and invariably frequents coral reefs and rocks.

Distribution.—Red Sea, Natal, Paumotus, Philippines, north-east coast of Australia. (Tryon.)

Locality.—Top of first inland cliff, about 300 feet above sea-level.

Number on specimen : 951.

Example : 1 (specimen associated with pectinoid and other bivalve shells of doubtful determination).

Cypræa, sp.

Description.—This is a small cast in a cream-coloured compact limestone, of cylindrical shape above but with a depressed base, exhibiting a sub - central, narrow, and longitudinal aperture; the lip bears a regular dentition along its entire length; a short canal is present at each end ; the spiral volutions are well exposed through a small fracture at the base.

Dimensions.—Length 25, width (max.) 15 mm.

Remarks.—From a comparison with recent forms this specimen appears to be allied to *C. carneola* of Linnæus, a species living in the Pacific and Indian Oceans.

Locality.—Flying Fish Cove ; about 500 feet above sea-level and above rocks of undoubted Miocene age.

Number on specimen : 841.

Examples : 1.

Turbo ?

Remarks. —Cast of a Gasteropod shell probably referable to *Turbo*, showing the two last whorls. The absence of sculpture and other characters renders this specimen of no account for determination purposes. Found in a cream-coloured limestone containing corals and other structures. The front or apertural part of the specimen is embedded in matrix.

Locality.—Top of first inland cliff, about 300 feet above sea-level.
Number on specimen: 951A.
Examples: 1.

INDETERMINABLE SPECIMENS.

First.—A fragment of white limestone weathering a slaty colour, with remains of a Gasteropod cast, probably of Trochoidal affinities, but not identifiable.

Locality.—North coast, about 50 feet above the sea-level.
Number on specimen: 1043.
Examples: 1.

Secondly.—A mass of light-coloured limestone contains several small forms of Gasteropod shells whose structures, having mostly dissolved away, leaving mere casts or impressions, are not capable of accurate determination. Among some of the shells represented in the block appear to be *Nassa* and a number of *Cerithium*-like forms with a granular ornamentation, probably belonging to the genus *Bittium*, etc.

Locality.—Top of first inland cliff, about 300 feet above sea-level.
Number on specimen: 951.
Examples: One block; composed entirely of small Gasteropods.

MOLLUSCA: LAMELLIBRANCHIATA.

Genus VENUS, Linnæus, 1758.

Systema Naturæ, 1758, 10th ed., p. 684.

Type.—*Venus verrucosa,* Linnæus.

Venus verrucosa, Linnæus.

Venus verrucosa, Linnæus: Systema Naturæ, 1758, 10th ed., p. 685; Philippi, Enum. Moll. Siciliæ, 1836, vol. i, p. 43; Römer (E.), Kritische Untersuch. *Venus,* 1857, p. 26; Fischer (P.), in Tchihatcheff's "Asia Mineure," 1866–69, volume on 'Paléontologie,' p. 365.

Description.—Shell sub-cordate and thick; sculpture exhibiting nearly equidistant concentric ridges, with a series of intermediate fine and closely-set striations; the ridges are tubercled or verrucose at the sides; a ribbed structure radiating from the beaks lies immediately below the outer coating with the concentric ridges, and where the concentric striations cross these a cancellated condition is set up ; margins crenulate ; ligamental furrow excavated, oblique; characters of lunule obscured by matrix ; no dentition seen.

Remarks.—The specimen referred to this species shows extremely well the chief characters of the shell. Both valves are in contact, but not quite *in situ*: the left illustrates structural ornamentation ; the right, represented by a cast, shows a posterior oblique ridge and adductor scar, but no sinus or pallial line are decipherable, probably on account of youth, as the specimen is small and apparently a young example. It is in a cream-coloured limestone.

Dimensions.—Height 28, length 31, diameter 25 mm.

Distribution.—Species of wide distribution occurring in the Post-Pliocene beds of the Clyde Basin, etc. ; in the Sicilian strata ; and recent examples in the Mediterranean ; Canary Islands ; America ; Indian Ocean (E. Römer); etc., etc.

Locality.—Top of first inland cliff, about 300 feet above sea-level.

Number on specimen : 1032.

Examples : 1.

Venus, sp.

A small block of cream-coloured limestone contains casts of a right and left valve of this genus. The position of the muscle marks and sinus, the characters of the posterior oblique area, and the convexity of the valves, appear to show a relationship to *Venus puerpera* of Linnæus, resembling, in fact, a figure called *V. puerpera*, var., in Chenu's "Manuel Conchyliologie," 1862, vol. ii, p. 82, fig. 352, although the absence of dental and sculptural characters renders the specimen of doubtful specific value.

Dimensions.—Height 55, length 65, depth of each valve 18 mm.

Locality.—Top of first inland cliff, about 300 feet above sea-level.

Number on specimen : 1032.

Examples : Two valves on one slab.

INDETERMINABLE SPECIMENS.

A small mass of a rather coarse-grained yellowish-white limestone, weathering a drab colour, largely composed of Lamellibranch shells, which occur as casts having little or no characters sufficient for identification. Some of the shells have a trigonal or nuculoid appearance.

Locality.—West end of island, about 725 feet above sea-level.

Number on specimen : 360.

Examples : 1.

THE FOSSIL CORALS OF CHRISTMAS ISLAND.

By Dr. J. W. Gregory, F.G.S., F.Z.S.

(PLATE XIX.)

The collection of fossil Corals made in Christmas Island by Mr. C. W. Andrews includes a little over seventy specimens, which were carefully collected, the exact stratigraphical position of each being recorded. The fauna is of interest, as I understand from Mr. Andrews that no fossils were obtained by previous visitors to Christmas Island, and that the only other fossils which he obtained were foraminifera and a few imperfect molluscan shells. Hence the determination of the geological age of the various limestones that build up the island must be dependent to a considerable extent on the evidence of the corals.

Many of the specimens, however, have been so altered, often by phosphatization, that they are specifically indeterminable; and the number of corals collected from the oldest limestones in Christmas Island is small, and the specimens fragmentary. But the most serious difficulty in the study of this fauna is that it comes from the borderland between the provinces of the neontologist and palæontologist. The identification of late Cainozoic fossil corals is always a difficult task. For the description of the recent specimens is based on the external form and superficial characters; whereas the description of the fossil corals refers to the essential structure of the corallites, as shown by transverse sections. Hence, consideration of the relations of the living and the latest extinct species of corals involves a comparison of incomparable terms.

A further difficulty in the case of the Christmas Island collections is introduced by the fact that the corals are mainly Astreans. And the Astreans in the Zoological Department are not yet arranged, so that I have not always been able to compare the fossil corals with specimens of the species to which they are referred.

The fauna includes representatives of nineteen determinable species, of which eight are new.

As regards the general character of the fauna, it is typically Indo-Pacific, all the previously known species coming from that region.

The corals are all reef-building species, and probably none of them grew at a greater depth than six or eight fathoms. The list of species and their distribution are given in the appended table. The horizons of the fossils have been divided into four

LIST OF SPECIES AND THEIR DISTRIBUTION.

| Species | Author | Distribution on Christmas Island. | | | | | Range of Species. |
| | | Recent. | Fossil. | | | | |
			Sea Cliffs.	Inland Cliffs.	Central Plateau.	Central Nucleus.	
Pocillopora, aff. brevicornis	Lam.	x	x	x			Indo-Pacific.
„ sp.	(Ed. & H.)			x	x	x	Indo-Pacific.
Mussa, aff. echinata	(Ell. & Sol.)	x	x	x			„
Leptoria phrygia	n.sp.						
Caloria andrewsi	„						
Meandrina equisepta	(Lam.)	x	x				Indo-Pacific.
Goniastraea retiformis	„	x	x				
Orbicella pleiades	(Ed. & H.), n.var.		x	x			?
„ quadrangularis, var. columnata	n.sp.						
„ murrayi	n.sp.						
„ herkloti	Dunc.			x ?	x		Miocene : Java.
„ praeheliopora	n.sp.				x	?	
Acanthastraea patula, var. paucidentata	Dana, n.var.	x	x				Indo-Pacific.
Prionastraea magnifica	(Blainv.)		x				
Anisocoenia murrayi	n.sp.			x			
„ favoidea	„						
Coscinaraea andrewsi	Ed. & H.					x	
Porites, aff. lutea	n.sp.		x	x		x	Indo-Pacific.
„ belli	Ed. & H.		x	x			Indo-Pacific.
Montipora, aff. danae	Ed. & H.			x			Indo-Pacific.

groups, in accordance with Mr. Andrews' account[1] of the structure of the island. The groups are the limestones of—

1. The sea cliffs.   3. The central plateau.
2. The inland cliffs.   4. The central nucleus.

The interpretation of the evidence of the fossil corals as to the ages and relations of the Christmas Island limestones is difficult, as so little is yet known of the coral fauna of Malaysia between early Miocene and recent times. Many Miocene corals from Java have been described by Duncan, von Reuss, and Martin; and the existing Malaysian coral fauna is fairly well known. But from the intervening period no corals have previously been described. Nevertheless, the evidence of Mr. Andrews' collection is tolerably clear.

The limestones of the sea cliff contain corals many of which are of the same species as those now growing on the fringing reef of Christmas Island; so that the date of those limestones is no doubt Pleistocene. At the other end of the series are the limestones of the central nucleus: they have yielded three determinable species, of which two are new, and the third (*Orbicella herklotsi*) is found in the older Miocene of Java; of the other two species one belongs to a genus elsewhere known only in the Miocene, and the other is a coral of an ancient aspect, though its genus was founded on a living species from the Red Sea. The limestones of the central nucleus are therefore probably Miocene in age. But the evidence of the corals is insufficient for positive opinion, or for the suggestion of a more precise date. As opportunities for further geological collecting in Christmas Island will probably arise, it may be worth while directing attention to the desirability of obtaining more specimens of corals from the central limestones.

On the central plateau reefs of recent limestone are said to occur; this age is assigned to the rocks on the evidence of the foraminifera. But there are no corals of recent species in the collection from the central plateau. The evidence of the corals renders it probable that outcrops of the central limestones occur on the floor of the plateau.

The majority of the specimens were obtained from the limestones of the inland cliffs. Most of the species from this zone are still living, and four of them also occur in the rocks of the sea cliffs. But others are of older aspect, and the occurrence of a weathered specimen of *Orbicella herklotsi* and *Anisocœnia faroidea* shows that the Miocene limestones are exposed in some parts of the inland cliffs. Whether the rest of the cliffs, containing the species

---

[1] C. W. Andrews, "A Description of Christmas Island (Indian Ocean)": Geogr. Journ., 1899, vol. xiii, pp. 20–24.

Mussa aff. *echinata, Cœloria andrewsi, Montipora* aff. *danœ*, etc., should be regarded as Pleistocene or Pliocene, the evidence is insufficient to show. It is only certain that these limestones are intermediate in age between the late Pleistocene of the sea cliffs and the Miocene of the central nucleus.

Family POCILLOPORIDÆ.

Pocillopora, aff. brevicornis, Lamarck, 1816.

Pocillopora is represented among the Christmas Island corals by several fragments included in a limestone from the foot of the first inland cliff on the North Coast (No. 867). One specimen is a cylindrical branch 45 mm. high and 8 mm. in diameter. Another is a low, massive, almost hemispherical branch.

Mr. Bernard has provisionally identified two recent *Pocilloporæ* from Christmas Island as *P. favosa* and *P. brevicornis*; the fossil specimens would agree with either in the characters of the corallites. A large number of recent species of this genus have been proposed by neontologists on variations in the shape of the branches. Ortmann,[1] however, has suggested that the recent species are mere individual variations. In describing a collection of thirty-three specimens he states that they form a complete transitional series, and fill up the gaps between the previously described species. Ortmann, therefore, did not give a specific name to any of the specimens.

Recently Mr. J. S. Gardiner[2] has also questioned whether "all these so-called species should not rather be described as varieties of one species," though he retains the conventional method of treatment of the group.

The most convenient name for the Christmas Island fossil specimens would be *P. brevicornis*, Lam.

Pocillopora, sp. indet.

No. 989. From second inland cliff, over Flying Fish Cove; alt. 500–600 feet.

No. 947. Broad reef on middle of the island; alt. 500–600 feet.

No. 925. High cliff over south end of Flying Fish Cove alt. 400 feet.

These three specimens are so altered that they are specifically indeterminable.

---

[1] Ortmann, Syst. und Verbr. Steinkor.: Zool. Jahrb., vol. iii, Syst. 1888, pp. 162–166.

[2] J. S. Gardiner, "Pocilloporidæ from S.W. Pacific ": Proc. Zool. Soc., 1897 (1898), p. 942.

Group ASTRÆIDÆ.

Mussa, aff. echinata (Edwards & Haime), 1849.

Lobophyllia echinata, Edwards & Haime, 1849. Mém. Astr., pt. ii: Ann. Sci.
          nat., Zool., ser. iii, vol. xi, p. 253.
Mussa   ,,   Edwards & Haime, 1857. Hist. nat. Cor., vol. ii,
          p. 337.

This species is represented in the collection by a fragment
(No. 203) 70 mm. high, 65 mm. long, and with the calices 28 mm.
wide. The specimen includes two confluent calices, and the walls
of the corallum are parallel in horizontal sections. As the upper
part of the septa is not shown, its absolute specific determination
is impossible. But so far as the evidence goes, the specimen
agrees with those collected by the "Challenger" in the Malay
Archipelago, and determined by Quelch as *M. echinata*. The only
doubtful point is, that in the transverse sections the septa do not
appear to be alternately thick and thin; but this arrangement
is probably masked by the secondary calcification of the specimen
during fossilization.

The Christmas Island specimen was collected from the first
inland cliff at the Zigzag, at the altitude of 90 feet.

Leptoria phrygia (Ell. & Sol.), 1786.

Madrepora phrygia, Ellis & Solander, 1786. Hist. Zooph., p. 162, pl. xlviii,
          fig. 2.
non Leptoria ,,   Edwards & Haime, 1849. Mém. Astr., pt. iii: Ann. Sci.
          nat., Zool., ser. iii, vol. xi, p. 292.
      ,,   *tenuis (non* Dana), Edwards & Haime, 1849. Ibid., p. 292.

The name of this species has been the subject of much confusion,
owing to an apparent inconsistency between Dana's figures and
description of this species and *L. tenuis* (Dana). Milne Edwards
and Haime apparently based their diagnoses on Dana's figures, and
thus inverted the main characters of the two species; for they
describe *L. tenuis* as having broader gyri and less crowded septa than
L. phrygia, and also as having stouter walls and columella. But
Dana does not state the magnification of his enlarged figures, and
it therefore appears wiser to base the distinctions between the two
species on his diagnoses. He therein states that the gyri of
L. phrygia are 2–2½ lines broad, while those of *M. tenuis* are
1½ lines broad. Moreover, in *L. phrygia* there are from 10 to 12
septa to the half-inch, whereas in *L. tenuis* there are about 20 septa
to the half-inch. Edwards & Haime, however, define *L. phrygia*
as having the gyri 3 mm. broad, against 4 mm. in *L. tenuis*, and
15 primary septa per centimetre, against 8 in *L. tenuis*.

Ortmann[1] appears, therefore, to be perfectly justified in concluding that Edwards & Haime reversed the names of these two species.

The Christmas Island collection includes three specimens of this species, which have the following dimensions :—

	No. 53.	No. 306.	No. 100.
Width of calicinal series	3 mm. ...	3–4 mm. ...	3–4 mm.
Number of primary septa per cm.	9 ...	7 ...	7–9

They are therefore referable to the *L. tenuis* of Edwards & Haime (*non* Dana) and the *L. phrygia* of Ellis & Solander, with whose figure they agree.

· A slide cut from specimen No. 306 affects the generic diagnosis · of *Leptoria*. As generally defined, the walls of adjacent corallites are said to unite directly; but, as shown on Fig. 1, the adjacent

Fig. 1.

series are, in places, united by costæ and exotheca, and not by the walls. This fact led me, on first examination of the slide, to feel some doubt whether the coral were a *Leptoria*. But it appears only necessary to modify the generic diagnosis to this slight extent; for the same mode of union of the series of corallites occurs in *L. tenuis* (Dana). Thus Dana's description of that species refers to the corallum as very cellular; and his figure of a transverse section (Dana, op. cit., pl. xii, fig. 7*d*) shows the compound nature of the walls.

Mr. Bernard's manuscript list of the recent corals collected by Mr. Andrews at Christmas Island shows that *L. phrygia* still lives on the neighbouring reefs.

---

[1] Ortmann : op. cit., p. 172.

The distribution of the fossil specimens on Christmas Island is as follows :—

No. 53. From top of sea cliff on the east coast.

No. 306. First inland cliff above West White Beach ; alt. 260 feet.

No. 100. From a limestone breccia on the first inland cliff at the height of 250 feet.

Cœloria andrewsi, sp.n.

Diagnosis.—Corallum, form unknown, but massive; the species is represented by a slab 80 mm. high, 55 mm. wide, and 20 mm. thick. Corallites in very short series and mostly isolated. The longest series is 7 mm. long, and includes three calicinal centres. The single, circumscribed corals occur in regular rows. Walls thick. Columella of stout trabeculæ, and for the genus fairly well developed. Septa stout; one cycle in young corallites; two incomplete cycles in mature corallites.

Distribution.—Represented in the collection by one specimen (No. 175), from the first inland cliff on the north coast ; approximate altitude 90 feet.

Figures.—Pl. XIX, Fig. 1. Part of a transverse section, × 2 dia.

Affinities.—The nearest ally of this species is the *Mæandrina delicatula*, Ortm.,[1] from Samoa, in which the valleys are from 5 to 12 mm. in length ; the septa occur in three cycles, and the columella is represented only by a trace. Owing to the shortness of the calicinal series the species belongs to the section of *Cœloria*, for which Edwards & Haime once founded the genus *Astroria*. This species is also allied to *Astroria esperi*, Ed. & H.,[2] which, however, has three incomplete cycles of septa, and calicinal valleys 3 centimetres long.

Mæandrina equisepta, sp.n.

Diagnosis.—Corallum massive. Calicinal series 5 mm. wide and fairly long (many of them being 3 cm. long); while there are many independent calices. Many of the calicinal series are straight, and others are bent into V-shape. Septa subequal, and about thirteen in number in 1 cm. ; small secondary septa occur at intervals. Columella usually a little under 1 mm. in width, but varying from ·5 to 1·5 mm.

Figure.—Pl. XIX, Fig. 2. Part of a transverse section, × 2 dia.

---

[1] Ortmann : op. cit., p. 171, pl. vi, fig. 6.

[2] Edwards & Haime, Mém. Astr., pt. ii : Ann. Sci. nat., Zool., ser. III, vol. xi (1849), p. 298.

Distribution.—Christmas Island. Fossil from the raised reefs of the sea cliff at Rocky Point. Also recent from fringing reef of Flying Fish Cove.

Affinities.—The main character of this species is the subequal size of its septa, which are alternately large and small in most species.

A recent specimen from Christmas Island has been provisionally named by Mr. Bernard *C.*, aff. *sinensis*, with which it agrees in some characters. But according to Edwards & Haime's diagnosis of *C. sinensis* the "valleys are extremely short; one sees few of them which are more than 2 cm. in length, and a great number of calices are independent (*se circonscrivent*)." The septa, moreover, are alternately large and small. *C. sinensis* is, indeed, placed by its founders in their genus *Astroria*, whereas the present species seems to me to be necessarily excluded from that section of *Cœloria*.

Another ally of *M. æquisepta* is *C. arabica*, Klz.[1] (*C. forskaeli*, Ed. & H.), which differs, among other characters, by the unequal size of the septa. *C. bottai*, Ed. & H.,[2] in this respect agrees with the Christmas Island species, but it has the columella " tout-à-fait rudimentaire."

Another coral with which this species has points of resemblance is the *Mæandrina heterogyra* of Ed. & H.;[3] but that species is described as having subequal septa of 2–3 cycles, a well developed columella, and 12–14 septa per cm. The locality of the type is unknown, and Quelch[4] maintains that it is a West Indian coral, and the name is a synonym of *M. strigosa*, Dana, i.e. *Mæandrina filograna* (Esper).

Reference to this *Mæandrina* raises the question of the retention of *Mæandrina* and *Cœloria*. The latter genus was founded by Milne Edwards & Haime[5] in 1848 for one species previously known as *Mæandrina dædalea*, which must therefore be taken as the type. *Cœloria* was separated from *Mæandrina* simply as in the former the columella is parietal and rudimentary, and in the latter is essential and spongy. In 1857 Edwards & Haime[6] retained the genera on the same grounds: they stated that in *Mæandrina* the columella is "bien développée," whereas *Cœloria* belongs to a group with the columella rudimentary or absent. Since that date those authors who have accepted *Cœloria* have

[1] Klunzinger: Korallth. Roth. Meer., iii, Steinkor., pt. 2 (1879), p. 17, pl. ii, figs. 1–3 and 8 ; pl. ix, fig. 10.
[2] Edwards & Haime, Mém. Astr., pt. ii: Ann. Sci. nat., Zool., ser. iii, vol. xi (1849), p. 295.
[3] Edwards & Haime, Mém. Astr., pt. ii: Ann. Sci. nat., Zool., ser. iii, vol. xi (1849), p. 281.
[4] Quelch. Reef Corals : Rep. Chall. Exped., Zool., vol. xvi, pt. 46, p. 93.
[5] Edwards & Haime, Classif. deux. trib. Astr.: Compt. Rend., vol. xlvi, p. 493.
[6] Edwards & Haime : Hist. nat. Cor., vol. ii, p. 289.

done so on the character of the columella. But in the type species of *Cœloria* the columella is quite well developed (see e.g. the original figure of Ellis & Solander, Hist. Zooph., pl. xlvi, figs. 1, 2); it is in fact better developed than in some species of *Mœandrina.*

The distinction based on the columella appears to me insufficient for the separation of the two genera. The length of the confluent calicinal series may, however, yield an adequate basis ; for those corals in which the calicinal series are very long may be conveniently kept distinct from those in which the calicinal series are short and independent calices predominate. *Cœloria,* with *C. dœdalea* as the type, would include the latter group. The naming of the former group is a difficult question. The most convenient name would be *Mœandrina,* but that name would have to be designated as Ed. & H., 1848, *non* Lamarck, 1801. For according to the original foundation of that genus its type is *Mœandrina pectinata,* Lam., which most authors have taken as the type of the genus *Pectinia.*

Whether the inconvenience of the change in the name *Mœandrina,* which observance of the laws of nomenclature would involve, be too serious for obedience to the law to be advisable, I leave zoologists to settle, and so provisionally retain it.

Goniastræa retiformis (Lamarck), 1816.

Astræa retiformis, Lamarck, 1816. Hist. nat. Anim. s. Vert., vol. ii, p. 266.
Goniastræa retiformis, Edwards & Haime, 1849. Mém. Astr., pt. iii : Ann. Sci. nat., Zool., ser. III, vol. xii, p. 161. .

This species is represented at Christmas Island by a recent specimen determined by Mr. Bernard and several fossil specimens. The latter show the following characters :—The corallites are from 3–4 mm. in dia. ; the walls are from ·5 mm. to something under 1 mm. in thickness ; the septa belong to three cycles, of which the third is incomplete ; the columella is loose and sometimes hollow ; the pali are indistinct ; the corallites are elliptical, quadrangular, pentagonal, or hexagonal in shape.

The corals agree closely with *G. capitata,* Stud.,[1] which, as Ortmann[2] suggests, is probably a variety of *G. retiformis* with thinner walls, somewhat exsert septa, and more open calices. The recent specimen from Christmas Island resembles the *capitata* form, the characters of which are not preserved in any of the fossils.

Distribution.—Christmas Island.
    Recent :
      · Fringing Reef, Flying Fish Cove.

---

[1] Th. Studer, Beitr. Fauna Steinkor. Singapore : Mitth. Naturf. Gesell. Bern., 1880 (1881), pp. 40, 41, fig. 8.
[2] Ortmann : op. cit., p. 173.

Fossil :

No. 1,042. Pinnacles at foot of first inland cliff at the Zigzag.

No. 969. Pedestal of block of foraminiferal limestone on top of the sea cliff.

No. —. Sea cliff at Rocky Point.

Orbicella herklotsi (Duncan), 1864.

Astræa herklotsi, Duncan, 1864. Coral from Mount Sela: Quart. Journ. Geol. Soc., vol. xx, p. 72, pl. vii, fig. 9.
Heliastræa tabulata, Martin, 1880. Tertiärsch. Java, p. 140, pl. xxiv, fig. 21, pl. xxvi, fig. 4.

Distribution.—Orbitoidal Limestone. Miocene at Radjamandala, near Tjisitu, Java ; and Mount Sela, Java.

Christmas Island.

No. 659. Limestone from south side of chalk-capped hill ; alt. 700 feet.

No. 954. From talus at foot of high cliff, east of Phosphate Hill.

No. 947. Broad reef near middle of the island.

? No. 996. An altered specimen from inland cliff, south coast ; alt. 200 feet.

? No. 626. A specimen in form of a cast, from the foot of the second inland cliff, east coast.

Figure.—Fig. 2. Part of a thin section of specimen, No. 659, × 7 dia.

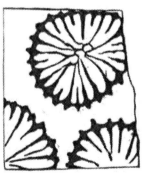

Fig. 2.

Orbicella murrayi, sp.n.

Diagnosis.—Corallum massive, with very large corallites, and very thick exothecal areas. The calices are from 9 to 10 mm. in dia., while the calicinal centres are from 15 to 25 mm. apart.

The septa occur in three complete cycles, and there is one order of the fourth. The columella is from 2 to 3 mm. in diameter.

The costæ are very long, and can be traced out through the compact exothecal tissue.

Distribution.—Christmas Island.

Fossil:

No. 996. From limestones of the inland cliff, on the south coast; alt. 200 feet.

? No. 903. Cast of probably the same species, from the sea-level on the east coast, above basalt and volcanic agglomerate.

Figure.—Pl. XIX, Fig. 3. Part of transverse section across No. 996, × 2 dia.

Affinities.—This species is characterized by the large size of the exothecal areas, which are wider than in any other species of *Orbicella* known to me. The better specimen was collected from the inland cliffs on the south coast, and may indicate an outcrop of the limestones of the central nucleus at that point.

Orbicella pleiades (Lamarck), 1816.

This well-known East Indian species is represented by several specimens, viz. :—

No. 122. Top of the sea cliff, east coast.

No. 978. Limestones of the inland cliff; alt. 200 feet. East coast.

No. 353. On the road, 212 chains south from West White Beach; alt. about 450 feet.

No. 867. Foot of first inland cliff, north coast; alt. 50–60 feet.

No. 212. Foot of the inland cliff, south end of Flying Fish Cove; alt. 50–60 feet.

No. — . Limestones of the sea cliff, Rocky Point.

The specimens have the corallites more closely packed than in the specimen shown in Ellis & Solander's original figure; but they agree in essential points with the species as generally accepted. The corallites are circular, and from 2 to 3 mm. in dia.; the septa in sections are usually twelve in number, but some representatives of an incomplete third cycle occur.

Orbicella, aff. quadrangularis (Edwards & Haime).

The collection includes a well-preserved fragment of an *Orbicella* with large subquadrangular corallites, distinct calicinal edges, well-marked costæ, narrow zones of very coarsely vesicular exotheca, and septa which are thick near the walls and become thin near the columella. In these respects it appears to be a member of this species, of which I have not seen either figures or specimens.

The Christmas Island specimens differ from Milne Edwards and Haime's diagnosis in three respects, which appear to me to be worthy of at least varietal recognition.

Var. columnata,[1] nov.

The variety differs from the typical form of the species by having deep open calices; the columella is very large; and the tertiary septa are not united to the secondary septa.

The diameter of the corallites is from 11–13 mm.; the diameter of the columella is about 5 mm.; and there are about 3½ cycles of septa.

Distribution.

a. Recent:

Locality of the type unknown.

b. Fossil:

Christmas Island. No. 322. Limestones of the seacliff series, mouth of Sidney's Dale.

Figure.—Fig. 3. Part of a transverse section, × 1⅓ dia.

Fig. 3.

Orbicella præheliopora, sp.n.

Diagnosis. — Corallum massive: external characters unknown. Corallites of medium size, being from 4–5 mm. in diameter, circular, and separated by from 1 to 2 mm. Columella very spongy, but large, being from 1–1·5 mm. in dia. Septa irregular; in some sectors of a corallite there may be representatives of an incomplete sixth order; whereas in the adjacent sector the septa of the fourth order are rudimentary and barely recognizable. The primary and

---

[1] *Columnatus,* furnished with a column, in reference to the large columella.

secondary septa are long and thin, the latter being considerably the shorter; both are connected to the columella, though in sections the connection may not be shown in all cases.

Distribution.—Christmas Island.

    Fossil :

        No. 946.   From the limestone pinnacles a little south of the middle of the island; alt. 550 feet.

        No. 511.   A specimen from top of the upper cliff, middle of the east coast.

Figure.—Pl. XIX, Fig. 4. Part of a transverse section of specimen No. 946, × 2 dia.

Affinities.—*Orbicella præheliopora* is a species intermediate in characters between the *Orbicella irregularis* (Mart.) from the Miocene of Java and *O. heliopora* (Lam.) from the Australian seas. It is probably nearer the former, which differs by having only four cycles of septa, and by having the corallites crowded together so that they are irregular and polygonal in shape. The two species agree in the irregularity of the septal sequence. In two adjacent sectors in one corallite of the type-specimen of *O. præheliopora* the sequence is as follows :—

$$1 \quad\quad 4 \quad\quad 3 \quad\quad 2 \ 5 \ 3 \quad\quad 1$$
$$1 \ 6 \ 4 \ 7 \ 3 \ 5 \ 2 \ 5 \ 3 \ 4 \ 1$$

According to Martin's diagram of *O. irregularis*, the sequence in three sectors in that species is :—

$$1 \quad\quad 3 \quad\quad 2 \quad\quad 3 \quad\quad 1$$
$$1 \ 4 \ 3 \ 5. \ 2 \quad\quad 3 \quad\quad 1$$
$$1 \quad\quad 3 \ 5 \ 2 \ 5 \ 3 \ 4 \ 1$$

From *O. heliopora* the Christmas Island coral differs by having a looser columella and less regular septal sequence; for *O. heliopora* is said to have four complete cycles. The primary, secondary, and tertiary septa are said, moreover, to be not very different in size in the living species.

Acanthastræa patula (Dana).

Orbicella patula, Dana, 1848. Zooph.: Expl. Exped. Wilkes, vol. viii, p. 209, pl. x, fig. 14.

Acanthastræa? *patula*, Edwards & Haime, 1857. Hist. nat. Cor., vol. ii, p. 505.

Var. paucidentata, nov.

The genus *Acanthastræa* is represented in the collection by a small fragment 70 mm. long; the corallites are from 9 to 12 mm. in diameter, the majority being 12 mm. The columella is small, and consists of a few denticles, though sections at first sight appear to have a long columella owing to the abundance of central

.endotheca. The corallites in internal sections are mostly circular, the majority are of the same size, the walls are thin. The septa include three complete, well-developed cycles; between them are .some obscure costæ,. corresponding to the septa of a fourth cycle.

The specimen agrees essentially with Dana's *O. patula*, except that the septa appear more distinct from one another than in his figure (Dana, pl. x, fig. 14*e*), and the columella contains fewer denticles. Whitelegge[1] has recently recorded the species from Funafuti; but he gives the corallites as from 5–10 mm. in diameter, and the walls from 2–6 mm. in thickness, with the septa varying from 12–36. He describes the columella as composed of a series of compressed denticles, which agrees with Dana's figure, though the dimensions of the Funafuti coral do not correspond very well.

Distribution.—Christmas Island.

Fossil: Pinnacles of the sea-cliff limestone. No. 166.

Figure.—Pl. XIX, Fig. 5. Part of a transverse section, × 2 dia. No. 166.

Prionastræa magnifica (De Blainville), 1830.

Favastrea magnifica, De Blainville, 1830. Zooph.: Dict. Sci. nat., vol. lx, p. 340; and 1834, Man. Act., pl. liv, fig. 3.

Astræa ,, Dana, 1848. Zooph.: Expl. Exped. Wilkes, vol. viii, p. 231, pl. xii, fig. 3.

Prionastræa ,, Edwards & Haime, 1850. Mém. Astr., pt. iii: Ann. Sci. nat., Zool., ser. iii, vol. xii, p. 129.

Fig. 4. (Nat. size.)

The collection contains one well-preserved specimen (No. 322) of *Prionastræa*, with corallites from 5–9 mm. in dia., a columella 2–3 mm. in dia., walls ·5 to 1 mm. thick, and three complete and

---

a fourth incomplete orders of septa. The corallites do not exhibit any tendency towards a serial arrangement, and the calices are polygonal.

The species must be compared with two living species, whose characters are as follows:—

	Dia. of corallites.	No. of septa.	Columella.	Calices.
australensis, Ed. & H.	10 mm.	36–38	rudimentary	oblong; sometimes in short series.
magnifica, Blv. ...	10 ,,	34	well developed	polygonal.

A transverse section of the Christmas Island coral is figured as Fig. 4, and it appears to be a typical form of *P. magnifica.* Two well-preserved specimens of the same species were collected by Mr. Andrews from the existing reefs. The fossil was found in the limestones of the sea cliff, at the mouth of Sidney's Dale.

Von Reuss[1] has described as *P. dubia* an allied species from the Javan Miocene.

Anisocœnia murrayi, sp.n.

Diagnosis.—Corallum massive. Corallites large, about 15 mm. in diameter, and closely united. Septa in five orders: those belonging to the different orders are of proportional lengths. The primary and secondary septa have internally thickened paliform lobes; the primary septa, in fact, appear clavate.

Distribution.—Orbitoidal Limestone of the central nucleus of the island, from fallen blocks from high cliff (400 feet) at south end of Flying Fish Cove (No. 964).

Figure.—Pl. XIX, Fig. 7. Part of a transverse section, × 2 dia.

Affinities.—This interesting coral is represented by one specimen in a compact and apparently structureless limestone. The coral is, however, well shown in thin sections. Its nearest ally is the Miocene *Anisocœnia crassisepta,* Reuss,[2] from which it differs by having the corallites more than twice the size; von Reuss gives their diameter as 7 mm.

Anisocœnia favoides, sp.n.

Diagnosis. — Corallum massive, with the corallites small and elongate; they vary in width from 2–3 mm. and in length from 3–7 mm. The corallites are closely united by a dense wall. Septa very short and thick, with well-marked dark lamina. The

---

[1] A. E. von Reuss, Foss. Kor. Java: Novara Reise, Geol. Th., 1867, vol. ii, p. 167, pl. i, fig. 3.
[2] A. E. von Reuss: ibid., p. 166, pl. i, fig. 2.

number of septa is about 14–16. Endotheca scanty, with the corallites traversed by a large axial cavity.

Distribution.—Christmas Island.

No. 919. Reef on top of the high cliff east of Phosphate Hill; alt. 600 feet.

Figure.—Pl. XIX, Fig. 6. Part of a transverse section, × 2 dia.

Affinities.—This species is of interest as helping to connect von Reuss's two genera *Anisocænia* and *Favoidea*, which, it seems to me, should be united, for they agree in all essential characters. The new species resembles *Favoidea junghuhni*, Rss.,[1] the type species of *Favoidea*, by having elongated corallites, which appear to divide by fission. A transverse section closely resembles von Reuss's figure of the corallum of his species. In the characters of the septa, however, this new species most closely resembles *Anisocænia*; for the septa are thick and short, and they are traversed by the central groove, clearly indicated in von Reuss's figure (op. cit., pl. i, fig. 2*b*). The main difference between this new species and those of von Reuss is, that in both the latter internal sections show that the corallites are united by an exothecal layer, whereas in the Christmas Island coral they unite directly. This difference does not seem to me of much importance in this case; it may be explained as due to comparison between slices at different depths in the corallum.

Group FUNGIDA.

Coscinaræa andrewsi, sp.n.

Diagnosis.—Corallum apparently massive. Corallites large, about 10 mm. in dia. (possibly in short series). Columella well developed, about 2 mm. in dia. Septa thick, trabeculate throughout. Three complete cycles, with representatives of the fourth; the septa of the third cycle are often unequal, and the sequence in the sectors is often asymmetrical. Synapticulæ rare.

Distribution.—Christmas Island. Orbitoidal Limestone of the central nucleus at Flying Fish Cove. No. 836.

Figures.—Pl. XIX, Fig. 8. Part of a transverse section, × 2 dia.

Affinities.—The species is founded on a small fragment, which, however, shows the characters of the corallites very distinctly. The genus is one of much interest, as it is one of the Fungids with very trabeculate septa. The species differs from the type *C. monile*, Forsk., by its larger corallites, which are less elongate and more regular in form. The septal sequence is irregular and somewhat indefinite.

---

[1] Von Reuss: op. cit., p. 168, pl. i, fig. 4.

Group PERFORATA.

Family PORITIDÆ.

Porites, aff. lutea, Edwards & Haime.

Porites *conglomerata*, var. *jaune*, Quoy & Gaimard, 1833.   Voy. Astrolabe,
        Zooph., vol. iv, p. 249.
,,   ,,   Dana, 1848.   Zooph.: Expl. Exp. Wilkes, vol. viii,
        p. 561, pl. lv, fig. 3.
,,   *lutea,*   Edwards & Haime, 1860.   Hist. nat. Cor., vol. iii, p. 180.

The genus *Porites* is now undergoing revision by Mr. Bernard, and until his work is issued, identifications of recent species of the genus must be regarded as provisional.   The Christmas Island collection includes two fossil *Porites*, with twelve well-marked septa, very thin and indistinct walls, inconspicuous columella, and the pali not well developed.   The diameter of the corallites is about 1·5 mm.   This association of characters renders it probable that the species is a close ally of *P. lutea*, which was founded by Edwards & Haime, practically on Dana's *P. conglomerata.* Mr. Stanley Gardner suggests that *P. lutea* should be regarded as a variety of *P. arenosa.*

Distribution.—On Christmas Island.

    Fossil: Sea cliff, Rocky Point.

        No. 161.   Top of the sea cliff, north coast.
        No. 165.   Lower part of the sea cliff.
        No. 997.   Southern slope of the island; alt. 350 feet.

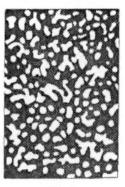

FIG. 5.

Figure.—Fig. 5.   Part of a transverse section of specimen from Rocky Point, × 9 dia.

Porites belli, sp.n.

Diagnosis. — Corallum massive. Corallites very small, being about 1·5 mm. in diameter. The walls are thin, but very distinct in sections. The intermediate tissue is very narrow. The septa are from 12 to 16 in number, and very sinuous and irregular. The columella is very small and indistinct, and so also are the pali.

Distribution.—On Christmas Island.

Fossil :

No. 132.	A much altered specimen from the second inland cliff. East coast; alt. 550 feet.	
No. 301.	An altered specimen with thickened walls. Inland cliff; alt. 250 feet.	
No. 306.	From inland cliff over West White Beach. North coast; alt. 260 feet.	
No. 853.	Shore plateau at top of sea cliff. North-East Point; alt. 40 feet.	
No. 980.	From 60–80 feet up the first inland cliff. North coast; alt. about 120 feet.	
No. 6.	From a large mass from south side of Flying Fish Cove.	
? No. 905.	An altered coral from top of the first inland cliff. South of the waterfall.	

Figure.—Fig. 6 : part of a section of specimen No. 609, × 9 dia. Fig. 7 : part of another specimen (No. 6), showing the walls burrowed by a boring alga.

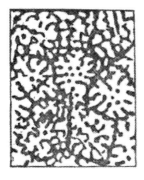

Fig. 6.

Fig. 7.

Affinities.—The Christmas Island corals, on which this species is founded, include several specimens from the limestones of the sea cliff and the inland cliff. The species has a well-marked but thin wall, which extends downward through the corallum, cutting it up into well-defined quadrangular or polygonal corallites. This wall is more definite internally than is the case in *P. gaimardi.* The species belongs to the group of which *P. arenosa* (Esp.) is a convenient type; that form differs, however, by its larger columella and more regular and equal septa; the corallum is said to be thin and encrusting in typical form of *arenosa*, though that point is probably unimportant.

In one specimen (No. 6, figd. Fig. 7) the walls are tunnelled by some boring alga.

Montipora, aff. danæ, Edwards & Haime.

Manopora tuberculosa (*non* Lam.), Dana, 1848. Zooph.: Expl. Exp. Wilkes,
vol. viii, p. 507, pl. xlvii, fig. 2.
Montipora danæ, Edwards & Haime, 1851. Mon. Porit.: Ann. Sci. nat., Zool.,
ser. iii, vol. xvi, p. 65.

Mr. Andrews' collection includes a specimen of a massive *Montipora*, with calices ·66 mm. in diameter, separated by

Fig. 8.

cœnenchyma of about the same width, and with six well-developed septa, and usually some representatives of the second cycle. In these characters it agrees with *M. danæ.* Specimens of the genus do not appear to have been previously met with as fossils.

The specimen (No. 364) was collected in the first inland cliff on the south from West White Beach at alt. of 120 feet.

FIGURES IN THE TEXT.

Fig. 1. *Leptoria phrygia* (Ell. & Sol.).   Part of transverse section, × 5 dia.
No. 306.

,, 2. *Orbicella herklotsi* (Dunc.).   Part of a transverse section, × 7 dia.
No. 659.

,, 3. *Orbicella quadrangularis* (Ed. & H.), var. *columnata.*   Part of
a transverse section, × 1½ dia. No. 322.

,, 4. *Prionastræa magnifica* (Blainv.).   Part of a transverse section,
× 2 dia. No. 322.

,, 5. *Porites,* aff. *lutea,* Ed. & H.   Part of a transverse section, × 9 dia.
No. 853.

,, 6. *Porites belli,* n.sp.   Part of a transverse section, × 9 dia. No. 609.

,, 7. *Porites belli,* n.sp.   Part of a transverse section bored by an alga,
× 9 dia. No. 6.

,, 8. *Montipora danæ,* Ed. & H.   Part of a transverse section, × 12 dia.
No. 364.

Q

ON THE FORAMINIFERA OF THE
ORBITOIDAL LIMESTONES AND REEF ROCKS
OF CHRISTMAS ISLAND.

By Professor T. Rupert Jones, F.R.S., etc., and
Frederick Chapman, A.L.S., F.R.M.S., etc.

(PLATES XX and XXI.)

The following has been written in elucidation of the foraminiferal
fauna of the rocks of Christmas Island (Indian Ocean), which
Mr. Andrews has kindly handed to us for description.

In submitting this report we wish to state that we have made
it as comprehensive as possible in the time at our disposal, and
hope at a later date to furnish further details with regard to this
interesting collection.

For the greater part of the work we have of necessity been
dependent upon thin sections for our study and determination of
the organisms; and this at best is somewhat unsatisfactory. It
is hoped, however, that by a careful examination of the various
slices of rock, showing the organisms in their different phases,
the facts here brought together will in some measure extend the
knowledge of the association and habits of growth of these small,
but most important, rock-builders.

It is now proposed to describe the general microscopic structure
both of the fossil and the recent limestones, in their order of age
as far as possible; and to give concise accounts of any foraminifera
which appear to be new.

Tertiary Limestones of Flying Fish Cove.

The most complete section of the older rocks of Christmas
Island is that seen in Flying Fish Cove; and for this reason
we chiefly confine our remarks to the foraminifera of the rocks
from this locality.

The oldest bed exposed is a yellow limestone (**No. 2**).[1] This
appears to be of much earlier date than the limestones found
higher in the sections. *Orbitoides* are found in all the limestones
of this section; but those of No. 2 are of the type associated
with rocks of Nummulitic (Eocene and Oligocene) age, whilst the
Orbitoidal limestones which follow are probably of Miocene age.

---

[1] These numbers are those employed in Mr. Andrews' collection of rocks.

This yellow limestone is composed largely of foraminifera; and, besides these, it contains polyzoa and *Lithothamnion*, both branching and massive. The organisms are imbedded in a fine-grained calcitic rock, which seems to have resulted from the crystallization of a fairly pure calcareous mud. It shows signs of having been indurated by the overlying basalt.

The foraminifera recognized in the thin slices of this rock are as follows :—

Cristellaria italica? (Defrance).

Saracenaria italica, Defrance, 1824, Dict. Sci. Nat., vol. xxxii, p. 177 ;
 vol. xlvii (1827), p. 344, Atlas Conch., pl. xiii, fig. 6.
Cristellaria italica (Defr.), Brady, 1884, Report Challenger, vol. ix, p. 544,
 pl. lxviii, figs. 17, 18, 20–23.

A nearly complete lateral and vertical section occurs in this slide (No. 2).

Cristellaria rotulata? (Lamarck).

Lenticulites rotulata, Lamarck, 1804, Annales du Muséum, vol. v, p. 188, No. 3 ;
 Tabl. Encycl. Méth., pl. 466, fig. 5.
Cristellaria rotulata (Lamarck), Brady, 1884, Rep. Chall., vol. ix, p. 547,
 pl. lxix, figs. 13a, b.

A vertical section, traversing from aperture to the opposite edge in the septal plane.

Globigerina bulloides, d'Orbigny.

G. bulloides, d'Orbigny, 1826, Ann. Sci. Nat., vol. vii, p. 277, No. 1 ; Modèle,
 No. 76 and (young) No. 17 ; Brady, 1884, Rep. Chall., vol. ix,
 p. 593, pl. lxxvii, and pl. lxxix, figs. 3–7.

A specimen somewhat fragmentary, but probably belonging to the above species.

Planorbulina mediterranensis, d'Orbigny.

P. mediterranensis, d'Orb., 1826, Ann. Sci. Nat., vol. vii, p. 280, No. 2, pl. xiv,
 figs. 4–6 ; Modèle, No. 79 ; Brady, 1884, Rep. Chall., vol. ix,
 p. 656, pl. xcii, figs. 1–3.

Several specimens, with a more or less neatly rounded contour, like that of the above species, appear in our rock-sections.

Truncatulina lobatula (Walker & Jacob).

Nautilus lobatulus, Walker & Jacob, 1798, Adams' Essays, Kanmacher's ed.,
 p. 642, pl. xiv, fig. 36.
Truncatulina lobatula, Brady, 1884, Rep. Chall., vol. ix, p. 660, pl. xcii, fig. 10 ;
 pl. xciii, figs. 1, 4, 5 ; pl. 105, figs. 4, 5.

This form is here represented by numerous examples cut in various directions; thus a good idea may be gathered of the actual shape of the test.

The shell-wall is fairly thin and simple, and the test is flat on the upper, and evenly inflated on the inferior, face. In the regularity of the chambers this form agrees very closely with the variety figured by d'Orbigny from the Miocene of Vienna under the name of *Truncatulina bouaana*,[1] which form has been included in the synonymy of *T. lobatula* by H. B. Brady. The chances that these sections represent a *Pulvinulina* are small, on account of the comparative thinness and simplicity of the outer walls of the chambers, although the two genera have isomorphous forms.

Pulvinulina repanda (Fichtel & Moll). (Pl. **XX**, Fig. 1.)

Nautilus repandus, Fichtel & Moll, 1798, Test. micr., p. 35, pl. iii, figs. *a–d.*
Rotalia repanda (F. & M.), Parker & Jones, 1860, Ann. Mag. Nat. Hist.,
    ser. iii, vol. v, p. 175, No. 25.
Pulvinula repanda (F. & M.), P. & J., in Carpenter, 1862, Introd. Foram.,
    p. 210.
Placentula repanda (F. & M.), Berthelin, 1878, Foram. Bourgneuf et Pornichet,
    p. 41, No. 68.
Pulvinulina repanda (F. & M.), Terrigi, 1880, Atti dell' Accad. Pontif.,
    ann. xxxiii, p. 206, pl. iii, fig. 61 ; Brady, 1884, Rep. Chall.,
    vol. ix, p. 684, pl. civ, figs. 18*a–c.*

Several good transverse and vertical sections of a pulvinuline form, with a thick *test*, and with characteristically coarse pores, have been noted in the yellow limestone (No. 2) [see photograph, Fig. 1]. The average diameter of the test is $\frac{1}{10}$ inch. These examples compare most closely with the above species, which is very frequent and large in the coral-sands at the present time. To aid the comparison, a section of a recent specimen has been made and examined, and bears out this conclusion.

Rotalia schroeteriana, Parker & Jones.

R. schroeteriana (Parker & Jones MS.), Carpenter, 1862, Introd. Foram.,
    p. 213, pl. xiii, figs. 7–9.
R. tuberosa, Karrer, 1867, Sitzungsb. k. Akad. Wiss. Wien, vol. lv, p. 349,
    pl. i, fig. 4.
R. schroeteriana, Parker & Jones, Brady, 1884, Rep. Chall., vol. ix, p. 707,
    pl. 105, figs. 7*a–c.*

Amongst the rotaline sections in specimen No. 2 there are some strongly developed examples, coarsely porous, sub-orbicular, and with the surface irregularly relieved with rounded prominences. These specimens appear to agree most nearly with the above species. *R. schroeteriana* has been described from Miocene deposits, and is also found living in the Eastern Archipelago.

---

[1] Foram. Foss. Vienne, 1846, p. 169, pl. ix, figs. 24–26.

Gypsina globulus (Reuss).

Ceriopora globulus, Reuss, 1847, Haidinger's Naturw. Abhandl., vol. ii, p. 33,
   pl. v, fig. 7.
Orbitolina lævis, Parker & Jones, 1860, Ann. Mag. Nat. Hist., ser. iii, vol. vi,
   p. 31, No. 7.
Tinoporus pilaris, Brady, 1876, Ann. Soc. Malac. Belg., vol. vi, p. 103.
Tinoporus baculatus (Montfort), var. *sphæroidalis,* Carter, 1877, Ann. Mag. Nat.
   Hist., ser. iv, vol. xix, p. 215, pl. xiii, figs. 18, 20.
Gypsina vesicularis (Parker & Jones), var. *sphæroidalis,* Carter, 1877, Ann. Mag.
   Nat. Hist., ser. iv, vol. xx, p. 173.
Gypsina globulus (Reuss), Brady, 1884, Rep. Chall., vol. ix, p. 717, pl. 101, fig. 8.

This well-known species is frequent in coral deposits throughout
the Tertiaries and in recent times. Their circular sections are
numerously represented in this limestone. The average diameter
of these specimens is about $\frac{1}{16}$ inch.

Amphistegina lessonii, d'Orbigny.

A. lessonii, d'Orbigny, 1826, Ann. Sci. Nat., vol. vii, p. 304, No. 3, pl. xvii,
   figs. 1–4.
A. lessonii, d'Orbigny : Brady, 1884, Rep. Chall., vol. ix, p. 740, pl. 111,
   figs. 1–7.

This species is common in the sections now described, and it is
of fairly average size. *A. lessonii* occurs in many of the Tertiary
strata dating from the Eocene ; and it is common at the present
time in tropical and sub-tropical seas.

Heterostegina depressa, d'Orbigny.   (Pl. XX, Fig. 1.)

H. depressa, d'Orbigny, 1826, Ann. Sci. Nat., vol. vii, p. 305, pl. xvii, figs. 5–7 ;
   Modèle, No. 99.
H. antillarum, d'Orbigny, 1839, Foram. Cuba, p. 121, pl. vii, figs. 24, 25.
H. helvetica, Kaufmann, 1867, Geol. Beschreib. des Pilatus, p. 153, pl. ix,
   figs. 6–10.
H. depressa, d'Orbigny : Brady, 1884, Rep. Chall., vol. ix, p. 746, pl. 112,
   figs. 14–20.

Numerous examples of the above species appear in the sections
of limestone No. 2. They are of moderately large size, averaging
one-sixth of an inch in width. These specimens also exhibit the
large flange-like portion strongly developed ; and which, when
isolated from the major part of the shell, may easily be mistaken
for one of the thick *Cycloclypeinæ.* The specimens seen in these
sections also show the transverse subdivision of the chambers into
chamberlets, thus being distinguished from the closely allied
Operculina.

Orbitoides (Discocyclina) dispansa (Sowerby).   (Pl. XX, Fig. 1.)

Lycophris dispansus, Sowerby (1837), Trans. Geol. Soc. Lond., ser. ii, vol.
   (1840), pp. 327 and 718, pl. xxiv, figs. 16 and 16a, b.

Orbitulites dispansa (Sow.), d'Archiac, 1850, Histoire progrès Géologie,
"Tableau de la Faune nummulitique," vol. iii, p. 230.
Lycophris dispansus, Sow., Carter, 1853, Ann. Mag. Nat. Hist., ser. II, vol. xi,
p. 172, pl. vii, figs. 23–29; (1853), Journ. Bombay Br. R. Asiatic
Soc., vol. v, pt. 18, p. 136, pl. ii, figs. 23–29; 1857, Geol. Papers
Western India, p. 451, pl. xviii, figs. 16, 16a, 16b, and p. 545,
pl. xxiii, figs. 23–29.
Orbitoides dispansa (Sow.), Carter, 1861, Ann. Mag. Nat. Hist., ser. III, vol. viii,
p. 447, pl. xvi, fig. 1; pl. xvii, fig. 1.
Orbitoides (*Discocyclina*) *dispansa* (Sow.), Gümbel, 1868 (1870), Abhandl.
m.-ph. Cl. k. bayer. Ak. Wiss., vol. x, p. 701, pl. iii, figs. 40–47.
Orbitoides dispansa (Sow.), Hantken, 1871, A magy. kir. földt. int. évkönyve,
vol. x, p. 132, pl. ii, figs. 10a, b; and Mitth. Jahrb. k. ungar.
geol. Anstalt, vol. i, p. 138, pl. ii, figs. 10a, b; Brady, 1875,
Geol. Mag., dec. II, vol. ii, p. 536, pl. xiv, figs. 2a, b, c;
Hantken, 1875 (1876), A magy. kir. földt. int. évkönyve, vol. iv,
p. 72, pl. xi, fig. 3; and Mitth. Jahrb. k. ungar. geol. Anstalt,
vol. iv, 1875 (1881), p. 82, pl. xi, fig. 3; Fritsch, 1878,
Palæontographica, Suppl. iii, Lief. i, p. 142, pl. xviii, fig. 10;
pl. xix, fig. 8; Brady, 1878, Jahrb. Mijn. Ned. Oost-Indie,
vol. vii, pt. 2, p. 164, pl. ii, figs. 2a–c; Medlicott & Blanford,
1879, Geol. India, pp. 340 and 459, pl. xv, fig. 8.
Orbitoides (*Discocyclina*) *dispansa* (Sow.), Bütschli, 1880, in Bronn, Klassen,
etc., Thier-Reichs, p. 215, pl. xii, fig. 16.
Orbitoides dispansa (Sow.), Martin, 1881, Samml. geol. Reichs-Mus. Leiden [1],
vol. i, Heft 2, p. 112, pl. vi, figs. 1–3.
Orbitoides (*Discocyclina*) *dispansa* (Sow.), Jennings, 1888, Geol. Mag., dec. III,
vol. v, p. 530, pl. xiv, fig. 6.
Orbitoides dispansa (Sow.), Verbeek, 1891, "Voorloopig Bericht over Nummu-
lieten, Orbitoiden, en Alveolinen van Java," Nat. Tijdschr.. v.
Nederl.-Indië, vol. li, p. 120, figs. 9a, b; Verbeek & Fennema,
1896, "Descr. géol. Java et Madoura," vol. i, pl. ix, figs.
148, 149; pl. x, figs. 158–160; vol. ii, p. 1173.

It has been noticed by previous authors, who have described
Orbitoides from the Eastern Archipelago and India, that the older
strata comprising the Eocene and Oligocene are characterized by
the type of *Orbitoides* limited by the subgenus *Discocyclina*, which
has the chambers of the median plane of a rectangular shape;
whilst the Miocene strata yield *Orbitoides* of the subgeneric type
Lepidocyclina, which has the median chambers lozenge-shaped or
subcircular.

The present section (No. 2) shows a few examples of *Orbitoides*
somewhat fractured on the flanged portion. Some of these fragments of the flange are turned in upon the plane of section, thus
accurately showing the shape of the median chambers, and
conclusively prove the affinity of the present species to the
Discocyclinæ. Special attention is drawn to this occurrence, since
the great mass of the Orbitoidal Limestone of Christmas Island
is composed of *Lepidocyclinæ*, and are therefore presumably of
Miocene age, whilst these now mentioned are possibly of Upper
Eocene or Oligocene age.

At the actual contact of the basalt with the limestone bed just described, the rock is composed of comminuted limestone intermingled with granules of glassy basalt or palagonite (specimen **No. 3**). In the limestone fragments of this rock foraminifera, such as *Heterostegina*, can still be distinguished, but they are much altered by the action of heat from the basalt.

The rock (**No. 522**) above the first basalt sheet is a yellowish limestone, not quite so dark as No. 2, and, as far as can be seen, is devoid of *Orbitoides*. The foraminifera are as a whole somewhat different from that of the preceding limestone (No. 2). Besides foraminifera, which are here numerous, there are remains of polyzoa, echinoderm spines, *Lithothamnion*, and other calcareous algæ. The rock is granular or hemicrystalline, whilst here and there it shows traces of travertine structure possibly due to the deposition of carbonate of lime from the flow of warm or heated currents of water.

The foraminifera observed in sections of this limestone (522) are as follows :—

? *Trochammina*, sp.

Textularia rugosa (Reuss).

Plecanium rugosum, Reuss, 1869, Sitzungsb. k. Ak. Wiss. Wien, vol. lix, p. 453, pl. i, figs. 3a, b.

The specimen in our section shows the irregular contour, similar to that of the above-mentioned species. It is usually found associated with coral reefs.

Bolivina beyrichi, Reuss.
Bolivina pygmæa, Brady. Rare.
? *Sphæroidina*. Spherical segments.
? *Pullenia*, sp. Very rare.

Truncatulina lobatula (Walker & Jacob).

As in the former rock-specimen, this species is fairly common in the sections. A few of the examples are higher in the vertical line, and therefore more nearly resembling *T. refulgens* (Montfort).

Pulvinulina repanda (F. & M.).

One or two examples of this species are present also in this rock.

Gypsina globulus (Reuss). Several fine specimens.

Rotalia schroeteriana (Parker & Jones).

Some very excellent sections, in both transverse and vertical direction, are seen in this specimen (No. 522).

Rotalia clathrata, Brady. (Pl. XX, Fig. 2.)

Rotalia clathrata, Brady, 1884, Rep. Chall., vol. ix, p. 709, pl. 107, figs. 8, 9.

One of the more striking forms in No. 522 may be referred to the above species. In section the surface reticulation is represented by square-ended projections. The shell-wall in this species, as in the other allied *Rotaliæ*, is coarsely tubulated. Longest diameter of the test $\frac{1}{16}$ inch.

This is not an isolated instance of a recent species occurring for the first time in the Miocene of Christmas Island, as will be seen by referring to subsequent pages. It is interesting to note that this rare form has been found only in the South Pacific, in shallow or moderately shallow water.

Gypsina globulus (Reuss).

This species is represented in this rock-section by several specimens. They are rather more irregular in internal structure than those of the preceding limestone (No. 2), and are altogether smaller in size.

Amphistegina lessonii, d'Orbigny.

This is again common in the section before us. It may be distinguished from *Pulvinulina elegans* (d'Orb.) by the sigmoid form of the septa and the alar extension of the chambers on the inferior surface.

Heterostegina depressa, d'Orbigny.

Frequent, but not so common as in the foregoing limestone (No. 2).

The last-mentioned limestone (No. 522) is succeeded by a second sheet of basalt with accompanying beds of tuff. The limestones which follow are of considerable thickness, and as a rule are crowded with *Orbitoides*; although there are some exceptions where these are rare.

The genus *Orbitoides* is represented, in the limestones now about to be described, by the Lepidocycline subgenus only, and this seems to indicate that the beds are related to others, in the same geographical area, which have been well investigated for their microzoic fauna and are of Miocene age.[1]

The first of the Miocene Orbitoidal Limestones is specimen **No. 924**, which was taken in contact with the basalt bed above referred to, and to the south of Flying Fish Cove at Smith Point. Thin slices of this rock exhibit layers of travertine, differing from the previous occurrence in being evenly stratified and not filling up angular cavities. This was probably formed by deposition from warm currents flowing over an evenly laid, sandy sea-bottom. The rock itself is roughly crystalline, with many organic particles interspersed; these latter are of an ash-grey colour, with the exception of the more gigantic forms as *Orbitoides* and *Carpenteria*, which are yellowish brown.

The organisms present in limestone No. 924 consist of polyzoa, echinoderm spines, foraminifera, and *Lithothamnion*.

The foraminifera are as follows:—

Spiroloculina, sp.

In the more finely grained material of this rock there are one or two examples of a small *Spiroloculina*, of the type of *Sp. asperula*, Karrer,[2] or *Sp. nitida*, d'Orbigny[3]; but, owing to the obscuration of the specimens by the surrounding material, it is difficult to say whether the test is finely arenaceous or not.

Miliolina trigonula (Lamarck).

Miliolites trigonula, Lamarck, 1804, Ann. du Mus, vol. v, p. 351, No. 3;
   1822, Anim. sans Vert., vol. vii, p. 612, No. 3.
Miliolina trigonula (Lam.), Brady, 1884, Rep. Chall., vol. ix, p. 164, pl. iii,
   figs. 14–16.

Several specimens occur in No. 924. It is a well-known Tertiary form; and in recent deposits is at home in depths down to 100 fathoms.

Miliolina subrotunda (Montagu).

Vermiculum subrotundum, Montagu, 1803, Test. Brit., pt. ii, p. 521.
Miliolina subrotunda (Montagu), Brady, 1884, Rep. Chall., vol. ix, p. 168, pl. v,
   figs. 10, 11.

This species is well seen in the sections and distinguished by its subcircular contour. It has occurred in other Miocene deposits, and is frequent as an inhabitant of moderately shallow water

---

[1] See Verbeek & Fennema, " Descr. géol. Java et Madoura," Appendix, vol. ii, 1896. Also Newton & Holland, Ann. Mag. Nat. Hist., ser. vii, vol. iii, pp. 256, 257.
[2] Sitzungsb. k. Ak. Wiss. Wien, vol. lvii, 1868, p. 136, pl. i, fig. 10.
[3] Ann. Sci. Nat., vol. vii, 1826, p. 298, No. 4.

around certain coasts; and it is especially common in some coral-sand deposits. In this limestone, No. 924, *M. subrotunda* is fairly common.

Miliolina ? oblonga (Montagu).

Vermiculum oblongum, Montagu, 1803, Test. Brit., p. 622, pl. xiv, fig. 9.
Miliolina oblonga (Montagu), Brady, 1884, Rep. Chall., vol. ix, p. 160, pl. v,
    figs. 4*a*, *b*.

A specimen occurs in this limestone, probably referable to the above species.

? *Uvigerina*, near *brunnensis*, Karrer.

Uvigerina brunnensis, Karrer, 1877, Geol. k. F.-J. Wasserleitung, p. 385,
    pl. xvi*b*, fig. 49; Brady, 1884, Rep. Chall., vol. ix, p. 577,
    pl. lxxv, figs. 4, 5.

This is a vertical section of a test which closely resembles a strongly inflated *Uvigerina*. In outline it may be compared with the above form, which was recorded by Karrer from Tertiary strata at Berchtoldsdorf, near Vienna. Our specimen has a rather large globose primordial chamber. The test measures $\frac{1}{24}$ inch (1·04 mm.) in length, which is equal to other recorded specimens.

Globigerina bulloides, d'Orbigny.

One specimen occurs in our slides of No. 924.

Globigerina conglobata, Brady. (Pl. XX, Fig. 3.)

Brady, 1879, Quart. Journ. Micr. Sci., new ser., vol. xix, p. 72; idem, 1884,
    Rep. Chall., vol. ix, p. 603, pl. lxxx, figs. 1–5; pl. lxxxii, fig. 5.

This appears to be the first recorded occurrence of the above species in the fossil condition. Two fine specimens were seen in our sections of No. 924.

Planorbulina, sp. near *acervalis*, Brady.

Growing upon some of the larger organisms, and also upon fragments of consolidated material in the rock, may be seen many specimens of an adherent foraminifer, possibly to be referred to the above species.[1] The chambers are more crowded or compressed in this form than in the somewhat similar *Gypsina inhærens*.

Truncatulina lobatula (W. & J.).

A solitary specimen of the above was noticed in our sections of No. 924.

---

[1] Rep. Chall., vol. ix, 1884, p. 657, pl. xcii, fig. 4.

Carpenteria, sp. near *C. lithothamnica*, Uhlig. ·

Carpenteria lithothamnica, Uhlig, 1886, Jahrb. k. k. geol. Reichsanstalt,
    vol. xxxvi, p. 189, pl. v, figs. 1–3.

A somewhat crushed specimen of *Carpenteria* occurs in a
section of No. 924. In some respects it agrees with Uhlig's
C. lithothamnica, of which he also figures a section (fig. 3, loc. cit.).
Our specimen also bears points of resemblance to *C. monticularis*,
Carter.[1] It is in lateral measurement one-eighth of an inch.

This occurrence of *Carpenteria* in rocks as old as the Miocene is
interesting ; and, until Uhlig's discovery of them in the Tertiary
beds of the Carpathians, and Sir John Murray's record of them
from the rocks of Malta,[2] they appear to have been unknown as
fossils.

Polytrema miniaceum (Pallas).

Millepora miniacea, Pallas, 1766, Elenchus Zoophytorum, p. 251.
M. miniacea (Pallas), Linné, 1788, Syst. Nat., 13th (Gmelin's) ed., vol. i, pt. 6,
    p. 3784, No. 6.
Polytrema miniaceum (Linné), Brady, 1884, Rep. Chall., vol. ix, p. 721, pl. 100,
    figs. 5–9 ; pl. 101, fig. 1.

In our section of No. 924 there are several conical foraminiferal
organisms, and tapering branchlets which strongly resemble the
sections of *P. miniaceum* seen in recent reef-rocks, and notably
those from the Funafuti atoll. The specimens here under notice
have a basis of rounded cellules, to which are added superficial
layers of chamberlets, elongated in the upward direction of growth.
There are apparently no reliable records of this genus from fossil
deposits.

Amphistegina lessonii, d'Orbigny.

This species is here very rare.

Heterostegina depressa, d'Orbigny.

This form is also very rare in this limestone.

Orbitoides (*Lepidocyclina*) *neodispansa*, sp. nov. (Pl. XX, Fig. 3.)

Test discoidal, thicker in the centre and surrounded by a peripheral flange. The curve from the centre to the edge makes
a more sudden sweep than it does in *O. papyracea* and its Miocene
analogue *O. verbeeki*. The surface of the test studded with bosses
of solid shell material, which are the salient bases of cones inserted

---

[1] Ann. Mag. Nat. Hist., ser. IV, vol. xix, 1877, pl. xiii, figs. 9–12.
[2] Scott. Geogr. Mag., 1890, p. 27 (sep. copy), and pl. i.

between the regular flattened and cylindrical chamberlets of the outer series in *Orbitoides.* The medium series of chamberlets are somewhat elliptical and alternate with one another. Average breadth $\frac{1}{4}$ inch (5 mm.); thickness $\frac{1}{16}$ inch (1·56 mm.). Very common in No. 924.

It is most probable that the form figured by Verbeek and Fennema (tom. cit., p. 1178, pl. xi, fig. 168) as *Lepidocyclina,* species *d,* is comparable with those we have just described. The dimensions of the former are stated to be 2¼ mm., which is about half the size of our specimens.

The limestone next in succession is from the middle of Flying Fish Cove at 480 feet, and its reference number is **571.**

It is a hard white limestone with dark spots, and it weathers with a pitted surface and becomes splintery. The rock is partially crystallized, but the organisms, especially the foraminifera, are not thereby obscured.

The organic contents of this specimen are fragments of *Lithothamnion,* foraminifera (*Orbitoides* absent), corals, and molluscan shells.

The foraminifera present in the sections of No. 571 are as follows :—

Miliolina ? *undosa* (Karrer).

Quinqueloculina undosa, Karrer, 1867, Sitz. k. Ak. Wiss. Wien, vol. lv, p. 361,
  pl. iii, fig. 3.
Miliolina undosa (Karrer), Brady, 1884, Rep. Chall., vol. ix, p. 176, pl. vi,
  figs. 6–9.

A transverse section of a flattened and furrowed *Miliolina* is seen in the slide of No. 571. It appears to agree most nearly with the above species.

Miliolina agglutinans (d'Orbigny).

Quinqueloculina agglutinans, d'Orbigny, 1839, Foram. Cuba, p. 168, pl. xii,
  figs. 11–13.
Miliolina agglutinans (d'Orb.), Brady, 1884, Rep. Chall., vol. ix, p. 180,
  pl. viii, figs. 6, 7.

A good transverse section of an arenaceous *Miliolina* comparable with *M. agglutinans* occurs in No. 571. The species is an inhabitant of shallow-water areas, and is frequent at the present day in coral-sands.

? *Gaudryina pupoides,* d'Orbigny.

A young individual resembling the above species is found in No. 571.

Planorbulina ? mediterranensis, d'Orbigny.

Several specimens of a *Planorbulina* are seen in the slides of No. 571, in some cases adherent to other objects. One of the specimens seen is attached to the flanged portion of a *Heterostegina.*

Carpenteria, spp.

This genus seems to have been important in the formation of some of these older limestones. One form here noticed closely resembles *C. monticularis* of Carter. Another form, of which there are two specimens present, has certain of the walls of the test strongly undulated on the outer surface. This modification may possibly agree with the coarser form *C. utricularis,* Carter.

Rotalia schroeteriana?, Parker & Jones.

Several sections of a *Rotalia,* possibly of the above species, occurs in No. 571.

Gypsina globulus (Reuss).

One very fine section of this form occurs here.

Amphistegina lessonii, d'Orbigny.

This species is here tolerably common and typical in form.

Heterostegina depressa, d'Orbigny.

The specimens of the above are numerous in No. 571, and are very complanate or outspread. The sections of the isolated, flanged portions of the test might easily be mistaken for *Cycloclypeus,* were the central parts of the test not present in the slides.

No. 861. Limestone in contact with basalt and palagonite in south of Cove. In the limestone portion are large masses of *Lithothamnion* intergrown with foraminifera (*Planorbulina*); there are also polyzoa and many foraminifera present. The surface of the basalt is coated with a layer of *Lithothamnion* and other adherent and encrusting organisms. Possibly this alga, which is a peculiar form of *Lithothamnion,* could grow on the rock whilst the latter was still warm.

Foraminifera :

Miliolina, sp.
Textularia rugosa (Reuss). Common.
Globigerina, sp., near *pachyderma* (Ehr.). Very rare.

Planorbulina mediterranensis, d'Orb.
Planorbulina larvata, P. & J.
(Both the above forms of *Planorbulina* are intergrown in this
specimen with a massive *Lithothamnion.*)
   Carpenteria lithothamnica?, Uhlig. Frequent.
Rupertia, sp. Basal segments adherent to a floor consisting of
Lithothamnion, which coats the surface of the basalt.
   Rotalia papillosa, var. *compressiuscula,* Brady. Very common.
Gypsina globulus (Reuss). Occasional.
Amphistegina lessonii, d'Orbigny. Frequent.
Heterostegina depressa, d'Orbigny. Several fragments.

Towards the side of the Cove whence the succession of rock
specimens now being described were taken, two specimens were
collected on either side of a basaltic mass, numbered 229 and
220 respectively.

Taking the specimen No. 229 first, it is seen to have many
points in common with the specimen No. 571 noticed above,
and although it differs from that rock in some slight degree of
minute structure, yet they contain so much in common and are in
themselves different from those rocks immediately below and above
that they are presumably different parts of the same bed.

No. 229 is a very hard, pale cream-coloured or whitish limestone.
Thin sections of the rock show it to be composed of *Lithothamnion*
in some quantity of the laminar and investing type, many foraminifera (but no *Orbitoides* present), echinoderm plates, and polyzoa.
The foraminifera in **No. 229** are as follows :—

Textularia rugosa (Reuss).

Several typical specimens are seen in this section.

Planorbulina acervalis?, Brady.

The specimens referred doubtfully to the above species are
adherent and forming a depressed layer, with thin-walled chambers.
They are fairly common in the section.

Carpenteria, sp. near *C. monticularis,* Carter.

Mostly fragmentary, but there is one example with a perfectly
enclosed chamber - cavity. The separate pieces of the test are
numerous in this section.

Pulvinulina repanda (Fichtel & Moll).

One good specimen was noticed in the slide of No. 229.

Amphistegina lessonii, d'Orbigny.

The specimens of this species arc both common and well-developed. Some of the tests are very thick and belong to the dome-shaped variety, which has been often noticed under separate specific names, from beds of Miocene age. This variety, however, is not confined to fossil deposits, it having been frequently seen in coral-sands of recent times.

Heterostegina depressa, d'Orbigny.

This species is here numerous and of a somewhat peculiar type, the central portion being much swollen, whilst the flanged portion is not so expansive as in specimens noticed earlier in this paper.

Limestone **No. 220** is the rock from the south side of the basalt mass mentioned, and is entirely different from the preceding specimen. It bears a strong resemblance to No. 924 previously described, and there cannot be much doubt that this specimen is an extension of No. 924.

It is a pale or cream-coloured limestone, full of *Orbitoides.*

Seen under the microscope parts of the rock appear somewhat brecciated. The rock is well crystallized, but nevertheless the organisms are perfectly preserved.

The rock is composed of a branching *Lithothamnion* (one specimen of *Orbitoides* has it growing upon the surface), foraminifera, echinoderm plates, polyzoa, and molluscan shell-fragments.

The foraminifera arc as follows :—

Carpenteria, sp.

This genus is here represented by numerous fragments of the shell-wall, but it is impossible to say to what species it may belong, although it bears the same general characters of the test as *C. monticularis.*

Gypsina inhærens? (Schultze).

There are numerous irregularly grown adherent foraminifera in specimen No. 220 which appear to belong to the above species.

Gypsina globulus (Reuss).

One specimen in No. 220.

Polytrema miniaceum (Pallas) and var. *involva,* Chapman, nov.

One of the adherent forms of the foraminifera in No. 220 is very similar in structure to the laminar or outspreading forms of

P. miniaceum found at Funafuti and elsewhere in coral rocks, in which the foraminifer alternates with other encrusting organisms. In this variety the chamberlets are elongated in the direction of growth or adherence, and the form shows little or no tendency to make the prolongations so characteristic of the type species. Some of the specimens of *Polytrema* here observed are more normal in appearance, having the conical branching habit of growth.

Amphistegina lessonii, d'Orbigny.

This species is common in No. 220.

Heterostegina depressa, d'Orbigny.

This form is rare, and not strongly developed in limestone No. 220.

Orbitoides neodispansa, sp. nov. (Pl. XX, Fig. 4.)

This species is very common in the specimen No. 220, constituting about one-third of the entire bulk of the rock. The specimens bear exactly the same characters as those of No. 924, and are in a similar condition of preservation.

No. 219. "Eastern edge of basalt mass, first inland cliff, Smith Point." Close to 220.

A limestone with veins of basalt and palagonite. This rock contains *Lithothamnion*, foraminifera, corals, and polyzoa.

Foraminifera:

Miliolina alveoliniformis, Brady. Rare.
Carpenteria, sp. Fragments.
Amphistegina lessonii, d'Orb. Rare.
Heterostegina depressa, d'Orb. Common.
Orbitoides (Lepidocyclina) ephippioides, sp. nov. Rare.

No. 595. A fine-grained limestone with included fragments of palagonitic material and many foraminifera. This rests upon the bed of palagonite tuff seen in the face of the Southern Cliff (Batoe merah[1]).

Foraminifera:

Orbulina universa, d'Orb. Frequent.
Globigerina bulloides, d'Orb. Common.
Globigerina dubia, Egger. One specimen.
Discorbina, sp. Rare.

---

[1] See p. 277.

Planorbulina, sp. Frequent.
Truncatulina lobatula (W. & J.). Rare.
Polytrema miniaceum (Pallas). Numerous fragments.
Amphistegina lessonii, d'Orb. Rare.

No. 598. Flying Fish Cove (Batoe merah[1]), above 595 and below 841.

An organic limestone with some secondary calcareous (aragonitic) layers. The organic contents are *Lithothamnion,* foraminifera, echinoderm remains, and polyzoa.

Foraminifera :

Textularia rugosa (Reuss). Rare.
Carpenteria utricularis, Carter. Frequent.
Rotalia schroeteriana, P. & J. Frequent.
Amphistegina lessonii, d'Orb. (thickened form). Frequent.
Heterostegina depressa, d'Orb. Common.

The next specimen to be described is **No. 845,** which comes from the southern end of Flying Fish Cove. It is a yellowish limestone composed very largely of massive *Lithothamnion.*

In the interstitial portion of the rock the following foraminifera were detected.

Planorbulina larvata, P. & J.

A few specimens of a flat adherent form referable to the above species.

Planorbulina acervalis, Brady.

Some of the adherent planorbuline forms are meandering and thin or much depressed, and resemble *P. acervalis* in all their characters.

Gypsina inhærens? (Schultze).

One or two of the adherent specimens are of wandering habit, and the chambers are large and inflated. They possibly belong to the above species.

Heterostegina depressa, d'Orbigny.

Our section shows one solitary example of this species cut through somewhat obliquely. The specimen is a rather large example of this form.

---

[1] See p. 277.

R

Following closely upon No. 845 is **No. 844**, which we next proceed to examine.

This is a white limestone with numerous large *Orbitoides* apparent on both weathered and fractured surfaces. It is finely crystallized, and the rock has been fractured here and there with the rifts now infilled with clear secondary calcite.

The organic contents of the rock are *Lithothamnion*, many foraminifera, amongst which the *Orbitoides* mentioned are conspicuous, and numerous polyzoa.

The foraminifera are as follows :—

Spiroloculina excavata, d'Orbigny.

Spiroloculina excavata, d'Orbigny, 1846, Foram. Foss. Vienne, p. 271, pl. xvi, figs. 19–21; Brady, 1884, Rep. Chall., vol. ix, p. 151, pl. ix, figs. 5, 6.

A very fine and perfect transverse section of the above form was noticed in No. 844.

Miliolina alveoliniformis, Brady.

One individual in transverse section appears in this slide.

Sigmoïlina, sp. near *S. celata* (Costa).

Spiroloculina celata, Costa, 1855, Mem. Accad. Napoli, vol. ii, p. 126, pl. i, fig. 14; 1856, Atti dell' Accad. Pont., vol. vii, pl. xxvi, fig. 5.
Planispirina celata (Costa), Brady, 1884, Rep. Chall., vol. ix, p. 197, pl. viii, figs. 1–4.
Sigmoïlina celata (Costa), Schlumberger, 1887, Bull. Soc. Zool. France, vol. xii, p. 111, pl. vii, figs. 12–14; Goës, 1896, Bull. Mus. Comp. Zool. Harvard Coll., vol. xxix, No. 1, pt. 20.

There is not much doubt that our section (cut transversely) is referable to the above species. Its earliest appearance as a fossil has hitherto been in the Pliocene of the Nicobar Islands.

Textularia rugosa (Reuss).

Very rare in rock-specimen No. 844.

Amphistegina lessonii, d'Orbigny.

The specimens in No. 844 are both common and characteristic.

Orbitoides (*Lepidocyclina*) *insulæ-natalis*, sp. nov. (Pl. XX, Fig. 5.)

Near "*Lepidocyclina*, spp. *c* and *c*," Verbeek & Fennema, 1896, Descr. géol. Java et Madoura, vol. i, pl. xi, figs. 166, 167; vol. ii, p. 1177.

This species is very conspicuous from the later Miocene limestones of Christmas Island. It is of large dimensions, being often

⅜ inch (19 mm.) in diameter. The form resembles a very large *O. dispansa*, and it further resembles this species in having the central area superficially studded with bosses of shell-material, which are the salient ends of inverted cones pointing towards the median plane. When the test is cut through tangentially these conical pillars appear as fibrous shell-substance surrounding the polygonal chamberlets. These cones cut longitudinally present a striking appearance from their fibrous (but non-tubulate) structure.

The chambers of the median plane are of that Lepidocycline type which appears as if imbricated, from the rounded ends of the chambers or chamberlets being alternate with those of the adjacent rows. The median series when cut through transversely is seen to be quite thin in the centre and to increase greatly in thickness or height towards the periphery. Another feature in the chamberlets of the median plane is the presence of stolon passages from one to another, thus giving a serrated appearance to the inner surfaces of the walls of each chamberlet. In this latter feature this species resembles the curious genus *Linderina*.[1]

Average diameter across the disc ½ inch (12·5 mm.); thickness ⅕ inch (5 mm.).

Next in order of succession we have **No. 562**, which is a pale cream-coloured limestone, very compact. This is from the upper cliff at about 500 feet. Viewed under the microscope the rock is seen to consist of clear crystalline calcite, which also fills the cracks appearing in various directions throughout the rock. This latter fact points to some disturbance of the rock-mass after consolidation. The rock is very full of organisms, consisting of *Lithothamnion*, foraminifera (amongst which the genus *Orbitoides* plays an important part), echinoderm plates, and polyzoa.

The following foraminifera were observed in specimen No. 562:—

Spiroloculina, sp.

One or two specimens of a neat *Spiroloculina* occur here, but it is impossible to say anything with regard to its specific relations from the sections.

Miliolina trigonula (Lamarck).

This is quite a common form in the sections of No. 562. Its relationship is clearly made out by the number of the specimens, cut in various directions.

---

[1] See Schlumberger, Bull. Soc. Géol. France, ser. III, vol. xxi, p. 120, figs. 3–5, woodcuts; pl. iii, figs. 7–9.

Miliolina alveoliniformis, Brady.

M. alveoliniformis, Brady, 1879, Quart. Journ. Micr. Sci., vol. xix, N.s., p. 54 ; idem, 1884, Rep. Chall., vol. ix, p. 181, pl. viii, figs. 15-20.

The specimen in our slides referred to the above species presents all the characters of the typical *M. alveoliniformis* in transverse section. It is interesting to note this occurrence of *M. alveoliniformis* in the Tertiary rocks for the first time as a fossil. It is a well-known form in coral sands, to which deposits it seems restricted.

Textularia rugosa (Reuss).

A few specimens of the above are seen in section No. 562.

Planorbulina mediterranensis?, d'Orbigny.

To this species we may with some reservation ascribe the neat adherent forms of *Planorbulinæ* seen in sections of No. 562.

Carpenteria, sp.

Numerous fragments of a *Carpenteria* occur in these sections (562). Since they have invariably been broken down into quite small pieces, it is not possible to say anything with regard to their specific relationship, excepting that they generally resemble the test of *Carpenteria monticularis*, Carter.

Amphistegina lessonii, d'Orbigny.

This is common in the limestone now being described.

Heterostegina depressa, d'Orbigny.

This species is frequent in No. 562.

Orbitoides (Lepidocyclina) sumatrensis, Brady. (Pl. XX, Fig. 6.)

Orbitoides sumatrensis, Brady, 1875, Geol. Mag., dec. ii, vol. ii, p. 536, pl. xiv, fig. 3 ; also Jaarb. Mijn. Ned. Ooste-Indië, 1878, vol. vii, pt. 2, p. 165, pl. ii, fig. 3.
Orbitoides (Lepidocyclina) sumatrensis, Brady : Newton & Holland, 1899, Ann. Mag. Nat. Hist., ser. vii, vol. iii, p. 259, pl. x, figs. 7-12.

This species was first described from the west coast of Sumatra, and Messrs. Newton & Holland have lately recorded the same form from the Miocene Limestone of Borneo.

The species resolves itself into two typical forms, one slightly different from the other in external shape and distinguished by the primordial chamber being megalospheric or . microspheric respectively. In this rock *O. sumatrensis* is associated with another form, not so numerously represented, referable to the species *O. verbeeki*, which, it is interesting to note, Newton & Holland described from their Bornean rocks as being associated with *O. sumatrensis*.

Orbitoides (Lepidocyclina) verbeeki, Newton & Holland.

Orbitoides papyracea, Brady, Geol. Mag., 1875, dec. II, vol. ii, p. 535, pl. xiv, fig. 1.
Lepidocyclina, sp. *g* and *k*, Verbeek & Fennema, Descr. géol. de Java et Madoura, 1896, vol. i, pl. xi, figs. 173–175, 177–180 ; vol. ii, p. 1178.
Orbitoides (Lepidocyclina) verbeeki, Newton & Holland, 1899, Ann. Mag. Nat. Hist., ser. VII, vol. iii, p. 259, pl. x, figs. 7–12.

One or two compressed forms of *Orbitoides* belonging to the above species were found in association with the preceding species.

Orbitoides (Lepidocyclina) neodispansa, sp. nov. (See p. 235.)

A few fragmentary specimens and one transverse section of the above form were found in this limestone No. 562. They appear to be slightly larger, however, than the typical forms described from rock-specimens Nos. 924 and 220.

No. 521 is a white limestone, somewhat cavernous, and with a pitted surface when weathered. From pinnacles at summit of cliff, at about 500 feet, immediately above No. 562. When viewed microscopically this rock varies from crystalline to finely granular or amorphous in different parts of the same slide. The constituent organisms of this limestone are *Lithothamnion*, many foraminifera, millepores, and echinoderm spines.

The following foraminifera were noticed in this rock :—

Miliolina trigonula (Lamarck).

Some typical sections of this form are present in our slides of No. 521.

Miliolina tricarinata (d'Orbigny).

Triloculina tricarinata, d'Orbigny, 1826, Ann. Sci. Nat., vol. vii, p. 299, No. 7; Modèle, No. 94.
Miliolina tricarinata (d'Orb.), Brady, 1884, Rep. Chall., vol. ix, p. 165, pl. iii, figs. 17*a*, *b*.

This species is a well-known Tertiary form ; it occurs in specimen No. 521, associated with the previous and other somewhat obscure species of *Miliolina*.

Carpenteria capitata, sp. nov. (Pl. XX, Fig. 7.)

Test normally adherent, of a somewhat erect habit of growth. The earliest - formed chambers are narrow and somewhat like those of the conical-shaped *Carpenteriæ*, and these are followed by a rudely spiral series of sub-globular chambers, the walls of which are thicker than those of the proximal portion. The later portion of the test is externally rough, appearing coarsely notched in section. This form has some affinities with *Rupertia* and possibly *Haddonia*. Height ¼ inch (6 mm.); greatest width 1/5 inch (4 mm.); thickness of the wall of the last chambers 1/5 inch (0·5 mm.).

Amphistegina lessonii, d'Orbigny.

This species is numerous in No. 521.

Heterostegina depressa, d'Orbigny.

The examples found in this limestone (521) are of extraordinary dimensions and have very extensive and thin flanges.

———

No. 646. Summit of Flying Fish Cove cliff ; from about the same horizon as 521. A limestone largely composed of *Lithothamnion*, foraminifera, and echinoderm remains.

Foraminifera :

Miliolina alveoliniformis, Brady. Rare.
Planorbulina larvata, P. & J. Frequent.
Gypsina globulus (Reuss). Rare.
Polytrema miniaceum (Pallas), var. *involva*, nov. (One large mass intergrown with *Lithothamnion*.)
Amphistegina lessonii, d'Orb. Common.
Heterostegina depressa, d'Orb. Frequent.
Orbitoides (*Lepidocyclina*) *sumatrensis*, Brady. Common.

———

The next specimen, **No. 550**, is a whitish limestone, compact, rather dense and amorphous, owing probably to the presence of granules derived from calcareous algæ. This is from about the same horizon as 562 (p. 243).

The organic remains constituting this rock are *Lithothamnion*, foraminifera, echinoderm spines, polyzoa, and lamellibranch shells.

The following foraminifera were observed in this rock :—

Miliolina bicornis? (Walker & Jacob).

Serpula bicornis, Walker & Jacob, 1798, Adams's Essays, Kanmacher's ed.,
    p. 633, pl. xiv, fig. 2.
Miliolina bicornis (W. & J.), Brady, 1884, Rep. Chall., vol. ix, p. 171, pl. vi,
    figs. 9, 11, 12.

A transverse section of a specimen closely resembling that of
M. bicornis is seen in the slide of No. 550. It is impossible,
however, to speak with certainty as to the exact species.

Miliolina trigonula (Lamarck).

Some examples of the above species are present in No. 550.

Textularia rugosa (Reuss).

Several specimens of this species occur in our slide.

Carpentaria, near *utricularis*, Carter.

Fragments of the tests of *Carpenteria* are rather numerous in
No. 550, and those with a distinctly pitted surface probably belong
to the above-named species. There are also some fragments with
more even surfaces which may belong to *C. monticularis*, Carter.

Rotalia schroeteriana?, Parker & Jones.

A species of *Rotalia* is common in this rock-specimen, which
with some reservation we may ascribe to the above form.

Gypsina globulus (Reuss).

This species occurs here in some numbers and is fairly large.

Amphistegina lessonii, d'Orbigny.

Common in the slides of No. 550.

Heterostegina depressa, d'Orbigny.

This species is represented in No. 550 by very large specimens,
some of which show a megalospheric commencement. The centre
of the disc in these specimens is very thick and often curved, giving
rise to sections showing both the vertical and tangential aspects
of the shell.

No. 551, at summit of cliff at about the same horizon as 521, is a white limestone with a somewhat crystalline texture. The organic contents may be put down as follows : *Lithothamnion*, sometimes encrusted with *Polytrema*; numerous foraminifera, including *Orbitoides*; and echinoderm spines.

The foraminifera are—

Spiroloculina, sp. near *asperula*, Czjzek.

An arenaceous form of *Spiroloculina* occurs in this limestone, which is perhaps referable to the above species. A similar form was noticed in No. 924.

Miliolina alveoliniformis, Brady.

Numerous sections of the above species occur in No. 551.

Polytrema miniaceum (Pallas), and var. *involva*, Chapman, nov.

Some free-growing specimens of the above form are seen in the slide of No. 551. One of the specimens is seen to be encrusting a nodular mass of *Lithothamnion*, after the manner of similar specimens we have observed in the material from the coral boring at Funafuti.

Heterostegina depressa, d'Orbigny.

Some occasional specimens were noticed in No. 551.

Orbitoides (Lepidocyclina) sumatrensis, Brady.

This species is common in No. 551.

Orbitoides (Lepidocyclina) insulæ-natalis, sp. nov.

A fragment or so of the above species occurs in this slide.

No. 841 occurs at the top of the cliff section at Flying Fish Cove, where the rock forms projecting pinnacles by weathering. It is a dense white limestone with some travertin, and composed chiefly of encrusting *Lithothamnion*. Many foraminifera are also present. Also many polyzoa and a *Serpula* were noticed in the section. This rock has a more recent aspect than any of those yet enumerated in the foregoing pages.

The foraminifera are—

Miliolina alveoliniformis, Brady.

Sections of the above form occur in No. 841, associated with other species of the same genus whose specific relationships cannot be easily made out.

Haddonia torresiensis, Chapman.

Haddonia torresiensis, Chapman, 1898, Journ. Linn. Soc. Lond., vol. xxvi, p. 452, pl. xxviii, and woodcut.

This interesting generic type was first found on coral rock from Torres Strait, and it has since occurred in many dredgings from the immediate vicinity of the Funafuti Atoll. The specimen seen in this section is a young individual attached to a fragment of limestone, and consists of three or four segments more or less creeping, the last of which is erect.

Textularia rugosa (Reuss).

Several specimens rather under the average size occur here.

Nodosaria radicula (Linné), var. *grandis*, nov. (Pl. XX, Fig. 8.)

A very fine section of a Nodosarian form cut accurately through the axial line is seen in the slide of No. 841. The apertures of the first-formed segments are well seen, and are elongated and tubular. The separate segments are well-marked by deeply impressed sutural divisions. There is no doubt of the affinity of this form. The thickness of the test and its exceptional size seem to merit a distinct varietal name.

Planorbulina acervalis, Brady.

This species is frequent in No. 841, and is seen to be attached to various fragments of shell and other material forming the rock.

Truncatulina, sp. near *lobatula* (W. & J.).

One or two examples of a thin-tested *Truncatulina* were noticed in this rock.

Carpenteria, sp.

Numerous fragments of a species of *Carpenteria* similar to *C. monticularis*, Carter, occur in No. 841.

Gypsina inhærens (Schultze).

This form occurs with some frequency in the slide of No. 841.

Polytrema miniaceum (Pallas), var. *involva*, Chapman, nov.

This form of the encrusting type before referred to occurs in some abundance in this rock.

Amphistegina lessonii, d'Orbigny.

The specimens here seen are both typical and common.

Heterostegina depressa, d'Orbigny.

This species is rare. One fine specimen, cut vertically, shows a megalospheric commencement.

No. 963. Blocks fallen from High Cliff, south of Flying Fish Cove; probably close to 841.

Rock composed of crystalline calcite. Some *Lithothamnion* and *Halimeda,* numerous foraminifera, and an echinoderm spine. This appears to be a transition rock between the Miocene and the recent limestones.

Foraminifera :

Globigerina bulloides, d'Orbigny. Several.
Globigerina conglobata, Brady. One specimen.
Planorbulina larvata, P. & J. Occasional.
Carpenteria monticularis, Carter. Fragments numerous.
Carpenteria utricularis, Carter. One good specimen.
Gypsina globulus (Reuss). One specimen.
Polytrema miniaceum (Pallas), var. *involva,* Chapman, nov. (encrusting form). Numerous.
Amphistegina lessonii, d'Orbigny. Frequent.
Orbitoides (*Lepidocyclina*) *verbeeki,* Newton & Holland. Fragments (? derived).

No. 549 is a specimen of the rock occurring at the base of the inland cliff at 500 feet, running south from the south-east end of Flying Fish Cove (see Map). It is a whitish or pale cream-coloured limestone, with some travertin. Besides many foraminifera (including *Orbitoides*) it contains *Lithothamnion* and polyzoa in small quantity.

The foraminifera noticed are as follows :—

Spiroloculina, sp.

Apparently an arenaceous form, but indeterminable.

Miliolina auberiana (d'Orbigny).

Quinqueloculina auberiana, d'Orbigny, 1839, Foram. Cuba, p. 167, pl. xii, figs. 1–3.
Miliolina auberiana (d'Orb.), Brady, 1884, Rep. Chall., vol. ix, p. 162, pl. v, figs. 8, 9 ; Goës, 1894, Kongl. Svenska Vet.-Akad. Handl., vol. xxv, p. 109, pl. xix, figs. 844a–d ; Millett, 1898, Journ. R. Micr. Soc., p. 505.

One specimen was seen in our slide of No. 549.

Miliolina ferussacii (d'Orbigny).

Quinqueloculina ferussacii, d'Orbigny, 1826, Ann. Sci. Nat., vol. vii, p. 301,.
No. 18; Modèle, No. 32.
Miliolina ferussacii (d'Orb.), Brady, 1884, Rep. Chall., vol. ix, p. 175, pl. 113,
figs. 17*a*, *b*; Chapman, 1891, Journ. R. Micr. Soc., p. 574,
pl. ix, fig. 8; Millett, 1898, Journ. R. Micr. Soc., p. 507, pl. xii,.
figs. 6*a*, *b*, 7*a-c*.

A common form in coral areas. The sections seen in our slide
are of the thin costate form. Not common in No. 549.

Textularia rugosa (Reuss).

This species is here somewhat common.

Textularia gramen, d'Orbigny.

Textularia gramen, d'Orbigny, 1846, Foram. Foss. Vienne, p. 248, pl. xv,.
figs. 4, 6; Brady, 1884, Rep. Chall., vol. ix, p. 365, pl. xliii,
figs. 9, 10.

One or two compressed *Textulariæ* occur here, which seem
referable to the above species.

Planorbulina mediterranensis, d'Orbigny.

Several attached specimens of the above *Planorbulina* were
noticed in the slide from No. 549.

Truncatulina refulgens (Montfort).

Cibicides refulgens, Montfort, 1808, Conchyl. System., vol. i, p. 122, 31ᵉ Genre.
Truncatulina refulgens (Montfort), d'Orbigny, 1826, Ann. Sci. Nat., vol. vii,
p. 279, pl. xiii, figs. 8–11; Modèle, No. 77; Brady, 1884, Rep.
Chall., vol. ix, p. 659, pl. xcii, figs. 7–9.

A *Truncatulina* with steep sides occurs with some frequency in
No. 549, which comes within the limits of the above form.

Amphistegina lessonii, d'Orbigny.

This species is common in No. 549.

Orbitoides (*Lepidocyclina*) *ephippioides*, sp. nov. (Pl. XX, Fig. 9.)

This species is a parallel form in the Lepidocycline group with
Orbitoides ephippium (Sow.),[1] of the Discocycline group. It bears.
some general resemblance to *O. insulæ-natalis*, but the more strongly

---

[1] *Lycophris ephippium*, Sowerby, 1837 [1840], Trans. Geol. Soc. Lond.,.
ser. II, vol. v, p. 327, pl. xxiv, figs. 15 and 15*a* and *b*.

bent individuals are, as one would suppose, nearer the parallel types
O. papyracea and *O. verbeeki.*
Average length ½ inch (12·5 mm.). Common in No. 549.

No. 993. Above Coffee Garden (see map, p. 280), in talus at
200 feet.
An Orbitoidal limestone with very little interstitial material, the
greater part consisting of foraminifera. Some *Lithothamnion* and
shell fragments. This limestone is mottled with veins and patches
of a grey colour.

Foraminifera:
Globigerina bulloides, d'Orb. Rare.
Gypsina globulus (Reuss). Frequent.
Heterostegina depressa, d'Orb. Common.
Orbitoides sumatrensis, Brady. Very abundant.
,,   *verbeeki,* Newton & Holland. Rare.
,,   *insulæ-natalis,* sp. nov.
,,   *ephippioides,* sp. nov.

No. 968. Foot of first inland cliff, Smith Point, about 60 feet
above sea.
A limestone partially crystalline. It is largely composed of
foraminifera, especially of the genus *Orbitoides,* and the alga
Lithothamnion.

Foraminifera:
Spiroloculina, sp. near *S. nitida,* d'Orbigny. Rare.
Miliolina ?auberiana, d'Orb. Rare.
,,   *trigonula* (Lam.). Rare.
,,   *circularis* (Born.). Rare.
,,   *alveoliniformis,* Brady. Several.
Orbitolites duplex, Carpenter. Several fragments.
Alveolina melo (F. & M.). Very rare.
Textularia rugosa (Reuss). Numerous.
Discorbina, sp. Rare.
Carpenteria monticularis, Carter. Fragments.
Gypsina inhærens (Schultze). Often growing in alternation with
Lithothamnion, forming nodules.
Amphistegina lessonii, d'Orbigny. Frequent, but small.
Heterostegina depressa, d'Orbigny. Numerous, but usually
fragmentary.
Orbitoides (Lepidocyclina) neodispansa, sp. nov. Rare.
,,   ,,   *verbeeki,* Newton & Holland. Rare.
,,   ,,   *ephippioides,* sp. nov. Frequent.
,,   ,,   *sumatrensis,* Brady. Very common.
,,   ,,   *murrayana,* sp. nov. (Pl. **XXI,**
Fig. 10.)

This species is exactly comparable in outline with the *O. stellata* of d'Archiac,[1] which, however, has rectangular chambers in the median plane and consequently belongs to the Discocycline series. On account of the difference of contour, this form being polygonal rather than discoidal, it was placed in a separate subgenus, *Astero-cyclina.* As Newton & Holland have shown, however (*loc. cit. supra*, p. 261), the more natural grouping of the *Orbitoides* is with the two subgenera *Discocyclina* and *Lepidocyclina.* The earlier known species having rectangular chambers in the median plane, we have named this form, which has the rounded imbricated chambers, distinctively as *Orbitoides (Lepidocyclina) murrayana*, after the originator of the expedition to Christmas Island which resulted in the collection of these specimens.

Our specimen has four rays, the contour between the rays being greatly incurved. The chambers of the median plane have straight sides and rounded or concave ends respectively. The chamberlets of the superficial layer are roughly spheroidal, especially towards the centre of the disc, becoming crowded, cylindrical, and greatly flattened towards the ends of the rays. The primordial chamber in our specimen is very large, measuring $\frac{1}{30}$ inch (·85 mm.) in diameter; it probably thus represents form A in the dimorphic sense. Diameter of the disc from point to point, $\frac{3}{8}$ inch (9·375 mm.).

No. 988. " From block in raised beach at north end of Flying Fish Cove."

A limestone, largely composed of a calcareous mud and rolled beach sand with *Orbitoides*, the latter having been chipped and worn, and afterwards enwrapped in a thick overgrowth of *Lithothamnion*, sometimes 4·5 mm. in thickness, which completely envelops all the large forms. (Pl. XXI, Fig. 16.)

The smaller specimens are free from the encrusting alga. The echinoderm fragments, *Lithothamnion*, *Globigerinæ*, and *Amphistegina* may be of more recent date.

Foraminifera :

Globigerina bulloides, d'Orbigny. Rare.
Amphistegina lessonii, d'Orbigny. Frequent.
Heterostegina depressa, d'Orbigny. Common.
Orbitoides (Lepidocyclina) verbeeki, Newton & Holland. Rare.
    ,,   ,,   *sumatrensis*, Brady. Common.
    ,,   ,,   *insulæ-natalis*, sp. nov. Common.

---

[1] *Calcarina stellata*, d'Archiac, 1846, Mém. Soc. géol. France, ser. ii, vol. ii, p. 199, pl. vii, figs. 1, 1a.

No. 347. "High Cliff, Sidney's Dale," south edge of narrow gorge, 250 feet above sea.

A somewhat reconstructed limestone (brecciated), with many adherent foraminifera. Probably of Upper Eocene or Oligocene age, approaching No. 2, described above, p. 226.

Foraminifera :

Planorbulina larvata, P. & J. Intergrown with *Lithothamnion*.
Carpenteria utricularis?, Carter. Several.
Rupertia stabilis, Wallich. Four specimens attached to fragments of limestone coated with *Lithothamnion*. (Pl. XXI, Fig. 11.)
Pulvinulina repanda (F. & M.). Common.
Rotalia schroeteriana, P. & J. Frequent.
Gypsina globulus (Reuss). Very fine. Common.
Amphistegina lessonii, d'Orbigny. Rare.
Orbitoides dispansa (Sow.). One specimen.

No. 318. Between basalt and limestone, Sidney's Dale.

A limestone with many organisms. The rock is somewhat decomposed and stained with a limonitic substance. The organic constituents are *Lithothamnion* and many foraminifera.

Foraminifera :

Pulvinulina repanda (F. & M.). Frequent.
Rotalia schroeteriana, P. & J. Frequent.
Heterostegina depressa, d'Orb. Rare.
Orbitoides (Discocyclina) dispansa (Sow.). Frequent. [One fragment shows the structure of the median chambers.]

No. 835. A limestone composed chiefly of *Orbitoides*, but in which traces of corals occur in places. There are also fragments of a branching *Lithothamnion* present. South of Flying Fish Cove, at 550 feet.

Foraminifera :

Miliolina, spp.
Planorbulina larvata, P. & J. Rare.
      „   *mediterranensis*, d'Orbigny. Rare.
Carpenteria monticularis, Carter. Large fragments.
      „   *utricularis*, Carter. Large fragments.
Amphistegina lessonii, d'Orbigny. Frequent.
Heterostegina depressa, d'Orbigny. Rare.
Orbitoides (Lepidocyclina) insulæ-natalis, sp. nov., var. *inæqualis*, nov. (Pl. XXI, Fig. 12.)

· This variety differs from the specific form in being altogether stouter, and more compressed in internal structure with regard to the peripheral chamberlets. It also differs essentially in being strongly undulated along the median plane, and sometimes in being unequally developed and much thicker on one side of the median layer. The undulated contour reminds one of *O.* (*L.*) *ephippioides,* but it is much thicker in the central disc than that species. Average diameter ¾ inch (16·8 mm.).

Orbitoides (*L.*) *andrewsiana,* sp. nov. Frequent.

No. 955. " Great block beneath High Cliff, North-East Point." An Orbitoidal limestone breccia, cemented by recent reef material, with the fragments overgrown with enormous encrusting Polytremata. This *Polytrema* is of great interest. It has also been met with by one of us in the recent reef rocks of the Funafuti Atoll, where it constitutes a large proportion of some of the limestones, and often found intergrown with *Lithothamnion.*

Foraminifera :
Globigerina bulloides, d'Orbigny. Rare.
Cymbalopora poeyi, d'Orb. Rare.
Polytrema miniaceum (Pallas), var. nov. *involva,* Chapman.
Amphistegina lessonii, d'Orbigny. Common.
Orbitoides (*Lepidocyclina*) *verbeeki,* Newton & Holland. Rare.
    ,,   ,,   *ephippioides,* sp. nov. One specimen.

Nos. 827 and **581.** " From low cliff of limestone resting on basalt, at head of valley, 500 feet, two miles south of Flying Fish Cove."

A limestone chiefly composed of *Orbitoides.* The material of the rock is well crystallized, and was originally deposited concentrically around the larger organisms.

Foraminifera :
Miliolina, sp. near *M. circularis* (Born.).
Alveolina melo (F. & M.). One specimen.
Truncatulina, sp. (thin-shelled), cf. *T. lobatula* (W. & J.) or *T. ungeriana* (d'Orb.). Frequent.
Carpenteria monticularis, Carter. Frequent.
Carpenteria utricularis, Carter. Rare.
Rotalia schroeteriana, P. & J. Common.
Amphistegina lessonii, d'Orb. Common.
Heterostegina depressa, d'Orb. Rare.
Orbitoides (*Lepidocyclina*) *andrewsiana,* sp. nov. (Pl. **XXI,** Fig. 14.)

O. andrewsiana is a very striking form in the Christmas Island limestones. The test is very thick in the centre, thinning off rapidly to a peripheral flange of some extent. In general contour it may be compared with *Orbitoides* (*Discocyclina*) *applanata.* Gümbel.[1] The chambers of the median plane are of the Lepidocycline character, and more rounded and crowded with one another than in some of the other forms of *Orbitoides* present in the same limestones. The chamberlets of the exterior are roughly discoidal and flattened, so that a tangential section affords a view of the chamberlets as large circular perforations, which is a marked feature in the sections. Many of the specimens noted are megalospheric. The internal structure of *O. andrewsiana* generally resembles *O. sumatrensis,* but the former is much larger, and has a very extensive peripheral flange. Average diameter ⅜ inch (9·375 mm.). Common.

Orbitoides (*Lepidocyclina*) *insulæ-natalis,* sp. nov. Common. (Pl. XXI, Fig. 13.)

O. (*L.*) *ephippioides,* sp. nov. Common. (Pl. XXI, Fig. 15.)

O. (*L.*) *verbeeki,* Newton & Holland. One specimen.

LIMESTONES FROM PLATEAU AND HILLS.

No. 143. Edge of cliff, South Point Hill, 1,020 feet.

A finely crystalline and calcareous rock, in which the organisms are almost entirely obliterated. A few echinus spines and foraminifera.

Foraminifera :

Truncatulina, sp.

Amphistegina lessonii, d'Orb.

No. 134. Top of upper cliff, southern end of east coast.

Limestones with few organisms; *Lithothamnion,* foraminifera, and echinus spines. In places this rock appears to be sheared.

Foraminifera :

Amphistegina lessonii, d'Orb.

Polytrema miniaceum (Pallas).

---

[1] Abhandl. m.-ph. Cl. k.-bayer. Ak. Wiss., vol. x, 1868 (1870), p. 700, pl. iii, figs. 17, 18, 35–7.

No. 131. Southern end of east coast, 400 feet.
A dolomitized limestone with foraminifera.

Foraminifera:
Amphistegina lessonii, d'Orbigny.
Heterostegina depressa, d'Orb. Abundant and somewhat broken.

No. 378. Murray Hill Summit.
A fine-grained dolomitized limestone, with traces of organisms
(? corals), in dull patches.
Foraminifera: *Polytrema miniaceum* (Pallas), var. *involva*,
Chapman. One specimen.

No. 935. Pinnacles on plateau at 800 feet, 1¼ miles W.S.W.
of 120 chain mark on South-East Road.[1]
A semi - crystalline limestone with branching *Lithothamnion*,
Halimeda, and foraminifera.

Foraminifera:
Miliolina, sp.
Clavulina, sp.
Carpenteria, sp. Numerous fragments; some very fine charac-
teristic pieces.

No. 658. A hard dolomitic limestone occurring with chalk-like
rock on plateau.
The material of this specimen is finely granular, and disseminated
throughout are fragmentary pieces of organic origin, which can be
determined as branching *Lithothamnion*, with many foraminifera,
usually badly preserved.
The foraminifera are undersized and thin-shelled as a rule,
and seem to indicate, together with the abundant and partially
decomposed calcareous algæ, that this rock represents the soft
mud of a shallow lagoon.

Foraminifera:
Spiroloculina, sp. Frequent.
Textularia rugosa (Rss.). Very rare.
? *Nodosaria* (*Dentalina*), sp. One example.
Discorbina, sp. (a small turbinoid form). Rare.
Planorbulina, sp., near *larvata*, P. & J. Frequent.

---

[1] On the chief road-clearings Mr. Ross has had the distances blazed on the
tree trunks every five or ten chains.

Truncatulina lobatula (W. & J.).   Several.
Carpenteria, sp.   Fragmentary.
Polytrema miniaceum (Pallas).   Small specimens; frequent.
Amphistegina lessonii, d'Orbigny.   Fragmentary; frequent.

No. 800.   " Immediately below phosphates, east slope of Phosphate Hill, 820 feet."
A partially dolomitized limestone with good crystals of zoned dolomite and calcite.   The matrix contains foraminifera (unaltered) and plates of echinoderms.
Foraminifera : *Amphistegina lessonii*, d'Orb.   Large and common.

LIMESTONES FROM SEA- AND INLAND CLIFFS.

No. 5.   "A rock filling cracks in basalt mass, south of Flying Fish Cove."
A basaltic and palagonitic breccia, with calcareous fragments and organisms, also bone fragments.   (Pl. XXI, Fig. 17.)
    Foraminifera :
Cristellaria, sp.   One specimen.
Globigerina bulloides, d'Orb.   Very common.
Carpenteria, sp.   Fragments.

No. 215.   Rock on basalt, top of shore cliff, Flying Fish Cove.
A recent limestone consisting of large *Halimeda* and encrusting *Lithothamnion*; also foraminifera and polyzoa, cemented by a deposition of travertin, probably resulting from differential currents or hot streams.
    Foraminifera :
Textularia rugosa (Reuss).   Frequent.
Carpenteria, sp.   Fragments.
Gypsina inhærens (Schultze).   Frequent.

No. 862.   Foot of first inland cliff, Smith Point.
A reef forming limestone, composed of *Halimeda*, *Lithothamnion*, foraminifera, corals, millepores, and echinoderm remains.
    Foraminifera :
Orbitolites, sp.
Globigerina bulloides, d'Orb.   Very rare.
Planorbulina acervalis, Brady.   Rare.
Carpenteria monticularis, Carter.   Rare.

No. 979. First inland cliff, two miles beyond Smith Point. A recent reef-rock with *Lithothamnion* and foraminifera.

Foraminifera :
Orbitolites complanata, Lam. One specimen.
Textularia sagittula, Defr. One specimen.
Cristellaria, sp. One specimen.
Globigerina bulloides, d'Orb. Common.
     ,,   *conglobata,* Brady. Rare.
Carpenteria, sp. Fragments.
Rotalia papillosa, Brady. One specimen.
Polytrema miniaceum (Pallas). Common.
     ,,   ,,   var. *involva,* Chapman. Common.
Amphistegina lessonii, d'Orb. Rare.

No. 52. East coast, on volcanic agglomerate in sea-cliff.
A limestone with branching *Lithothamnion* and foraminifera in a slightly calcareous matrix. An included fragment of a palagonitic or basic rock occurs in this specimen.

Foraminifera :
Miliolina ? *trigonula* (Lam.).
Truncatulina refulgens (Montf.). Common.
Carpenteria, sp. Fragments.
Gypsina globulus (Reuss). Rare.

No. 116. "Junction of limestone and basalt, in bay south of Waterfall, east coast."
An indurated limestone of a deep yellow colour, in conjunction with an intrusion or flow of basalt. The infilling of the organisms in the limestone is coarsely crystalline. At the junction of the limestone with the basalt there is a layer of minute pellets (calcareous algæ ?). In the body of the limestone there are numerous clear augite crystals worked out of the basalt. The organic contents of the limestone are *Lithothamnion,* foraminifera, echinoderm spines, and molluscan shells. This limestone passes rapidly into a fine-grained chalky rock, with delicate foraminifera and partially decomposed *Lithothamnion.*

Foraminifera :
Miliolina ? *trigonula* (Lam.). Rare.
Bolivina, sp. ? One specimen.
Truncatulina lobatula (W. & J.), in chalky portion. Frequent.
Carpenteria, sp. Rare.
Rotalia papillosa, var. *compressiuscula,* Brady. Frequent.

No. 525. Rock which forms knolls on basalt, near streams, east coast.

A limestone with included particles of basalt and strings of palagonitic matter. With *Lithothamnion*, foraminifera, echinoderm fragments, and polyzoa.

Foraminifera:

Textularia rugosa (Reuss). Rare.
Truncatulina lobatula (W. & J.). Frequent.
Rotalia schroeteriana, P. & J. Very abundant.

No. 859. At foot of first inland cliff at Steep Point.

A limestone with much secondary calcareous crystallization (aragonitic). The rock was originally partially or mainly organic, but only traces of organisms now remain, of *Lithothamnion* and foraminifera.

Foraminifera: *Heterostegina depressa*, d'Orb. Fragments.

No. 1,002. First inland cliff, south of Steep Point.

This is a much brecciated rock containing algæ, foraminifera, corals, and echinoderm fragments. It is cemented by granular and clear calcareous matter. A talus rock.

Foraminifera:

Alveolina melo (Fichtel & Moll). One specimen.
Discorbina, sp.
Carpenteria utricularis, Carter. Fragments numerous.
Polytrema miniaceum (Pallas), var. *involva*, Chapman, encrusting a cemented brecciated fragment.
Amphistegina lessonii, d'Orbigny. Very rare.

No. 1,005. First inland cliff, south of Steep Point, 250 feet.

A reef-limestone with *Lithothamnion*, millepores, and foraminifera.

Foraminifera:

Carpenteria utricularis, Carter. Abundant.
Amphistegina lessonii, d'Orb. Common.
Heterostegina depressa, d'Orb. Rare.

No. 1,006. "First inland cliff, south of Steep Point, 250 feet."

A limestone showing evidence of disturbance; a rift in the rock is filled in with palagonitic mud and aragonite. It contains *Lithothamnion*, foraminifera, and lamellibranch shells.

Foraminifera:
Miliolina trigonula (Lam.). Several.
Orbitolites, sp., cf. *O. marginalis* (Lam.).
Carpenteria monticularis, Carter. Numerous fragments.
Polytrema miniaceum (Pallas). Occasional.
? *Cycloclypeus*, sp. Worn fragment.
Orbitoides ? verbeeki, Newton & Holland. Fragments.

No. 900. "Foot of cliff (first inland), inner side of Steep Point Valley."
A limestone composed of branching *Lithothamnion* and foraminifera, cemented by granular and crystalline calcite.

Foraminifera:
Miliolina, sp., cf. *M. circularis* (Born.). Rare.
Textularia rugosa (Reuss). Frequent.
Carpenteria utricularis, Carter. Very common.
Gypsina vesicularis (P. & J.). One specimen.
Gypsina inhærens (Schultze). Frequent.
Polytrema miniaceum (Pallas), var. *involva*, Chapman. Common, and very fine specimens.
Amphistegina lessonii, d'Orb. Very common.

No. 403A. "Along lines of fracture, north of Steep Point Hill."
A fine-grained dolomite or magnesite, against which rests a brecciated rock composed of reef material and phosphatic concretions. In the reef-rock are *Halimeda, Lithothamnion*, foraminifera, and echinoderm spines.

Foraminifera:
Carpenteria, sp. Fragments very abundant.
Gypsina inhærens (Schultze). Rare.

No. 940. Middle cliff, North-East Point.
A partially phosphatized limestone, with branching *Lithothamnion* and foraminifera.

Foraminifera:
Sigmoïlina, sp. One specimen.
Bigenerina digitata, d'Orb. One specimen.
Globigerina bulloides, d'Orb. Numerous.
Planorbulina, sp. Frequent.
Gypsina, sp. Fragmentary, occasional.
Polytrema miniaceum (Pallas). Some fragments.

No. 943. "North-East Point, above reef."

A limestone largely formed of coral, with calcareous mud infillings. Also *Lithothamnion* and foraminifera.

Foraminifera :

Miliolina, sp.
Carpenteria, sp. Fragmentary.
Amphistegina lessonii, d'Orbigny. Rare.
? *Cycloclypeus* or ? *Heterostegina.* Fragments.

No. 937. Inland cliff, North-East Point.

A limestone containing polyzoa or coral and foraminifera. The interspaces filled in by rapid crystallization with calcareous material as aragonite. The infilled portions are regular or parallel-sided, suggesting local earth-movements, producing rifts.

Foraminifera :

? *Sphæroidina.*
Heterostegina depressa, d'Orbigny.

No. 335. "South Valley, west coast and cliff, southern side at 150 feet."

A coral-reef rock with many organisms, somewhat comminuted.

Foraminifera :

Textularia rugosa (Reuss). Frequent.
Globigerina bulloides, d'Orbigny. Frequent.
Globigerina conglobata, Brady. Rare.
Truncatulina lobatula (W. & J.). Rare.
Carpenteria, sp. Fragmentary ; rare.
Rotalia schroeteriana, P. & J. Common.
Heterostegina depressa, d'Orb. Frequent.

No. 864. Cliff over Coffee Garden, Flying Fish Cove (see Map), about 200 feet.

A recent coral-reef rock with branching *Lithothamnion,* foraminifera, and echinoderm remains.

Foraminifera :

Miliolina ? *bicornis* (W. & J.). One specimen.
Truncatulina lobatula (W. & J.). Rare.
Carpenteria, sp. Fragments.
Polytrema miniaceum (Pallas). Rare.

No. 200. A coarse fragmental limestone cemented with aragonite. Some corals, *Halimeda, Lithothamnion,* gastropods, and foraminifera. Probably recent. From outer part of a reef.

Foraminifera :
Globigerina bulloides, d'Orbigny. Frequent.
Carpenteria monticularis, Carter.
Polytrema miniaceum (Pallas).

No. 202. " Zigzag,[1] just above 80 feet."
Coral rock with interspaces infilled with foraminiferal mud. Occasional joints of *Halimeda.*

Foraminifera :
Textularia rugosa (Reuss).
Globigerina bulloides, d'Orbigny. Very abundant.
Carpenteria, sp. ? Frequent.
Pulvinulina repanda? (F. & M.). Rare.

No. 208. " Zigzag, 200 feet." Coral rock with interspaces filled with chalky organic mud, with *Halimeda* and foraminifera.

Foraminifera :
Globigerina bulloides, d'Orbigny. Numerous.
Carpenteria, sp. Frequent.
Gypsina inhærens (Schultze). Rare.
Gypsina globulus (Reuss). Rare.
Polytrema miniaceum (Pallas). Fragments.
Heterostegina depressa, d'Orb. Occasional.

No. 209. " Zigzag, 210 feet."
A recent reef-rock. A microconglomerate, i.e. with large proportion of cement. Contains *Lithothamnion, Halimeda,* foraminifera, corals, echinoderm spines and plates, and polyzoa.

Foraminifera :
Carpenteria monticularis, Carter. In great abundance.
Gypsina globulus (Reuss). Occasional.
Polytrema miniaceum (Pallas), var. *involva,* Chapman. (Encrusting form.)

No. 211. " Zigzag, 250 feet."
A recent reef-rock with corals and foraminifera.

---

[1] The " Zigzag " is a path up the first inland cliff, about a quarter of a mile north of the settlement. (See Fig. 6 on p. 280.)

Foraminifera :

Textularia rugosa (Reuss). Very rare.
Globigerina bulloides, d'Orb. Numerous and well preserved.
Carpenteria monticularis, Carter. Numerous fragments.

No. 1,032. "Top of Zigzag, 280–300 feet." A limestone
composed of calcareous algæ and foraminifera, with a crystalline
calcitic cement, but in places amorphous or muddy. The organic
contents are *Lithothamnion, Halimeda*, foraminifera, corals, echinoderm plates and spines, polyzoa, and lamellibranch shells.

Foraminifera :

? *Spiroloculina*, sp.
Globigerina bulloides, d'Orb. Frequent.
Carpenteria, sp. near *monticularis*, Carter. Fragments.
Carpenteria proteiformis, Goës. One specimen.
Polytrema miniaceum (Pallas). Frequent.
Polytrema miniaceum, var. *involva*, Chapman. Frequent.

LIST OF SPECIES OF *Orbitoides*.

The species of *Orbitoides* found in the Tertiary rocks of
Christmas Island, Indian Ocean, with their distribution :—

1. *Orbitoides (Discocyclina) dispansa* (Sowerby). { Java, Sumatra, India (Scinde), Persia, Bavarian Alps, Italy, Spain, South of France, Antigua, Jamaica, St. Thomas.
2. *O. (Lepidocyclina) neodispansa*, sp. nov. Christmas Island.
3. *O. (L.) verbecki*, Newton & Holland. Sumatra, Borneo.
4. *O. (L.) ephippioides*, sp. nov. Christmas Island.
5. *O. (L.) insulæ-natalis*, sp. nov. Christmas Island.
6. *O. (L.) insulæ-natalis*, var. *inæqualis*, var. nov.
7. *O. (L.) sumatrensis*, Brady. Sumatra, Borneo.
8. *O. (L.) andrewsiana*, sp. nov. Christmas Island.
9. *O. (L.) murrayana*, sp. nov. Christmas Island.

NOTE ON THE
COMPOSITION OF SOME DOLOMITIC AND OTHER LIMESTONES FROM CHRISTMAS ISLAND.

By E. W. Skeats, B.Sc., F.G.S.

No. 134. Summit of upper cliff on East Coast. 800 feet.
Composition: $CaCO_3 = 97.56 \%$, $MgCO_3 = 2.44 \%$, $Ca_3P_2O_8 = .15 \%$. *Total* = 100.15.

A compact cream-coloured limestone, with no evident crystalline structure in the hand specimen. The rock originally consisted of organisms and small lumps of undifferentiated material set in a cement of calcareous silt. Subsequent alteration consists in the change of a small quantity of the fine silt into calcite crystals. Some of the crystals occur in the form of definite rhombohedra, with angles of 105° approximately. Empty lozenge-shaped spaces in the rock possibly represent the positions of rhombohedra which fell out probably during the grinding of the slice.

The calcite can be recognized by its cleavage and polarization colours. Sections of some of the organisms show long fibrous crystals which may be fibrous calcite, but are possibly the rhombic form aragonite. Minute scalenohedral (?) crystals of calcite occasionally project into cavities formed by contraction during recrystallization.

The organic remains are comparatively few. They include more than one species of the Calcareous Alga *Lithothamnion*. The only other organisms are foraminifera, including *Globigerina* (?) and the Rotaliiform genera *Truncatulina* and *Planorbulina* (?). The shallow-water affinities of the two latter organisms suggest that this deposit may have been laid down in the lagoon.

No. 963. Limestone (Miocene) from high cliff over Flying Fish Cove. 500 feet.
Composition: $CaCO_3 = 97.29 \%$, $MgCO_3 = 3.19 \%$. *Total* = 100.48. A white, very compact limestone.

A piece of unaltered rock (consisting of organic fragments embedded in silt) may possibly be a fallen fragment; its structure serves as a contrast to that of the main mass of the rock. The original silty matrix has very largely been replaced (as a result possibly of consolidation under pressure and percolation of water) by a clear mosaic of calcite surrounding the still unaltered large organic fragments.

Some of these fragments are, however, losing their distinctive boundaries as a result of the extension of this recrystallization into the bodies of the organisms. In certain parts of the slides, empty spaces (with scalenohedral? calcite crystals projecting into them) occur as a result of contraction during recrystallization. The unaltered organisms are numerous. The Calcareous Alga *Lithothamnion* is represented by several species.

A section of a shell (lamellibranch?) occurs in one part of the slide. The remaining organisms are foraminifera belonging to the genera *Bolivina*, *Globigerina* (*conglobata* and *bulloides*), *Polytrema*, *Gypsina*, *Carpenteria*, and *Amphistegina*.

From the presence of *Carpenteria* and some pelagic forms, this deposit was probably formed in water of a moderate depth, and on the seaward side of the reef.

No. 179. Top of second inland cliff, North-East Point. 600 feet. *Composition :* $CaCO_3 = 97\cdot72\ \%$, $MgCO_3 = 1\cdot72\ \%$, $Ca_3 P_2 O_8 = \cdot20\ \%$. *Total* $= 99\cdot64$. A very compact limestone, which in the hand specimen does not show signs of recrystallization.

The original rock consisted of organisms, more or less fragmentary, and a matrix of silt, the finely comminuted product of trituration of these organisms. This structure is still seen in the unaltered parts of the slide, but in places the more finely divided material has been recrystallized. The contraction due to recrystallization has caused empty spaces to occur. These spaces have been partially, and in some cases wholly, filled by subsequently deposited scaleno-hedral (?) crystals of calcite. Further evidence of the secondary formation of calcite is afforded by the fact that cracks which were formed in the rock have been subsequently filled with a calcite mosaic. The partial recrystallization of the matrix has in one or two instances invaded the substance of the contiguous organisms, whose outlines have consequently been rendered indistinct. The unaltered organic remains constitute a considerable proportion of the rock. Several species of the Calcareous Alga *Lithothamnion* occur in abundance.

The Foraminifera present include *Carpenteria*, *Truncatulina*, *Polytrema*, *Amphistegina*, and a doubtful specimen of *Gaudryina*.

The presence of *Carpenteria* would seem to suggest that the deposit was formed at a moderate depth, as this genus rarely occurs within the limits of wave-action.

Specimens : 804, 800, 811, 308, 658, 378, and 514. These are all dolomitic limestones whose microscopical structure is very similar. The rocks are more or less porous : empty spaces having arisen as a result of recrystallization. The cavities are lined by dolomite crystals, which are usually clear, and show as blunt rhombohedra having angles of 105° approximately.

These dolomitic limestones are described in a definite order, the first (804) having the largest percentage of calcium carbonate and the last (514) the largest percentage of magnesium carbonate. Dolomite consists of 54 $\%$ $CaCO_3$ and 46 $\%$ $MgCO_3$, consequently in the rocks first described there is an excess of unchanged calcite amounting to more than 20 $\%$, while in the last this excess is no more than 6 $\%$. Recognizable crystals of calcite are few in number, but it is possible that this excess of calcite may occur in the semi-opaque material which is found in all the slides, either as a dark zoning to the rhombohedra of dolomite or irregularly distributed throughout the rock.

No. 804. Cliff forming east flank of Phosphate Hill.

Composition : Ca C O$_8$ = 67·88 $\%$, Mg C O$_4$ = 31·96 $\%$. *Total* = 99·84. A white limestone compact in parts, but some portion is porous.

The slice is taken through the porous region, and the cavities are so large and numerous that it is difficult to explain their presence entirely by assuming that they were formed during recrystallization. Many of these cavities are lined with colourless dolomite crystals. The amount of semi-opaque material is large, and consists either of zones in dolomite crystals, or more usually it occurs irregularly distributed throughout the slide.

No recognizable traces of organisms are present.

No. 800. Rock immediately beneath bed of phosphate on Phosphate Hill. 850 feet.

Composition : Ca C O$_4$ = 65·05, Mg C O$_4$ = 34·77. *Total* = 99·82. A very compact, recrystallized, hard rock.

The usual cavities occur and are sometimes lined by clear crystals. A large quantity of semi-opaque material is present, and is occasionally seen forming long acute crystals (calcite ?), but is usually enclosed as zones in dolomite rhombohedra. Many of the crystals show two or three zones parallel to the external boundary. A few remains of organisms such as *Lithothamnion* occur in places.

No. 811. Immediately below phosphate at the summit of Phosphate Hill.

Composition : Ca C O$_8$ = 61·79, Mg C O$_8$ = 37·96. *Total* = 99·75. A hard, compact, recrystallized dolomite limestone.

Cavities are fairly numerous, and are usually lined with clear dolomite crystals. There is a fair quantity of irregularly distributed semi-opaque material, but most of the slide consists of clear crystals of dolomite with small centres of semi-opaque material.

No. 308. From low cliff in valley on West Coast, at 350 feet.

Composition : Ca C O$_8$ = 60·63, Mg C O$_8$ = 39·27, Ca$_8$ P$_2$ O$_8$ = ·15. *Total* = 100·05. A fine - grained white rock, with many minute regular-shaped cavities.

The main part of the slide consists of small rhombohedral crystals of dolomite, a few of which are zoned. Nearly all traces of organisms are obliterated, but occasionally the dark remains of fragments of organisms which have resisted recrystallization are seen.

No. 658. A hard rock associated with chalk-like rock on plateau. *Composition:* Ca C O$_s$ = 60·27, Mg C O$_s$ = 39·57. *Total* = 99·84. A crumbling, porous, white limestone.

The slide consists almost entirely of idiomorphic zoned crystals of dolomite. The irregular empty spaces and cracks which occur are, however, usually bordered by clear crystals. Most of the organisms have been obliterated, but one or two specimens of *Amphistegina* and possibly *Polytrema* occur. The dolomite crystals usually have dark centres, from which small, dark, acute crystals (? calcite) are projecting in some cases. In other places organic fragments are recrystallizing in the form of these long dark (? scalenohedral) crystals of (? calcite).

No. 378. Highest rock collected from Murray Hill, at about 1,100 feet. *Composition:* Ca C O$_s$ = 60·34, Mg C O$_s$ = 40·02. *Total* = 100·36. A cream-coloured, hard, compact rock.

Irregular cavities and cracks occur, and both are filled, or partially filled, with large clear rhombohedral crystals. A fair amount of semi-opaque material remains irregularly distributed over the slide. Very few of the rhombohedra are zoned, and most are very small. A few organisms remain, especially a meandrine form (? *Polytrema*), and some organic fragments are recrystallizing, showing acute crystals of calcite (?) projecting at right angles to the length of the fragment.

No. 514. Near the summit over Flying Fish Cove, at 880 feet. *Composition:* Ca C O$_s$ = 59·33, Mg C O$_s$ = 40·88. *Total* = 100·21. A cream-coloured spongy limestone.

Very similar to **No. 378**, but the dolomite crystals are larger and less semi-opaque material is present, but zoning is not well seen. The only remaining organisms are meandrine forms (? *Polytrema*) and fragments undergoing recrystallization.

ANALYSES OF ROCK-SPECIMENS FROM CHRISTMAS ISLAND.

Number.		Ca C O$_3$.	Mg C O$_3$.	Ca$_3$ P$_2$ O$_8$.	Total.
134	... ...	97·56 ...	2·44 ...	·15 ...	100·15
179	... ...	97·72 ...	1·72 ...	·20 ...	99·64
308	... ...	60·63 ...	39·27 ...	·15 ...	100·05
378	... ...	60·34 ...	40·02 ...	— ...	100·36
514 { 1st sample	...	59·33 ...	40·88 ...	— ...	100·21 }
{ 2nd sample	...	61·12 ...	39·36 ...	— ...	100·48 }
658	... ...	60·27 ...	39·57 ...	— ...	99·84
800	... ...	65·05 ...	34·77 ...	— ...	99·82
804	... ...	67·88 ...	31·96 ...	— ...	99·84
811	... ...	61·79 ...	37·96 ...	— ...	99·75
963	... ...	97·29 ...	3·19 ...	— ...	100·48

GEOLOGY.

By C. W. ANDREWS, B.Sc., F.G.S.

FROM the description of the physical features of Christmas Island given at the beginning of this volume, it will be gathered that the island may be considered as probably an ancient atoll which has been raised to a considerable height above the level of the sea. The chief reasons for so regarding it are, firstly, the general form of the plateau with its outer border of slightly higher land, and secondly, the nature of some of the rocks occurring on the more elevated points. In the present section a brief sketch of the general geological structure is given, a fuller account being deferred till the nature of the rocks, especially of the later limestones, has been more completely investigated, both with the microscope and by chemical analysis.

The difficulties in the way of a detailed examination of the geology of the island were considerable. The density of the vegetation both rendered locomotion slow and difficult, and, at the same time, concealed much that it was desirable to see (Fig. 1). Moreover, the want of sufficient men for carrying water made it impossible to stay more than a day or two in places remote from the settlement or from the streams on the east coast. In consequence of this the south of the island was not fully examined; but since in those parts which were traversed it was like the northern and eastern regions, and since the appearance of its seaward slopes was the same as that of the other coasts, it seems improbable that the structure of this region differs in any important respect from that of the rest of the island. Much, however, remains to be done, and now that several roads have been cut and a number of men could be employed, further exploration would be comparatively easy.

One of the chief objects of the expedition to Christmas Island was to find out whether its structure would throw any light upon the vexed question of the nature of the foundations of atolls. The various views that have been put forward in this controversy are so well known that it is unnecessary to give any account of them here. From the description which follows, it will be seen that at Christmas Island at least we do not find the great thickness of reef-limestone required by the Darwinian theory of atoll-formation, and although there may be some evidence that subsidence did occur in the earlier history of the island it is clear that it was neither continuous for any long period nor of any great extent. It may, of course, be objected that Christmas Island was never a typical atoll, and to this objection no answer is possible, but since it can be shown that at one time it must have consisted of reefs and islands approximating very nearly to those seen in atolls which are regarded as typical, the determination of the nature of the foundations upon which those reefs and islands rested is at least a step in the right direction. From the account that follows, it will be seen that in this case the basis of the island is almost certainly a volcanic

Fig. 1.—Forest on the Plateau.

peak the foot of which is now some 2,400 fathoms below the level of the sea, and that on its summit and flanks great accumulations of Tertiary limestones have been deposited, and in some cases are interstratified with the products of the eruptions, probably for the most part submarine, which took place from time to time. The oldest of the volcanic rocks are trachytic, the newer basaltic. The last of the eruptions was accompanied by the formation of thick beds of volcanic ash (palagonite tuffs), and it is upon these that the great mass of the Miocene (Orbitoidal) limestones rests.

The later deposits which have accumulated on the basis thus constituted are very difficult to describe. They may be said to consist of reef-limestones and detrital limestones formed on the submarine slopes of the island, but since after each movement of elevation fresh reefs seem to have grown round more or less of the new shore-lines, the whole structure is very complex. Another source of difficulty is the almost complete obliteration of all organisms in many of the limestones, chiefly in consequence of dolomitization.

Perhaps the most remarkable of the rocks of Christmas Island are the thick deposits of nearly pure phosphate of lime which cap several of the higher hills. This substance is probably derived from ancient (? Pliocene) guano beds formed on the low islets which existed before the first elevation of the island, and is the insoluble residue of beds of limestone altered by this guano. On Murray Hill there is a bed of rock, consisting largely of phosphates of alumina and iron, which has perhaps been produced by the alteration of a bed of volcanic ash by an overlying mass of guano, since completely disappeared.

It will be convenient to describe the geology of the island under the following heads :—

1. The central nucleus.
2. The plateau and hills.
3. The inland cliffs.
4. The sea cliff.

At the same time it will be impossible to keep these sections entirely distinct from one another, e.g. in cases where the inland cliffs have been cut back into the central nucleus and consist of tertiary rocks.

The Central Nucleus. — By far the most important exposure of the central core of the island is at Flying Fish Cove (see Map). In this locality, behind the platform upon which the settlement is situated, a steep slope rises to a height of from 400 to 500 feet. In its northern portion it consists of a succession of cliffs separated by steep talus slopes, while towards the southern end there is a talus slope up to about 250 feet, and above this a vertical or even overhanging cliff of from 200 to 250 feet. At the northern end of the cove the cliffs run nearly N. to S., but as they are followed southward their direction changes first N.N.E.-S.S.W., then N.E. to S.W., E.N.E. to W.S.W., and finally S.E.-N.W. (see Figs. 2 and 6).

The general structure of the cliff is shown on the sections in Figs. 2 and 5 (pp. 272 and 276). The oldest limestone visible (A in sections) is exposed at the southern end of the cove, at the

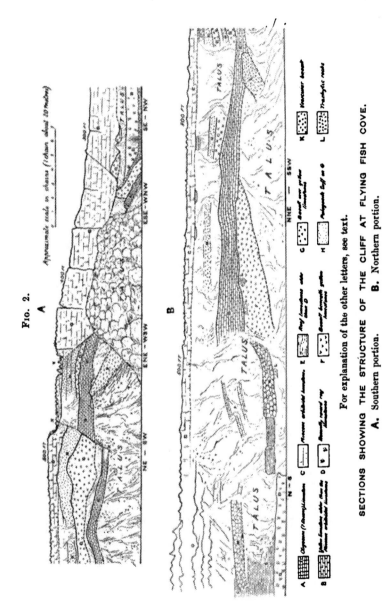

Fig. 2.

For explanation of the other letters, see text.

SECTIONS SHOWING THE STRUCTURE OF THE CLIFF AT FLYING FISH COVE.

A. Southern portion.   B. Northern portion.

The broken lines indicate that the base of the beds is hidden beneath talus.

commencement of the sea cliff which forms the southern boundary of the bay. It is a very hard compact yellow limestone, showing little or no traces of bedding or jointing. Its upper surface dips at about 40° a little to the W. of N., and it disappears beneath the beach of coral fragments that has been thrown up at this point on the landward side of the narrow fringing reef. On the land side it can be traced up the cliff for about sixty yards, when it disappears under the talus which entirely conceals its base. This limestone is described above (No. 2, p. 226), and is of Eocene or Oligocene age; it was probably deposited in comparatively shallow water, and before the great accumulations of the Miocene and later limestones of the higher parts of the island could have been formed considerable subsidence must have taken place. In the rocks of corresponding age in Java, several species of *Nummulites* are said to occur in abundance, but, strangely enough, according to Messrs. Jones & Chapman this genus is entirely wanting in Christmas Island; its place seems to have been taken by large Heterostegines.

Above this limestone is a thick bed of compact black basalt (No. 1; see Fig. 3 and G in Fig. 2, A). The junction is marked by a bed of soft rock some five or six inches thick, in which harder nodules are embedded. These nodules consist of limestone containing foraminifera like those of the rock below, together with fragments of much altered basic glass (No. 3, p. 231). The soft matrix in which these nodules are embedded is a much decomposed rock consisting mainly of fragments of basic glass. The basalt mass measured along the shore is about 40 feet thick; it is roughly jointed into spheroidal masses, and seems to have been exposed on the sea bottom, the joint cracks being filled with a hard yellow rock, consisting of lime and fine detritus, derived from basic volcanic rocks and including numbers of various species of *Globigerina*. This rock (No. 5) is described on p. 258, and is figured on Pl. XXI, Fig. 17.

The basalt[1] itself is a compact black rock, very fresh-looking. The ground-mass consists of microliths of plagioclase, many small prisms of purple augite, and much magnetite. There are porphyritic crystals of olivine, more or less altered into serpentine and viridite. The skeleton crystals of magnetite are often arranged parallel to one another, and at right angles to the axis of the olivines. There are numerous rounded cavities, lined, and in some cases filled, with a strongly pleochroic green mineral, forming radial aggregates which show a black cross between crossed nicols.

The upper surface of this basalt flow is covered with thick masses of Miocene Orbitoidal limestone (C in Figs. 2 and 5), which, near the junction, contains numerous fragments of the basalt overgrown

---

[1] In the description of the volcanic rocks I am indebted to Mr. G. T. Prior, of the Department of Mineralogy, for much assistance.

Fig. 4.—Mass of Porites (about 30 feet high) in Sea Cliff South of Flying Fish Cove.

Fig. 3.—Bed of Basalt resting on older Tertiary Limestone, South side of Flying Fish Cove.

with *Lithothamnion* and *Polytrema* : this circumstance indicates that this basalt was exposed upon the sea bottom in early Miocene, or perhaps pre-Miocene times. On the right hand of section A on p. 272 this basalt is marked G, and is made to correspond to the upper basalt overlying the limestone B in the rest of the section; this is perhaps a mistake, since it agrees very nearly with the basalt F underlying that limestone, which, together with the overlying basalt and ash beds, seems to be wanting on this southern end of the cove. It may, however, be remarked that the limestone A is very similar in character to B (No. 522, p. 231), and if it were not that its fossil contents (see No. 2, p. 226) are said to be rather different and point to a possibly somewhat greater age, I should have regarded it as the southern continuation of B : in that case the basalt would be correctly lettered. Indeed, I believe this last interpretation to be correct.

The upper yellow limestone (B) just referred to forms a prominent cliff throughout about the middle two-thirds of the cove. At its southern end it seems to have been cut out by the fault marked Y–Y (Fig. 2, A), but its termination is largely concealed by the talus derived from the lofty cliffs of Miocene limestone (C). A little farther to the north this cliff is again interrupted by another fault, X–X (Fig. 2, A), the downthrow side of which is towards the north ; this causes the limestone to terminate abruptly against basalt and ash, and to reappear at a lower level, where it again forms a nearly continuous cliff, low at first, but increasing in height towards the north, where it sometimes reaches 60 feet. At its northern extremity it becomes broken up into minor cliffs (P, Fig. 2, B) separated by soil-clad slopes, beneath which it finally disappears. The foot of the cliff is from 200 to 250 feet above the sea, but except in one or two places where it rests on volcanic rocks (e.g. at L and F), the base of this limestone is concealed beneath talus which forms a steep rock-strewn slope to the shore platform. This limestone is described on p. 231 as No. 522; it is remarkable for the absence of *Orbitoides*, which is found in the rocks both above and below. The beds dip slightly seaward (at from 5° to 10°), and are broken up by joint planes into great cubical masses, many of which strew the platform below, of which, moreover, they probably form the chief foundation ; blocks of the same limestone also appear on the foreshore in the middle of the cove.

As already mentioned, the base of this limestone is mostly concealed beneath talus, but at a few points it can be seen to rest upon volcanic rocks ; in all cases it seems to have been deposited upon these rocks long after their consolidation, and near the junction often contains fragments of them. Of these volcanic rocks there are two series—an older, trachytic, and a later, basaltic. The chief exposure of the former occurs near the middle of the cove (at L on the right-hand side of section B in Fig. 2), where it forms a great boss projecting into the overlying limestone. The extent of the mass cannot be determined, since its borders are mostly concealed by talus. The surface of this rock in contact with the limestone seems to have been greatly altered before the latter was deposited. In the centre of the mass the rock (No. 929) is light-grey, fine-grained, and made up of a felt of small lath-shaped felspar crystals, giving straight extinctions and showing flow structure round vesicular cavities which themselves show a more or less linear arrangement. There are some traces of a much altered ferro-magnesian mineral between the meshes of the felspars. Professor Judd has kindly had the specific gravity of this rock determined for me; it is 2·45.

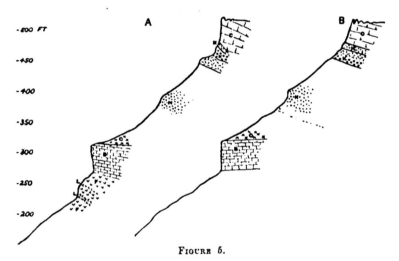

FIGURE 5.

SECTIONS SHOWING THE STRUCTURE OF THE CLIFF AT FLYING FISH COVE.

A. At middle of section B, Fig. 2.
B. At right-hand end of section B, Fig. 2.

For explanation of lettering see Fig. 2 (p. 272).

A few chains farther north trachytic rock again appears, but in this case under peculiar conditions. Here the trachyte forms two or three large masses, apparently completely included in the great bed of basalt which there immediately underlies the yellow limestone. The trachyte is here much altered, and consists of angular nodules separated by a brown powdery substance, apparently produced by the decomposition of the rock along cracks. In one place the basalt sends a finger-like process into the midst of one of the trachytic masses, and in another it appears to have penetrated the trachyte horizontally for some distance, so as to appear to be interbedded with it. The whole structure seems to be the result of the eruption of a mass of basalt along the same line as that along which an eruption of trachyte had taken place at an earlier date, and the inclusion of portions of the older lava in the newer. The trachyte at this point is made up of a felt of small lath-shaped felspar crystals, giving straight extinctions and sometimes showing traces of a radial arrangement in groups. There are no porphyritic constituents and there are scattered grains of magnetite.

The basalt (marked F in section B, Figs. 2 and 5) varies much in character in different parts of the mass. For the most part it is a fine-grained rock, consisting of small lath-shaped crystals of felspar, a little granular augite, and much magnetite. Flow structure is shown in the arrangement of the felspar crystals; there are no porphyritic crystals. Where this rock forms a narrow tongue penetrating the trachyte it becomes more glassy. In one place the mass of fine-grained basalt is traversed by a vein or dyke of a basalt with large porphyritic crystals of pinkish-brown augite, often showing the characteristic octagonal sections, large fragments of olivine sometimes showing traces of crystal forms and altered into viridite along cracks only, and finally large lath-shaped crystals of felspars with traces of zoning; in one or two instances felspars are included in the augite crystals. The ground-mass consists of felspar microliths, small augites, and much magnetite. This coarser rock was probably injected into a fissure from the deeper portion of the mass.

South of the fault X-X the limestone B rests on the upper end of a great mass of basalt (F), which can be traced down nearly to the sea-level. At its upper end it penetrates the limestone, and is repeated twice owing to slight faulting parallel to the main fault X-X.

Wherever the talus is wanting it can be seen that the yellow limestone (B) is overlaid by a bed of glassy basalt (G), varying greatly in thickness and attaining its greatest development towards the southern end of the bay (nearly above the letters N.E.-S.W. in section A, Fig. 2). At this point it forms the lower portion of a lofty overhanging cliff, which, from the red staining of the lime-stone forming its summit and the colour of the volcanic ash beneath, is called by the people the " Batoe merah " or the " red rock." To the north of this point the basalt bed can be seen at intervals only, and to the south it is interrupted (see Fig. 2) by the fault X-X and is finally cut out by the slip Y-Y, the Miocene Orbitoidal limestones (C) resting on its end.

The basalt of this bed is a somewhat glassy rock, the ground-mass of which is full of microliths of felspar and granules of magnetite; there is a considerable quantity of olivine, which except in a few cases is entirely altered into serpentinous material. Numerous rounded vesicles more or less completely filled with a bottle-green substance are present. In the higher part of the bed this rock has undergone further alteration, the whole of the olivine being replaced by serpentine and the green material filling the vesicles apparently altered into a similar substance, while the glassy base has become palagonitic. The higher parts of the bed also seem to have been more glassy than the lower.

The thickness of this basalt is, as already noticed, very variable, and the upper surface is nowhere clearly defined. It is covered by beds of palagonite tuffs, which in places attain a thickness of at least 50 feet. The passage from the basalt to the ash beds seems to be marked by an ill-defined band of a peculiar rock consisting of angular fragments of basic glass, some an inch across, embedded in a copious cement of crystalline calcite or, in places, of non-crystalline lime, containing fragments of palagonite (probably merely the smaller fragments of glass completely altered), and occasionally foraminifera ; the cementing substance sometimes makes up a great portion of the rock. Seen on a fractured surface the basic glass is black in colour, of a resinoid lustre, and has an irregular splintery fracture. In thin sections it is seen to be a yellowish brown, and the fragments are usually altered along their edges to an orange-yellow palagonite ; embedded in the glass are many small nodules and imperfect crystals of olivine and some very small crystals of augite. This rock was not actually seen *in situ*, but it invariably occurred in the talus immediately beneath the beds of palagonite tuff, which it almost certainly separated from the basalt below.

The palagonite tuffs (H, Figs. 2 and 5), like the underlying basalt, vary considerably in thickness in different parts of the section. Between the faults X-X and Y-Y (see Fig. 2) they probably attain a thickness of quite 50 feet. Further towards the middle of Flying Fish Cove they are mostly concealed by talus, but here and there form a low cliff of red or red and green mottled rock, which crumbles beneath the feet. Under the microscope it is seen that the rock consists of small fragments of a highly vesicular basic glass, which has been completely converted into palagonite ; the whole is cemented together into a compact mass by crystalline calcite, and here and there the shells of foraminifera occur. The palagonite forms bands of different colours parallel to the outlines of the fragments or of the vesicles, and there are often zones clouded with immense numbers of small granules, which under a low power appear perfectly opaque. Sometimes these dark zones are numerous, but usually there is one within a narrow band of clear palagonite. In a few instances the whole of the interior of the fragments is clouded with the opaque granules. According to Mr. Chapman the foraminifera which occur scattered through the mass are usually species of *Pulvinulina*.

The glassy basalt, the rock composed of fragments of basic glass, and the thick masses of palagonite tuff above described seem to have been the products of a submarine eruption, the fragments of basic glass being derived from the shattering of the chilled upper surface of the basalt flow, and the palagonite tuffs being composed of the finer fragments of vesicular glass derived from the same source and mingled to some extent with sediment containing marine organisms. These rocks are very similar to specimens described by Murray and Renard in the "Challenger" Report on Deep-sea Deposits as forming the nuclei of manganese nodules dredged from depths of more than 2,000 fathoms in the Indian and Pacific Oceans. Thus the more altered portion of the glassy basalt is very similar to that figured in the volume quoted on pl. xix, fig. 4; the palagonite tuff to those shown on pl. xviii, figs. 1, 2, 3; and the basic glass (No. 400) to that figured on pl. xvii, fig. 3; and no doubt they were produced under similar conditions. The degree to which the palagonite tuffs are exposed on the cliff is shown in Fig. 2, where also it will be seen that, like the basalt, these ash beds are cut off by the fault Y-Y and have Miocene Orbitoidal limestones resting on their southern extremity.

Inland, about half a mile south of Flying Fish Cove (Fig. 6), we come upon an extensive exposure of this upper basalt. The eastern edge of the exposure runs a little to the west of south, approximately along the 500 feet contour-line; to the westward (that is, the seaward) side the basalt forms a series of steep rounded slopes separated by narrow valleys and running down to about the 300 feet contour-line; here it again disappears beneath limestones, chiefly Miocene and containing *Orbitoides*, but in some places of more recent origin. This belt of basalt is about a third of a mile wide at its northern end, and can be followed south for about a mile, beyond which it is completely covered with Miocene limestones: this is the most extensive exposure of volcanic rock in the island. As already mentioned, the upper surface of the exposure roughly follows the 500 feet contour-line where it disappears beneath the overlying Miocene limestones. The palagonite tuffs found in the cliff section are here almost entirely absent and usually represented only by a bed of impure limestone, often stained and banded red and yellow by water percolating along the surface of the volcanic rock, and containing fragments of palagonite and basalt, sometimes in such quantities as to form a kind of breccia.

Towards the southern end of this exposure of basalt there are several patches of Orbitoidal limestone at from 500 to 550 feet above the sea; these rest directly on the basalt, many fragments of which are included in their basal portion, which may present the appearance of a breccia of basalt fragments. Some of these limestones (Nos. 835, 827, 581) are described on pp. 254 and 255.

Returning to the cliff section, we find that the upper surface of the palagonite tuff bed may be covered directly by Miocene Orbitoidal limestone, or in a few places (e.g. at the points where the sections in Fig. 2 were taken) a thin band of basalt, which is often highly vesicular and contains large crystals of augite; above this may be a thin band of palagonite tuff, or in places a volcanic breccia consisting of fragments of highly altered basic glass and basalt embedded in a ground-mass of yellowish limestone which may contain foraminifera.

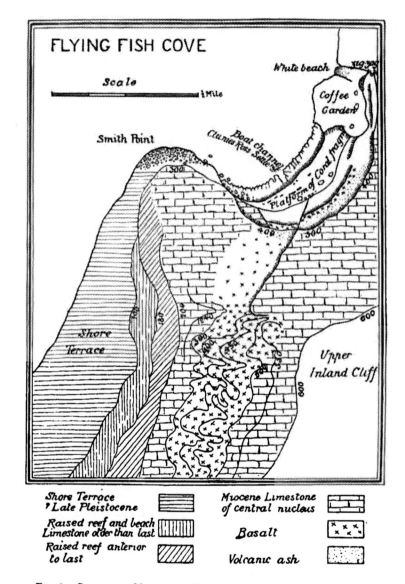

FIG. 6.—GEOLOGICAL MAP OF THE NEIGHBOURHOOD OF FLYING FISH COVE.

The Miocene Orbitoidal limestones, which rest upon the upper volcanic series, take a very large part in the formation of the basis upon which the higher and later limestones rest, and extensive exposures of them occur in several localities. Along the summit of the northern half of the Flying Fish Cove cliff they form a vertical face, varying from 10 to 30 feet in height. On the terrace above they are exposed in low pinnacles roughly ranged in rows parallel to the cliff edge, and at the fault X-X (Fig. 2) they form a prominent cliff running inland for about the third of a mile and terminating at its southern end against the basalt mass described above (see Fig. 6). This cliff occurs on the downthrow side of the fault, the limestone on the upthrow side having apparently slipped down the seaward slope; the line marked Y-Y indicates the position of a portion of the slip. South of Y-Y (Fig. 2, A) these limestones thicken out greatly and form cliffs at least 200 feet in height, the mass being split by a series of vertical fissures roughly parallel to the coast south of Smith Point. These fissures mark small slips, which on the terrace above are indicated by a series of small step-like displacements; the high cliff on the south of the cove (Fig. 2, A, between the letters W.S.W. and N.W.) is, in fact, a section across the ends of these terraces. In the extreme south of the cove these limestones have been affected by two or three small faults, which involve the underlying basalt (G) and cause the repetition of the basalt bed in two places in the base of the cliff; the limestones from either side of one of these faults are described above under the numbers 229 (p. 238), 220 (p. 239), 219 (p. 240), 861 (p. 237). The last specimen shows conclusively that these limestones were deposited on a basalt surface exposed beneath the sea and thickly coated with *Lithothamnion* and other encrusting organisms. Nos. 229 and 571 (p. 236) are probably from the same bed, both being taken close to the underlying basalt, and both being devoid of *Orbitoides*; 571, however, is from a point about 480 feet above the sea, in the middle of the cove, while 229 is from only about 100 feet at the south end, the difference of height being accounted for partly by the slope on which the beds are deposited causing a general dip seaward and partly by the slipping that has occurred. No. 924 (p. 233) closely resembles 220, and is likewise taken from close to the basalt, but in this *Orbitoides* are present, and the same is the case with 968 (p. 252), from a little farther west, at a height of about 60 feet above the sea. Of the rest of the limestones from this locality described above by Messrs. Jones & Chapman, 595 (p. 240) and 845 (p. 241) are from immediately above the line of slip Y-Y; 596 (p. 241) and 844 (p. 242), from above the last; and 841 (p. 248) and 963 (p. 250) are from the summit of the high cliff at this point. The two last are stated to be probably of more recent origin than the Miocene rocks below, and may represent a remnant of some much later deposit which formerly covered them. From the north of the fault X-X the specimens

550 (p. 246) and 562 (p. 243) were taken close to the underlying volcanic rock, and 521 (p. 245), 551 (p. 248), and 646 (p. 246), from pinnacles at the summit of the cliff (about 500 feet). It will be seen that rocks nearly on the same horizon may exhibit considerable diversity in their fossil contents, but since in most cases the fossils were determined from a single section the diversity may be more apparent than real.

The whole of these Miocene Orbitoidal limestones were probably deposited in shallow water on the summit and flanks of a submarine bank. I never found *Orbitoides* on any rock more than about 600 feet above the sea, although corals of Miocene age are said to occur at much greater elevations (see p. 208). Before these higher rocks could have been formed probably a certain amount of subsidence had taken place.

It will be convenient to describe here the northern end of the Flying Fish Cove section (left-hand end of B in Fig. 2), although in so doing it will be necessary to refer to some of the later rocks. It has already been mentioned that at its northern end the cliff of yellow limestone (marked B) becomes broken into minor cliffs (P), which dip somewhat downward and are soon concealed beneath a soil-clad talus slope. At a point slightly to the north of where the main cliff of limestone breaks up, the basalt likewise disappears, being partly concealed by soil, but mostly by a consolidated talus composed of blocks of Miocene Orbitoidal limestone, with some pebbles of volcanic rock. This forms a cliff (see N in section) which can be seen to rest upon basaltic and trachytic rocks. At its southern end, which is at a rather higher level than the main face, the talus blocks are angular, but throughout the greater part of its extent they are perfectly rolled and rounded, and there can be no doubt that we have here a section of an old beach which was formed when the sea was 80 or 100 feet higher than now. Still farther north this disappears under a coral-reef rock, probably formed about the same time. Above the point in the section marked N–S traces of beds of Miocene Orbitoidal limestone occur only about 200 feet up the cliff, showing that here also rocks of this age overlap the earlier rocks as in the south. These in turn are concealed beneath a great mass of cemented talus (M in section), which has been cut back into a lofty cliff, M (80–100 feet in places). The rocks comprising this talus include blocks of Orbitoidal limestone, but seem to be mostly of later date. At its northern end this cliff disappears beneath the limestones, forming the first inland cliff at the Zigzag (see note on p. 263), and its foot is concealed by a reef-rock (E) which partly covers the slope below it. In the talus beneath the high cliff are numerous blocks of basalt and palagonite tuffs, showing that the beds of these rocks are continued to the northern end of the cove, where they also pass beneath M and E. The lowest part of the section shows the face of the sea cliff (D), consisting of late Pleistocene or possibly recent limestones.

In this section we appear to have a fair representation of what would be seen in vertical sections through the island at right angles to the coast at any point, the succession being as follows : (1) A central core of older volcanic and Eocene or Oligocene limestones ; (2) beds of basalt, volcanic ash, and thick masses of Orbitoidal limestones enwrapping 1 ; (3) masses of talus, derived mainly from the Miocene rocks and covered by (4) a thick detrital limestone, which is derived from the wear of the reefs which cover the higher portions of the island; (5) a raised reef of much later date, which covers the foot of the cliffs and slopes composed of 4 ; and (6) finally, the late Pleistocene, or even recent, limestones of the sea cliff, which cling to the base of any of the older formations which may be exposed.

Rocks of the Central Nucleus in other localities.—As far as I know, the only other locality in the island where there is an exposure of the Eocene or Oligocene limestone containing Discocycline *Orbitoides* is in Sidney's Dale (see Map), a deep gorge on the west coast. This valley is one of several which, beginning at a height of between 400 and 500 feet, runs down to the sea in a generally south-west direction. In some cases (e g. Sidney's Dale) they cut through the sea cliff and terminate at the sea-level (Fig. 7), in others (e.g. Hugh's Dale) they open out on the top of the lowest terrace. These valleys seem to have been originally formed along lines of cracking and faulting; as a rule, on one side they are shut in by vertical cliffs, on the other by steep slopes. The floor is often formed by basaltic rock, and in one or two instances (e.g. in the lower part of Sidney's Dale Valley) it appears to form an upper edge of a narrow dyke running along the direction of the valley and showing signs of columnar structure at right angles to it (see Fig. 8). In all cases there are signs that in the rainy season a considerable torrent runs down these valleys, and no doubt has contributed to a considerable extent to their present form. I believe that where the sea cliff has been cut through to the sea-level this is entirely the work of the running water, and that the movements which first gave rise to these gorges did not affect the lowest terrace, which in fact was formed subsequently to them (see Fig. 7).

In Sidney's Dale, at about 250 feet above and 25 chains from the sea, the southern wall of the gorge is formed by cliffs varying from 60 to 100 feet in height; the northern side is very steep and in places cliff-like, while the total width of the floor is not more than 20 or 30 feet, and is mostly occupied by the rounded and water-worn rocks which indicate the existence of a rapid stream at some seasons. When I visited the valley in October it was perfectly dry. The cliffs to the south consist of a basal portion of basalt, about 10 feet high, then a narrow band of soft rock some 18 inches thick, and above this to the summit of the cliff hard yellow Eocene or Oligocene limestone. The basalt has a ground-mass crowded with lath-shaped crystals of plagioclase, some augites, and numerous skeleton crystals of magnetite; there is some glassy base. A few porphyritic crystals of pale purple augite and some porphyritic felspars replaced by calcite occur. This basalt is extensively exposed in the neighbourhood and is different from the basalt above referred to as forming a dyke on the floor of the dale.

The soft rock (No. 318) forming the thin band separating the basalt from the limestone above, and the massive limestone (No. 347), are described on p. 254. In both, the Lower Tertiary type of *Orbitoides* is present. Unfortunately the relations of this bed of ancient limestone were not worked out, because in the first

Fig. 7.—Mouth of Sidney's Dale, West Coast

place my stay in the neighbourhood was very brief, and in the second without microscopic examination the age of the beds was not recognizable. It will be noted that, as at Flying Fish Cove, this old limestone occurs at a comparatively low level, not being more than about 250 feet above the sea.

The volcanic rocks are exposed over a considerable area on the east coast in the neighbourhood of the fresh-water stream and waterfall marked on the Map. There they do not occur more than about 150 feet at most above the sea-level; but towards the southern end of this coast, a little north of Ross Hill, I found basalt pebbles up to 400 feet.

In the neighbourhood of the fresh-water stream are some rounded knolls, and in a shallow valley between these I found an exposure of a trachytic rock similar to that described from Flying Fish Cove. This exposure was of small extent, and seemed to be completely surrounded by basalt, of which the knolls are composed ; the relations of the two could not be made out, the ground being for the most part covered with a dense jungle of screw-pines, very difficult to penetrate. The basalt at this point forms a great part of the shore terrace, and appears on the shore in the waterfall bay and in another bay a little to the south. At the stream it is covered by thick beds of red palagonite tuffs, and it is to the presence of these volcanic rocks that the existence of the two or three small brooks is due. The palagonite tuffs are covered with coral limestones, the age of which is not known. At the waterfall (Panchorán Bay) the basalt forms an extensive sea-worn platform (Fig. 9), and on the beach forms a projecting ledge over which a perennial stream of excellent water flows. The basalt at this point, which is near the centre of the mass, contains porphyritic crystals of felspar, augite, and olivine. There seem to be two kinds of porphyritic felspars, one in well-defined twinned crystals, probably labradorite, the other less well-defined and with distinct zonal banding ; this is probably more acid. The olivine is usually altered into a pleochroic fibrous serpentinous mineral. Ground-mass of microliths of felspars, augite, and magnetite. Above the basalt at this point is a bed of volcanic conglomerate, consisting of blocks of basic rock, some vesicular, some compact and glassy, mostly more or less rounded ; these are embedded in a ground-mass of red volcanic ash with much lime ; in fact, at the top of the bed the pebbles of basaltic rock are embedded in hard limestone. The greatest thickness of this bed measured was about 10 feet. Upon it is a bed of hard yellow limestone, the age of which is doubtful. The absence of *Orbitoides* (see No. 52, p. 259) is against its Miocene age, but on the other hand Dr. Gregory has doubtfully referred a coral from this bed to a species (*Orbicella murrayi*, p. 216) found elsewhere in the Orbitoidal limestone. Upon it is a thick mass of limestone breccia, the blocks composing which are of all sizes and cemented by finer material, often filled with phosphatic nodules ; probably the whole is a submarine talus of comparatively recent date derived from the cliffs behind. This is capped in turn by a reef-limestone of quite recent date (probably late Pleistocene). The cliff at the north and south of this bay is therefore formed (from below up) by (1) basalt, (2) volcanic agglomerate, (3) yellow limestone (4 or 5 feet), perhaps of Miocene ge, (4) limestone breccia, an old talus, (5) late reef-limestone with corals like those now living on the coast.

A few hundred yards farther south the sea-washed platform is composed of a basalt of a very different character from that

FIG. 8.—DYKE OF BASALT, FLOOR OF SIDNEY'S DALE, WEST COAST.

FIG. 9.—SEA-WORN BASALT IN WATERFALL (PANCHORÁN) BAY, EAST COAST.

just described. This is a much altered glassy basalt with small porphyritic felspars and augites. The base has been for the most part altered into a yellowish and greenish brown palagonite-like substance which contains many microliths of plagioclase. There are some vesicles filled with concentric layers of a transparent substance showing a black cross between crossed nicols. The lower part of the bed is divided into fairly regular hexagonal vertical prisms, the summits of which have been broken into small angular fragments and recemented with crystalline calcite, the resulting rock having a remarkable appearance owing to the sharp contrast between the black basalt and the white lime. This extends up the cliff for about 40 feet, and is in some places capped by a foot or two of a fine-grained brown rock, apparently an ash, and on the top of the cliff there is a thick bed of red palagonite tuff. In a cliff a little to the south a clean section of the basalt shows that it is divided into four or five beds separated by indurated and brecciated limestone. The whole is covered by a conglomerate of blocks of limestone, some of great size, probably a consolidated talus from the inland cliffs.

South of Steep Point the base of the sea cliff is formed of basalt divided into hexagonal columns, in one case apparently curved.

Still farther south there are extensive exposures of basalt, which may be distinguished at a long distance from the summits of the inland cliffs by the great size of the sago-palms (*Arenga listeri*) which grow upon them; in this locality volcanic rocks may occur up to 400 feet above the sea.

In some localities on the east coast the Miocene Orbitoidal limestones are magnificently developed. The most notable exposure is near North-East Point, where the whole of the first inland cliff for more than half a mile consists of limestones of this age, crowded with the characteristic fossils. This cliff is about 250 feet high, and it appears to have been formed by a slipping away of a portion of the eastern flank of the island. A little farther south a much more extensive slip has taken place, giving rise to a cliff upwards of 500 feet in height and consisting apparently almost wholly of Miocene rocks. Towards the summit (about 400 feet) is found the rock which Messrs. Jones & Chapman have described above (No. 955, p. 255) as a breccia of fragments of Orbitoidal limestone cemented by recent reef material, but I am inclined to doubt whether the brecciation and recementing of the rock may not both be of Miocene date.

The base of these cliffs is concealed by a talus of great blocks and also in the northern part by comparatively recent reef-limestones which once formed a narrow fringing reef along their foot; it cannot therefore be seen whether here, as at Flying Fish Cove, these Miocene limestones rest on a volcanic basis or not; but since in the immediate neighbourhood pebbles of basaltic rock occur in the shore platform, and since at the same level and only about a mile further south the basalts and tuffs are present and of considerable thickness, it seems almost certain that this is the case. Cliffs composed of these Orbitoidal limestones are easily distinguishable from those formed of later reef-limestones, by their flat smooth faces and the straightness of all their lines, which is the consequence of the system of jointing which splits the mass up into roughly cubical blocks. The magnificent range of cliffs (first inland) which forms the fine headland, Egeria Point, are no doubt of this age, and so perhaps are those of South Point.

On the plateau and higher cliffs no Orbitoidal limestones at all occur, but according to Dr. Gregory some of the corals (e g. *Orbicella herklotsi*) collected from the reefs on the central plateau are of Miocene type. If this is so it indicates that in these localities the basis of older rocks has been exposed by denudation ; but since no rocks containing *Orbitoides* were seen and, on the other hand, traces of volcanic rocks were found, it seems probable that the Orbitoidal limestones never completely covered the volcanic basis, for had they done so traces of them should remain on the plateau.

THE ROCKS OF THE CENTRAL PLATEAU AND HILLS.

The general characters of the central plateau and of the hills which occur on its borders are described above in the introductory section (pp. 11–13). As already mentioned, some of the limestones exposed in the interior contain corals of Miocene type (see p. 208), and therefore most probably form part of the central nucleus which has been exposed by the very extensive denudation that the island must have undergone. Other reasons for supposing that this may be the case are, that in the middle of the island occasional pebbles of volcanic rock may be found, and that, as mentioned on p. 18, the great depth of the reddish-brown soil covering much of the central region has certainly been derived from the decomposition of volcanic rock, at least in great part. It is unfortunate that the Miocene age of some of the rocks of the plateau could not be determined by me while on the island, since a careful examination of their relations, and fuller collections of their fossils, might have thrown much light on the age of the highest limestones and on the date of the first elevation of the island above the sea. This event was no doubt post-Miocene, but that it was not long subsequent to that period seems to be rendered probable by the fact that since it took place a series of negative movements of the shore-line has occurred, a succession of inland cliffs has been cut back, and enormous masses of calcareous rock, both reef-limestones and more especially detrital limestones which cover much of the flanks of the island, have been formed.

The latest of the limestones covering the highest parts of the island and forming, in my opinion, an atoll reef and island, have been either to a large extent removed by denudation or have undergone great alteration, which has led to the destruction of the contained organisms. The rocks composing the summit of Murray Hill, Phosphate Hill, and the highest land over Flying Fish Cove are dolomitic limestones, containing 34 to 41 per cent. of carbonate of magnesia. Descriptions and analyses of these rocks (Nos. 378, 514, 800, 811) are given above by Mr. E. W. Skeats (pp. 267–268); and Messrs. Jones & Chapman have described the organisms contained in 378 (p. 257) and 800 (p. 258), and also in No. 143 (p. 256), a similar rock from the summit of Ross Hill. In all cases the fossils are nearly obliterated, and only imperfect remains of a few foraminifera and fragments of *Lithothamnion*, which resists destruction to the last, are to be seen : in the rock from Murray Hill there may be traces of coral structure. The rocks forming the rim between the hills are of a similar character both on the seaward side and on the landward slope, or low cliff, which, according to the view expressed above, faced the lagoon. In these, although their general appearance and mode of occurrence point to an origin from a coral reef, yet traces of coral are rarely seen. In some places, where the limestones contain little carbonate of magnesia, the foraminifera are fairly distinct: an example of such a rock is No. 134 (pp. 256 and 265), which was collected a little below the summit of the upper cliff on the east coast.

The rocks of the central plateau have been examined only in part. One of the most interesting is from pinnacles projecting from the soil at about 800 feet above the sea (No. 935, p. 257) : it is a crystalline limestone crowded with fragments of *Lithothamnion* and *Halimeda*, together with a few foraminifera, and it seems to be a shallow-water rock, such as might well accumulate in a lagoon. At no great distance from this there is another rock which points more strongly to lagoon conditions. This is a fine white limestone, which for the most part is of a powdery chalk-like consistency, is composed entirely of carbonate of lime, and usually contains no organisms : scattered in it are irregular hardened masses which include numerous foraminifera, which are described above (No. 658, p. 257) as being undersized and thin-shelled, and the nature of the rock as a whole is stated to indicate that it was once the soft mud of a shallow lagoon, an interpretation which the position in which it is found strongly supports. Some of the hard masses closely associated with this rock are dolomitized and the organisms obliterated. (See No. 658, p. 268.)

The most important evidence that the higher points on the northern and eastern rim of the plateau once formed islets is the existence upon several of them of thick beds of phosphate of lime, for it is difficult to account for the great accumulation of this substance at these points otherwise than by supposing that it is derived from thick beds of guano deposited on these elevations under conditions very different from those now prevailing. The necessary conditions would seem to have been fulfilled if these hills formed low treeless islets, whether these consisted merely of accumulations of coral thrown upon the reef by the action of the waves, or were the highest points along the line of reefs which had been exposed by a change in the relative levels of the land and sea. Another condition favourable for the accumulation of guano is absence, or at least scantiness, of rainfall, and the low and, as they must at first have been, treeless islets would certainly have a much smaller rainfall than at present occurs. Moreover, at the time when the first upward movement took place, the conditions prevailing in the Malay Archipelago were very different from at present. In Java, for instance, late Miocene or early Pliocene deposits are found at an elevation of 900 metres, so that a smaller land-area was then exposed, and, furthermore, the volcanic mountains were much less elevated than now. These circumstances may have considerably modified the meteorological conditions of Christmas Island, which lies near the southern edge of the region affected by the monsoon (see p. 17).

The phosphates, as they now exist, are probably the remains of beds of limestone, which have been altered by the overlying guano, the carbonate of lime being replaced by phosphate. The phosphatization occurred somewhat irregularly, and the removal of the more soluble portions of the beds by the action of percolating water has left behind a thick bed of blocks and nodules of phosphate, which covers a large area and extends to a considerable depth (upwards of 10 feet in places). The most important of these deposits is at Phosphate Hill, where a large area is covered by them, but other beds are to be found on some of the hills on the east coast. Moreover, at the present day small nodules of phosphate of lime are scattered widely over the plateau, and particularly on the outer slopes of the island. These nodules also occur embedded in the later limestones, and sometimes may have been formed *in situ* by segregation, but in most cases are simply derived from the higher beds. In any case the terraces, particularly the shore terrace, are in places thickly strewn with a sort of shingle of nodules of phosphate of lime, which have either weathered out of the limestones or fallen from the beds above.

In many places on the plateau the level surface of the soil is thickly strewn with small round black bodies varying in size from that of No. 10 shot to that of small peas. Mr. R. Irvine informs me that these pellets consist of a central nucleus of phosphate of lime, surrounded by a fairly thick coat of manganese dioxide, the whole being again covered with a thin layer of phosphate; they contain about 18 per cent. of manganese dioxide. This is probably derived from the volcanic tuffs which were extensively exposed on the higher parts of the island, and, as already mentioned, must be to a large extent the parent rock from which the thick soil of the island is derived. Their decomposition may have given rise to mud deposits on the lagoon bottom.

The phosphate itself is a very peculiar substance. It is intensely hard (between 6 and 7), and this, combined with the waxy lustre of a newly fractured surface, gives the impression that it is siliceous, though as a matter of fact it contains little or no silica (less than

1 per cent.). Under the microscope it can be seen that the rock, which has been phosphatized, was a fragmental one; obscure traces of contained organisms (foraminifera) may be observed occasionally, and in some specimens fragments of bone occur. There are numerous irregular cracks and cavities, which are usually lined with nearly transparent phosphate of lime, showing a beautifully banded agate-like structure. The colour of the rock is as a rule a brownish white, but some specimens are of a darker tint. In some cases the rock is found to consist of fragments of dark and light coloured phosphatized rock, embedded in a cement of transparent yellowish phosphate of lime, apparently deposited from solution in concentric layers round the fragments. Under crossed nicols this banded substance is found to be doubly refractive, polarizes feebly in tints of grey and shows traces of the black cross, the banded structure being rendered very prominent. In many respects this phosphatic rock closely resembles in its structure some of the phosphatic nodules from deep water described by Murray & Renard in the "Challenger" Report on Deep-sea Deposits (p. 391 et seq.). These nodules are described as having been formed as segregations of phosphate of lime replacing carbonate in certain marine deposits. This mode of origin may perhaps account for the presence of some of the small nodules found scattered over the island, but cannot be responsible for the formation of the great masses occurring at Phosphate Hill and elsewhere. The average composition of the phosphate is about 39 per cent. phosphoric acid; 51·5 per cent. lime; 3·5 per cent. carbonic acid; 2 per cent. iron and alumina; the remaining 4 per cent. being made of magnesia, water, fluorine, and other substances; there is only about ·2 per cent. of silica. The brown soil in the neighbourhood of these deposits also contains a considerable amount of phosphoric acid, often amounting to more than 30 per cent.

On Murray Hill is a bed of a remarkable rock which seems to have been produced by the phosphatization of a volcanic rock, probably a bed of tuff. It consists of small brown spherules of phosphatic matter cemented by doubly refractive phosphate of (?) lime: under the lens it presents somewhat the appearance of an oolite. It contains 39 per cent. of phosphoric acid, only 2·5 per cent. of lime, 32·5 per cent. of iron and alumina, nearly 5 per cent. of silica, the remainder being almost all water, either free or combined.

The rock upon which the phosphate beds rest is, in most places, a dolomitic limestone, which, in the specimens examined, curiously enough seems to contain no trace of phosphate of lime. Descriptions and analyses of some of these dolomitic rocks from Phosphate Hill (Nos. 800, 804, 811) are given on p. 267.

THE UPPER CLIFFS AND TERRACES.

The rocks composing the upper inland cliffs have not been fully examined, but enough has been done to show that in different places rocks of very different characters occur. These upper cliffs would perhaps be more fitly called talus slopes, since it is rare or an actual cliff face to be seen, the usual form being a steep (30°–40°) slope strewn with jagged blocks of limestone sometimes arranged more or less in a succession of small terraces. A general account of them has been given on p. 11. The upper cliff consists entirely of white and cream-coloured limestones, which towards the summit are often more or less dolomitized, and are nearly always more or less cavernous, owing partly to the crystallization which has usually taken place to a greater or less extent. Traces of coral are rare, but in one or two cases I found a rock apparently made up of broken pieces of a branching coral. Some of the beds consist largely of foraminifera, fragments of mollusca, and other organisms. At 725 feet over West White Beach I found a bed composed almost exclusively of a small lamellibranch, but this was on the south-west side of Murray Hill and perhaps belongs rather to the plateau than the upper cliff. Many of the rocks are clearly of fragmental origin, and consist of angular fragments of older limestones in a later calcareous matrix. No Orbitoides were seen. The rocks on the whole are such as might have accumulated on the submarine slopes outside a living reef, and, in fact, are probably largely composed of the débris derived from the wear of the rocks described above as forming the rim of the plateau. This upper slope is separated from the one below by a level terrace of varying width, usually soil-clad, but occasionally studded with blocks and pinnacles of limestone.

The second inland cliff, like the upper one, is generally reduced to a mere slope covered with talus, but in a few places, e.g. to the north of Steep Point on the east coast, it forms a vertical face. In it coral is found much more often than in the upper cliff, and at the locality just referred to numerous masses of it can be seen embedded in the limestone. Fragmental limestones are again common, and pieces of echinoid spines and molluscan shells are frequently met with; in some cases foraminifera are very numerous. The limestones are occasionally more or less dolomitic (see 131, p. 257), and in a few cases are partly phosphatized (940, p. 261). In this last case the limestone in question occurs below Phosphate Hill, and the contained phosphate was no doubt derived from that covering the slopes above. No. 131 is from a narrow valley on the summit of the first inland cliff, between its outer edge and the foot of the second inland cliff.

FIRST INLAND CLIFF.

The general characters of this cliff have been described above on p. 10 : both in its mode of origin and composition it is much more complex than the slopes above. It may consist either of (1) limestones of the central nucleus, containing *Orbitoides*, as at North-East Point, or (2) limestones of later date, largely made up of corals, molluscan shells, echinoid fragments, foraminifera, and other organisms, which together with other reef débris have accumulated on the flanks of the island; this is the prevailing type, and is found on all sides of the island where this cliff is well developed. The cases where the Miocene rocks are exposed have been noticed above. Rocks forming a cliff of the second type are described by Professor Rupert Jones and Mr. Chapman under the numbers 979 (p. 259), 859, 1002, 1005, 1006 (p. 260), 900, 403A (p. 261), 937, 864 (p. 262), 200, 202, 208, 209 (p. 263), and 1032 (p. 264). It will be seen that some of these are described as being brecciated or as forming a 'microconglomerate,' and as a matter of fact they all seem to me to be mainly of detrital origin. Again, several are described as 'recent,' but this can only be regarded as a relative term, since they are probably older than the Pleistocene. It should be noticed, however, that the corals described by Dr. Gregory from this cliff are either recent forms or very closely allied to recent forms (see p. 210 et seqq.), and usually occur also in the sea cliff, but on this point see below (p. 294). Nos. 1002, 1005-6 may be taken as fairly typical of the rocks of the vertical face (200 feet high) of this cliff as developed on the east coast. No. 900 was from the bottom of a cliff forming the western side of the deep cleft by which Steep Point Hill has been cut off from the main mass, and may be taken as typical of deeper parts of this limestone; in this specimen minute fragments of bone are not uncommon. Nos. 200, 202, 208, 209, 211, and 1032 are from the first inland cliff, just north of Flying Fish Cove, and form part of a series of specimens collected every few feet from the bottom to the top. No. 1032 is crowded with organisms, and must have been formed close to a living reef. This series may be taken as giving a fairly good idea of the kind of rocks of which this cliff is, as a rule, composed.

The first inland cliff appears to owe its origin to two different causes in different localities. In the first place it may be a fault cliff formed by the foundering of some portion of the outer edge of the island, as described above; this type is as a rule confined to places where the Miocene limestones are exposed, e.g. east coast near North-East Point and probably Egeria Point (south side), where the cliff can be seen to have been formed by one main slip and a number of subsidiary ones, some of which may extend for a short distance only, and form a number of short low cliffs at different levels above the main face. In the second case the cliff is the result of wave action; this is the commonest type, and the cliffs of the north and east coast are excellent examples of it. In many places it is clear that it has been formed by wave action at two or three levels (see p. 10), and that the sea has stood at several horizons along this cliff is abundantly proved by the fact that in places where the cliff is wanting raised reefs occur at different elevations.

For instance, south of Smith Point (see Fig. 6, p. 280) there is such a reef terrace on the 180 feet contour-line, and at the foot of this a still later one at about 100 feet. Again, between Flying Fish Cove and North-East Point, for the greater part of the distance the single high cliff which is found at the Zigzag (see Fig. 6) is replaced by two or three irregular step-like cliffs of reef-limestone, often interrupted by talus slopes, gaps, and channels, and in fact representing the remains of a series of fringing reefs, each of which in turn was raised and cut back by the sea, while at its foot its successor grew up on the talus derived from the cliffs above. Whether a single vertical cliff face or a succession of terraces was formed depended upon the steepness of the submarine slopes. If these were gentle enough to allow talus material to accumulate and afford a foundation for a fringing reef the terraced condition followed, but if on the other hand the slopes were steep and no reef could grow, a vertical cliff was formed. It should be noted that all intermediate conditions occur, the commonest being that in which the upper 150 feet or so form a vertical face, while the foot, from the shore terrace up to about 100 feet above the sea, is formed by a narrow belt of reef. This corresponds to the terrace between the 100 feet and 180 feet contour-lines in Fig. 6, and is the most persistent of these minor terraces. In some places shore conglomerate was observed on its surface, and great limestone blocks fallen upon it from the cliffs above rest on a sort of pedestal of cemented coral fragments like that which is found at the base of the blocks lying on the present fringing reef. Of course these raised fringing reefs are of later date than the rocks in which the first inland cliff has been carved by the sea, and the lower ones may be but little older than the reef forming the present sea cliff and terrace. This probably accounts for the fact that some of the corals labelled as from the first inland cliff are similar to those found in the sea cliff and to recent forms.

THE SHORE CLIFF AND TERRACE.

The shore terrace and cliff (see pp. 6–10) are formed by the elevated fringing reef that grew round the island before the last negative movement of the shore-line took place. It is the most persistent of the terraces, and, with the exception of about a quarter of a mile in two localities, it runs round the whole island. In some places, as above mentioned, it may be in part formed by the volcanic and other rocks of the central nucleus, but elsewhere it may be described as consisting of a thin capping of coral limestone, resting on a foundation of consolidated talus derived from what are now the inland cliffs, and, of course, varying in characters as the rocks composing those cliffs vary. For instance, on the east coast, in the neighbourhood of the fresh-water stream both the talus foundations and the reef-limestone overlying it are full of blocks of basalt derived from the exposure on the slopes behind.

The shore cliff forming the southern boundary of Flying Fish Cove may be taken as fairly typical of the shore cliff in general. It will be seen (Fig. 2 A, p. 272) that the basalt marked A, which runs down beneath the sea-level, has its upper surface covered with an old talus consisting of blocks derived from the cliffs of Miocene limestone behind, lying in a matrix of smaller limestone fragments mingled with the débris of the basalts and palagonite tuffs which occur in the neighbourhood, and often including the shells of foraminifera. A similar talus forms the foot of the cliff (see Fig. 2 A, above the letters S.E.–N.W.), where, being very hard, it forms a projecting ledge which is some 6 or 10 feet high. Upon it is about 50 feet of very fresh-looking coral limestone, in which the individual coral stocks, in the position of growth, may often be distinguished. One mass of *Porites* is between 20 and 30 feet high and nearly as broad (see Fig. 4, p. 274). A fine section of the sea cliff is exposed where it is cut through at the mouth of Sidney's Dale (Fig. 7, p. 284). Here also it is seen to consist very largely of recent species of corals, some of which, both from this and other localities, have been noticed by Dr. J. W. Gregory (pp. 206–225).

If the terrace at the top of the sea cliff be examined it will be found in many places to consist of two parts, an outer broader zone, which is the summit of the raised reef, and wherever the rock is free from soil and vegetation can be seen to consist mainly of fresh-looking corals, and an inner, much narrower zone, running along the foot of the inland cliff and consisting of the same material, being, in fact, the base of the portion which has been cut back by the waves.

The present fringing reef forms a narrow shelf round the island, being only interrupted where deep water occurs close to the foot of the sea cliff; and, if a further negative movement of some fifty feet were to take place, it would form a cliff and terrace much like that just described.

Summary and Conclusions.

From the foregoing account it will be seen that Christmas Island presents some important peculiarities which differentiate it from other oceanic islands, and are difficult to explain. The island is, in fact, the flat summit of a submarine mountain more than 15,000 feet high, the depth of the platform from which it rises being about 14,400 feet, and its height above the sea being upwards of 1,000 feet. The submarine slopes are steep, for depths of 1,100 fathoms occur less than four (in one case less than three) miles, and the foot of the mountain (about 2,400 fathoms) within twenty miles of the coast of the island. As far as the soundings go, they show that the slopes of the upper part of the peak are nearly alike on all sides, being about 2 in 5. Soundings made in the neighbourhood of the island at depths of more than 1,000 fathoms usually show the bottom to be covered with *Globigerina* ooze ; off the south-east corner of the island coral-sand was met with in depths of more than 900 fathoms, and this sand is no doubt derived from the wear of the cliffs of this part of the island, which is exposed to the full force of the swell of the Southern Ocean. Round the rest of the coast fragments of volcanic rocks and pieces of manganese dioxide are recorded from various depths up to 1,100 fathoms: two soundings of 385 and 925 fathoms respectively brought up calcareous algæ. Between the island and Java lies a long narrow trough, which is one of the abysses of the Indian Ocean, being upwards of 3,000 fathoms deep in places. Its long axis lies parallel to the south coast of Java, the submarine slopes of which appear to be formed by a great fault and are very steep, the 2,000-fathom line being only a few miles from the land.

Forming the flat summit of the Christmas Island peak we meet with a succession of limestones ranging from the Eocene (or Oligocene) up to recent reef deposits, and accompanying the older Tertiary deposits are various volcanic rocks, most important of which are basalts and trachytes lying beneath the Eocene (or Oligocene) limestone, while above it are basalts and basic tuffs separating it from the Miocene Orbitoidal limestone which seems to make up the great mass of the island. The total thickness of these older Tertiary and the interstratified volcanic rocks is, as far as can be ascertained, about 600 feet, but it is probable, as above stated, that some of the rocks exposed on the plateau may be Miocene, in which case the series is considerably thicker. The occurrence of such a series of Tertiary deposits on an oceanic island is, I believe, unknown elsewhere, although Wallace mentions that Upper Miocene deposits occur in the Azores. Another point of importance in the case of these Tertiary rocks is that they, especially the Miocene Orbitoidal limestones, end abruptly on the coast in vertical cliffs sometimes 250 feet high, so that it is clear that the area which they originally covered must have been much larger than the present island, and that it has been cut down to its present dimensions by repeated faulting and slipping down of its peripheral region. All these limestones must have been deposited in shallow water, probably less than 100 fathoms deep. At present the Eocene limestones are found up to about 250–300 feet, the Miocene Orbitoidal limestones up to about 550 feet, while the summit rises 1,200 feet above the sea. If we suppose the Eocene limestones to have been deposited in 100 fathoms (and it was probably much less), the range of the oscillation with reference to the sea-level which the island can be proved to have undergone is between 200 and 300 fathoms, a small proportion of the total depth to the ocean floor. Speaking generally, this oscillation appears to have consisted, first, of a gradual depression, allowing of the accumulation of the Miocene Orbitoidal limestones and those composing the higher land, then a period of rest, followed by a succession of movements of elevation (or better, negative movements of the shore-line), which have given rise to the terraced structure of the island and continued to the present time. The period of rest between the upward and downward movement of the sea-level must have been a prolonged one, for it was during this time that the atoll condition existed, and the great bulk of the detrital limestone derived from the destruction of the living reefs, and now forming the mass of the first inland cliff, was deposited : the great accumulation of guano that must have taken place would also have required a vast period of time for its formation.

In Java the later Eocene deposits include limestones, in which is found the Discocycline *Orbitoides dispansa* as in Christmas Island, but accompanied by numerous Nummulites, which, curiously enough, according to Messrs. Jones & Chapman, are entirely wanting in the limestones described by them, while on the other hand large Heterostegines occur abundantly. Above these Eocene deposits comes a great mass of volcanic rocks, including andesites, diabases, and other lavas, some derived from submarine eruptions. This volcanic series seems to correspond in time to the basalts and tuffs which overlie the older limestone at Flying Fish Cove. The Miocene rocks consist of three divisions, the lower made up chiefly of volcanic breccias, the middle of soft marls, the upper of calcareous rocks with some dolomites and marls. In Christmas Island these are probably all represented by the massive Orbitoidal limestone, the absence of terrigenous material being only what might be expected. In both areas the calcareous rock is crowded with Lepidocycline Orbitoides, but although some of the Christmas Island forms occur in Sumatra and Borneo none are recorded from Java, and most are described as new ; the fact that the Orbitoides of the two areas have been described by different authors may in part account for the discrepancy.

It will be seen that the rocks of South Java, if we make allowance for the proximity to land at the time of their deposition, resemble in their general characters and succession those of Christmas Island, and like them they often terminate on the south coast in abrupt faces, or show other indications that they formerly extended farther south, but have been cut back by faulting and slipping. As to the possibility that these rocks in the two localities were deposited in a continuous area, it can only be said that the difficulties in the way of supposing this to have been the case are very great. If it were so it must be imagined that the enormous depth between the two islands has been attained since the Miocene by a general depression of the sea bottom south of the fault line forming the southern margin of the Malayan platform ; and further, that during this depression the small area which forms the elevation on which Christmas Island now stands escaped the movement, and in fact forms a ' horst,' on all sides of which the sea bottom has been faulted down about 2,400 fathoms. These suppositions, however, appear untenable, and most of the difficulties are avoided by regarding the base of Christmas Island as a volcanic peak which has accumulated in consequence of repeated eruptions. In this case, since upon its summit shallow-water deposits of Eocene age occur, the depth of the floor of the ocean in the neighbourhood can have undergone little alteration since the Eocene times, unless, indeed, it has been lowered equally round the foot of the mountain by a system of cross faults. This volcano, like those of Java and Sumatra, etc., probably owes its origin to the movements along the line of the great fault forming the south boundary of the Malayan area in pre-Eocene times. Some post-Eocene movements probably caused the eruptions, the products of which form the base of the Miocene both in Christmas Island and Java, and may have resulted in the deepening of the abyss between the two areas. Movements are still in progress, as the eruptions of the Malayan islands show, and in Christmas Island also two slight earthquakes have been recorded by Mr. A. Clunies Ross within the last few years: the last of these, on October 20th, 1895, was sufficiently severe to loosen great masses of rock from the cliff. This seems to have been felt in the Cocos-Keeling Islands also, a point of some interest, since these islands almost certainly rest on a volcanic peak which may owe its origin to the same causes as that of Christmas Island.

In the foregoing pages I have frequently spoken of the elevation and depression of the island. This is, of course, merely elevation and depression in reference to the sea-level, and it would probably have been better to have employed the terms suggested by Suess, namely, "negative and positive movements of the shore-line," since in some cases, at least, particularly in the formation of the later cliffs, it seems very probable that it is the general level of the surface of the sea that has been altered, and not merely a local upheaval of a limited land-area that has taken place.

The above description of the geology of Christmas Island must be regarded merely as a first essay, for owing to the fact that the age of many of the limestones could not be recognized by me on the spot, and to other difficulties referred to above, much remains to be done, and in the light of my present knowledge, both of the localities and of the rocks, if it were possible to revisit the island for even a few days, many questions could be definitely settled which during my former visit puzzled me greatly, after repeated examination. One point of special interest may be referred to, namely, the possibility of finding still earlier, perhaps Cretaceous, limestones beneath the Eocene (or Oligocene) limestone in Sidney's Dale on the west coast.

THE GEOGRAPHICAL RELATIONS OF
THE FLORA AND FAUNA OF CHRISTMAS ISLAND.

By C. W. Andrews, B.Sc., F.G.S.

Among the most interesting subjects of inquiry in connection with an oceanic island are the relations of its flora and fauna to those of the neighbouring lands, the means by which it has been colonized, and the degree to which the changed conditions under which the colonists are placed have led to modifications and have given rise to new species. In the present section these points are briefly discussed, and a list of all the recorded species is appended, together with their approximate distribution or that of their allies.

The fauna and flora of Christmas Island are on the whole, as might be expected, most nearly related to those of the Indo-Malayan islands, but to this there are some exceptions in the case of certain groups. Of the 319 species of animals recorded, 145 or about 45 per cent. are described as endemic : this remarkably high percentage of peculiar forms is, however, no doubt largely due to the fact that in some groups, particularly the insects, the species inhabiting Java and the neighbouring islands are still imperfectly known, and many now described for the first time from Christmas Island will no doubt probably be found to exist also in other localities.

Of the mammals all are peculiar species except one, and that is a well-marked variety of a species inhabiting Further India. The nearest allies of the Rats and Fruit-bat are found in the Austro-Malayan islands, a circumstance for which an explanation is offered below.

The birds may be divided into four groups. (1) The resident land birds, which are all peculiar species, more nearly allied to Austro-Malayan than to Indo-Malayan forms (Lister, Proc. Zool. Soc., 1888, p. 530). (2) The sea birds, mostly widely spread forms, but in one case, *Sula abbotti*, previously recorded from Assumption Island only, and in another, *Phaethon fulvus*, described from specimens of which the locality is not known. (3) The migrants, which reach the island during the rainy season, corresponding to the northern winter. (4) Accidental visitors, to which division *Chalcococcyx basalis* and *Myristicivorus bicolor* may probably be referred.

Of the six reptiles four are peculiar, but belong to widely distributed genera, and the other two occur in Java.

Of the fourteen species of land-shells described, six are peculiar, but allied forms are widely distributed in the neighbouring lands. The same may be said of most of the other species, but two or three are not known from the Indo-Malayan islands, and may have reached the island from the eastward in the same way as some of the mammals.

Nine species of butterflies are recorded, of which three are peculiar, while another is a distinct variety of a Javanese species. The others are Indo-Malayan, except two, which may be Australian.

Of the larger moths sixty-five species are described, ten of which are peculiar. Of the remainder, most occur in the neighbouring islands, but there is a considerable group of species found in Ceylon, and another from the Austro-Malayan and Pacific islands. Out of nine species of Microlepidoptera six are new, two of the others belong to the Australian region, while the third is recorded from Africa.

Of the Hymenoptera nine out of eleven species are said to be peculiar. All belong to widely distributed genera.

The Coleoptera are represented by a much greater number of species than any of the other orders of insects, eighty-four in all being described, while ten others have been referred to their genera only. Fifty-six species are said to be peculiar to the island, but this remarkably high proportion (nearly 67 per cent.) is no doubt due to the fact that the beetles of Java are still incompletely known. The remaining species are mostly either widely distributed forms or are Indo-Malayan. As in the case of the moths, a few are identical with species from Ceylon.

All the Homoptera are described as new. Several are related to Austro-Malayan forms. Of the Hemiptera four out of six are new, the remaining two are pelagic. The two new species of Neuroptera belong to widely distributed genera, and the three remaining species are common in the Oriental region.

Of the Orthoptera twenty-two species are described, fourteen being endemic, but nearly all belonging to widely distributed genera. The remainder are either cosmopolitan, or at any rate Oriental forms.

Of three species of Chilopoda, one is Palæarctic (this was not collected by me), the other two Oriental. Two out of three species of Diplopoda are peculiar, the third being a cosmopolitan form. Twelve species of Arachnids have been described, three being new. The remainder, with the exception of one Australian form, are Oriental, mostly occurring in the Indo-Malayan islands. The land Crustacea are all widely distributed on the Indo-Pacific coasts.

Finally, of the four species of earth-worms two are peculiar, one having allies in the Aru Islands and Ceylon, the other in Sumatra. The other two species occur both in the Oriental and Australian regions.

One hundred and eleven species of Dicotyledonous plants are recorded, and of these ten only are referred to as new, but a considerable number, while not specifically distinct, differ markedly from specimens from other localities, and may be regarded as local varieties. In fact, as has been pointed out on the authority of Professor Oliver, we are probably here dealing with species in the making [6, 10]. Most of the other plants either occur in the Indo-Malayan islands or are widely distributed tropical forms.

Of the Monocotyledons seven out of eighteen species are endemic, the remainder being either Indo-Malayan or widely distributed.

The single Gymnosperm, *Cycas circinalis*, is found both in the Indo- and Austro-Malayan islands. The ferns are either Indo-Malayan or common tropical forms: only two are described as endemic. The remaining Cryptogams are all, with the exception of one peculiar species of fungus, either Indo-Malayan or widely distributed species.

The causes which have been instrumental in the introduction of the fauna and flora have been, as usual, the winds and ocean currents, the work of the former being much the more important. The prevailing wind is the south-east trade, which blows on an average 300 days in the year. The nearest land in the direction from which it comes is the north-west coast of Australia, about 900 miles away, so that, as might be supposed, the number of species possibly introduced by this means is very small ; perhaps one or two of the butterflies may have reached the island in this way. In fact, as Wallace [1] long ago pointed out in the case of the Azores, the introduction of plants and animals into remote islands is due not so much to ordinary or normal as to extraordinary or exceptional causes. These latter, in the case of Christmas Island, are the storms which, during the rainy season, blow occasionally from the northern quarter, and it is after these, or sometimes even after a few days' steady breeze from this direction, that birds of passage, dragon-flies, various moths and butterflies, and other insects reach the island. It is no doubt, therefore, to these occasional northern winds and storms, that by far the greater number of the species of plants and animals owe their introduction, and, indeed, considering that new arrivals were observed after nearly every gale, it seems rather remarkable that a greater number of forms have not gained a permanent footing. In the case of the birds most of the newcomers were migrants coming south to avoid the northern winter, and would not, in any case, be likely to remain permanently ; the rails, of which at least two species were seen, would probably find it impossible to breed in the island on account of the rats. Several of the species recorded were only represented

---

[1] "Island Life," 2nd ed., p. 261.

by single individuals, which were picked up in a dying condition; this was the case with the specimens of *Chalcococcyx basalis* and of *Hirundo gutturalis.* Since I left the island several individuals of a black and white fruit-pigeon (*Myristicivorus bicolor*) have been observed on the island, and I heard reports that similar cases had occurred previously; but it seems unlikely that this species could become a permanent inhabitant, for it would probably come into direct competition with the native fruit - pigeon, which itself sometimes dies in large numbers for want of sufficient food and water. Several other birds, of which I did not obtain specimens, have been observed. Mr. Andrew Ross told me he had shot a small duck and that a fishing hawk had been seen on the coast. I myself saw a number of white-headed swifts which remained for some days. Whatever the reason may be, it is certain that for an extremely long period of time no bird has become a permanent denizen of the island, for all the land birds which breed there are peculiar species, whose ancestors must have arrived long ago. It should be noted, moreover, that according to Mr. Lister, who has ably discussed the geographical relations of the Christmas Island birds [5], they are more nearly related to Austro-Malayan than to Javanese types. This circumstance may be accounted for by supposing that when their ancestors reached the island different meteorological conditions prevailed, or that they may owe their introduction to some. other cause, e.g. drifting on rafts of floating trees such as not uncommonly occur in these seas.

Of the insects the dragon-flies, which arrive in swarms, usually disappear in a few days, most likely because of the absence of standing water. The butterflies and moths were generally much battered during their transit, and it can only rarely happen that the conditions necessary for their establishment as permanent inhabitants are fulfilled. Of the other less conspicuous insects it is impossible to speak, because I was unable to distinguish the new arrivals from the natives, but no doubt many species must from time to time be blown across from Java during these gales.

Of the plants, according to Mr. Ridley [8], very few are introduced by the wind, the most important being the various Cryptogams, of which the small spores are easily blown long distances; orchids, of which the seeds are very small; *Hoya* and *Blumea*, the seeds of which are plumed; and to these perhaps may be added *Berria* and *Dipterocarpus*, the winged fruits of which are sometimes carried high into the air and may be blown long distances.

The ocean current which passes the island is the equatorial drift, which comes down from the Timor Sea and receives tributaries through the Straits between the islands of the Archipelago (Bali, Lombok, etc.). It is to the transport of rafts of trees by this current that the rats, the fruit-bat, and possibly some of the land birds, very probably owe their introduction to the island, and this circumstance would account for the similarity of many of them to

Austro-Malayan forms. Some at least of the Reptilia and Land Mollusca no doubt reached the island by the same means.

In the case of the plants this means of transport is perhaps the most important of all, as is shown by the very large number of species which have seeds capable of resisting long immersion in sea-water. To this division belong most of the sea-loving trees (e.g. *Calophyllum, Hibiscus, Scævola, Cordia,* etc.), as well as many of those found in the forests generally (e.g. *Barringtonia, Cryptocarya, Inocarpus, Ochrosia,* etc.). Many of the smaller plants also may have been introduced by this means either as seeds or perhaps, in the case of epiphytic plants, attached to floating trees.

Several other means by which plants may reach an oceanic island are excellently illustrated in the flora of Christmas Island. Thus a considerable proportion of the trees bear fruits which are eaten by the pigeons and other birds, and may have been brought across the sea by them. It is by no means necessary that the birds themselves should survive in order that the seeds may get a footing,[1] so that from time to time plants may have been introduced by species of birds which are not now found in the island.

Another mode of distribution is by seeds and fruits, which, either by means of a sticky secretion or by hooks, can cling to the plumage of birds. Several species have no doubt been introduced in this manner, the most notable being *Pisonia,* the fruits of which are extremely sticky, and sometimes clog the feathers of the sea birds to such an extent as to impede their movements.

The plants and animals already introduced by man are referred to on p. 20, but considerable additions to these will no doubt quickly follow. In the case of plants especially the reduction in the number of rats near the settlement will render possible the cultivation of many species which hitherto have been destroyed before the fruits could ripen.

The following table consists of a list of the species of animals and plants at present recorded from Christmas Island, together with their distribution or, in the case of peculiar species, the distribution of their nearest allies. Species peculiar to the island are marked 'x' in the first column, and the regions in which their nearest allies occur are indicated in the succeeding columns by numbers distinguished by an asterisk; in the case of species not peculiar to the island the same numbers are employed without the asterisk. The geographical divisions adopted are those employed

---

[1] See Clement Reid, "Crgin of the British Flora," p. 30, 1899.

by Wallace in his "Distribution of Animals," and the numbers refer to his subdivisions of those areas, as follows :—

(*a*) ORIENTAL REGION.

1. Hindostan.
2. Ceylon.
3. Indo-China.
4. Indo-Malaya.

(*b*) AUSTRALIAN REGION.

1. Austro-Malaya.
2. Australia.
3. Polynesia.
4. New Zealand.

(*c*) ETHIOPIAN REGION.

1. East Africa.
2. West Africa.
3. South Africa.
4. Madagascar.

In the last column the occurrence of species in localities other than those indicated in the preceding columns is noted, and various remarks are appended. The whole of the regions in which a species or its allies occur are not in all cases mentioned, but as far as possible the district nearest to Christmas Island in which they are found is noticed.

FAUNA OF CHRISTMAS ISLAND.

LIST OF SPECIES.

	Peculiar to the Island.	Oriental Region.	Australian Region.	Ethiopian Region.	Various localities and remarks.
MAMMALIA.					
Pteropus natalis	x	...	•1	...	Lombok.
Pipistrellus murrayi ...	x	...	...	...	Allies widely distributed.
Crocidura fuliginosa, var.					
trichura	var. x	3			
Mus nativitatis	x	...	? •1		
Mus macleari	x	•4	. •1		
AVES.					
Carpophaga whartoni ...	x	...	•1, •3		
Myristicivorus bicolor ...	...	3, 4	1		
Chalcophaps natalis ...	x	•1, 2, 3, 4	•1		
Limnobænus fuscus ...	...	1, 2, 3, 4	1		
Anous stolidus ...	...	...	...	...	Tropical and sub-tropical seas.
Glareola orientalis	...	...	...	...	Migrant wintering in Malay Archipelago and Australia.
Charadrius dominicus ...	...	...	...	...	Ditto.
Ochthodromus geoffroyi ...	...	...	...	...	Ditto.
Numenius variegatus ...	...	...	...	...	Ditto.
Heteractitis brevipes	...	...	...	...	Ditto.
Tringoides hypoleucus	...	...	...	...	Migrant wintering in S. Africa, India, and Australia.
Calidris arenaria ...	...	...	...	...	Nearly cosmopolitan.
Limonites ruficollis	...	...	...	...	Migrant wintering in Burmah, Malay Archipelago, and Australia.
Gallinago sthenura	...	...	...	...	Migrant wintering in India and Malay Archipelago.
Demiegretta sacra ...	...	1, 3, 4	1, 2, 3		Tropical and sub-tropical oceans.
Fregata aquila ...	...	...	...	...	Indian and Pacific Oceans.
Fregata ariel ...	...	...	...	...	Tropical and sub-tropical oceans.
Sula sula	...	...	...		Assumption Island.
Sula abbotti ...	...	...	...	...	
Sula piscatrix ...	...	...	...		Tropical and sub-tropical oceans.
Phaethon rubricauda	...	...	...		Tropical regions of Indian and Pacific Oceans.
Phaethon fulvus ...	...	...	...	...	Other localities unknown.
Astur natalis ...	x	...	•1		
Ninox natalis ...	x	...	•1, •2		
Collocalia natalis ...	x	...	•1		
Chalcococcyx basalis ...	...	4	1, 2		
Motacilla melanope	...	...	...	...	Palæarctic in summer, going south in winter.
Motacilla flava ...	...	...	...	...	Ditto.

x

	Peculiar to the Island.	Oriental Region.	Australian Region.	Ethiopian Region.	Various localities and remarks.
Zosterops natalis	x	...	•1		
Merula erythropleura ...	x	? •4	? •3		
Hirundo gutturalis ...	...	...	...	...	Nests in N.E. Asia; migrates as far south as Australia in winter.
REPTILIA.					
Gymnodactylus marmoratus	...	4			
Gecko listeri	x	...	•1		
Lygosoma atrocostatum ...	...	4	1		
Lygosoma nativitatis ...	x				
Ablepharus egeriæ ...	x	...	...	...	Allies widely distributed.
Typhlops exocæti	x				
LAND MOLLUSCA.					
Lamprocystis normani ...	x	•4	•1, •2, •3		
Lamprocystis mabelæ ...	x	•4	•1, 2, 3		
Lamprocystis mildredæ ...	x	•4	•1, 2, 3		
Succinea solidula ...	...	...	...	...	Habitat previously unknown.
Succinea solitaria	x	...	...	...	Allies widely distributed.
Succinea listeri	x	...	...	...	Ditto.
Opeas subula	...	...	...	...	Probably introduced.
Pythia scarabæus	...	4	1, 3		
Melampus luteus	...	...	1, 2, 3		
Melampus fasciatus ...	...	...	1, 2, 3		
Melampus castaneus ...	...	...	3		
Leptopoma mouhoti ...	...	3			
Truncatella valida ...	...	...	1, 3	...	Allies Oriental.
Assiminea andrewsiana ...	x	•1			
LEPIDOPTERA RHOPALOCERA.					
Limnas petilia	...	4	2		
Vadebra macleari	x	•4			
Melanitis ismene, var. *determinata*	...	4	...	...	Wide range.
Charaxes andrewsi ...	x	...	•1		
Junonia villida	...	...	2		
Hypolimnas misippus ...	...	4			
Hypolimnas nerina, var. *listeri*	var. x	•4			
Nacaduba aluta	...	3, 4	1		
Terias amplexa	x	...	...	...	Allies widely distributed in Asia and Africa.
LEPIDOPTERA PHALÆNÆ.					
Euchromia horsfieldi ...	...	4	1		
Nola distributa	...	1, 3, 4	...	4	
Deiopeia pulchella ...	...	...	...	...	Old World.
Argina cribraria ...	...	3, 4	1	4	

	Peculiar to the Island.	Oriental Region.	Australian Region.	Ethiopian Region.	Various localities and remarks.
LEPIDOPTERA, *continued.*					
Mimeusemia econia ...	x	•4			
Dipterygia vagivitta ...	...	3, 4			
Amyna selenampha ...	...	1, 2, 3, 4	...	3, 4	
Amyna octo ...	...	...	...	...	Tropics.
Prodenia littoralis ...	...	...	...	...	Mediterranean sub-region, tropics, sub-tropics.
Leocyma tibialis ...	...	1, 3	1, 3		
Armactia columbina ...	...	...	2		
Brana calopasa ...	...	2	1		
Patula macrops ...	...	1, 2, 3		1,2,3,4	
Ophiusa honesta ...	...	1, 2, 3, 4			
Ophiusa coronata ...	...	1, 2, 3, 4	2		
Ophiusa serva ...	...	1, 2, 3, 4	1, 2		
Bocula limbata	x				
Acantholipes similis ...	...	1, 4			
Thermesia rubricans ...	...	1, 2, 3, 4	1, 3	1,2,3,4	
Ophideres salaminia ...	...	1, 2, 3, 4	1, 2, 3	4	
Ophideres ancilla ...	...	1, 2, 3			
Ophideres fullonica ...	...	1, 2, 3, 4	1, 2	1, 2, 3	
Ophideres materna ...	...	...	...	...	Tropical Africa.
Cosmophila erosa ...	...	...	...	...	Widely distributed.
Cosmophila vitiensis ...	...	...	3		
Eutelia delatrix ...	...	1, 2, 3, 4	2		
Stictoptera describens ...	...	2, 4			
Hydrillodes vexillifera ...	x				
Maliattha signifera ...	...	1, 2, 3, 4	2		
Erastria griseomixta ...	x				
Tarache olivacea ...	...	3			
Earias chromataria ...	...	1, 2, 3, 4	...	1, 2, 3	
Porthesia pulverea ...	x	•4			
Orgyia postica ...	...	1, 2, 3, 4	1, 2		
Chaerocampa erotus ...	...	3	2, 3		
Chaerocampa vigil ...	...	1, 2, 3, 4	1, 2		
Theretra lucasi ...	...	1, 2, 3, 4	1, 2		
Pseudosphinx discistriga ...	...	1, 2, 3, 4	2	...	Japan.
Cephonodes hylas ...	...	1, 2, 3, 4	2, 3	2, 3	Specimens of a type recorded only from S. Africa.
Hyperythra lutea ...	...	1, 2, 3, 4	1, 2		
Boarmia acaciaria ...	...	1, 2, 3, 4	1, 2	2, 3, 4	
Boarmia scotozonea ...	x	•1, •2			
Sauris hirudinata ...	...	1, 2, 3, 4	2, 3	3	
Thalassodes veraria ...	...	1, 2, 4			
Craspedia optivata ...	...	2			
Craspedia, sp.					
Epiplema inhians ...	...	3			
Doloessa castanella ...	...	2			
Corcyra cephalonica ...	...	2	...	...	Europe, West Indies. Probably introduced.
Homoeosoma nimbella ...	...	...	...	3	United States, Europe, Syria.
Ephestia scotella ...	x				
Heterographis singhalella ...		2			
Eusophera cinerosella ...	...	...	...	...	Europe. Probably introduced.
Epicrocis aegnusalis ...	...	1, 2, 3, 4	2	4	

	Peculiar to the Island.	Oriental Region.	Australian Region.	Ethiopian Region.	Various localities and remarks.
LEPIDOPTERA, *continued.*					
Endotricha listeri	x				
Herculia nannodes	...	3, 4			
Zinckenia nigerrimalis ...	x				
Zinckenia fascialis	...	...	...	...	Nearly cosmopolitan.
Dichocrosis surusalis ...	...	2, 4	1		
Dichocrosis auritineta ...	...	4	1		
Sylepta lunalis	...	1, 2, 3, 4	1		
Glyphodes holophæalis ...	x	...	...	...	Nearest allies neotropical.
Glyphodes indica	...	1, 2, 3, 4	1, 2, 3	1,2,3,4	
Glyphodes suralis	...	3	1, 3		
Hellula undalis	...	1, 2, 3, 4	...	1,2,3,4	United States and Mediterranean sub-region.
MICRO-LEPIDOPTERA.					
Oxychirota paradoxa ...	...	...	2		
Cosmoclostis quadriquadra	...	...	1, 2		
Brenthia elachista ...	x	...	...	...	Resembling American forms.
Simaethis ornaticornis ...	x	...	...	...	Near a European species.
Phycodes adjectella ...	...	...	...	2	
Tortricomorpha chlorolepis	x				
Epagoge halysidota ...	x	*4	*1, *2	*2	
Cænognosis incisa	x		*2		
Dendroneura punctata ...	x	...	...	...	Genus widely distributed, said to accompany banana and sugar-cane.
HYMENOPTERA.					
Mantibaria anomala ...	x				
Ophion flavocephalus ...	x	...	...	...	Genus widely distributed.
Lobopelta diminuta ...	...	...	...	...	Oriental.
Camponotus melichloros ...	x	...	...	...	Genus widely distributed.
Notogonia alecto	...	...	...	...	Ditto.
Odynerus polyphemus ...	x	*4	...	...	Ditto.
Polistes balder	x	*1, *3, *4	...	...	Ditto.
Halictus andrewsi ...	x	*3	...	...	Ditto.
Halictus binghami ...	x	...	...	...	Ditto.
Megachile rotundipennis ...	x	*1	...	...	Ditto.
Megachile nivescens ...	x	...	...	...	Ditto.
COLEOPTERA.					
Morio orientalis	...	3, 4			
Harpalus, sp.	...	...	...	...	Genus widely distributed.
Trechus, sp.	...	...	...	...	Ditto.
Gyrophæna, sp.	...	...	...	...	Ditto.
Philonthus, sp.	...	...	...	...	Ditto.
Lithocharis, sp.	...	...	...	...	Ditto.
Pæderus listeri	x	*4			
Lispinus castaneus ...	...	...	1		

	Peculiar to the Island.	Oriental Region.	Australian Region.	Ethiopian Region.	Various localities and remarks.
COLEOPTERA, *continued.*					
Dactylosternum abdominalis	...	2, 3, 4	3	1, 3, 4	Brazil, Madeira, Cape Verde, and Canaries.
Hololepta malleata ...	x	*1			
Platysoma lignarium ...	x				
Paromalus, sp.					
Prometopia quadrimaculata	...	2, 4			
Stelidota orientalis					
Shoguna polita	x	*3	*1	*4	
Shoguna striata	x	*3	*1	*4	
Oniscomorpha marmorata...	x				
Xuthia maura	...		1		
Bothrideres strigatus ...	x	2, 3, 4	...	1	
Psammœcus concinnula					
Dermestes felinus	...	...	...	...	Cosmopolitan.
Epilachna indica	...	...	...	...	Asiatic.
Epilachna nativitatis ...	x				
Scymnus, sp.					
Aphanocephalus, sp.					
Euxestus parki	...	...	...	4	Madeira.
Parægus listeri	x				
Figulus rossi	x				
Leptaulax, sp.					
Rhyssemus inscitus ...	...	2			
Trichyorhyssemus hirsutus	x				
Phileurus convexus ...	x	*1, *2			
Protætia andrewsi ...	x	*4			
Chrysodema simplex ...	x				
Chrysobothris andrewsi ...	x				
Fornax, sp.					
Tetrigus murrayi	x	*1, *2	...	*3	
Anchastus discoidalis ...	x	*2			
Megapenthes andrewsi ...	x	*3			
Melanoxanthus dolosus ...	...	2			
Melanoxanthus litura ...	...	2			
Laius tibialis	x	...	...	...	Genus Oriental and Australian.
Lasioderma testacea ...	...	...	...	...	Nearly cosmopolitan.
Neoptinus parvus	x				
Paranobium posticum ...	x	*3	...	*3	
Aspidiphorus orbiculatus...	...	4			
Dinoderus minutus ...	...	4	1	...	Widely distributed.
Minthea rugicollis ...	...	2	...	...	Saylee.
Opatrum dubium	x	...	...	...	Genus cosmopolitan.
Bradymerus seminitidus ...	x	...	*1	...	Genus Oriental also.
Alphitobius piceus ...	...	...	...	...	Cosmopolitan.
Palorus depressus ...	...	...	...	...	Ditto.
Toxicum antilope	x	*4	...	...	Genus widely distributed.
Nyctobates carbonaria ...	x				
Amarygmus funebris ...	x	...	*1	...	Genus Oriental and Australian.
Sessinia andrewsi	x	...	...	...	Genus widely spread.
Sessinia listeri	x	...	*3		
Rhyncholobus rossi ...	x				
Rhyncholobus discoidalis ...	x				

	Peculiar to the Island.	Oriental Region.	Australian Region.	Ethiopian Region.	Various localities and remarks.
COLEOPTERA, *continued*.					
Rhyncholobus vittatus ...	x				
Rhyncholobus andrewsi ...	x				
Acicnemis andrewsi ...	x				
Camptorhinus crinipes ...	x	...	•1		
Mecopus bispinosus ...	...	...	...	...	Widely spread in Malay Archipelago.
Trochorhopalus strangulatus	...	3, 4	1		
Rhabdocnemis fausti ...	x	...	...	...	Allies in Oriental region and in the Pacific Islands.
Cossonus variipennis ...	x	...	...	...	Genus cosmopolitan.
Phlæophagosoma dubium ...	x				
Pachyops incertus	x				
Dryophthorus assimilis ...	x	...	•3		
Platypus solidus	...	2			
Xyleborus perforans					
Xyleborus parvulus ...	...	2, 3	1	...	Probably widely spread in Oriental region.
Orychodes andrewsi ...	x	...	...	...	Oriental region.
Xenocerus nativitatis ...	x	•4	•1		
Litocerus jordani	x	•4			
Apatenia apicalis	x				
Aræocerus, sp.					
Prinobius coxalis	x	•3	•1		
Ceresium quadrimaculatum	x	...	...	...	Genus Oriental.
Ceresium nigrum	x				
Examnes affinis	x	•4			
Monohammus nativitatis ...	x				
Olenecamptus basalis ...	x	...	...	...	Allied to *O. bilobus*, ranging from China to N. Australia.
Pterolophia perplexa ...	x	...	...	...	Genus Oriental.
Prosoplus banksi	...	1, 2, 3, 4	1, 2, 3		
Apomecyna nigritarsis ...	x	...	...	...	Genus African and Oriental.
Ægocidnus exiguus ...	x	...	...	...	Genus Malayan.
Crioceris impressa ...	...	4	1		
Rhyparida rossi	x				
Rhyparida modesta ...	x	•4			
Demotina lateralis ...	x	...	...	...	Genus ranges from China and Japan to New Guinea.
Scelodonta nitidula ...	...	1, 2, 4			
Psylliodes tenuepunctata ...	x	...	...	...	Allies Oriental.
HOMOPTERA.					
Pæcilopsaltria calypso ...	x	•1,•2,•3,•4	•1		
Ricania flavifrontalis ...	x	...	...	...	Allies widely distributed.
Paurostauria delicata ...	x	...	•2	•1, •4	
Varcia flavicostalis ...	x	...	•2		
Nogodina affinis	x	...	•1		
Nogodina hyalina ...	x				
Nogodina subviridis ...	x				
Bidis aristella	x	...	•1		

	Peculiar to the Island.	Oriental Region.	Australian Region.	Ethiopian Region.	Various localities and remarks.
HOMOPTERA, *continued.*					
Clovia eximia	x	*4			
Issus andrewsi	x	*1			
Idiocerus punctatus ...	x	...	*1		
HEMIPTERA HETEROPTERA.					
Æthus nitens	x	...	...	...	Genus widely distributed.
Pentatoma grossepunctatum	x	...	...	...	Ditto.
Lygæus subrufescens ...	x	...	*1	...	Ditto.
Brachyrhynchus lignicolus	x	*1, *2, *3	*1, *2		
Halobates princeps ...	...	...	1		
Halobates proavus ...	...	...	1		
NEUROPTERA.					
Pantala flavescens	...	...	...	...	Widely distributed in Tropics.
Trithemis trivialis ...	...	1, 2	...	...	Widely distributed in Oriental Region.
Anax guttatus	...	1, 2, 3, 4	1, 3	...	Ditto.
Formicaleo morpheus ...	x	...	...	...	Genus widely distributed.
Myrmeleon iridescens ...	x	...	...	...	Ditto.
Termes, sp.	...	...	*1	...	Ditto.
ORTHOPTERA.					
Labidura nigricornis ...	x	...	...	...	Genus widely distributed.
Platylabia dimidiata ...	...	4	1		
Anisolabis stäli	...	4	...	...	Genus widely distributed.
Labia murrayi	x	...	...	...	Genus cosmopolitan.
Labia incerta	x				
Labia indistincta	x				
Labia subarmata	x	...	...	...	Resembles some American species.
Anechura, sp.	...	...	...	...	Genus cosmopolitan.
Temnopteryx fulva ...	...	4	...	...	Ditto.
Phyllodromia supellectilium	...	...	...	...	Cosmopolitan.
Periplaneta americana ...	...	...	...	...	Ditto, carried by ships.
Leucophœa surinamensis ...	...	...	...	...	Ditto, ditto.
Panesthia javanica ...	...	4	1		
Hierodula dispar	x	*4	...	...	Genus in warmer parts of Old World.
Clitumnus stilpnoides ...	x	*1, *2, *3, *4			Nearest ally in Mauritius. Genus widely distributed.
Ectadoderus flavipalpis ...	x	...	...	...	
Gryllacris rufovaria ...	x	*4	...	...	Genus widely distributed.
Pseudorhynchus lessoni ...	...	4	1		
Phisis listeri	x	*2	*1, *3		

	Peculiar to the Island.	Oriental Region.	Australian Region.	Ethiopian Region.	Various localities and remarks.
ORTHOPTERA, *continued.*					
Psyra pomona	x	•4	•1		
Oxya orientalis	x	...	...	...	Widely distributed.
Cyrtacanthacris disparilis	x	•4	...	...	Ditto.
Epacromia rufostriata ...	x	...	...	...	Ditto.
CHILOPODA.					
Cryptops hortensis ...	...	...	...	...	Palæarctic.
Cryptops inermipes ...	...	3			
Mecistocephalus castaneiceps	...	3, 4	3		
DIPLOPODA.					
Orthomorpha coarctata					
Cylindrodesmus hirsutus ...	x	...	...	...	Cosmopolitan.
Iulomorpha exocœti ...	x	•4	•3		
ARACHNIDA.					
Hormurus australasiæ ...	...	3, 4	1, 2, 3		
Trachychernes claviger ...	...	3			
Chelifer javanus	...	4			
Chelifer murrayi ...	x	•3, •4			
Ariadna natalis	x	•4			
Scytodes venusta	...	4			
Smeringopus elongatus ...	...	...	...	...	Widely distributed in Tropics.
Argiope reinwardti ...	...	4	1		
Cyrtophora unicolor ...	...	1, 2, 3, 4	1		
Nephila nigritarsis ...	...	...	2		
Cyclosa mulmeinensis ...	...	1, 3, 4	...	3	
Heteropoda listeri	x				
LAND CRUSTACEA.					
Geearcinus lagostomus ...	...	...	...	...	Tropics generally.
Cardisoma carnifex ...	...	...	...	...	Indian and Pacific Oceans.
Ocypoda ceratophthalma ...	...	...	...	...	Ditto.
Birgus latro	...	...	...	...	Ditto.
Cænobita clypeata ...	...	...	...	...	Ditto.
VERMES.					
Pontodrilus ephippiger ...	x	...	...	...	Allied to species from Aru Islands, Ceylon, Japan.
Perichæta brevis	x	...	...	...	Allied to species in Sumatra.
Perichæta posthuma ...	...	1	1	...	? Bahamas.
Megascolex armatus ...	...	1, 3, 4	1	...	Seychelles.

FLORA OF CHRISTMAS ISLAND.

LIST OF SPECIES.

	Peculiar to the Island.	Oriental Region.	Australian Region.	Ethiopian Region.	Various localities and remarks.
DICOTYLEDONS.					
Tiliacora racemosa ...	...	1, 2, 4			
Pedicellaria pentaphylla ...	...	...	...	...	Widely spread in Tropics.
Pittosporum nativitatis ...	x				
Ochrocarpus ovalifolius ...	...	4	1, 3		
Calophyllum inophyllum ...	...	...	...	...	Ditto.
Malvastrum tricuspidatum	...	...	...	...	Ditto.
Abutilon auritum	...	...	...	...	Ditto.
Abutilon listeri ...	x				
Hibiscus vitifolius	...	...	...	...	Ditto.
Hibiscus tiliaceus ...	...	...	...	...	Ditto.
Hibiscus, sp.					
Kleinhovia hospita	...	...	...	...	Tropical Asia.
Berria ammonilla					
Grewia lævigata ...	...	1, 4			
Grewia, sp.					
Acronychia andrewsia ...	x				
Melia azedarach					
Dysoxylum amooroides ...	...	4	1		
Celastrus paniculatus	...	1, 4			
Colubrina pedunculata ...	x	•4			
Cissus repens ...	...	...	2	...	Tropical Asia.
Cissus pedata ...	...	1, 2, 3, 4			
Leea sambucina ...	...	1, 3, 4	2		
Leea horrida					
Allophylus cobbe, forma glaber	...	1, 2, 3, 4	2		
Erythrina indica ...	...	1, 3, 4	1, 3	...	Sea-shore from Sunderbuns to Malay Archipelago.
Strongylodon ruber ...	...	2	3		
Galactia tenuiflora ...	...	1, 2, 3, 4	2	1	
Canavalia ensiformis ...	...	...	...	...	Widely spread in Tropics.
Phaseolus lunatus...	...	...	...	...	American species now widely spread.
Cajanus indicus ...	...	...	...	...	Widely cultivated in Tropics.
Pongamia glabra ...	...	1, 2, 3, 4	1, 2, 3	4	All coasts from Mascarene Islands to Polynesia.
Inocarpus edulis ...	...	4	1, 3		
Guilandina bonducella	...	...	...	...	Widely spread in Tropics.
Cassia siamea ...	...	...	...	...	Introduced.
Entada scandens ...	...	...	...	...	Widely spread in Tropics.
Terminalia catappa ...	...	1, 3, 4	1		
Combretum acuminatum ...	...	1, 4			
Gyrocarpus asiaticus	...	...	...	...	Widely spread in Tropics.
Quisqualis indica ...	...	1, 2, 3, 4	...	...	Tropical Africa.
Eugenia, sp.					

	Peculiar to the Island.	Oriental Region.	Australian Region.	Ethiopian Region.	Various localities and remarks.
DICOTYLEDONS, *continued.*					
Barringtonia racemosa		4	1, 3		
Pemphis acidula		...	...	...	Tropical coasts, Old World.
Momordica charantia ... ...:		1, 3, 4	? 1	...	Tropical Africa.
Melothria mucronata ...		1, 4	? 1		
Melothria, sp.					
Heptapleurum ellipticum					
Randia densiflora		1, 2, 3	1, 2		
Guettarda speciosa		...	...	...	Tropical shores, Old and New Worlds.
Morinda citrifolia		1, 4	1, 2, 3		
Saprosma nativitatis	x				
Ageratum conyzoides		...	...	...	All hot countries.
Blumea spectabilis		1, 2			
Wedelia biflora		...	...	...	Shores of Tropical Eastern Asia.
Synedrella nodiflora		1, 3	...	...	Tropical America.
Scœvola koenigii		3, 4	1, 2, 3	...	Tropical East Asia generally.
Ardisia complanata		3, 4			
Sideroxylon sundaicum		...	1		
Jasminum sambac		1, 4	1		
Cerbera odollam		1, 3, 4	1, 2, 3		
Ochrosia ackeringæ, var. angustifolia		4			
Hoya aldrichii	x				
Tournefortia argente		2, 4	2	4	
Cordia subcordata... ...		...	2, 3	...	South-East Asia, Tropical Africa.
Thretia buxifolia		1, 3, 4			
Ipomœa pes-capræ		...	...	...	Tropical coasts.
Ipomœa grandiflora		...	2		
Ipomœa peltata		4	3	4	
Ipomœa digitata		...	...	...	Widely spread in Tropics.
Convolvulus parviflorus ...		...	...	...	Ditto of Old World.
Solanum biflorum		3, 4			
Solanum ferox		1, 4			
Physalis minima		...	...	...	Tropical Asia, Africa, Australia.
Datura alba		1			
Ruellia prostrata, var. dejecta		1, 2	...	1	
Asystasia coromandeliana ...		1, 4	...	...	Africa, Arabia.
Dicliptera macleari ...	x				
Stachytarpheta indica ...		...	...	...	Tropical Asia and America.
Callicarpa longifolia		1, 4	1, 2		
Premna lucidula		4			
Anisomeles ovata		1, 3, 4			
Leucas javanica		4			
Boerhaavia diffusa, var. pubescens		...	...	...	Tropics generally.
Pisonia grandis		...	2, 3	...	
Pisonia excelsa		4	1		
Deeringia celosioides		1, 4	1, 2		
Celosia argentea		...	...	...	Tropical Asia and Africa.
Achyranthes aspera		...	...	...	Tropics generally.
Peperomia lævifolia		4			

	Peculiar to the Island.	Oriental Region.	Australian Region.	Ethiopian Region.	Various localities and remarks.
DICOTYLEDONS, *continued.*					
Peperomia rossi	x				
Cryptocarya nativitatis ...	x	...	*2		
Hernandia peltata ...		1, 4	1, 3		
Euphorbia hypericifolia ...		...	...	...	Tropics generally.
Euphorbia pilulifera ...	...	...	...	...	Tropics and sub-tropics.
Phyllanthus niruri ...	...	...	...	...	Tropics generally.
Jatropha curcas	...	...	...	...	Ditto.
Croton caudatus ...	...	1, 4			
Claoxylon rubescens ...	...	4	1, 3		
Acalypha wightiana ...	...	1, 4			
Cleidion javanicum	...	1, 4			
Macaranga tanarius ...	...	4	1		
Celtis cinnamomea... ...	...	1, 4			
Sponia amboinensis ...	...	...	2, 3	...	Tropical Asia.
Ficus retusa ...	...	1, 4	1, 2		
Ficus saxophila	...	4			
Cudrania javanensis ...	...	...	...	...	Old World Tropics.
Fleurya ruderalis ...	...	4	1, 3		
Laportea crenulata ...	...	1, 4			
Laportea murrayana ...	x				
Procris pedunculata ...	...	4	1, 3	4	
Boehmeria platyphylla ...	...	1, 3, 4	1, 3		
MONOCOTYLEDONS.					
Dendrobium crumenatum ...	...	3, 4	1		
Dendrobium macræi ...	...	1, 4			
Phreatia listeri	x				
Phreatia congesta ...	x				
Saccolabium archytas ...	x				
Sarcochilus carinatifolia ...	x				
Corymbis veratrifolia ...	...	1, 2, 3, 4	1		
Crinum asiaticum	...	...	...	...	Tropical Asia to Japan and N. Australia.
Arenga listeri	x				
Pandanus, sp.					
Remusatia vivipara ...	...	1, 2, 3, 4			
Fimbristylis cymosa ...	...	4	1, 2, 3		
Ischæmum foliosum, var. *leiophyllum*	x	...	...	...	Asiatic.
Digitaria sanguinalis ...	...	...	...	...	Cosmopolitan.
Panicum andrewsi ...	x				
Oplismenus compositus ...	...	...	...	...	Tropics generally.
Eleusine indica	...	...	...	...	Old World Tropics.
Eragrostis plumosa ...	...	...	...	...	Tropical Asia and Africa.
GYMNOSPERMS.					
Cycas circinalis	...	4	1		

	Peculiar to the Island.	Oriental Region.	Australian Region.	Ethiopian Region.	Various localities and remarks.

CRYPTOGAMS.

FERNS.

	Peculiar to the Island.	Oriental Region.	Australian Region.	Ethiopian Region.	Various localities and remarks.
Trichomanes parvulum		4	3	4	
Davallia solida		3, 4	3		
Davallia dissecta		4			
Davallia speluncæ		...	...	...	Tropics and sub-tropics.
Asplenium nidus		...	...	...	Ditto of Old World.
Asplenium falcatum		1, 4	1, 2, 3	1, 2, 3	
Asplenium centrifugale	x				
Nephrodium syrmaticum		1, 4			
Nephrodium dissectum		1, 4	3	4	
Nephrodium intermedium		1, 4	1	...	Japan.
Nephrodium truncatum		1, 4	2, 3		
Nephrodium polymorphum		1, 4	1		
Aspidium membranaceum		2, 3, 4			
Nephrolepis exaltata		...	...	...	Tropics generally.
Nephrolepis acuta		...	...	...	Ditto.
Nephrolepis ramosa		...	...	...	Ditto.
Polypodium adnascens		1, 3, 4	1, 3	1, 2	
Polypodium irioides		1, 3, 4	1, 2, 3	1, 2	
Vittaria elongata		1, 3, 4	1, 2, 3	1, 2	
Acrostichum flagelliferum		1, 4			
Acrostichum listeri	x				
Lycopodium phlegmaria		...	...	...	Tropics of Old World.

MOSSES.

	Peculiar to the Island.	Oriental Region.	Australian Region.	Ethiopian Region.	Various localities and remarks.
Leucobryum chlorophyllosum		4	1		
Octoblepharum albidum		...	...	...	Tropics.
Thyridium fasciculatum		1, 4	3	4	Chile.
Trachymitrium revolutum		4			
Neckera lepiniana		4	1, 3	4	
Thuidium plumulosum		2, 4	3		
Hypnum montagnei		4			

HEPATIC.

	Peculiar to the Island.	Oriental Region.	Australian Region.	Ethiopian Region.	Various localities and remarks.
Ptychanthus squarrosus		4	1		

LICHENS.

	Peculiar to the Island.	Oriental Region.	Australian Region.	Ethiopian Region.	Various localities and remarks.
Parmelia tinctorum		...	...	...	Widely distributed, Asia, Africa, Australia, etc.
Parmelia appendiculata		...	...	1	
Physcia picta		...	...	...	Very widely distributed.
Pyxine sorediata		...	...	...	Africa, S. America, Japan, Tahiti.
Pannaria rubiginosa		...	...	...	Very widely distributed.
Lecanora varia		...	...	...	Ditto.
Ramalina fraxinea		...	...	...	Europe, N. and S. America.
Lecidea lutea		...	...	...	Very widely distributed.
Leptogium phyllocarpum		...	...	...	Ditto.

	Peculiar to the Island.	Oriental Region.	Australian Region.	Ethiopian Region.	Various localities and remarks.

CRYPTOGAMS, *continued.*

FUNGI.

Schizophyllum commune ...	...	...	...	...	Cosmopolitan.
Polyporus confluens ...	...	...	2	...	Europe and N. America.
Fomes lucidus	...	...	...	...	Cosmopolitan.
Fomes australis	...	2	1, 2	...	Europe, Venezuela.
Polystictus flabelliformis ...	...	1, 2, 3, 4	1	...	S. America, Cuba.
Polystictus xanthopus ...	...	...	...	...	Tropics generally.
Polystictus luteo-olivaceus	...	...	2		
Polystictus sanguineus ...	...	1, 4	1, 2, 3	1, 2, 3	America.
Hexagonia polygramma ...	...	1, 2	1, 2	...	Central America.
Daedalea tenuis	...	4	2		
Favolus boucheanus ...	...	...	2	...	Europe and N. America.
Laschia cæspitosa ...	...	...	2		
Hirneola polytricha ...	...	1, 2, 4	2	...	Mexico, Cuba.
Hirneola auricula-judæ ...	...	...	...	...	Widely distributed.
Guepinia sparassoides ...	...	...	...	3	
Cyathus montagnei ...	...	2	2	...	Cuba, S. America.
Geaster andrewsi	x				
Trichoscypha tricholoma ...	...	2		...	S. America, West Indies.
Stilbum javanicum ...	...	4			

MYCETOZOA.

Stemonitis splendens, Rost., var. *a, genuina* ...	...	4	2, 3	...	Europe, America.
Arcyria flava, Pers.	...	4	...	...	Europe, N. America.
Lycogala miniatum, Pers.	...	4	...	...	Europe, N. and S. America.

LIST OF THE PRINCIPAL PAPERS RELATING TO CHRISTMAS ISLAND.

1. **Dampier's Voyages.** Edition 1829, vol. i, p. 472. London.

2. **A Voyage to and from the Island of Borneo in the East Indies, etc.** By Capt. DANIEL BEEKMAN. London, 1718. (See Pinkerton's Voyages, vol. xi, p. 103.)

3. **Report on a Zoological Collection made by the Officers of H.M.S. "Flying Fish" at Christmas Island, Indian Ocean.** Proc. Zool. Soc., 1887, p. 507. (This includes the report of Captain J. P. Maclear, of H.M.S. "Flying Fish," on the visit to the island, and descriptions of the collections by Dr. A. G. Butler, Dr. R. B. Sharpe, O. Thomas, G. A. Boulenger, E. A. Smith, R. I. Pocock, C. O. Waterhouse, F. J. Bell, and A. Dendy.)

4. **Report on Christmas Island (Indian Ocean), H.M.S. "Egeria," 1887.** By Captain PELHAM ALDRICH. (With map.) (Admiralty Reports.)

5. **On the Natural History of Christmas Island in the Indian Ocean.** By J. J. LISTER, M.A., F.R.S. Proc. Zool. Soc., 1888, p. 512. (This is accompanied by reports on the collections by O. Thomas, G. A. Boulenger, E. A. Smith, C. J. Gahan, A. G. Butler, W. F. Kirby, and R. I. Pocock.)

6. **Report on the Botanical Collections from Christmas Island, Indian Ocean, made by Captain J. P. Maclear, Mr. J. J. Lister, and the Officers of H.M.S. "Egeria."** By W. BOTTING HEMSLEY. Journ. Linn. Soc. (Botany), vol. xxv (1890), p. 351.

7. **Account of Christmas Island (Indian Ocean).** By Rear-Admiral Sir W. J. L. WHARTON, F.R.S. Proc. Roy. Geogr. Society, vol. x (N.S.), 1888, p. 613.

8. **A Day at Christmas Island.** By H. N. RIDLEY, F.L.S. Journ. Straits Branch Roy. Asiatic Soc., p. 123, June, 1891. (This paper is accompanied by a list of the plants and animals known from the island at that date.)

9. **Report on Christmas Island.** By Rear-Admiral Sir W. J. L. WHARTON, F.R.S., and Captain J. P. MACLEAR. Nature, vol. xxxvi (1887), p. 12.

10. **Note on the Flora of Christmas Island.** By Sir W. T. THISELTON-DYER, K.C.M.G., F.R.S. Nature, vol. xxxvi (1887), p. 78.

11. **Presidential Address, Section D, Bath Meeting of British Association, 1888, p. 690.** By Sir W. T. THISELTON-DYER, K.C.M.G., F.R.S.

12. **Letter relating to Christmas Island.** J. J. LISTER, F.R.S. Nature, vol. xxxvii (1888), p. 203.

13. **Letter relating to Christmas Island.** Rear-Admiral Sir W. J. L. WHARTON, F.R.S. Nature, vol. xxxvii (1888), p. 204.

14. **Letter relating to Christmas Island.** H. B. GUPPY. Nature, vol. xxxvii (1888), p. 222.

15. **Die Theorieen über die Entstehung der Koralleninseln und Korallenriffe.** By R. LANGENBECK. Leipzig, 1890, p. 136.

16. **Description Géologique de Java et Madoura.** By R. D. M. VERBEEK and R. FENNEMA (1896), vol. ii, p. 1031.

17. **Straits Settlements. Papers relating to the Cocos-Keeling and Christmas Islands, 1897.** (Parliamentary Papers, C 8367.)

18. **Colonial Reports. Annual, No. 216. Cocos-Keeling and Christmas Islands. Report on the Annual Visit for 1897.** (1897, C 8650-14.)

19. **Colonial Reports. Annual, No. 257. Cocos-Keeling and Christmas Islands. Report on the Annual Visit for 1898.** (1899, C 9046-25.)

20. **A Description of Christmas Island (Indian Ocean).** By C. W. ANDREWS. Geogr. Journ., vol. xiii (1899), p. 17. (With map.)

21. **Notes on a Collection of Gephyrean Worms found at Christmas Island (Indian Ocean) by Mr. C. W. Andrews.** By A. E. SHIPLEY, M.A., F.R.S. Proc. Zool. Soc., 1899, p. 54. (Papers on the Marine Mollusca, Sponges, Corals, and Foraminifera will appear later in Proc. Zool. Soc. for 1900.)

APPENDIX.

A small collection of birds and insects made by Mr. Hugh Ross since I left the island has recently reached England. The species are nearly all described above, but there are two birds and one beetle new to the island, and also a beetle that is new to science.— C. W. A.

The birds are :—

AVES.

COLUMBIFORMES.

Myristicivorus bicolor.

Adult male. Flying Fish Cove, February 4, 1899. Several individuals of this species were observed; probably they had been blown to the island during migration.

CHARADRIIFORMES.

Heteractitis brevipes.

Female. Flying Fish Cove, September 22, 1898.

INSECTA.

The beetles are described below by Messrs. Waterhouse & Arrow.

? Crioceris impressa, Fab., var.

A single example sent to Mr. Andrews may provisionally be regarded as a variety of *C. impressa*, Fab. The body underneath, the head (except at the occiput), legs, and antennæ are black, the prothorax and elytra testaceous. The prothorax has a rather distinct transverse impression just a little in front of the base, and this is the only character of importance to suggest the specific distinctness of this new form.

C. impressa is a variable and rather widely distributed species, occurring in most of the Indo-Malayan islands, and in India, Burma, and China.

Phileurus convexus, Arrow, sp.n.

P. nitidus, angustus, haud depressus ; capite rugose punctato, acuminato, fronte cornu parvo conico armata ; prothorace sub-quadrato parum transverso, angulis posticis fere rectis, anticis parum approximatis, disco leviter punctato, lateribus paulo crebrius, medio antice et postice carinæ vestigiis vix apparentibus ; elytris longis, grosse lineato - punctatis, interstitiis minutissime punctatis ; abdomine cum pygidio fere polito, propygidio coriaceo. ♀ long. 14¼ mm.

Hab.—Flying Fish Cove.

This new species is formed for the first representative of the important family Dynastidæ so far found in the island, a single specimen having been recently discovered by Mr. H. Ross.

This species is less flattened, and somewhat longer than usual, but does not differ structurally from the larger described forms of Continental Asia, where all its hitherto known allies are found, for the Ceylon insect described by Walker is evidently wrongly placed. M. Fairmaire has referred to a '*P. javanus,*' apparently the *Heteronychus javanus*, Burm., which although allied is hardly congeneric. But the genus *Phileurus* will probably be eventually restricted to the American insects and new genera formed for the Oriental species.

The only other insect new to the island is a large moth : *Patula macrops* (Linn.), (Syst. Nat., 12th ed., iii, p. 225). Africa, Madagascar, Ceylon, India, Burmah.

INDEX.

STEPHEN AUSTIN AND SONS, PRINTERS, HERTFORD.

EXPLANATION OF PLATES.

PLATE I.

Pteropus natalis, Thomas. Adult male. (p. 23.)

P.J. Smit. del et lith. Mintern Bros Chromo

Pteropus natalis, Thomas.

PLATE II.

Mus nativitatis, Thomas.   Adult male.   (p. 28.)

Pl.II.

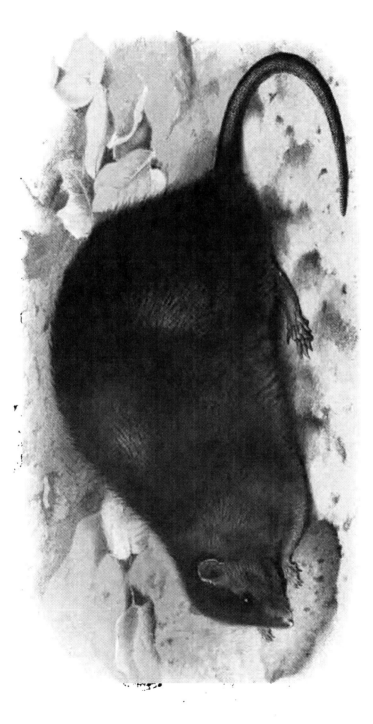

P.J.Smit del et lith.

Mintern.Bros.Chromo.

Mus nativitatis, Thomas.

PLATE II (*bis*).

Mus macleari, Thomas. Figs. 1, 3, 6, 7, 8. ⎱ (p. 34.)
Mus nativitatis, Thomas. Figs. 2, 4, 5, 9, 10. ⎰

Figs. 1 and 2, cranium from above ; Figs. 3 and 4, from below ;
Figs. 5 and 6, side view with lower jaw ; Figs. 7-9, right
upper molar series ; Figs. 8 and 10, right lower molar series.

Figs. 7-10 × 4 ; the others natural size.

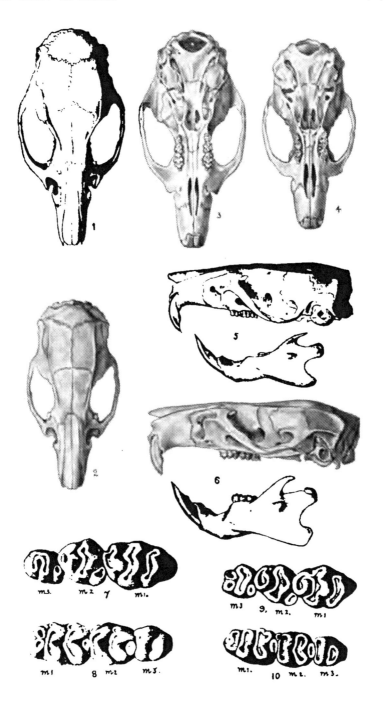

Skulls and Teeth of *Mus macleari* and *Mus nativitatis.*

PLATE III.

Phaethon fulvus, Brandt.   (p. 45.)

Pl. III.

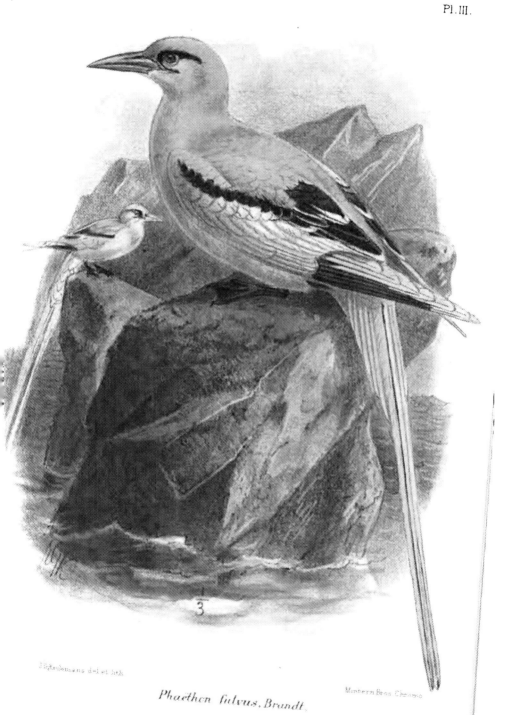

J. G. Keulemans del et lith.

Mintern Bros Chromo

Phaëthon fulvus, Brandt.

PLATE IV.

Ninox natalis, Lister. (p. 47.)

J.G.Keulemans del. et lith.   Mintern Bros Chromo

Ninox natalis. Lister.

PLATE V.

Astur natalis (Lister).   (p. 46.)

J.G Keulemans del et lith

Mintern Bros Chromo

Astur natalis. Lister, sp.

PLATE VI.

Zosterops natalis, Lister.   (p. 49.)

.J.G.Keulemans del et lith   Mintern Bros.Chromo

Zosterops natalis, Lister.

PLATE VII.

Reptilia.

Fig. 1. *Gecko listeri*, Boulenger. (p. 51.)

Figs. 2, 2a, 2b. *Lygosoma nativitatis*, Boulenger. (p. 52.)

Figs. 3, 3a, 3b. *Ablepharus egeriæ*, Boulenger. (p. 53.)

2b.

3b.

3a.

2a.

J Green del et lith

Mintern Bros imp

1.Gecko listeri. 2.Lygosoma nativitatis. 3.Ablepharus egeriæ

PLATE VIII.

LAND SHELLS.

Pl. VIII.

J Green del. et lith.

Mintern Bros imp.

Land Mollusca.

PLATE IX.

Lepidoptera.

Figs. 1, 1a. *Bocula limbata*, Butler. (p. 66.)

Fig. 2. *Epiplema inhians*, Warr. (p. 72.)

Fig. 3. *Endotricha listeri*, Butler. (p. 73.)

Fig. 4. *Boarmia scotozonea*, Hampson, sp.n. (p. 71.)

Fig. 5. *Erastria grisæomixta*, Hampson, sp.n. (p. 68.)

Fig. 6. *Hydrillodes vexillifera*, Hampson, sp.n. (p. 68.)

Fig. 7. *Mimeusemia econia*, Hampson, sp.n. (p. 64.)

Fig. 8. *Charaxes andrewsi*, Butler, sp.n. (p. 61.)

Fig. 9. *Porthesia pulverea*, Hampson, sp.n. (p. 69.)

Fig. 10. *Zinckenia nigerrimalis*, Hampson, sp.n. (p. 73.)

Fig. 11. *Glyphodes (Phacellura) holophœalis*, Hampson, sp.n. (p. 74.)

Fig. 12. *Cosmophila vitiensis*, Butler. (p. 67.)

Fig. 13. *Ephestia scotella*, Hampson, sp.n. (p. 72.)

Fig. 14. *Dichocrocis auritincta*, Butler, sp.n. (p. 74.)

Fig. 15. *Boarmia scotozonea*, Butler. (p. 71.)

E.C. Knight ad. nat. lith   West, Newman Chr

Lepidoptera.

PLATE X.

COLEOPTERA.

Pl. X.

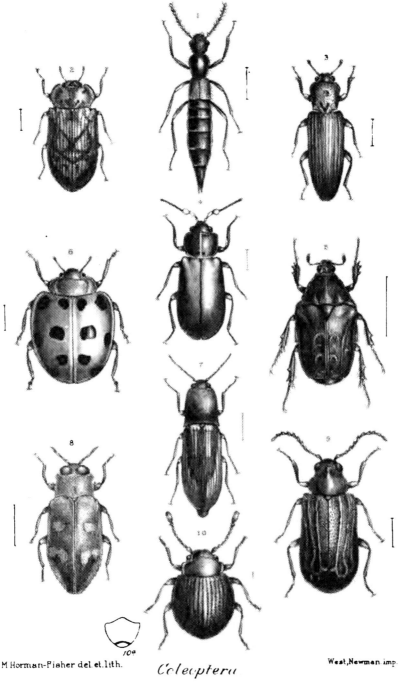

M Horman-Fisher del.et.lith.

Coleoptera

West,Newman.imp.

PLATE XI.

COLEOPTERA.

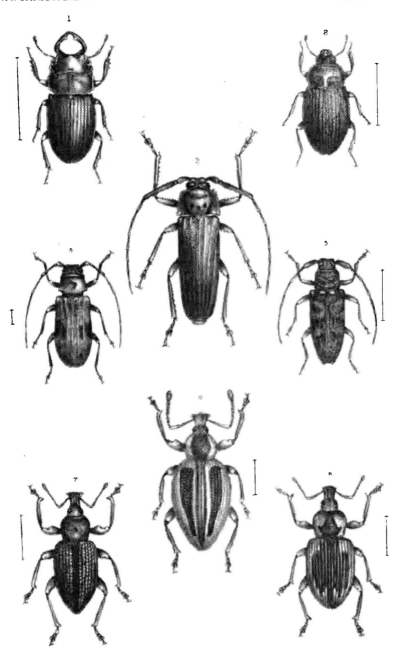

PLATE XII.

ORTHOPTERA.

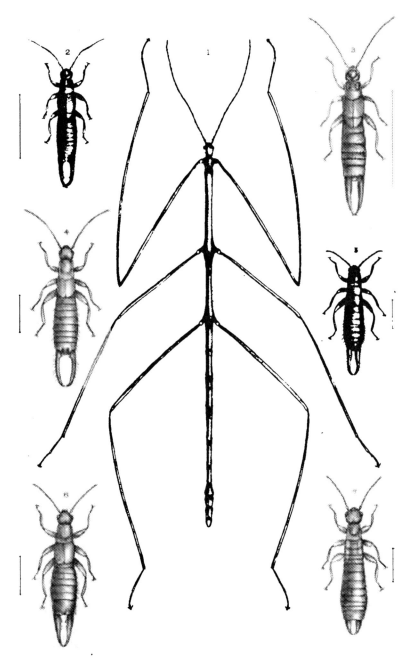

M.Horman-Fisher del et lith

West, Newman imp

Orthoptera.

PLATE XIII.

ORTHOPTERA.

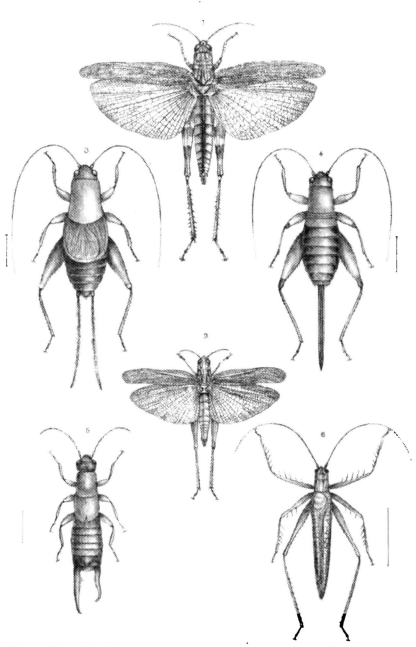

M.Horman-Fisher del et lith

West, Newman imp

Orthoptera.

PLATE XIV.

ORTHOPTERA, NEUROPTERA, AND HYMENOPTERA.

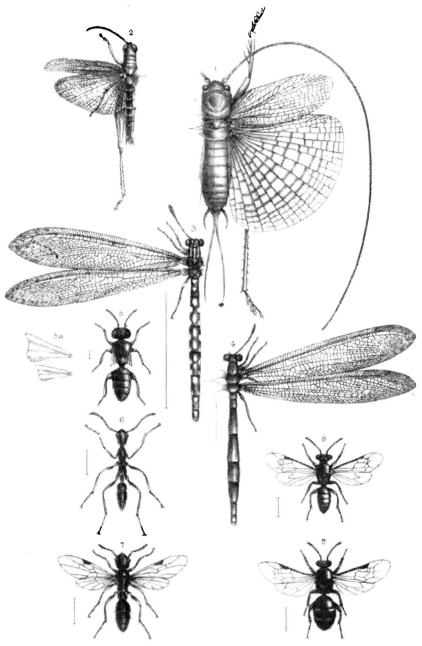

M.Horman-Fisher del.et lith.   West, Newman imp

Orthoptera, Neuroptera,
and Hymenoptera.

PLATE XV.

HOMOPTERA AND HEMIPTERA.

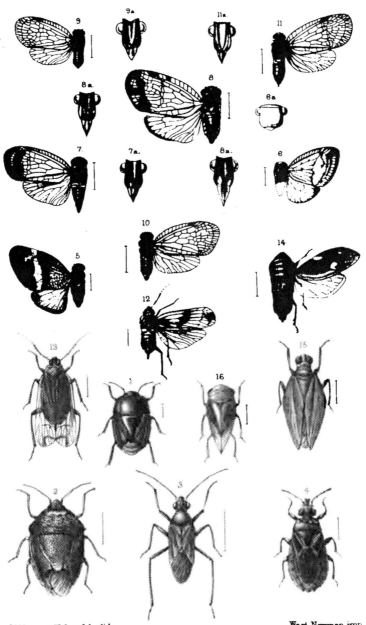

M.Horman-Fisher del.et lith.   West, Newman imp.

Homoptera.
and Hemiptera.

PLATE XVI.

ARACHNIDA.

FIG. 1. *Chelifer murrayi*, Pocock, sp.n. Much magnified. (p. 156.)

FIG. 1a. *Chelifer murrayi*. Flagellum of movable digit of mandible. (p. 156.)

FIG. 2. *Argiope reinwardti* (Dol.). Enlarged one-fourth. (p. 159.)

FIG. 3. *Cyrtophora unicolor* (Dol.). Enlarged one-fourth. (p. 160.)

[This figure and that of *Argiope reinwardti* are taken from specimens preserved in alcohol. According to Mr. Andrews the abdomen in living examples is more voluminous, and in the case of *C. unicolor* the anterior prominences project much less than here represented.]

FIG. 4. *Heteropoda listeri*, Pocock, sp.n. Face and mandibles. (p. 161.)

[The beard of bristles clothing the front of the upper half of the mandibles stands out more clearly in the actual specimen than in the figure.]

FIG. 4a. *Heteropoda listeri*. Vulva. ♀. (p. 161.)

FIG. 4b. *Heteropoda listeri*. Tarsus and distal end of palpus of ♂ from below. (p. 161.)

FIG. 4c. *Heteropoda listeri*. Bifid tip of flagellum and its sheath of palpal organ. (p. 161.)

FIG. 4d. *Heteropoda listeri*. Tibial spine of palp of ♂ from the side. (p. 161.)

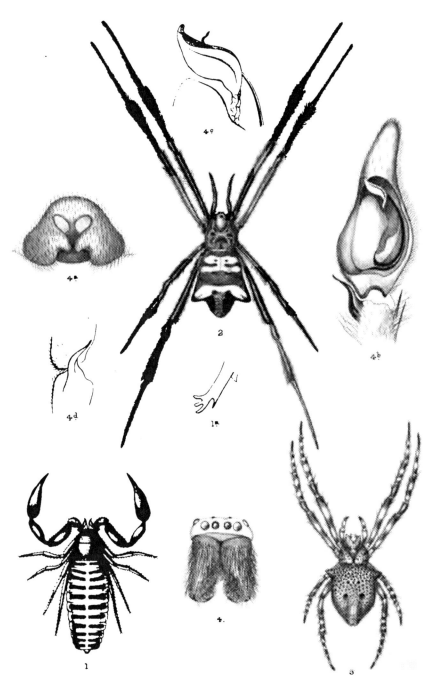

F O Pickard - Cambridge del et lith

West, Newman imp.

Arachnida.

PLATE XVII.

Pittosporum nativitatis, Baker, *fil,* sp.n. (p. 171.)

FIG. 1. Branchlet showing inflorescence (natural size).

FIG. 2. Flower (× 5).

FIG. 3. Sepal (× 5).

FIG. 4. Petal (× 5).

FIG. 5. Stamens and ovary not fully developed (× 5).

FIG. 6. Ovary not fully developed (× 5).

FIG. 7. Bract (× 5).

R.Morgan del.et lith.

West, Newman imp.

Pittosporum nativitatis. *Baker fil.*

PLATE XVIII.

Panicum andrewsi, Rendle, sp.n.   (p. 192.)

FIG. 1. Barren glume, i, viewed from inside.

FIG. 2. Barren glume, ii, viewed from inside.

FIG. 3. Barren glume, iii, viewed from inside and showing the empty pale.

FIG. 4. Fertile glume.   Dorsal view.

Natural size.   Figs. 1–4, parts of spikelet, × 18.

R.Morgan del.et lith.
A.B.Rendle anal.

West.Newman imp

Panicum andrewsi, *Rendle*.

PLATE XIX.

Fossil Corals.

Fig. 1. *Cæloria andrewsi*, Gregory, sp.n. Transverse section.

Fig. 2. *Mæandrina equisepta*, Gregory, sp.n. Transverse section.

Fig. 3. *Orbicella murrayi*, Gregory, sp.n. Transverse section.

Fig. 4. *Orbicella præheliopora*, Gregory, sp.n. Transverse section.

Fig. 5. *Acanthastræa patula*, Gregory, var. nov. *paucidentata.* Transverse section.

Fig. 6. *Anisocænia favoides*, Gregory, sp.n. Transverse section.

Fig. 7. *Anisocænia murrayi*, Gregory, sp.n. Transverse section.

Fig. 8. *Coscinaræa andrewsi*, Gregory, sp.n. Transverse section.

All the figures twice natural size.

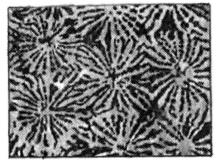

E. Drake ad nat.lith.   West, Newman imp

Fossil Corals

All ×2 diam.

PLATE XX.

Foraminiferal Limestones.

Fig. 1.   No. 2.   Oldest Limestone (Eocene or Oligocene) from south end of Flying Fish Cove.   × 15.   (p. 226.)

Fig. 2.   No. 522.   ? Oligocene Limestone, B of section, Flying Fish Cove.   × 15.   (p. 231.)

Fig. 3.   No. 924.   Miocene Orbitoidal Limestone, Flying Fish Cove.   × 15.   (p. 233.)

Fig. 4.   No. 220.   Miocene Orbitoidal Limestone, Flying Fish Cove.   × 15.   (p. 239.)

Fig. 5.   No. 844.   Miocene Orbitoidal Limestone, Flying Fish Cove.   × 5.   (p. 242.)

Fig. 6.   No. 562.   Miocene Orbitoidal Limestone, Flying Fish Cove.   × 10.   (p. 243.)

Fig. 7.   No. 521.   White Limestone from pinnacles at 500 feet over Flying Fish Cove.   × 5½.   (p. 245.)

Fig. 8.   No. 841.   White Limestone from pinnacles at 500 feet over Flying Fish Cove.   × 6.   (p. 248.)

Fig. 9.   No. 549.   Miocene Orbitoidal Limestone, Flying Fish Cove.   × 6.   (p. 250.)

F. CHAPMAN, PHOTO.   MORGAN & KIDD, COLLOTYPE.

FORAMINIFERAL ROCKS : CHRISTMAS ISLAND.

PLATE XXI.

FORAMINIFERAL LIMESTONES.

FIG. 10. Specimen No. 968. Miocene Orbitoidal Limestone, south of Flying Fish Cove. × 6. (p. 252.)

FIG. 11. Specimen No. 347. Eocene or Oligocene Limestone from high cliff in Sidney's Dale (see map). × 15. (p. 254.)

FIG. 12. Specimen No. 835. Miocene Orbitoidal Limestone, south of Flying Fish Cove. × 5. (p. 254.)

FIG. 13. Specimen No. 827. Miocene Orbitoidal Limestone, south of Flying Fish Cove. × 4½. (p. 255.)

FIG. 14. Specimen No. 827. Miocene Orbitoidal Limestone, south of Flying Fish Cove. × 6. (p. 255.)

FIG. 15. Specimen No. 581. Miocene Orbitoidal Limestone. × 5. (p. 255.)

FIG. 16. Specimen No. 986. Pebble of Orbitoidal Limestone in raised beach, north of Flying Fish Cove. × 2. (p. 253.)

FIG. 17. Specimen No. 5. From cracks in basalt on south side of Flying Fish Cove. × 15. (p. 258.)

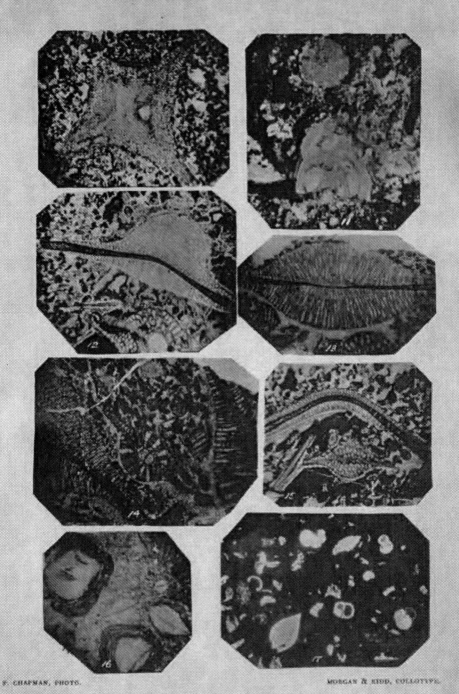

F. CHAPMAN, PHOTO.   MORGAN & KIDD, COLLOTYPE.

FORAMINIFERAL ROCKS : CHRISTMAS ISLAND.

NATURAL HISTORY PUBLICATIONS
OF THE TRUSTEES OF THE
BRITISH MUSEUM.

The following publications can be purchased through the Agency of *Messrs.* LONGMANS & CO., 39, *Paternoster Row* ; *Mr.* QUARITCH, 15, *Piccadilly* ; *Messrs.* KEGAN PAUL, TRENCH, TRÜBNER & CO., *Paternoster House, Charing Cross Road* ; and *Messrs.* DULAU & CO., 37, *Soho Square ;* or at the NATURAL HISTORY MUSEUM, *Cromwell Road, London, S.W.*

Catalogue of the Specimens and Drawings of Mammals, Birds, Reptiles, and Fishes of Nepal and Tibet. Presented by B. H. Hodgson, Esq., to the British Musuem. 2nd edition. By John Edward Gray. Pp. xii., 90. [With an account of the Collection by Mr Hodgson.] 1863, 12mo. 2s. 3d.

Catalogue of the Mammalia and Birds of New Guinea in the Collection of the British Museum. [With list of Species of New Guinea Birds, and those of the neighbouring Localities.] By John Edward Gray, Ph.D., F.R.S., and George Robert Gray, F.L.S., &c. Pp. 63. Woodcuts. 1859, 8vo. 1s. 6d.

Report on the Zoological Collections made in the Indo-Pacific Ocean during the voyage of H.M.S. " Alert," 1881-2. Pp. xxv., 684. 54 Plates. 1884, 8vo.

Summary of the Voyage	...	By Dr. R. W. Coppinger.
Mammalia	... ...	„ O. Thomas.
Aves	... ...	„ R. B. Sharpe.
Reptilia, Batrachia, Pisces	...	„ A. Günther.
Mollusca	... ...	„ E. A. Smith.
Echinodermata	... ...	„ F. J. Bell.
Crustacea	... ...	„ E. J. Miers.
Coleoptera	.. ..	„ C. O. Waterhouse.
Lepidoptera	... ...	„ A. G. Butler.
Alcyonaria and Spongiida	...	„ S. O. Ridley.

1l. 10s.

MAMMALS.

List of the Specimens of Mammalia in the Collection of the British Museum. By Dr. J. E. Gray, F.R.S. Pp. xxviii., 216. [With Systematic List of the Genera of Mammalia, Index of Donations, and Alphabetical Index.] 1843, 12mo. 2s. 6d.

Catalogue of the Bones of Mammalia in the Collection of the British Museum. By Edward Gerrard. Pp. iv., 296. 1862, 8vo. 5s.

Catalogue of Monkeys, Lemurs, and Fruit-eating Bats in the Collection of the British Museum. By Dr. J. E. Gray, F.R.S., &c. Pp. viii., 137. 21 Woodcuts. 1870, 8vo. 4s.

Catalogue of Carnivorous, Pachydermatous, and Edentate Mammalia in the British Museum. By John Edward Gray, F.R.S., &c. Pp. vii., 398. 47 Woodcuts. 1869, 8vo. 6s. 6d.

Catalogue of Seals and Whales in the British Museum. By John Edward Gray, F.R.S., &c. 2nd edition. Pp. vii., 402. 101 Woodcuts. 1866, 8vo. 8s.

——— Supplement. By John Edward Gray, F,R.S., &c. Pp. vi., 103. 11 Woodcuts. 1871, 8vo. 2s. 6d.

List of the Specimens of Cetacea in the Zoological Department of the British Museum. By William Henry Flower, LL.D., F.R.S., &c. [With Systematic and Alphabetical Indexes.] Pp. iv., 36. 1885, 8vo. 1s. 6d.

Catalogue of Ruminant Mammalia (Pecora, Linnæus) in the British Museum. By John Edward Gray, F.R.S., &c. Pp. viii., 102. 4 Plates. 1872, 8vo. 3s. 6d.

Catalogue of the Marsupialia and Monotremata in the Collection of the British Museum. By Oldfield Thomas. Pp. xiii., 401. 4 coloured and 24 plain Plates. [With Systematic and Alphabetical Indexes.] 1888, 8vo. 1l. 8s.

BIRDS.

Catalogue of the Birds in the British Museum :—

Vol. VI. Catalogue of the Passeriformes, or Perching Birds, in the Collection of the British Museum. *Cichlomorphæ* : Part III., containing the first portion of the family Timeliidæ (Babbling Thrushes). By R. Bowdler Sharpe. Pp. xiii., 420. Woodcuts and 18 coloured Plates. [With Systematic and Alphabetical Indexes.] 1881, 8vo. 1l.

Vol. VII. Catalogue of the Passeriformes, or Perching Birds, in the Collection of the British Museum. *Cichlomorphæ* : Part IV., containing the concluding portion of the family Timeliidæ (Babbling Thrushes).

Catalogue of the Birds in the British Museum—*continued.*

By R. Bowdler Sharpe. Pp. xvi., 698. Woodcuts and 15 coloured Plates. [With Systematic and Alphabetical Indexes.] 1883, 8vo. 1*l*. 6*s*.

Vol. VIII. Catalogue of the Passeriformes, or Perching Birds, in the Collection of the British Museum. *Cichlomorphæ*: Part V., containing the families Paridæ and Laniidæ (Titmice and Shrikes); and *Certhiomorphæ* (Creepers and Nuthatches). By Hans Gadow, M.A., Ph.D. Pp. xiii., 386. Woodcuts and 9 coloured Plates. [With Systematic and Alphabetical Indexes.] 1883, 8vo. 17*s*.

Vol. IX. Catalogue of the Passeriformes, or Perching Birds, in the Collection of the British Museum. *Cinnyrimorphæ*, containing the families Nectariniidæ and Meliphagidæ (Sun Birds and Honey-eaters). By Hans Gadow, M.A., Ph.D. Pp. xii., 310. Woodcuts and 7 coloured Plates. [With Systematic and Alphabetical Indexes.] 1884, 8vo. 14*s*.

Vol. X. Catalogue of the Passeriformes, or Perching Birds, in the Collection of the British Museum. *Fringilliformes*: Part I., containing the families Dicæidæ, Hirundinidæ, Ampelidæ, Mniotiltidæ, and Motacillidæ. By R. Bowdler Sharpe. Pp. xiii., 682. Woodcuts and 12 coloured Plates. [With Systematic and Alphabetical Indexes.] 1885, 8vo. 1*l*. 2*s*.

Vol. XI. Catalogue of the Passeriformes, or Perching Birds, in the Collection of the British Museum. *Fringilliformes*: Part II., containing the families Cœrebidæ, Tanagridæ, and Icteridæ. By Philip Lutley Sclater, M.A., F.R.S. Pp. xvii., 431. [With Systematic and Alphabetical Indexes.] Woodcuts and 18 coloured Plates. 1886, 8vo. 1*l*.

Vol. XII. Catalogue of the Passeriformes, or Perching Birds, in the Collection of the British Museum. *Fringilliformes*: Part III., containing the family Fringillidæ. By R. Bowdler Sharpe. Pp. xv., 871. Woodcuts and 16 coloured Plates. [With Systematic and Alphabetical Indexes.] 1888, 8vo. 1*l*. 8*s*.

Vol. XIII. Catalogue of the Passeriformes, or Perching Birds, in the Collection of the British Museum. *Sturniformes*, containing the families Artamidæ, Sturnidæ, Ploceidæ, and Alaudidæ. Also the families Atrichiidæ and Menuridæ. By R. Bowdler Sharpe. Pp. xvi., 701. Woodcuts and 15 coloured Plates. [With Systematic and Alphabetical Indexes.] 1890, 8vo., 1*l*. 8*s*.

Vol. XIV. Catalogue of the Passeriformes, or Perching Birds, in the Collection of the British Museum. *Oligomyodæ*, or the families Tyrannidæ, Oxyrhamphidæ, Pipridæ, Cotingidæ, Phytotomidæ, Philepittidæ,

Catalogue of the Birds in the British Museum—*continued.*

Pittidæ, Xenicidæ, and Eurylæmidæ. By Philip
Lutley Sclater, M.A., F.R.S. Pp. xix., 494. Woodcuts
and 26 coloured Plates. [With Systematic and Alphabetical Indexes.] 1888, 8vo. 1*l.* 4*s.*

Vol. XV. Catalogue of the Passeriformes, or Perching
Birds, in the Collection of the British Museum.
Tracheophonæ. or the families Dendrocolaptidæ,
Formicariidæ, Conopophagidæ, and Pteroptochidæ.
By Philip Lutley Sclater, M.A., F.R.S. Pp. xvii., 371.
Woodcuts and 20 coloured Plates. [With Systematic
and Alphabetical Indexes.] 1890, 8vo. 1*l.*

Vol. XVI. Catalogue of the Picariæ in the Collection of
the British Museum. *Upupæ* and *Trochili*, by Osbert
Salvin. *Coraciæ*, of the families Cypselidæ, Capri-
mulgidæ, Podargidæ, and Steatornithidæ, by Ernst
Hartert. Pp. xvi., 703. Woodcuts and 14 coloured
Plates. [With Systematic and Alphabetical Indexes.]
1892, 8vo. 1*l.* 16*s.*

Vol. XVII. Catalogue of the Picariæ in the Collection
of the British Museum. *Coraciæ* (contin.) and
Halcyones, with the families Leptosomatidæ, Coraciidæ,
Meropidæ, Alcedinidæ, Momotidæ, Totidæ and Coliidæ,
by R. Bowdler Sharpe. *Bucerotes* and *Trogones* by
W. R. Ogilvie Grant. Pp. xi., 522. Woodcuts and 17
coloured Plates. [With Systematic and Alphabetical
Indexes.] 1892, 8vo. 1*l.* 10*s.*

Vol. XVIII. Catalogue of the Picariæ in the Collection
of the British Museum. *Scansores*, containing the
family Picidæ. By Edward Hargitt. Pp. xv., 597.
Woodcuts and 15 coloured Plates. [With Systematic
and Alphabetical Indexes.] 1890, 8vo. 1*l.* 6*s.*

Vol. XIX. Catalogue of the Picariæ in the Collection of
the British Museum. *Scansores* and *Coccyges* : containing the families Rhamphastidæ, Galbulidæ, and
Bucconidæ, by P. L. Sclater; and the families Indi-
catoridæ, Capitonidæ, Cuculidæ, and Musophagidæ, by
G. E. Shelley. Pp. xii., 484 : 13 coloured Plates.
[With Systematic and Alphabetical Indexes.] 1891,
8vo. 1*l.* 5*s.*

Vol. XX. Catalogue of the Psittaci, or Parrots, in the
Collection of the British Museum. By T. Salvadori.
Pp. xvii., 658 : Woodcuts and 18 coloured Plates.
[With Systematic and Alphabetical Indexes.] 1891,
8vo. 1*l.* 10*s.*

Vol. XXI. Catalogue of the Columbæ, or Pigeons, in
the Collection of the British Museum. By T. Salvadori.
Pp. xvii., 676 : 15 coloured Plates. [With Systematic
and Alphabetical Indexes.] 1893, 8vo. 1*l.* 10*s.*

Vol. XXII. Catalogue of the Game Birds (*Pterocletes,
Gallinæ, Opisthocomi, Hemipodii*) in the Collection of

Catalogue of the Birds in the British Museum—*continued*.
the British Museum. By W. R. Ogilvie Grant.
Pp. xvi., 585 : 8 coloured Plates. [With Systematic
and Alphabetical Indexes.] 1893, 8vo. 1*l*. 6*s*.

Vol. XXIII. Catalogue of the Fulicariæ (Rallidæ and
Heliornithidæ) and Alectorides (Aramidæ, Eurypy-
gidæ, Mesitidæ, Rhinochetidæ, Gruidæ, Psophiidæ,
and Otididæ) in the Collection of the British Museum.
By R. Bowdler Sharpe. Pp. xiii., 353 : 9 coloured
Plates. [With Systematic and Alphabetical Indexes.]
1894, 8vo. 20*s*.

Vol. XXIV. Catalogue of the Limicolæ in the Collection
of the British Museum. By R. Bowdler Sharpe.
Pp. xii., 794. Woodcuts and 7 coloured Plates. [With
Systematic and Alphabetical Indexes.] 1896, 8vo.
1*l*. 5*s*.

Vol. XXV. Catalogue of the Gaviæ and Tubinares in
the Collection of the British Museum. Gaviæ (Terns,
Gulls, and Skuas,) by Howard Saunders. Tubinares
(Petrels and Albatrosses), by Osbert Salvin. Pp. xv.,
475 ; woodcuts and 8 coloured Plates. [With Systematic and Alphabetical Indexes.] 1896, 8vo. 1*l*. 1*s*.

Vol. XXVI. Catalogue of the Plataleæ, Herodiones,
Steganopodes, Pygopodes, Alcæ, and Impennes in the
Collection of the British Museum. Plataleæ (Ibises
and Spoonbills) and Herodiones (Herons and Storks),
by R. Bowdler Sharpe. Steganopodes (Cormorants,
Gannets, Frigate-birds, Tropic-birds, and Pelicans),
Pygopodes (Divers and Grebes), Alcæ (Auks), and Impennes (Penguins), by W. R. Ogilvie-Grant. Pp. xvii.,
687 : Woodcuts and 14 coloured Plates. [With Systematic and Alphabetical Indexes.] 1898, 8vo. 1*l*. 5*s*.

Vol. XXVII. Catalogue of the Chenomorphæ (Pala-
medeæ, Phoenicopteri, Anseres), Crypturi, and Ratitæ
in the Collection of the British Museum. By T
Salvadori. Pp. xv., 636 : 19 coloured Plates. [With
Systematic and Alphabetical Indexes.] 1895, 8vo.
1*l*. 12*s*.

A Hand-list of the Genera and Species of Birds. [Nomen-
clator Avium tum Fossilium tum Viventium.] By R.
Bowdler Sharpe, LL.D. Vol. I. Pp. xxi., 303. [With
Systematic Index.] 1899, 8vo. 10*s*.

List of the Specimens of Birds in the Collection of the
British Museum. By George Robert Gray :—
Part III., Section I. Ramphastidæ Pp. 16. [With
Index.] 1855, 12mo. 6*d*.
Part III., Section II. Psittacidæ. Pp. 110. [With
Index.] 1859, 12mo. 2*s*.
Part III., Sections III. and IV. Capitonidæ and Picidæ.
Pp. 137. [With Index.] 1868, 12mo. 1*s*. 6*d*.

List of the Specimens of Birds in the Collectioh of the British Museum—*continued.*

Part IV. Columbæ. Pp. 73. [With Index.] 1856, 12mo. 1*s.* 9*d.*

Part V. Gallinæ. Pp. iv., 120. [With an Alphabetical Index.] 1867, 12mo. 1*s.* 6*d.*

Catalogue of the Birds of the Tropical Islands of the Pacific Ocean in the Collection of the British Museum. By George Robert Gray, F.L.S., &c. Pp. 72. [With an Alphabetical Index.] 1859, 8vo. 1*s.* 6*d.*

REPTILES.

Catalogue of the Tortoises, Crocodiles, and Amphisbænians in the Collection of the British Museum. By Dr. J. E. Gray, F.R.S., &c. Pp. viii., 80. [With an Alphabetical Index.] 1844, 12mo. 1*s.*

Catalogue of Shield Reptiles in the Collection of the British Museum. By John Edward Gray, F.R.S., &c.:—

Appendix. Pp. 28. 1872, 4to. 2*s.* 6*d.*

Part II. Emydosaurians, Rhynchocephalia, and Amphisbænians. Pp. vi., 41. 25 Woodcuts. 1872, 4to. 3*s.* 6*d.*

Hand-List of the Specimens of Shield Reptiles in the British Museum. By Dr. J. E. Gray, F.R.S., F.L.S., &c. Pp. iv., 124. [With an Alphabetical Index.] 1873, 8vo. 4*s.*

Catalogue of the Chelonians, Rhynchocephalians, and Crocodiles in the British Museum (Natural History). New Edition. By George Albert Boulenger. Pp. x., 311. 73 Woodcuts and 6 Plates. [With Systematic and Alphabetical Indexes.] 1889, 8vo. 15*s.*

Catalogue of the Lizards in the British Museum (Natural History). Second Edition. By George Albert Boulenger :—

Vol. I. Geckonidæ, Eublepharidæ, Uroplatidæ, Pygopodidæ, Agamidæ. Pp. xii., 436. 32 Plates. [With Systematic and Alphabetical Indexes.] 1885, 8vo. 20*s.*

Vol. II. Iguanidæ, Xenosauridæ, Zonuridæ, Anguidæ, Anniellidæ, Helodermatidæ, Varanidæ, Xantusiidæ, Teiidæ, Amphisbænidæ. Pp. xiii., 497. 24 Plates. [With Systematic and Alphabetical Indexes.] 1885, 8vo. 20*s.*

Vol. III. Lacertidæ, Gerrhosauridæ, Scincidæ, Anelytropidæ, Dibamidæ, Chamæleontidæ. Pp. xii., 575. 40 Plates. [With a Systematic Index and an Alphabetical Index to the three volumes.] 1887, 8vo. 1*l.* 6*s.*

Catalogue of the Snakes in the British Museum (Natural
History). By George Albert Boulenger, F.R.S. :—

Vol. I., containing the families Typhlopidæ, Glauconiidæ,
Boidæ, Ilysiidæ, Uropeltidæ, Xenopeltidæ, and Colubridæ aglyphæ, part. Pp. xiii., 448 : 26 Woodcuts
and 28 Plates. [With Systematic and Alphabetical
Indexes.] 1893, 8vo. 1l. 1s.

Vol. II., containing the conclusion of the Colubridæ
aglyphæ. Pp. xi., 382 : 25 Woodcuts and 20 Plates.
[With Systematic and Alphabetical Indexes.] 1894,
8vo. 17s. 6d.

Vol. III., containing the Colubridæ (Opisthoglyphæ and
Proteroglyphæ), Amblycephalidæ, and Viperidæ.
Pp. xiv., 727 : 37 Woodcuts and 25 Plates. [With
Systematic Index, and Alphabetical Index to the 3
volumes.] 1896, 8vo. 1l. 6s.

Catalogue of Colubrine Snakes in the Collection of the
British Museum. By Dr. Albert Günther. Pp. xvi., 281.
[With Geographic, Systematic, and Alphabetical Indexes.]
1858, 12mo. 4s.

BATRACHIANS.

Catalogue of the Batrachia Salientia in the Collection cf the
British Museum. By Dr. Albert Günther. Pp. xvi., 160.
12 Plates. [With Systematic, Geographic, and Alphabetical
Indexes.] 1858, 8vo. 6s.

FISHES.

Catalogue of the Fishes in the British Museum. Second
edition. Vol. I. Catalogue of the Perciform Fishes in the
British Museum. Vol. I. Containing the Centrarchidæ,
Percidæ, and Serranidæ (part). By George Albert
Boulenger, F.R.S. Pp. xix., 394. Woodcuts and 15 Plates.
[With Systematic and Alphabetical Indexes.] 1895, 8vo.
15s.

List of the Specimens of Fish in the Collection of the British
Museum. Part I. Chondropterygii. By J. E. Gray.
Pp. x., 160. 2 Plates. [With Systematic and Alphabetical
Indexes.] 1851, 12mo. 3s.

Catalogue of Fish collected and described by Laurence
Theodore Gronow, now in the British Museum. Pp. vii.,
196. [With a Systematic Index.] 1854, 12mo. 3s. 6d.

Catalogue of Apodal Fish in the Collection of the British
Museum. By Dr. Kaup. Pp. viii., 163. 11 Woodcuts and
19 Plates. 1856, 8vo. 10s.

Catalogue of Lophobranchiate Fish in the Collection of the
British Museum. By J. J. Kaup, Ph.D., &c. Pp. iv., 80.
4 Plates. [With an Alphabetical Index.] 1856, 12mo. 2s.

MOLLUSCA.

Guide to the Systematic Distribution of Mollusca in the
British Museum. Part I. By John Edward Gray, Ph.D.,
F.R.S., &c. Pp. xii., 230. 121 Woodcuts. 1857, 8vo. 5s.

List of the Shells of the Canaries in the Collection of the
British Museum, collected by MM. Webb and Berthelot
Described and figured by Prof. Alcide D'Orbigny in the
"Histoire Naturelle des Iles Canaries." Pp. 32. 1854,
12mo. 1s.

List of the Shells of Cuba in the Collection of the British
Museum, collected by M. Ramon de la Sagra. Described
by Prof. Alcide d'Orbigny in the "Histoire de l'Ile de
Cuba." Pp. 48. 1854, 12mo. 1s.

List of the Shells of South America in the Collection of the
British Museum. Collected and described by M. Alcide
D'Orbigny in the "Voyage dans l'Amérique Méridionale."
Pp. 89. 1854, 12mo. 2s.

Catalogue of the Collection of Mazatlan Shells in the British
Museum, collected by Frederick Reigen. Described by
Philip P. Carpenter. Pp. xvi., 552. 1857, 12mo. 8s.

List of Mollusca and Shells in the Collection of the British
Museum, collected and described by MM. Eydoux and
Souleyet in the "Voyage autour du Monde, exécuté
"pendant les années 1836 et 1837, sur la Corvette 'La
"Bonite,'" and in the "Histoire naturelle des Mollusques
"Ptéropodes." Par MM. P. C. A. L. Rang et Souleyet.
Pp. iv., 27. 1855, 12mo. 8d.

Catalogue of the Phaneropneumona, or Terrestial Operculated
Mollusca, in the Collection of the British Museum. By
Dr. L. Pfeiffer. Pp. 324. [With an Alphabetical Index.]
1852, 12mo. 5s.

Catalogue of Pulmonata, or Air Breathing Mollusca, in the
Collection of the British Museum. Part I. By Dr. Louis
Pfeiffer. Pp. iv., 192. Woodcuts. 1855, 12mo. 2s. 6d.

Catalogue of the Auriculidæ, Proserpinidæ, and Truncatellidæ
in the Collection of the British Museum. By Dr. Louis
Pfeiffer. Pp. iv., 150. Woodcuts. 1857, 12mo. 1s. 9d.

List of the Mollusca in the Collection of the British Museum.
By John Edward Gray, Ph.D., F.R.S., &c.
Part I. Volutidæ. Pp. 23. 1855, 12mo. 6d.
Part II. Olividæ. Pp. 41. 1865, 12mo. 1s.

Catalogue of the Conchifera, or Bivalve Shells, in the Collection of the British Museum. By M. Deshayes :— Part I. Veneridæ, Cyprinidæ, Glauconomidæ, and Petricoladæ. Pp. iv., 216. 1853, 12mo. 3s. Part II. Petricoladæ (concluded); Corbiculadæ. Pp. 217-292. [With an Alphabetical Index to the two parts.] 1854, 12mo. 6d.

BRACHIOPODA.

Catalogue of Brachiopoda Ancylopoda or Lamp Shells in the Collection of the British Museum. [Issued as "Catalogue of the Mollusca, Part IV."] Pp. iv., 128. 25 Woodcuts. [With an Alphabetical Index.] 1853, 12mo. 3s.

POLYZOA.

Catalogue of Marine Polyzoa in the Collection of the British Museum. Part III. Cyclostomata. By George Busk, F.R.S. Pp. viii., 39. 38 Plates. [With a Systematic Index.] 1875, 8vo. 5s.

CRUSTACEA.

Catalogue of the Specimens of Amphipodous Crustacea in the Collection of the British Museum. By C. Spence Bate, F.R.S., &c. Pp. iv., 399. 58 Plates. [With an Alphabetical Index.] 1862, 8vo. 1l. 5s.

ARACHNIDA.

Descriptive Catalogue of the Spiders of Burma, based upon the Collection made by Eugene W. Oates and preserved in the British Museum. By T. Thorell. Pp. xxxvi., 406. [With Systematic List and Alphabetical Index.] 1895, 8vo. 10s. 6d.

MYRIOPODA.

Catalogue of the Myriapoda in the Collection of the British Museum. By George Newport, F.R.S., P.E.S., &c. Part I. Chilopoda. Pp. iv., 96. [With an Alphabetical Index.] 1856, 12mo. 1s. 9d.

INSECTS.

Coleopterous Insects.

Nomenclature of Coleopterous Insects in the Collection of the British Museum :—
Part VI. Passalidæ. By Frederick Smith. Pp. iv., 23. 1 Plate. [With Index.] 1852, 12mo. 8d.
Part VII. Longicornia, I. By Adam White. Pp. iv., 174. 4 Plates. 1853, 12mo. 2s. 6d.
Part VIII. Longicornia, II. By Adam White. Pp. 237. 6 Plates. 1855, 12mo. 3s. 6d.
Part IX. Cassididæ. By Charles H. Boheman, Professor of Natural History, Stockholm. Pp. 225. [With Index.] 1856, 12mo. 3s.

Illustrations of Typical Specimens of Coleoptera in the
Collection of the British Museum. Part I. Lycidæ. By
Charles Owen Waterhouse. Pp. x., 83. 18 Coloured
Plates. [With Systematic and Alphabetical Indexes.]
1879, 8vo. 16s.

Catalogue of the Coleopterous Insects of Madeira in the
Collection of the British Museum. By T. Vernon
Wollaston, M.A., F.L.S. Pp. xvi., 234 : 1 Plate. [With
a Topographical Catalogue and an Alphabetical Index.]
1857, 8vo. 3s.

Catalogue of the Coleopterous Insects of the Canaries in the
Collection of the British Museum. By T. Vernon
Wollaston, M.A., F.L.S. Pp. xiii., 648. [With Topo-
graphical and Alphabetical Indexes.] 1864, 8vo. 10s. 6d.

Catalogue of Halticidæ in the Collection of the British
Museum. By the Rev. Hamlet Clark, M.A., F.L.S.
Physapodes and Œdipodes. Part I. Pp. xii., 301.
Frontispiece and 9 Plates. 1860, 8vo. 7s.

Catalogue of Hispidæ in the Collection of the British
Museum. By Joseph S. Baly, M.E.S., &c. Part I. Pp. x.,
172. 9 Plates. [With an Alphabetical Index.] 1858,
8vo. 6s.

Hymenopterous Insects.

List of the Specimens of Hymenopterous Insects in the
Collection of the British Museum. By Francis Walker,
F.L.S. :—

Part II. Chalcidites. Additional Species. Appendix.
Pp. iv., 99–237. 1848, 12mo. 2s.

Catalogue of Hymenopterous Insects in the Collection of the
British Museum. By Frederick Smith. 12mo. :—

Part I. Andrenidæ and Apidæ. Pp. 197. 6 Plates.
1853, 2s. 6d.

Part II. Apidæ. Pp. 199–465. 6 Plates. [With an
Alphabetical Index.] 1854, 6s.

Part III. Mutillidæ and Pompilidæ. Pp. 206. 6 Plates.
1855, 6s.

Part IV. Sphegidæ, Larridæ, and Crabronidæ. Pp. 207–
497. 6 Plates. [With an Alphabetical Index.] 1856,
6s.

Part V. Vespidæ. Pp. 147. 6 Plates. [With an Alphabetical Index.] 1857, 6s.

Part VI. Formicidæ. Pp. 216. 14 Plates. [With an
Alphabetical Index.] 1858, 6s.

Part VII. Dorylidæ and Thynnidæ. Pp. 76. 3 Plates.
[With an Alphabetical Index.] 1859, 2s.

Descriptions of New Species of Hymenoptera in the Collection of the British Museum. By Frederick Smith. Pp. xxi., 240. [With Systematic and Alphabetical Indexes.] 1879, 8vo. 10s.

List of Hymenoptera, with descriptions and figures of the Typical Specimens in the British Museum. Vol. I., Tenthredinidæ and Siricidæ. By W. F. Kirby. Pp. xxviii., 450. 16 Coloured Plates. [With Systematic and Alphabetical Indexes.] 1882, 8vo. 1l. 18s.

Dipterous Insects.

List of the Specimens of Dipterous Insects in the Collection of the British Museum. By Francis Walker, F.L.S. Part VII. Supplement III. Asilidæ. Pp. ii., 507-775. 1855, 12mo. 3s. 6d.

Lepidopterous Insects.

Catalogue of the Lepidoptera Phalænæ in the British Museum. Vol. I. Catalogue of the Syntomidæ in the Collection of the British Museum. By Sir George F. Hampson, Bart. Pp. xxi., 559. 285 Woodcuts. [With Systematic and Alphabetical Indexes, and Table of the Phylogeny of the Syntomidæ.] 1898, 8vo., 15s.

————Atlas of 17 Coloured Plates, 8vo., 15s.

Illustrations of Typical Specimens of Lepidoptera Heterocera in the Collection of the British Museum:—

Part III. By Arthur Gardiner Butler. Pp. xviii., 82. 41-60 Coloured Plates. [With a Systematic Index.] 1879, 4to. 2l. 10s.

Part V. By Arthur Gardiner Butler. Pp. xii., 74. 78-100 Coloured Plates. [With a Systematic Index.] 1881, 4to. 2l. 10s.

Part VI. By Arthur Gardiner Butler. Pp. xv., 89. 101-120 Coloured Plates. [With a Systematic Index.] 1886, 4to. 2l. 4s.

Part VII. By Arthur Gardiner Butler. Pp. iv., 124. 121-138 Coloured Plates. [With a Systematic List.] 1889, 4to. 2l.

Part VIII. The Lepidoptera Heterocera of the Nilgiri District. By George Francis Hampson. Pp. iv., 144. 139-156 Coloured Plates. [With a Systematic List.] 1891, 4to. 2l.

Part IX. The Macrolepidoptera Heterocera of Ceylon. By George Francis Hampson. Pp. v., 182. 157-176. Coloured Plates. [With a General Systematic List of Species collected in, or recorded from, Ceylon.] 1893, 4to. 2l. 2s.

Catalogue of Diurnal Lepidoptera of the family Satyridæ in the Collection of the British Museum. By Arthur Gardiner Butler, F.L.S., &c. Pp. vi., 211. 5 Plates. [With an Alphabetical Index.] 1868, 8vo. 5s. 6d.

Catalogue of Diurnal Lepidoptera described by Fabricius in the Collection of the British Museum. By Arthur Gardiner Butler, F.L.S., &c. Pp. iv., 303. 3 Plates. 1869, 8vo. 7s. 6d.

Specimen of a Catalogue of Lycænidæ in the British Museum. By W. C. Hewitson. Pp. 15. 8 Coloured Plates. 1862, 4to. 1l. 1s.

List of Lepidopterous Insects in the Collection of the British Museum. Part I. Papilionidæ. By G. R. Gray, F.L.S. Pp. 106. [With an Alphabetical Index.] 1856, 12mo. 2s.

List of the Specimens of Lepidopterous Insects in the Collection of the British Museum. By Francis Walker. 12mo. :—

    Part XIX. Pyralides. Pp. 799–1036. [With an Alphabetical Index to Parts XVI.–XIX.] 1859, 3s. 6d.

    Part XX. Geometrites. Pp. 1–276. 1860. 4s.

    Part XXI. ————— Pp. 277–498. 1860, 3s.

    Part XXII. ————— Pp. 499–755. 1861, 3s. 6d.

    Part XXIII. ————— Pp. 756–1020. 1861, 3s. 6d.

    Part XXIV. ————— Pp. 1021–1280. 1862, 3s. 6d.

    Part XXV. ————— Pp. 1281–1477. 1862, 3s.

    Part XXVI. ————— Pp. 1478–1796. [With an Alphabetical Index to Parts XX.–XXVI.] 1862, 4s. 6d.

    Part XXVII. Crambites and Tortricites. Pp. 1–286. 1863, 4s.

    Part XXVIII. Tortricites and Tineites. Pp. 287–561. 1863, 4s.

    Part XXIX. Tineites. Pp. 562–835. 1864, 4s.

    Part XXX. ————— Pp. 836–1096. [With an Alphabetical Index to Parts XXVII.–XXX.] 1864, 4s.

    Part XXXI. Supplement. Pp. 1–321. 1864, 5s.

    Part XXXII. ———— Part 2. Pp. 322–706. 1865, 5s.

    Part XXXIII.———— Part 3. Pp. 707–1120. 1865, 6s.

    Part XXXIV.———— Part 4. Pp. 1121–1533. 1865, 5s. 6d.

    Part XXXV. ———— Part 5. Pp. 1534–2040. [With an Alphabetical Index to Parts XXXI.–XXXV.] 1866, 7s.

Neuropterous Insects.

Catalogue of the Specimens of Neuropterous Insects in the Collection of the British Museum. By Francis Walker. 12mo. :—

    Part I. Phryganides—Perlides. Pp. iv., 192. 1852, 2s. 6d.

    Part II. Sialidæ—Nemopterides. Pp. ii., 193–476. 1853, 3s. 6d.

    Part III. Termitidæ—Ephemeridæ. Pp. ii., 477–585. 1853, 1s. 6d.

Catalogue of the Specimens of Neuropterous Insects in the Collection of the British Museum. By Dr. H. Hagen. Part I. Termitina. Pp. 34. 1858, 12mo. 6d.

Orthopterous Insects.

Catalogue of Orthopterous Insects in the Collection of the British Museum. Part I. Phasmidæ. By John Obadiah Westwood, F.L.S., &c. Pp. 195. 48 Plates. [With an Alphabetical Index]. 1859, 4to. 3l.

Catalogue of the Specimens of Blattariæ in the Collection of the British Museum. By Francis Walker, F.L.S., &c. Pp. 239. [With an Alphabetical Index.] 1868, 8vo. 5s. 6d.

Catalogue of the Specimens of Dermaptera Saltatoria [Part I.] and Supplement to the Blattariæ in the Collection of the British Museum. Gryllidæ. Blattariæ. Locustidæ. By Francis Walker, F.L.S., &c. Pp. 224. [With an Alphabetical Index.] 1869, 8vo. 5s.

Catalogue of the Specimens of Dermaptera Saltatoria in the Collection of the British Museum. By Francis Walker, F.L.S., &c.—

Part II. Locustidæ (continued). Pp. 225–423. [With an Alphabetical Index.] 1869, 8vo. 4s. 6d.

Part III. Locustidæ (continued).—Acrididæ. Pp. 425–604. [With an Alphabetical Index.] 1870, 8vo. 4s.

Part IV. Acrididæ (continued). Pp. 605–809. [With an Alphabetical Index.] 1870, 8vo. 6s.

Part V. Tettigidæ.—Supplement to the Catalogue of Blattariæ.—Supplement to the Catalogue of Dermaptera Saltatoria (with remarks on the Geographical Distribution of Dermaptera). Pp. 811–850; 43; 116. [With Alphabetical Indexes.] 1870, 8vo. 6s.

Hemipterous Insects.

Catalogue of the Specimens of Heteropterous Hemiptera in the Collection of the British Museum. By Francis Walker, F.L.S., &c. 8vo. :—

Part I. Scutata. Pp. 240. 1867. 5s.

Part II. Scutata (continued). Pp. 241–417. 1867. 4s.

Part III. Pp. 418–599. [With an Alphabetical Index to Parts I., II., III., and a Summary of Geographical Distribution of the Species mentioned.] 1868. 4s. 6d.

Part IV. Pp. 211. [Alphabetical Index.] 1871. 6s.
Part V. Pp. 202. ——————— 1872. 5s.
Part VI. Pp. 210. ——— ———— 1873. 5s.
Part VII. Pp. 213. ——————— 1873. 6s.
Part VIII. Pp. 220. ——————— 1873. 6s. 6d.

Homopterous Insects.

List of the Specimens of Homopterous Insects in the Collection of the British Museum. By Francis Walker. Supplement. Pp. ii., 369. [With an Alphabetical Index.] 1858, 12mo., 4s. 6d.

VERMES.

Catalogue of the Species of Entozoa, or Intestinal Worms, contained in the Collection of the British Museum. By Dr. Baird. Pp. iv., 132. 2 Plates. [With an Index of the Animals in which the Entozoa mentioned in the Catalogue are found, and an Index of Genera and Species.] 1853, 12mo. 2s.

ANTHOZOA.

Catalogue of Sea-pens or Pennatulariidæ in the Collection of the British Museum. By J. E. Gray, F.R.S., &c. Pp. iv., 40. 2 Woodcuts. 1870, 8vo. 1s. 6d.

Catalogue of Lithophytes or Stony Corals in the Collection of the British Museum. By J. E. Gray, F.R.S., &c. Pp. iv., 51. 14 Woodcuts. 1870, 8vo. 3s.

Catalogue of the Madreporarian Corals in the British Museum (Natural History) :—

> Vol. I. The Genus Madrepora. By George Brook. Pp. xi., 212. 35 Collotype Plates. [With Systematic and Alphabetical Indexes and Explanation of the Plates.] 1893, 4to. 1l. 4s.
>
> Vol. II. The Genus Turbinaria ; the Genus Astræopora. By Henry M. Bernard, M.A. Cantab., F.L.S., F.Z.S. Pp. iv., 106. 30 Collotype and 3 Lithographic Plates. [With Index of Generic and Specific Names, and Explanation of the Plates.] 1896, 4to. 18s.
>
> Vol. III. The Genus Montipora ; the Genus Anacropora. By Henry M. Bernard, M.A. Pp. vii., 192. 30 Collotype and 4 Lithographic Plates. [With Systematic Index, Index of Generic and Specific Names, and Explanation of the Plates.] 1897. 4to. 1l. 4s.

BRITISH ANIMALS.

Catalogue of British Birds in the Collection of the British Museum. By George Robert Gray, F.L.S., F.Z.S., &c. Pp. xii., 248. [With a List of Species.] 1863, 8vo. 3s. 6d.

Catalogue of British Hymenoptera in the Collection of the British Museum. Second edition. Part I. Andrenidæ and Apidæ. By Frederick Smith, M.E.S. New Issue. Pp. xi., 236. 11 Plates. [With Systematic and Alphabetical Indexes.] 1891, 8vo. 6s.

Catalogue of British Fossorial Hymenoptera, Formicidæ, and
. Vespidæ in the Collection of the British Museum. By
Frederick Smith, V.P.E.S. Pp. 236. 6 Plates. [With an
Alphabetical Index.] 1858, 12mo. 6s.
A Catalogue of the British Non-parasitical Worms in the
Collection of the British Museum. By George Johnston,
M.D., Edin., F.R.C.L., Ed., LL.D., Marischal Coll., Aber-
deen, &c. Pp. 365. Woodcuts and 24 Plates. [With an
Alphabetical Index.] 1865, 8vo. 7s.
Catalogue of the British Echinoderms in the British Museum
(Natural History). By F. Jeffrey Bell, M.A. Pp. xvii., 202.
Woodcuts and 16 Plates (2 Coloured). [With Table of
Contents, Tables of Distribution, Alphabetical Index,
Description of the Plates, &c.] 1892, 8vo. 12s. 6d.
List of the Specimens of British Animals in the Collection
of the British Museum : with Synonyma and References
to figures. 12mo.:—
Part IV. Crustacea. By A. White. Pp. iv., 141. (With
an Index.) 1850. 2s. 6d.
Part V. Lepidoptera. By J. F. Stephens. 2nd Edition.
Revised by H. T. Stainton and E. Shepherd. Pp. iv.,
224. 1856, 1s. 9d.
Part VI. Hymenoptera. By F. Smith. Pp. 134. 1851. 2s.
Part VII. Mollusca, Acephala and Brachiopoda. By
Dr. J. E. Gray. Pp. iv., 167. 1851, 3s. 6d.
Part VIII. Fish. By Adam White. Pp. xxiii., 164.
(With Index and List of Donors.) 1851, 3s. 6d.
Part IX. Eggs of British Birds. By George Robert
Gray. Pp. 143. 1852, 2s. 6d.
Part XI. Anoplura, or Parasitic Insects. By H. Denny.
Pp. iv., 51. 1852, 1s.
Part XII. Lepidoptera (continued). By James F.
Stephens. Pp. iv., 54. 1852, 9d.
Part XIII. Nomenclature of Hymenoptera. By
Frederick Smith. Pp. iv., 74. 1853, 1s. 4d.
Part XIV. Nomenclature of Neuroptera. By Adam
White. Pp. iv., 16. 1853, 6d.
Part XV. Nomenclature of Diptera, 1. By Adam
White. Pp. iv., 42. 1853, 1s.
Part XVI. Lepidoptera (completed). By H. T. Stainton.
Pp. 199. [With an Index.] 1854, 3s.
Part XVII. Nomenclature of Anoplura, Euplexoptera,
and Orthoptera. By Adam White. Pp. iv., 17.
1855, 6d.

PLANTS.

Catalogue of the African Plants collected by Dr. Friedrich
Welwitsch in 1853–61.—Dicotyledons. By William Philip
Hiern, M.A., F.L.S., &c. :—
Part I. [Ranunculaceæ to Rhizophoraceæ.] Pp. xxvi.,
336. [With Portrait of Dr. Welwitsch, Introduction,
Bibliography, and Index of Genera.] 1896, 8vo. 7s. 6d.

Catalogue of African Plants—*continued.*

    Part II. Combretaceæ to Rubiaceæ. Pp. 337–510.
    [With Index of Genera.] 1898, 8vo. 4*s.*

    Part III. Dipsaceæ to Scrophulariaceæ. Pp. 511–784.
    [With Index of Genera.] 1898, 8vo. 5*s.*

    Vol. II., Part I. Monocotyledons and Gymnosperms.
    By Alfred Barton Rendle, M.A., D.Sc. F.L.S., Assistant,
    Department of Botany. Pp. 260. [With Index of
    Genera.] 1899, 8vo. 6*s.*

A Monograph of Lichens found in Britain : being a Descriptive Catalogue of the Species in the Herbarium of the British Museum. By the Rev. James M. Crombie, M.A., F.L.S., F.G.S., &c. Part I. Pp. viii., 519 : 74 Woodcuts. [With Glossary, Synopsis, Tabular Conspectus, and Index.] 1894, 8vo. 16*s.*

A Monograph of the Mycetozoa : being a Descriptive Catalogue of the Species in the Herbarium of the British Museum. By Arthur Lister, F.L.S. Pp. 224. 78 Plates and 51 Woodcuts. [With Synopsis of Genera and List of Species, and Index.] 1894, 8vo. 15*s.*

List of British Diatomaceæ in the Collection of the British Museum. By the Rev. W. Smith, F.L.S., &c. Pp. iv., 55. 1859, 12mo. 1*s.*

FOSSILS.

Catalogue of the Fossil Mammalia in the British Museum (Natural History). By Richard Lydekker, B.A., F.G.S. :—

    Part I. Containing the Orders Primates, Chiroptera, Insectivora, Carnivora, and Rodentia. Pp. xxx., 268. 33 Woodcuts. [With Systematic and Alphabetical Indexes.] 1885, 8vo. 5*s.*

    Part II. Containing the Order Ungulata, Suborder Artiodactyla. Pp. xxii., 324. 39 Woodcuts. [With Systematic and Alphabetical Indexes.] 1885, 8vo. 6*s.*

    Part III. Containing the Order Ungulata, Suborders Perissodactyla, Toxodontia, Condylarthra, and Amblypoda. Pp. xvi., 186. 30 Woodcuts. [With Systematic Index, and Alphabetical Index of Genera and Species, including Synonyms.] 1886, 8vo. 4*s.*

    Part IV. Containing the Order Ungulata, Suborder Proboscidea. Pp. xxiv., 235. 32 Woodcuts. [With Systematic Index, and Alphabetical Index of Genera and Species, including Synonyms.] 1886, 8vo. 5*s.*

    Part V. Containing the Group Tillodontia, the Orders Sirenia, Cetacea, Edentata, Marsupialia, Monotremata, and Supplement. Pp. xxxv., 345. 55 Woodcuts. [With Systematic Index, and Alphabetical Index of Genera and Species, including Synonyms.] 1887, 8vo. 6*s.*

Catalogue of the Fossil Birds in the British Museum (Natural History). By Richard Lydekker, B.A. Pp. xxvii., 368. 75 Woodcuts. [With Systematic Index, and Alphabetical Index of Genera and Species, including Synonyms.] 1891, 8vo. 10*s.* 6*d.*

Catalogue of the Fossil Reptilia and Amphibia in the British Museum (Natural History). By Richard Lydekker, B.A., F.G.S. :—

Part I. Containing the Orders Ornithosauria, Crocodilia, Dinosauria, Squamata, Rhynchocephalia, and Proterosauria. Pp. xxviii., 309. 69 Woodcuts. [With Systematic Index, and Alphabetical Index of Genera and Species, including Synonyms.] 1888, 8vo. 7s. 6d.

Part II. Containing the Orders Ichthyopterygia and Sauropterygia. Pp. xxi., 307. 85 Woodcuts. [With Systematic Index, and Alphabetical Index of Genera and Species, including Synonyms.] 1889, 8vo. 7s. 6d.

Part III. Containing the Order Chelonia. Pp. xviii., 239. 53 Woodcuts. [With Systematic Index, and Alphabetical Index of Genera and Species, including Synonyms.] 1889, 8vo. 7s. 6d.

Part IV. Containing the Orders Anomodontia, Ecaudata, Caudata, and Labyrinthodontia; and Supplement. Pp. xxiii., 295. 66 Woodcuts. [With Systematic Index, Alphabetical Index of Genera and Species, including Synonyms, and Alphabetical Index of Genera and Species to the entire work.] 1890, 8vo. 7s. 6d.

Catalogue of the Fossil Fishes in the British Museum (Natural History). By Arthur Smith Woodward, F.G.S., F.Z.S. :—

Part I. Containing the Elasmobranchii. Pp. xlvii., 474. 13 Woodcuts and 17 Plates. [With Alphabetical Index, and Systematic Index of Genera and Species.] 1889, 8vo. 21s.

Part II. Containing the Elasmobranchii (Acanthodii), Holocephali, Ichthyodorulites, Ostracodermi, Dipnoi, and Teleostomi (Crossopterygii and Chondrostean Actinopterygii). Pp. xliv., 567. 58 Woodcuts and 16 Plates. [With Alphabetical Index, and Systematic Index of Genera and Species.] 1891, 8vo. 21s.

Part III. Containing the Actinopterygian Teleostomi of the Orders Chondrostei (concluded), Protospondyli, Aetheospondyli, and Isospondyli (in part). Pp. xlii., 544. 45 Woodcuts and 18 Plates. [With Alphabetical Index, and Systematic Index of Genera and Species.] 1895, 8vo. 21s.

Systematic List of the Edwards Collection of British Oligocene and Eocene Mollusca in the British Museum (Natural History), with references to the type-specimens from similar horizons contained in other collections belonging to the Geological Department of the Museum. By Richard Bullen Newton, F.G.S. Pp. xxviii., 365. [With table of Families and Genera, Bibliography, Correlation-table, Appendix, and Alphabetical Index.] 1891, 8vo. 6s.

4337r   B

Catalogue of Tertiary Mollusca in the Department of Geology,
British Museum (Natural History). Part I. The Australasian Tertiary Mollusca. By George F. Harris, F.G.S., etc.
Pp. xxvi., 407. 8 Plates. [With Table of Families, Genera,
and Subgenera, and Index.] 1897, 8vo. 10s.

Catalogue of the Fossil Cephalopoda in the British Museum
(Natural History) :—

   Part I. Containing part of the Suborder Nautiloidea, con-
sisting of the families Orthoceratidæ, Endoceratidæ,
Actinoceratidæ, Gomphoceratidæ, Ascoceratidæ,
Poterioceratidæ, Cyrtoceratidæ, and Supplement. By
Arthur H. Foord, F.G.S. Pp. xxxi., 344. 51 Woodcuts.
[With Systematic Index, and Alphabetical Index of
Genera and Species, including Synonyms.] 1888,
8vo. 10s. 6d.

   Part II. Containing the remainder of the Suborder
Nautiloidea, consisting of the families Lituitidæ,
Trochoceratidæ, Nautilidæ, and Supplement. By
Arthur H. Foord, F.G.S. Pp. xxviii., 407. 86 Wood-
cuts. [With Systematic Index, and Alphabetical
Index of Genera and Species, including Synonyms.]
1891, 8vo. 15s.

   Part III. Containing the Bactritidæ, and part of the
Subarder Ammonoidea. By Arthur H. Foord, Ph.D.,
F.G.S., and George Charles Crick, A.R.S.M., F.G.S.
Pp. xxxiii., 303. 146 Woodcuts. [With Systematic
Index of Genera and Species, and Alphabetical Index.]
1897, 8vo. 12s. 6d.

List of the Types and Figured Specimens of Fossil Cephalopoda
in the British Museum (Natural History). By G. C. Crick,
F.G.S. Pp. 103. [With Index.] 1898, 8vo. 2s. 6d.

A Catalogue of British Fossil Crustacea, with their Synonyms
and the Range in Time of each Genus and Order. By
Henry Woodward, F.R.S. Pp. xii., 155. [With an
Alphabetical Index.] 1877, 8vo. 5s.

Catalogue of the Fossil Bryozoa in the Department of
Geology, British Museum (Natural History):—The Jurassic
Bryozoa. By J. W. Gregory, D.Sc., F.G.S., F.Z.S. Pp.
[viii.,] 239. 22 Woodcuts and 11 Plates. [With List of
Species and Distribution, Bibliography, Index, and
Explanation of Plates.] 1896, 8vo. 10s.

A Catalogue of the Fossil Bryozoa in the Department of
Geology, British Museum (Natural History) :—The Cretaceous Bryozoa. Vol. I. By J. W. Gregory, D.Sc., F.G.S.,
Pp. viii., 457. 64 Woodcuts and 17 Plates. [With Index
and Explanation of Plates.] 1899, 8vo. 16s.

Catalogue of the Blastoidea in the Geological Department of
the British Museum (Natural History), with an account of
the morphology and systematic position of the group, and
a revision of the genera and species. By Robert Etheridge,
jun., of the Department of Geology, British Museum
(Natural History), and P. Herbert Carpenter, D.Sc., F.R.S.,
F.L.S. (of Eton College). Pp. xv., 322. 20 Plates. [With
Preface by Dr. H. Woodward, Table of Contents, General
Index, Explanations of the Plates, &c.] 1886, 4:o. 25s.

Printed in the United States
139906LV00009B/13/A

9 781436 741033